THE POWER OF
COMICS

THE POWER OF

COMICS

History, Form, and Culture

Randy Duncan and Matthew J. Smith

continuum

Continuum International Publishing Group
80 Maiden Lane, New York, NY 10038
The Tower Building, 11 York Road, London SE1 7NX

www.continuumbooks.com

Index by Randall W. Scott

Printed and bound in the United States of America

Library of Congress Cataloging-in-Publication Data

A catalog record for this book is available from the Library of Congress.

Contents

Preface

This is a textbook about comic books.

But don't just accept our word that comic books are a medium worthy of being considered with scholarly attention. Just ask any of the growing number of scholars who, since the early 1970s, have been teaching about the social implications, artistic merits, and cultural significance of this medium. Just ask any of the creators, who, over the last two decades especially, have brought forth some of the most mature and fertile combinations of words and pictures ever printed. Just ask yourself when, perhaps, you have read a few chapters of this introduction to the field of comics arts studies and can better appreciate the power of the medium.

Unlike many other books about comic books, our book is not just a history, or only focused on theory, or wholly devoted to an aspect of the culture of the medium. Ours is a synthesis of all of that, written for an audience unfamiliar with the language and customs surrounding the culture of creating and reading comic books. Our goal in authoring this textbook is to establish a coherent and comprehensive—but by no means definitive—explanation of comic books: their history, their communication techniques, the research into their meanings and effects, and the characteristics of the people who make and consume them. Our approach is borne of our backgrounds in communication and literary studies, but incorporates scholarly efforts from a host of disciplines, including art, history, sociology, economics, psychology, and many more.

We freely admit that our approach is focused principally on American comic books, as one means to keep this expansive and ever-expanding field manageable. However, we do present a chapter on comics in other cultures, as it is impossible to talk about American comic books without acknowledging the international talents and trends that have come to influence them.

We also want to note our bias towards print comic books amidst the growth of online comics. Our rationale for this bias includes print's long history, the generally held perception of what constitutes a comic book, and the fact that differences in form and techniques employed (trails rather than pages, transitional devices such as dissolves, the potential to use animation and sound, etc.) arguably make many online comics a different art form than the print comic book.

We acknowledge that this book is a product of so many more people than just its two authors, and we owe a debt of thanks to those who lent their expertise and keen eyes to the production of this edition. We are grateful to our colleagues on the Comix-Scholars Discussion List, Peter Coogan, Alec Hosterman, Charles Hatfield, and Leonard Rifas, among many other comics scholars. Our gratitude goes to David Stoddard for our cover design and artwork (which includes a Pyroman by legendary cover artist Alex Shomburg). We are also grateful for the support and assistance we received from Continuum Publishing from David Barker, Katie Gallof, Gabriella Page-Fort, Max Novick, John Mark Boling, Claire Heitlinger, Benn Linfield, Ryan Masteller and Carol Sawyer, as well as Randy Scott, indexer.

Randy would like to thank Brian Camp, Deborah Sessor, Carl Miller, and Travis Langley for meticulous and insightful comments on chapters; Robert O'Nale, Tommy Cash, and all the other students in Comics as Communication classes through the years who gave feedback on those very rough and fragmentary handouts that were the seeds from which this project grew; and the various Henderson State University committees that supported this book with a sabbatical leave and research funding. And last, but certainly not least, thanks to the friends who were always willing to provide much-needed relief from work in the form of tennis and poker-like card games.

Matt wishes to thank his friend and colleague Andrew F. Wood, who inspired Matt to pursue this project, and his ever-patient wife, Susan Sheridan Smith, who endured through the actual writing of it. Matt is also grateful to the students in his Fall 2005 Seminar in Media Research, who helped with the initial identification of resources: Lara Bachelder, Michael Burk, Josh Cohick, Ashley Corry, Claudia Dattilo, Susan Feuer, Jessica Fisher, Sarah Gearhart, Emily Hiscar, Laura Lachman, Steve Less, Brian McCoach, Hiedi Mowrey, Tregg Nardecchia, Jerrod Swanton, and Lauren Wilson. Additional help came from students Jocelin Baker, Jamie Daugherty, and Jeff Dern, as well as institutional support from librarian Ken Irwin and the Wittenberg University Faculty Research Fund Board.

Professionals, historians, and fans from the comics community who generously gave of their time and expertise include Alan Asherman, Jerry Bails, Robert Beerbohm, Karen Berger, Larry Clowers, Shel Dorf, Mike Friedrich, Kathleen Glosan, Gary Groth, Denis Kitchen, Paul Levitz, John Jackson Miller, Chuck Rozanski, Jeff Smith, Bill Spicer, Roy Thomas, Maggie Thompson, Hames Ware, Bill Williams, John Wheat, and two legends we were fortunate to know when they walked among us—Will Eisner and Julie Schwartz.

Randy dedicates this volume to his two best friends, Trina Bright and Jody Duncan Burge, for encouraging him to dive in and for giving him the buoyant support to make it to the far shore.

Matt's dedication is to his twin sons, Trevor and Kent, who share with him the wonder of discovering the worlds of reading and imagination that comic books open.

There was a lot more we wanted to say about comic books but couldn't fit into this book. We invite you to visit us at *www.powerofcomics.com* for additional material that didn't make our print edition.

Introduction

by Paul Levitz

There's something oxymoronic about a comics textbook. If ever there was a medium characterized by its unexamined self-expression, it would be comics. For decades after the medium's birth, it was free of organized critical analysis, its creators generally disinclined to self-analysis or formal documentation. The average reader didn't know who created the comics, or how or why, and except for a uniquely destructive period during America's witch-hunting of the 1950s, didn't seem to care. As the medium has matured, however, and the creativity of comics begun to touch the mainstream of popular culture in many ways, curiosity has followed, leading to journalism and eventually scholarship, and so here we are.

For those of you who simply wanted to take a course about comics as a way to read more of them, my apologies and sympathies. Apologies, because in a way this text is partially my fault—apparently when I published an article entitled "A Call for Higher Criticism" in *The Comics Journal* almost thirty years ago, it caught the eye of a young communication grad student named Randy Duncan, who pursued the question in his dissertation, his teaching, his involvement in co-founding an academic conference on comics scholarship, and now his collaboration on this text. This is a fine example of the vitally important Law of Unintended Consequences. Another example would be the result of printing salesman Max Gaines putting 10¢ stickers on a handful of reprint flyers of newspaper comic strips, intended as premium giveaways, and then placing them on a newsstand to see if they would sell. Gaines could never have imagined, much less intended, the industry that resulted and the diverse creative art form that emerged.

I offer my sympathies because, as informative and interesting as this textbook is, it's hardly as much fun as the best of comics. But it, in turn, may have the unintended result of creating better comics. Understanding the medium you work in has always been an important step toward expanding its potential and improving your own work. When I came into the world of comics almost forty years ago, it still operated much like a medieval guild, with the form being taught to new apprentices by masters, while the young people worked alongside, starting with the simplest tasks. Virtually all of American comics were created by a couple hundred people in the New York metro area, and finding your way in to this group was a daunting and difficult task. Not only were there no text-books analyzing the field, there were almost no books detailing its history, cataloging the works, or providing any guidance in any way. That has all changed, and this volume is just another step in a very rapid and exciting evolution.

But while the fun starts (and, for many, still happily ends) with simply reading and enjoying comics, it doesn't need to stop there. The exploration you're taking into the world of comics may lead you further than you expect. As you learn about it, you'll discover that it is one of the more fertile and open fields of expression around: blessed with low barriers to entry even before the digital revolution (and lower still afterward), in an early and vigorous stage of both creative and commercial growth as it reaches out to new and wider audiences, and inventive in its adoption of many different forms of collaboration, allowing people with various different gifts to participate. In Japan, the ultimate form of this is a twice-annual gathering called Comiket, which a half million people attend to purchase manga (the Japanese form of comics) created by approximately 35,000 individual creators, who bring enough copies to sell to finance their creation. In America, there's an explosion of webcomics going on, as well as opportunities to work with everyone from traditional book publishers, to the larger comic publishers, to the many, many small presses, including those formed around a single creator's efforts.

If your journey does not take you as far into our world as the creation of comics yourself, understanding the history, evolution, and dynamic present flowering of the medium in America, Japan, and France will increase your enjoyment of what you read. Like all media, and perhaps more than some, comics have their hidden meanings, encoded "Easter Eggs" to delight their serious fans, and the broad scope of this volume will enable you to catch up if you haven't spent enough time with them. These elements often spill over into the films and television shows based on the comics, and sometimes into the culture beyond, particularly as comics' creators have moved into many other media in recent years.

If, in the end, you want nothing other than to sit down and enjoy a good comic book, whether it calls itself a graphic novel or any other label, you'll find mention in this text of many of the best to pull off the shelf, along with discussions of a fair share of the greatly talented people who have written and drawn them. As you learn about the context in which they worked, you may approach these creators' stories with a bit more appreciation, and in the process enjoy them all the more. Or maybe you'll ignore the credits, the context, and everything but the comic, and settle down to nestle your imagination in its pages. And that's just fine, too.

Paul Levitz is a comic book fan (editor/publisher of *Etcetera* and *The Comic Reader*), historian (member of the editorial board of the first edition of *Who's Who in American Comic Books*), writer (*Legion of Super-Heroes* and many other titles), editor (*Batman* and other titles), and publisher (currently President & Publisher of DC Comics).

Defining Comic Books
as a Medium

"Once regarded as one of the lower forms of mass entertainment, comic books are today widely considered to be potentially capable of complex and profound expression as both literary and visual art forms."

—Nancy Dziedric and Scot Peacock, literary critics, 1997

Art Spiegelman's graphic novel *Maus* won a special Pulitzer Prize for literature in 1992. The Pulitzer is considered to be one of the highest honors in writing, and for a comic book to be recognized alongside the year's best work in literature and journalism was previously unthinkable. But *Maus* is not just any comic book. It tells the true story of a Holocaust survivor through an unconventional cast of animals, recounting both the horrors of the Nazi persecution of the Jews in Europe and the enduring pain of survivors and their children. It brilliantly demonstrates the power of the comics to communicate ideas through a poignant combination of words and pictures.

While *Maus* was widely praised, the opening line of English professor Lawrence L. Langer's review, in *The New York Times Book Review*, was fairly typical of how the literary community dealt with the fact that *Maus* was a comic book: "Art Spiegelman doesn't draw comics" (17). Forget that the narrative consisted of hand drawings and word balloons presented in a series of panels; it seems that it could not be a comic book because it was good. Unfortunately, this still reflects the common conception of comic books. It is not even that misguided an idea. The majority of comic books produced in America have been quickly created, lowest-common-denominator, mass media products targeted at eleven-year-olds.

Nowadays, the average person has to go out of their way to even see a comic book, and if they do it will likely be of the costumed superhero variety. But, these books do not accurately represent the variety or potential of the **medium**. A medium is a channel for communicating, and includes familiar favorites such as radio, television, or the printed page. When we use the term *medium* in this book, we are addressing the social reality of comic books, such as their function as economic commodities. We will also speak of comic books as an **art form**. In

FIGURE 1.1. There are two related stories in *Maus*. The first is that of Art interviewing his father, Vladek, in the present. The second, told through a series of flashbacks, chronicles Vladek's struggle to survive the Holocaust in Nazi Europe. From *Maus II: A Survivor's Tale: And Here My Troubles Began* by Art Spiegelman. ©1986, 1989, 1990, 1991 by Art Spiegelman. Used by persmission of Pantheon Books, a division of Random House, Inc.

choosing this reference, we mean to emphasize the creative aspects of communicating meaning through the comic book form. Even the worst of the lot may be talked about as an art form because there is always a set of materials, techniques, and limitations involved in how such work is created. At their best, comic books can accommodate content as profound, moving, and enduring as that found in any of the more celebrated vehicles for human expression. Comic books can attract creators who aspire to art and literature, who create works of complexity, passion, and depth. *Maus* received national attention, but many excellent works—such as *The Tale of One Bad Rat*, *It's a Good Life if You Don't Weaken*, *A Contract with God*, and many, many more—are virtually unknown outside the small community of comic book readers and are just waiting to be discovered.

OBJECTIVES

In this chapter you will learn:

1. about the relationships between comic books and other forms of sequential art;
2. the essential differences between a comic strip and a comic book;
3. a model for the communication process of putting meaning into and taking meaning from comic books; and
4. reasons why comic books should be studied.

What exactly is a comic book? Why do we consider *Maus* to be one? We will get to some definitions in short order, but for now let us begin by acknowledging that we are dealing with a particular kind of **sequential art**. Unlike static or stand-alone pieces of art, which are quite often focused on capturing a moment or invoking an emotional response, sequential art is, with some exceptions, concerned with storytelling. As you will see in the next section, there are a number of different manifestations of sequential art, and we find the comic book to be among the most intriguing of them in terms of its storytelling potential. Thereafter, we will sort out the differences among many of the terms associated with this medium before looking more closely at some of the ways the medium works. We conclude with some arguments as to why we think exploring comic books is worth your time and interest.

CARTOONS, COMICS, AND SEQUENTIAL ART

The search for a definition must begin with disentangling the comic book medium from the semantic confusion of the term *comics*. First of all, there is no distinct medium known as comics. **Comics** is a useful general term for designating the phenomenon of juxtaposing images in a sequence. (To *juxtapose* means to place two things side by side.) As comics theorist Scott McCloud points out, this umbrella term has been used to cover comic strips, comic books, cave paintings, Grecian urns, tapestries, stained glass windows, and more (*Understanding*). These disparate forms of communication have been treated as a single medium for a number of reasons. Perhaps there is a natural tendency to lump them together because they have some similarities of form. All of the examples given above tell a story by presenting carefully selected moments of varying length within panels. A **panel** is simply a discernible area that contains a moment of the story.

Another formal similarity is the potential for use of compositional elements. Perceived distance, angle of view, color, arrangement of elements, simulated lighting effects, and other elements of composition could be used in all of the forms of visual communication mentioned above. They all draw upon the same visual vocabulary. Of course, for the most part, it has been for strategic and political reasons that comics have been defined to include historical artifacts like Grecian urns and the **Bayeux Tapestry**. This famed tapestry is a horizontal strip of embroidered linen 231 feet long and twenty inches high, created circa 1100 BC, that depicts the Norman conquest of England in a sequence of juxtaposed scenes. These and other works of art lend respectability to an otherwise denigrated form of expression. It is a strategic ploy for respectability by association.

This has been especially true for comic books, which are elevated in prestige even by being associated with comic strips. In the early days of comics scholarship, perhaps the study of comic books was kept under the protective umbrella of comics for fear that on its own the medium would receive nothing but scorn from the academy. This attempt to protect comic book scholarship by hiding it amongst its more respectable cousins has actually marginalized the study of comic books. Yet of all the visual communication media that have been called comics, comic books are currently among the most vibrant and ambitious.

With this sense of potential in mind, we offer the following working definition as a means for identifying what a **comic book** is. As an art form, a comic book is a volume in which all aspects of the narrative are represented by pictorial and linguistic images encapsulated in a sequence of juxtaposed panels and pages. Some of the terms within that definition bear some explication. By *volume* we mean a collection of sheets of paper bound together. So a comic book might be as brief as only a few sheets or as expansive as a several-hundred-page omnibus edition. In the near future the term *volume* might be used more metaphorically to include comic books on an e-book reader such as the Kindle. The aspects of the narrative that we are talking about are the people, objects, sounds, sensations, and thoughts that play a role in the storytelling. A **narrative**, of course, is an account of an event or a series of events. Our definition has a certain utility in helping us to begin talking about comic books; however, we acknowledge that it functions best in describing typical or pure cases of the art form. There are some cases lying on the boundaries that may vary from the definition but still meet enough of the criteria to be recognized as comic books.

Why call such objects *comic books*, though? The content of *Maus* is certainly not comical, and comic book magazines do not appear to be as handsomely bound or durable as a traditional book. As you will see in greater detail in the next chapter, most of the early American comic books started out as collections of re-pasted newspaper comic strips. By the time that innovation took hold, the label of "comics" had already been semantically stuck to that art form, even though adventure and science fiction stories not told for laughs had become popular features among them. For more than eight decades the label has endured, although it does seem to be a sizeable misnomer, given the fact that comic books address many more types of stories than just humorous ones, and many comic books are produced on rather flimsy materials.

In recent times a number of people have attempted to rehabilitate the image of comic books by using a different term, *graphic novel*, to describe the more ambitious works in the art form. For creators, labeling their work a graphic novel allows them to distance themselves from the commercial and periodical connotations associated with comic books. For publishers, *graphic novel* is a term that helps elevate the status of their product and has allowed them entrée into bookstores, libraries, and the academy. In practice, graphic novels may be longer than the typical comic book and most often feature self-contained, rather than continuing, stories. While we too use that term in this book, you may well note that the graphic novel meets the definition of the comic book introduced above. For our intents and purposes, a graphic novel is a comic book. Yet while we find a close kinship between comic books and graphic novels, we find some broader divisions between a comic book and a comic strip, as we shall explore in the next section.

DIFFERENTIATING THE COMIC BOOK FROM THE COMIC STRIP MEDIUM

Few formal defintions of comic books have been previously offered because there has been little recognition of comic strips and comic books as distinct mediums. However, scholar Joseph Witek refers to strips and books as the "two most common forms of sequential art expression in our culture," and raises strenuous objections to subsuming strips and books under the label "the comics" because it "obscures the important differences between them" (*Comic Books* 6). In fact, the similarities and differences between comic strips and comic books can be explored from at least four perspectives, in terms of production, distribution, the art form, and culture.

Production Perspective

A medium can be defined by the technology that is used to mass produce its products. There is little differentiation between comic books and comic strips under this definition. While the paper used varies in size and quality, comic strips and comic books are both essentially products of the printing press, and the only significant difference in production is that comic books are bound. The real differences between the two media occur prior to reproduction (in the creative process) and after reproduction (in their distribution and use).

Distribution Perspective

When we consider the specific means of mass production and distribution, comic strips and comic books were once subsumed under larger media categories: Comic strips were a component of the newspaper medium, while comic books were a component of the magazine medium. However, since the development of the direct market and comic book specialty shops, the majority of comic books do not find their way to consumers through the magazine distribution system. More recently, computer technology has provided new options for both the production and distribution of sequential art. Digital comic strips and comic books not only bypass traditional distribution systems, but appear in new formats that make the two media virtually indistinguishable. Their uniqueness does not become apparent until we consider definitions based on creation and use.

Art Form Perspective

This approach emphasizes the unique formal aspects or "language" of a medium. While it is true that both strips and books use **encapsulation**—the selection of key moments of action—layout, and composition, they use them in very different ways.

FIGURE 1.2. Charles Schultz is widely regarded as a master of the comic strip medium because of his work for more than half a century on his daily *Peanuts* strip. Comic strips face different constraints than comic books in terms of how they can communicate. © 2008 United Feature Syndicate

Comic Strip	Comic Book
1. very few panels	many panels
2. the panel is the only unit of encapsulation	units of encapsulation include the panel, the page, the two-page spread and inset panels
3. layout is normally rigid	layout can be creative
4. composition is usually simple	composition can be complex

The ancient Greeks considered an art form (a *techne*) to be "a body of principles that can generate an artifact, a work of creation" (Smith, Craig 2). Comic books and comic strips are different types of artifacts, created by different bodies of principles. Even though there might be sharing of *vocabulary*, each is a medium with its own unique *language*.

Cultural Perspective

Perhaps the clearest difference between comic strips and comic books is their differing roles in our culture. They exist for different reasons and serve different audiences and purposes. It should be noted that the distinctions below are generalizations, and while most comic strips still exist to increase newspaper circulation, there are an increasing number of online strips that exist independent of any coporate agenda. In addition, existing primarily as a sales tool does not preclude strips like *Krazy Kat* and *Calvin and Hobbes* from having literary and artistic merit.

Comic Strips	Comic Books
1. exist to sell newspapers	exist as products in their own right, as promotional tie-ins, and even as literary and artistic expressions
2. come to readers "unbidden," as a supplement within the newspaper	readers must actively seek them out
3. most Americans read comic strips	fewer and fewer people read comic books
4. readers derive brief pleasure and go on about their lives	can be a way of life for fans (fandom subculture)

There are many more differences in the uses for and gratifications derived from these two media, but suffice it to say that they occupy radically different cultural spaces. Future chapters will examine the cultural characteristics and uses of comic books in greater detail. Another approach to defining a communication act like comic books is to explore the process of communication.

A COMMUNICATION MODEL OF COMIC BOOKS

Comic books are acts of communication. They exist because someone has a set of ideas to share, and they thrive when an audience takes note of those ideas. The basic model for a communication act was first developed by a pair of mathematicians named Claude Shannon and Warren Weaver, whose *The Mathematical Theory of Communication* gave rise to the field of information theory. Their model, with its familiar components of source-message-channel-receiver, is often taught as a foundational concept in communication studies. We begin our model of comic book communication building on the foundation of what Shannon and Weaver first proposed.

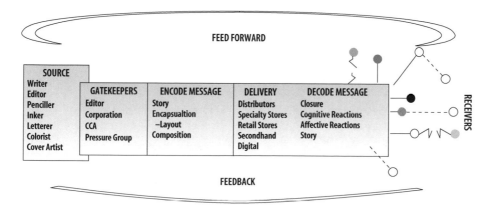

FIGURE 1.3. This model of comic book communication builds on information theory.

Source

In this model, the corporate or small business structure that finances the publication of the comic book is treated as part of the gatekeeping mechanism through which the message must pass, but not as the actual source of the message. The **source** is the comic book creator or creators. The order in which the creative components are presented is deliberate, beginning with those creative roles that are most directly related to invention (idea, purpose, story). Most often the idea begins with the *writer*, a wordsmith who outlines the plot, describes scenes and actions, and provides dialogue for the characters and narrator. However, some *editors* also take an active role in plotting stories. An editor coordinates the publication of a comic book, including hiring the creative talent and supervising the various stages of production. Some writer and *penciller* (a **penciller** is the artist who does the pencil drawings of the images in a comic book story) teams collaborate very closely on the creation of stories. However it is generally the writer who creates the story, whether in the form of a one-paragraph synopsis or detailed panel-by-panel descriptions. Legend has it that writer/editor Stan Lee would simply describe his story ideas to pencillers over the phone in a few minutes. On the other hand, writer Alan Moore often takes pages to describe a single panel, and even accompanies some of his descriptions with thumbnail sketches.

The second most important creative component is the graphic representation of the story. It is the job of the penciller to create these pictures. However, some pencillers provide such loose sketches that the **inker** (the person who goes over the pencil sketches with ink) must take an active role in the composition of the panel. Even when the penciller provides very tight, detailed drawings, the inker still makes an important contribution to the style of the message, which can influence the readers' affective (emotive) and cognitive (thinking) reactions to the art style. The **letterer** (the person who adds text to the panels) creates a visual **paralanguage** for the writer's words. It is the letterer's craft, to a great extent, that determines how the writer's words will be interpreted. Especially with modern color processes that allow for more subtle and sophisticated use of color, the **colorist** also contributes to the message. Receivers can have affective reactions to color: reds and oranges can agitate, blues and greens can calm, and so forth. Colors also have cognitive associations (e.g., purple for royalty) that can be exploited to create meanings. Bright primary colors were an essential element in constructing the mythology of comic book superheroes such as Superman, just as a muted palette was essential to the darker heroes and anti-heroes.

While the **cover artist** has no direct contribution to the story, he or she creates the first impression of the comic, one that plays an important part in the marketing of the book. The cover also creates a context for the reading of the story. No receiver can help but begin reading with the expectations created by the cover.

Feedforward

Discussion about the comic book message takes place not only among the receivers, but also between the sources and the receivers. **Feedforward** consists of messages about the forthcoming comic book that are sent from the source to some of the receivers. Comic books are often advertised in other comic books by the same publisher, on posters in comic book specialty stores, and in distributors' newsletters and order forms. Another type of feedforward is the interviews with writers and artists that are presented in the fan press. **Fans** are consumers of comic books who have a manifest commitment to the medium (e.g., they purchase the same comic book titles month after month). Some fans attend comic book conventions where they can view photocopies of works in progress, see promotional slideshows or videos, engage in interpersonal communication with the creators, and receive promotional flyers, buttons, etc. An increasingly important form of feedforward is computer-mediated communication. A number of internet discussion groups have comic book professionals among their subscribers, and many professionals maintain their own home pages and blogs. These professionals often engage in dialogue about their forthcoming works, furthering feedforward.

Feedback

Feedback—messages sent from receivers to sources—can occur in many of the same forms as feedforward. For decades, comic books contained a page or two of letters from fans, though some of the larger publishers have displaced this feature in recent years, opting to include advertising instead. Most fan publications also have a letters section. Fans who attend comic book conventions or belong to internet discussion groups often share their reactions to a product with its creators or publishers. These shared forums of communication create a sense of community among comic book creators and fans.

Gatekeepers

The messages that can be delivered to receivers are determined to some degree by the individuals and entities that serve as the **gatekeepers** of comic book communication. These gatekeepers can be within the structure of production or they can be outside forces. The gatekeepers most directly involved with the production of the message are the editors, though many independently produced comic books have no editor. At some of the smaller companies, which publish creator-owned properties, the editor operates as little more than a proofreader. However, at the larger, more mainstream companies (Marvel, DC, Archie Comic Publications), editors often hire the creative staff, plan the general direction of the title, and even co-plot some individual issues. Companies such as Marvel and DC also operate within a corporate structure that imposes certain limitations (usually based on consistency with corporate image or stockholder tolerance). In such companies it falls to the editor to enforce the guidelines set down by the corporate parent.

Some editors must also enforce the guidelines established by the **Comics Code Authority** (CCA). The Code is a voluntary self-regulation process begun by comic book publishers in 1954 to preempt any government regulation of the industry. Over the years many of the restrictions have been eliminated, and fewer and fewer comic books are voluntarily submitted for CCA's seal of approval. Pressure groups, from the Christian right to Native American tribal councils, are occasionally a force for the restriction of comic book content. Of course, they have no direct effect but must achieve their ends through influencing internal gatekeepers at the corporate or editorial level.

Encoded Messages

This portion of the model deals with the unique "language" by which messages are communicated through the medium of comic books. On the broadest level, there is the story or narrative—what happens. However, a comic book does not visually, or even verbally, present each moment of action in the narrative. Instead, certain moments of prime action from the narrative are selected by the writer or artist and encapsulated in a discrete space, which in comics is called a *panel*, irrespective of whether or not there are actual panel borders. The process of **encapsulating** certain moments involves creative decisions that are central to comic book communication. Choosing the size of the panel can affect the emphasis given to a moment in the panel, as compared to moments in other panels. The size of the panel can also affect the amount of time of that moment, both in terms of reading time and the relative time span within the overall narrative. Choosing the sequence of moments to encapsulate is important, because adjacent panels can interact to create a level of meaning that does not exist in individual panels alone. Finally, the choice of which and how many moments to encapsulate on a particular page determines, to a great extent, how successfully the page operates as a unit. Encapsulation is perhaps the most distinctive and essential act in the creation of a comic book message.

The final level of encoding the message is the act of **composing** individual panels. Film borrowed from theatre the concept of mise-en-scène, "putting in the scene." Most of the mise-en-scène elements present on stage or screen—color, lighting, distance, angle, movement, setting, and décor—can be depicted in a comic book panel. However, there are also some elements of composition that are unique to comics. First, variations in the shape of the frame can affect the meaning of what is framed. Second, the expressive potential of lines means that the brush strokes with which a picture is inked can create affective and/or cognitive reactions to an image. Third, any sound that is introduced into a comic book story has to be visual and is therefore an element of composition. Fourth, comic books must effectively blend words and pictures.

The elements of composition help communicate the message by acting as signs. A **sign** is simply one thing intended to represent another thing. Most of the drawings in comic books are **icon signs**—they represent what they look like. However, because comic books are an extremely *additive* medium—requiring receivers to add their own experience or imagination to the encapsulated moments in order to construct the story—many elements of a comic book can operate as

FIGURE 1.4. The first image is an example of a icon sign. Archie's girlfriends Betty and Veronica are not real people; they are icons of idealized teenagers as envisioned by Dan DeCarlo. In the second image, one does not need a narrator's caption to understand the fear this family is experiencing in a panel from *Vault of Horror* #15 (1950) drawn by Johnny Craig; fear can be read in the index sign captured in their expressions. You may recognize the third image as Superman's chest emblem, depicted here by Alex Ross, but the highly stylized design is also a symbol sign. (Cartoonist John Byrne grew up reading black-and-white *Superman* reprints and thought the emblem depicted two fish swimming past one another. Talk about arbitrary symbols!) ™ & © 2008 Archie Comic Publications, Inc. Used with permission. © William M. Gaines, Agent, Inc. Used with permission. Superman © DC Comics

index signs, meaning that they indicate the existence of something that is not explicitly depicted, such as an emotion or sensation. Most facial expressions in comic books are **index signs** of the characters' emotions. Index signs are either commonplaces (e.g., shivering to indicate that it is cold), or conventions (e.g., crashing waves to intimate lovemaking). **Symbol signs** are more abstract and subjective. These are arbitrary patterns, such as words in our language. Different receivers will have different interpretation of symbol signs, and can perceive symbol signs where the comic book creator(s) intended none.

Delivery

Although often taken for granted in the communication process, the means by which the message is actually delivered to the receivers can affect reception of the message. This model does not include direct subscriptions from the publisher; with the growth of comics distributors and specialty stores, subscription has become a fairly insignificant means of delivery. Also, as subscriptions are such a direct transmission of the message, there is little of the interaction or amplification of the message that can result from other delivery systems. The five remaining methods of delivery that are listed in the model can all involve varying degrees of interaction with the message, and can also engage receivers in the processes of feedforward and feedback. Operators of comics specialty stores are often fans themselves and are willing to engage in dialogue about the merits of artists, writers, characters, and stories. Occasionally, the same is true of the people involved in such secondhand delivery methods as used book stores, flea markets, and garage sales. Distributors and subscription services usually have no interpersonal contact with receivers, but they do maintain a dialogue of sorts through their websites or newsletters that accompany the order forms. In addition to providing a summary of the content of forthcoming comic books, these forums provide behind-the-scenes news, reviews, interviews, and chatty editorials. Many also publish letters from their customers, and will even add to their offerings based on customers' suggestions. Retail outlets, such as newsstands, grocery stores, and Wal-Marts, rarely provide for any dialogue of feedforward and feedback. However, this delivery system can still involve an amplification of the comic book communication experience. The comic book fan's affective reaction upon approaching a display of comic books seems to be generated from varying degrees of ritual, pleasure anticipated, and pleasure remembered. A longtime comic book fan, upon encountering the array of gaudy covers, can still experience the tingly excitement he or she felt as an adolescent standing before the big blue vending machines or the circular racks that proclaimed, "Hey kids, comics!"

Decoded Message

In any act of communication, the **meaning** (the decoded message) ultimately resides with the receivers. The elements of the decoded message parallel those of the encoded message, but in reverse order. The receiver has **cognitive reactions** (knowing) and **affective reactions** (feeling) to the signs that are communicated by the compositional elements within panels. The receiver performs **closure** between the encapsulated moments in order to create a completed whole out of fragments. Perhaps one of the most important standards for the critical evaluation of a comic book is whether or not the encapsulation choices of the writer and artist produced successful closure. At the highest level of decoded meaning the receiver creates a continuous story out of discrete panels. However, this involves more than simply understanding *what happens*—it also requires an understanding of *what it means*, or the comic's subtext. Every element of the communication process depicted in this model flows into and affects the ultimate meaning that each receiver derives from the comic book communication act.

Noise

Noise is any interference that distorts the message. **Channel noise** refers to a technical problem with the transmission of the message. For example, an artist might not draw characters distinctly enough for a reader to tell them apart, or a page layout might be so confusing that a reader is not certain of the reading order of the panels. **Environmental noise** is physical noise in the receiver's surroundings. A person reading a comic book while babysitting is likely to experience some environmental intrusions. **Semantic noise** occurs when a receiver attributes a different meaning to a word than what was intended by the source of the message. A reader who does not know the definition for the word *acquiesce* might find it frustrating when a character utters the unfamiliar word. In this model, varying degrees of noise are indicated by the jagged patches along some of the solid lines to receivers.

Amplification

The dotted lines between receivers represent an **amplification** of the original message. Many comic book readers tend to engage in dialogue about the comic books they read. This can happen in comic book clubs, in **fanzines**, in **APAs** (amateur press alliances), at comic book conventions, in online forums, or simply informally among friends. This amplification usually occurs among two or more people who have read the same comic book, but it is also possible for a reader to relate portions of the comic book message to someone who has not encountered it firsthand. The significance of this amplification is that the final meaning that resides with a receiver might be the product of both the reading itself and the discussion that followed, or, in the case of secondhand receivers, it could be the product solely of the discussion.

Like definitions, models cannot be more than simplified representations of complex processes. While the preceding model is by no means an exhaustive or definitive description, it can stimulate a more in-depth examination and understanding of comic book communication. Given a more serious attempt to understand what is going on in the communication process, we begin to appreciate more fully how comic books are a viable medium for the communication of ideas. There are additional reasons why comic books are worth our attention, and those are explored in the next section.

ANALYZING: WHY STUDY COMIC BOOKS?

As noted previously, most people hold a low opinion of comic books. To many, comic books are little more than cheap, disposable artifacts of popular culture that are not worth serious reflection or investigation. Given these opinions, what justification might there be for studying comic books in the context of a course? In this concluding section we present four explanations for why the medium is worth such attention.

First Reason: Originality of the Art Form

Comic books are a unique and powerful form of communication. Perhaps long-time comic book writer Jim Shooter was a bit carried away by his enthusiasm when he claimed, "What we've got is the most portable, limitless, intense, personal, focused, intimate, compelling, wonderful visual medium in creation" (6). However, it is true that comic books tell stories and involve readers in ways that no other art form—not plays, novels, or film—can duplicate. Historian Ron Goulart notes: "What I'd noticed early on was that comics were telling stories in a new way" (*Great History* v).

However, one variation on this justification claims that comic books do not tell stories in new ways, but that "The art of the pictorial narrative is, in fact, the original art form. Painting, sculpture and their analogous crafts are all offspring of the narrative work. Today narratives are called comics" (Steranko, *History* 5). Proponents point to Paleolithic cave drawings with sequences of images depicting a hunt as the first "comics." While clearly not what we think of as comics, and certainly not comic books, these primitive works are the beginning of the tradition of narrative art that led to the modern comic book.

A less ambitious variation on this justification is that comics are an American original. "Perhaps a major reason for recognizing and studying the comics," writes M. Thomas Inge, "is the fact that they are one of the few native American art forms" (*American Comic Book* xv). It should be noted that Inge is writing about comic strips, and he is echoing the so-called **Yellow Kid Thesis**, which states that the birth of a new art form was heralded by Richard Felton Outcault's late-nineteenth-century single-panel "comic strip" *Hogan's Alley* (which came to feature an urchin popularly known as the Yellow Kid). As we will see in the next chapter, taking a broader historical and cultural perspective seriously undermines the Yellow Kid Thesis.

Even without the justification of ancient lineage or native origin, comic books are worth studying because, as scholar Roger Sabin points out, "they are a language, with their own grammar, syntax and punctuation. They are not some hybrid form halfway between 'literature' and 'art' (whatever those words might mean), but a medium in their own right" (*Adult* 9).

Second Reason: The New Literacy

Reading in the twenty-first century often involves more than the mere understanding of words. As author Tom Wolf notes, "reading of words is but a subset of a much more general human activity which includes symbol decoding, information integration and organization" (427). The very concept of literacy has been revolutionized and broadened. Visual literacy, the ability to understand pictorial information, became one of the basic skills required for communication in the latter half of the twentieth century. As comic book pioneer Will Eisner points out, "Comics are at the center of the phenomenon" (*Graphic* 3).

The existence of the comic book has done more than just help undermine the primacy of the printed word. Comic books break down, or at least blur, boundaries between word texts and picture texts. Reading comic books requires a different type of literacy because on the comic book page the drawn word and the drawn picture are both images to be read as a single integrated text. Of course, comic books can vary in the degree to which they successfully integrate these two elements, and, as we shall see in later chapters, some theorists propose using the degree of interdependence or interanimation of the linguistic and the pictorial as the primary aesthetic standard for evaluating comic books.

"The comic book occupies a curious and unique position in the 20th century electronic media revolution," contends academic Ronald Schmitt. "It represents a transitional medium that directly transforms the printed word and the framed picture, paving the way for a new type of literacy which combines these and other traditional texts (spoken word, music) in the ultimate of intertextual media forms: television" (160). Writing in 1992, perhaps Schmitt did not anticipate the ascendancy of another intertextual media form—the website. Certainly the habits and skills developed by reading comics have helped make the Web both more acceptable and more comprehensible for many people. Comic books and comic strips themselves are making a new evolutionary leap as they move to the Web in ever-increasing numbers. Writing in 1985, Inge asked, "What could be a more natural form of creative expression for the future than one that effectively combines the written word with the visual symbol? Perhaps comic books or visual novels are a major literary form for the twenty-first century" (*American Comic Book* 5). Adding confirmation to Inge's vision was the 2008 winner of the prestigous Caldecott Medal for excellence in children's literature. Brian Selznick's *The Invention of Hugo Cabret* (2007) proved to be an innovative mixture of prose, comics, and illutrations that further affirmed the trend toward a new visual literacy.

Third Reason: Historical Significance

There was a time when virtually every kid in America, and quite a few adults, read comic books (Nyberg 1). Until the television became a fixture in most American homes, the comic book was "the dominant element in the culture of American children" (Lupoff and Thompson 11). Consider these estimates of comic book readership:

> Between the ages of six and eleven 95 per cent [*sic*] of boys and 91 per cent of girls buy comic books for a steady reading diet. Between twelve and seventeen, the figure falls to 87 per cent of boys and 81 per cent of girls. Between eighteen and thirty, the figure is 41 per cent of men and 28 per cent of women; after thirty, it is down to 16 and 12. But remember, these are steady readers. (Waugh, 334)

It was probably a fairly accurate statement in 1989 when comic book historian Mike Benton wrote that "the American comic book has touched the lives of nearly everyone alive today" (*Comic Book* 11).

Discovering: The Development of Comic Books as Literature

1940s	*The Spirit* by Will Eisner introduces emotional resonance and depth. Eisner told human interest stories within the confines of the adventure genre. While these adventure tales had very little subtext, Eisner's experiments with the form and seven-page story limit resulted in an unprecedented degree of narrative density and complexity.
1950s	Harvey Kurtzman produces the EC war comic books, perhaps the first comic books to have, to some degree, all of the virtues of literature: Kurtzman used his mastery of narrative breakdown and composition to create realistic, emotional anti-war stories that worked on multiple levels.

Cont'd

Late 1960s	While most simply attack and undermine establishment values, the best of the underground comix provide social commentary and pointed satire.
Early 1970s	Realism asserts itself in the emergence of autobiographical subject matter.
1976	*American Splendor* by Harvey Pekar provides the sustained work of personal vision.
1978	Considered the first definitive graphic novel, *A Contract with God* by Will Eisner is a ground-level work that strives to be literature.
1980	*Raw* by Art Spiegelman and Françoise Mouly introduces a conscious attempt to create comic books as art.
1983	Alan Moore begins writing *Swamp Thing*, incorporating subtext, social commentary, and emotional resonance into a mainstream DC comic book.
1982	*Love and Rockets* by Jaime and Gilbert Hernandez becomes the first major ground-level series, proving that there is an adult audience for comic books.
1986	*Maus* by Art Spiegelman is received as the most highly acclaimed work in the history of the medium. Still, many critics refuse to recognize it as a comic book.
1986	DC breaks with traditional conceptions of the superhero by publishing Frank Miller's *Batman: The Dark Knight* and Alan Moore and Dave Gibbons' *Watchmen*.
1988	DC's new *Sandman* series written by Neil Gaiman begins its run as a sustained literary effort in a mainstream comic book. The work attracts both praise from the mainstream media and new adult readers for comic books. Perhaps even more than *Maus*, this series enhanced the credibility of the medium because no one could deny that this was indeed a comic book.
1994	Paul Karasik and David Mazzucchelli adapt Paul Auster's novella *City of Glass* into graphic novel form, reimaging elements of the narrative and in the process demonstrating the potential of the comics form as a distinct storytelling medium.
2001	The American Book Awards recognizes Chris Ware's *Jimmy Corrigan: The Smartest Kid on Earth* for "outstanding literary achievement."
2006	*Time* magazine names Alison Bechdel's memoir *Fun Home: A Family Tragicomic* the best book of 2006.

Fourth Reason: Potential of the Medium

In an October 15, 1986 appearance on *Late Night with David Letterman*, Harvey Pekar, writer of the autobiographical comic book *American Splendor*, expressed the potential of the comic book medium in clear, simple terms: "It's words and pictures. You can do anything you want with words and pictures" (qtd. in Witek, *Comic Books* 154). Pekar's words proved prophetic, for, as we will see in Chapter 3, 1986 was a watershed year in comic books, and thereafter more and more creators proved that they in fact *could* do anything they wanted with words and pictures.

Notable works since that year have ranged from Alan Moore and Dave Gibbons' deconstruction of the superhero mythos in *Watchmen* (1986), to Martin Rowson's melding of T.S. Eliot and Raymond Chandler in *Wasteland* (1990), to Will Eisner's poignant autobiographical novel *To the Heart of the Storm* (1991). In 1989, scholar Joseph Witek noted that "a growing number of contemporary American comic books are being written as literature aimed at a general readership of adults" (*Comic Books* 3). Eric Drooker's nearly wordless fable of the artist in the modern metropolis, *Flood!* (1992); Howard Cruse's honest portrayal of a gay man's coming of age in the 1960s American south in *Stuck Rubber Baby* (1995); Jason Lutes' *Jar of Fools* (1994), a sparse tale of love, loss, and magic; and Greg Rucka and Steve Lieber's riveting Antarctica murder mystery *Whiteout* (1998) are just a few of the literate works that are beginning to fulfill the potential of the medium.

This chapter began with a disparaging quote from Lawrence L. Langer's review of *Maus*. While Langer is loath to acknowledge the work as a comic, he does admit that it is "a serious form of pictorial literature" (17). And *Maus* is but one of scores of serious literary works that have shown the medium to be worthy of greater attention and study. However, in the introduction to *Comics: Anatomy of a Mass Medium*, scholars Reinhold Reitberger and Wolfgang Fuchs make one simple point that cannot be overlooked: "Comics are important because we love to read them!" (7).

Discussion Questions

1. One approach to defining comic books is to establish the essential and identifying characteristics of the medium (and the art form). Engage your classmates in an open dialogue concerning the essential nature of the comic book using the following questions:

   - Does it have to be more than one page?
   - Does it have to have pictures?
   - Must it be on paper?
   - Does it have to have words?
   - Does it have to have panels?
   - Does it have to have more than one panel per page on at least some of the pages?
   - Must there be a juxtaposition of words and pictures in the same compositional unit (e.g., page, panel)?
   - Can the answers to the above questions lead you to your own definition of the comic book?

2. Besides the examples given in the chapter, what other types of channel noise can occur in a comic book? In what ways can noise change the received meaning of a message?

3. Other than comic books and comic strips, what examples of sequential art have you personally encountered? In what ways were they similar and dissimilar to comic books?

Activities

1. Conduct a small, informal survey about knowledge of comic books. Interview at least ten people. Try to get a good variety of ages among the respondents (e.g., two teenagers, two people in their twenties, two people in their thirties, etc.). In addition to the questions suggested below, you should come up with some of your own.

   - Have you ever heard of *Maus* by Art Spiegelman?
   - What is a graphic novel?
   - Name two comic books that do not have anything to do with Superman, Batman, or Spider-Man.

   Prepare to compare your results with those of your classmates to see how comic books are perceived.

2. The very name of the medium—*comic books*—works against a broader acceptance. Most people have a preconceived notion of a comic book as cheap (if not trashy) juvenile entertainment. Thus, to disassociate their work from this preconception, various comics creators and proponents of the comic book have proposed other names for the medium, such as:

   - Comix
   - Commix
   - Drawn Books
   - Drawn Stories
   - Dual-Writing
   - Encapsulated Narrative
   - Graphic Literature
   - Pictorial Literature
   - Picto-fiction
   - Picture Stories
   - Rendered Writing
   - Sequential Art

   Rank these names according to the ones you think most most accurately describe the medium. Which would be most useful for gaining wider acceptance? What are the flaws (inaccuracies, misrepresentations, confusing terminology, etc.) with each of these names?

Recommended Readings

Comics:

Moore, Alan, and Dave Gibbons. *Watchmen*. 1986–1987. New York: DC Comics, 2005.

In order to fully appreciate how artfully *Watchmen* deconstructs the superhero genre, you must first read a few traditional superhero narratives. Alan Moore's masterful plotting of this psychological drama irrevocably placed him among comicdom's all-time greatest writers.

Spiegelman, Art. *The Complete Maus*. 1986–1991. London: Penguin, 2003.

The most honored American comic book should be read by every student of the medium. Spiegelman reveals the pain of surviving the Holocaust by recounting flash-backs to the wartime experiences of his father, Vladek, as well as his own struggle to come to terms with living with his scarred parent.

Scholarly Sources:

Talon, Durwin S. *Panel Discussions: Design in Sequential Art Storytelling*. Raleigh, NC: TwoMorrows Publishing, 2003.

Talon presents perspectives on the art of effective storytelling from a host of comic book professionals, including editors, writers, pencillers, inkers, and cover artists. Illustrations from the creators' own works help to demonstrate how they have used the techniques of the medium to achieve mastery.

Witek, Joseph. *Comic Books as History: The Narrative Art of Jack Jackson, Art Spiegelman, and Harvey Pekar*. Jackson, MS: University of Mississippi Press, 1989.

Witeck produced one of the earliest in-depth analyses of comic books, treating them as acts of literary expression and their creators as artists.

The History of Comic Books,
Part I: Developing a Medium

"Comics were not created—they evolved."

—LES DANIELS, HISTORIAN, 1971

There is some debate about when people first started making comics, but William Hogarth (1697–1764), clearly laid the foundations for popularizing sequential art. Comics historian Maurice Horn claims that Hogarth's "drawings can be acknowledged as the first direct forerunners of the comic strip" ("Hogarth" 321). At least some of the "drawings" that Horn refers to were actually engraved copies of paintings. Early in his career, Hogarth was a painter who promoted himself as an artist and made considerable supplemental income by selling prints of his paintings. Hogarth produced seven sets of sequential narratives on "Modern Moral Subjects." The first three of these sets were originally done in the form of paintings: "A Harlot's Progress" (1731), "The Rake's Progress" (1735), and "Marriage a la Mode" (1743). While the six paintings (or prints) in "A Harlot's Progress" do have a deliberate sequence and do tell a rudimentary story when they are juxtaposed, as comics historian Mike Kidson points out, the visual sequencing within each image "is confused and inconsistent," and "we understand the series as a narrative because of what it depicts, not because of the way in which it is composed" (79). However, Hogarth refined his narrative technique. "The Rake's Progress" displays a "much more considered approach towards visual sequencing," and "Marriage a La Mode" has a "much more strip-like and consistent left-to-right construction" (Kidson 79–80).

Prints of Hogarth's work were quite popular with London's upper class, but he seemed to want to reach a broader audience, so Hogarth himself authorized copies that could be sold at a fraction of the cost of the originals. By the fourth series, "Industry and Idleness" (1747), Hogarth was reducing his initial investment of time and money by skipping the painting altogether and converting from copperplate engraving to a sort of "enhanced" etching. However, Hogarth's authorized prints were still too expensive for most of London's middle class. But due in part to the availability of cheap pirated prints, Hogarth's work did cross class boundaries. It may well be that Hogarth's importance in the

FIGURE 2.1. William Hogarth first marketed sequential art through prints of his painting series "A Harlot's Progress" (1731). The first plate shows the lead character's arrival in London and the second her role as a kept woman. By the last plate, scavengers are picking over her estate after her death from syphilis.

history of comics stems as much from his marketing ability and his marketability as it does from his artistic or storytelling ability.

OBJECTIVES

In this chapter you will learn:

1. the continental roots of comics as an art form;
2. the ways in which comic strips and pulps contributed to the emergence of the American comic book;
3. how publishers turned comic books into a stand-alone medium, building on the success of the superhero genre and the shop system; and
4. how subsequent cycles of boom and bust have been influenced by the audience and the editorial direction of the major publishers.

Sequential art dates back to the beginning of humanity's artistic expression. Between 10,000 and 25,000 years ago, juxtaposed images in sequence used to convey simple narratives were painted or scratched onto cave walls in France and Spain. Since that time humanity has engaged in a wide array of image sequencing practices, or sequential art, ranging from Egyptian tomb paintings (circa 1300 BC), to the Bayeux Tapestry (circa 1100 AD), to Mexican codices (circa 1500 AD).

However, the sequences of images painted on cave walls, carved into stone, baked onto clay, or woven into elaborate tapestries are far removed from the modern manifestations of sequential art—comic strips and comic books—in terms of production, distribution, and function. Perhaps comics, in the broadest sense of the term, have existed as an art form for millennia, but sequential art forms employed as popular entertainment media are, as art historian David Kunzle puts it, "children of the printing press" (133).

As the movable-type printing press technology spread throughout Europe, so did a new form of popular entertainment—the **broadsheet**, a single large piece of paper with a series of images on it, usually accompanied by text. Although the text was placed above or below the image rather than incorporated into it, the broadsheet manifested the essential form and function of the modern comic strip. Broadsheets were the first type of sequential art to create a balance and a degree of interdependence between picture and text. Broadsheets were popular in Germany, France, England, and Holland from about 1450 to 1800, and they were often sold at fairs and festivals. Governments and churches even attempted to use this powerful new medium to disseminate news and teach moral lessons.

There is not space in this brief introduction to comic book history to explore the myriad influences on the evolution of sequential art. Indeed, many of the techniques of sequential art that we associate with comics were developed piecemeal by dozens of medieval book illustrators. Art historian Daniele Alexander-Bidon has demonstrated that in these copiously illustrated, single-copy manuscripts created for the very wealthy, "one finds page lay-outs, balloons for words or thought, onomatopoeia, movement lines, containment by frames or going outside them, fast movements split into several images, and graphic relations between contiguous images" (qtd. in Groensteen, "Töpffer" 108–109). However, we can proceed with a survey of some of the major eras and influential figures who have helped shape the medium as it now manifests itself in twenty-first-century America. In this chapter, we'll examine how the art form further developed from its European publishing roots and evolved to become a major contributor to popular culture by the mid-twentieth century.

Discovering: Eras of the American Comic Book

It is always somewhat artificial to divide artistic and commercial phenomena into eras, and it is totally unrealistic to expect the stages of an art form or industry to have tidy beginning and ending points. The classification system detailed below allows for the overlapping of eras, with the defining characteristics of a new era beginning to appear as the characteristics of the old era are still fading. Within the fan community itself, you are likely to encounter references to the "Golden Age" of comics during the 1940s or the "Silver Age" in the 1960s. This classification system, while not universally agreed upon, tends to be based on first appearances or deaths of key characters in mainstream, primarily superhero, comic books. We have opted to organize our history of American comic books into eras defined by major changes in comic book content or industry practices. Below we name these eras—and we expand upon them throughout this and the next chapter—introducing them in terms of the following details:

Cont'd

Inception—the initial development of the characteristics that define the era

Flashpoint—the works that embody the characteristics of the era and stand as models for other works to follow or actions that truly "ignite" the era

Lasting Effects—considerations of how the medium was altered by the era

Era of Invention

Inception: 1842	*The Adventures of Obadiah Oldbuck* (translation of Rodolphe Töpffer's *Les Amours de Monsieur Vieux Bois*)
Flashpoint: 1897	*The Yellow Kid in McFadden's Flats* [*Yellow Kid Magazine*]
Lasting Effects:	Established the characteristics of the art form (gutter, balloons, etc.) and the medium (cheap, disposable)

Era of Proliferation

Inception: 1934	*Famous Funnies* #1
Flashpoint: 1938	*Action Comics* #1
Lasting Effects:	The superhero became strongly associated with the comic book

Era of Diversification

Inception: 1940	*Planet Comics* #1 (science fiction) *Wings Comics* #1 (aviation) *Walt Disney's Comics & Stories* (funny animals)
Flashpoint: 1947	William Gaines inherits Educational Comics
Lasting Effects:	Established a number of different genres that have been repeated and revised by subsequent creators

Era of Retrenchment

Inception: 1952	Competition from television/peak and decline of industry
Flashpoint: 1954	*Seduction of the Innocent* and the Comics Code Authority
Lasting Effects:	Constraints on the content of mainstream comic books, limiting the complexity of storytelling

Era of Connection

Inception: 1956	*Showcase* #4
Flashpoint: 1962	*Amazing Fantasy* #15
Lasting Effects:	The more fallible hero eventually led to the antihero, and comics fandom comes into being

Cont'd

Era of Independence

Inception: 1958	Kurtzman's *Humbug*
Flashpoint: 1968	*Zap* #1
	His Name Is Savage
Lasting Effects:	Alternative and small press comic books emerge, allowing varying degrees of freedom from the traditional mainstream constraints

Era of Ambition

Inception: 1978	A Contract with God
Flashpoint: 1986	*Maus*
	Watchmen
	The Dark Knight Returns
Lasting Effects:	Ambitious works that garner mainstream media attention

Era of Reiteration

Inception: 1986	*The Man of Steel*
Flashpoint: 1994	*Marvels*
	Zero Hour
Lasting effects:	Mainstream publishers continue to cater to a smaller, highly specialized audience

There is possibly a case for splitting the timeline into Mainstream and Independent branches. Characterizing the most recent era as reiteration focuses on the mainstream, but there is much original work being done in the independent press and with mass market book publishers. However, it looks as if one of the undercurrents of this era will be the blurring of the distinction between independent and mainstream. There are mainstream imprints with an "indie sensibility," and more and more independent creators being recruited by the mainstream.

THE ERA OF INVENTION

Rodolphe Töpffer: Father of the Comic Book

The son of a well-known artist, Rodolphe Töpffer (1799–1846) had a lifelong desire to be a painter. Yet art was never to be more than a sideline for Töpffer. He became a teaching-director of a boys' preparatory school and engaged his creativity in scholarly writing. It was his scholarship, particularly a translation of *Demosthenes* (1824) and a study of the *Iliad* (1831), that earned him the chair of Rhetoric and Belles-Lettres at the Academy in Geneva. Töpffer went on to write more scholarly treatises and a number of critically acclaimed short stories. However, he is best known for what began as "doodlings" done to give his artistic yearnings an outlet and to delight his students at the prep school.

It was with these *la litterature en estampes* (picture-stories), as he called them, that Töpffer made "a decisive break with older formats and that he initiated a new form of expression." (Groensteen, "Töpffer" 107–108). Töpffer created at least seven picture-stories between 1827 and 1844. The first, *Les Amours de M. Vieux-Bois*, was created in 1827, but not printed until 1837. Töpffer's first published album was *Histoire de M. Jabot*, drawn in 1831, printed in 1833, and published in 1835. These picture-stories were usually published as oblong albums, some close to one hundred pages long.

One of Töpffer's innovations was that he used the medium of sequential art to tell entertaining fictional stories. Morality tales and propaganda were replaced by slapstick tales of absurdist antiheroes who struggled against the whims of fate. Yet his greatest innovations were not in content, but in form. Historian John Geipel speculates that it was due to his poor eyesight that Töpffer developed "the 'shorthand,' epigrammatic style of drawing that became the stock-in-trade of the later strip cartoonists" (136). This sketchy (cartoon) style allowed Töpffer's panel compositions and panel sequences to be much more dynamic than any work that had preceded him. "He made broken lines more suggestive than continuous ones, and by abandoning the academic concept of three-dimensional, anatomical drawing, he learned how to render movement. His art is all movement, breathless, relentless; it is the movement for the movement's sake" (Kunzle 139).

His work might not have been preserved if not for the positive comments of German writer Johann Wolfgang von Goethe. As Goethe wrote about Töpffer in a letter to Eckermann: "If, for the future, he would choose a less frivolous subject and restrict himself a little, he would produce things beyond all conception" (503). The content of Töpffer's work never became serious, but he began to take the form itself seriously. In his *Essai de physiognomonie (Essay on Physiognomy)*, written in 1845, Töpffer proclaimed that "the picture-story, which critics disregard and scholars scarcely notice, has greater influence at all times, perhaps even more than written literature" (3). He also recognized that he had created a truly blended art form, where pictures without text would have only vague meaning, and text without pictures would have virtually no meaning. Likewise, each segment (or panel) derives its meaning from what has gone before and what follows. With Töpffer, "the transition from illustration in the Hogarthian sense to composition of an entire story in pictorial terms was complete" (Wiese xvii).

Töpffer's works were rather quickly translated into a number of different languages, including English. One of the English translations, perhaps a pirated copy of a British edition, made its way to America in the early 1840s as *The Adventures of Obadiah Oldbuck*. The American edition was 8½ × 11 and forty pages in length. It was printed on both sides of the paper, with six to twelve panels per page. In other words, it looked a lot like a modern comic book (Beerbohm, *Obadiah*). After only a few of his albums had been published, Töpffer began to inspire imitators, including the famed illustrator Gustave Doré (1832–1883),

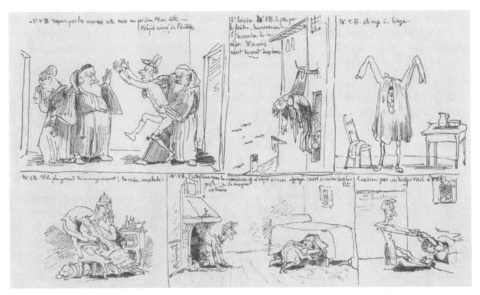

FIGURE 2.2. Rodolphe Töpffer's *Les Amours de M. Vieux-Bois* (1837) represents one of the earliest experiments with publishing sequential art. Humor ensues as Mr. Vieux-Bois alternates between fouling up suicide attempts (note he is attempting to hang himself in the second panel) and chasing his beloved (she tries to hide from him in the fifth panel).

whose *The Labours of Hercules* (1847) was a picture-story album that followed the Töpffer model in form, tone, and style, but was superior in draftsmanship. Töpffer had created the art form, now it just awaited a medium of transmission, a means of production and distribution.

Comic Strips and Pulp Fiction

The American comic book industry subsequently grew out of two roots: newspaper comic strips and pulp magazines. The format and commercial infrastructure grew primarily out of a repackaging of the comic book's closest cousin, the comic strip. Part of the investment capital, the talent, and even some of the heroic archetypes were diverted from the pulps.

The first characters to populate the comic book pages did not wear capes or leap tall buildings. They tended to be youngsters with names like Buster Brown, Little Nemo, and the Katzenjammer Kids. The first mass media products that began to look like modern comic books—and were called comic books—were actually reprint collections of popular newspaper comic strips. More than a thousand books of comic strip reprints were published between 1897 and 1932 (Beerbohm and Olson 367). The first and most famous of the comic strips kids to have a collection of his adventures reprinted in book form is the Yellow Kid. The strip that became known as *The Yellow Kid* began as a single-panel cartoon by Richard Felton Outcault (1863–1928). In 1894 Outcault began doing weekly drawings of slum life for the *Sunday World* newspaper. It was not until May 5, 1895 that he titled his cartoon *Hogan's Alley*. Most of the urchins and street toughs he drew wore the conventional clothing of tenement kids. However, one bald, barefooted, jug-eared kid by the name of Mickey Dugan inexplicably wore a nightshirt. As Mickey gained prominence in the strip, he became the chief source of dialogue, and the dialogue appeared not in a word balloon, but written on his nightshirt. Legend has it that a printer used Mickey's nightshirt as the test area for a new yellow ink, and thereafter he became known to readers as the Yellow Kid. The Yellow Kid was an immensely popular character, and he was widely merchandised. In March 1897, the publication of the *Yellow Kid Magazine* marked "the first published collection of an American comic strip" (Benton, *Comic Book* 14). Since *The Yellow Kid* had demonstrated that comics could dramatically increase newspaper circulation, he was soon joined on the comics page by *The Katzenjammer Kids, Mutt & Jeff, Foxy Grandpa*, and many others. The most popular of the comic strips were collected and reprinted in a variety of formats. Then, in 1919, the publishing company of Cupples & Leon introduced black-and-white reprint books that were 9½ inches square with a flexible cardboard cover. These were sold on newsstands and passenger trains for 25 cents (or 75 cents for the Big Book editions) (Beerbohm and Olson 374). This was the dominant reprint format until 1934, when Cupples & Leon abandoned comic strip reprints to concentrate on their successful children's book series (Tom Swift, the Hardy Boys, etc.).

By 1922 hundreds of books of newspaper strips had been published, but in January of that year the Embee Distributing Company of New York experimented with a new approach to marketing sequential art. *Comic Monthly* offered the usual strip reprints, and it looked very similar to the standard Cupples & Leon format (with a slight size modification to 8½ × 10 inches), but the soft paper cover and cheaper interior paper allowed for a cheaper price of only 10 cents. Most significantly, it was the first monthly newsstand comic publication, appearing once a month for all of 1922. The experiment lasted exactly one year, but it was a few steps closer to the product that would launch the comic book industry.

At the dawn of the twentieth century, pulp magazines were beginning to replace dime novels as a form of cheap entertainment for the middle class and educated lower class. Beneath their often lurid covers, pulp magazines contained rough-edged wood-pulp pages filled with crude but powerful storytelling that helped establish most genres of popular fiction and launched the careers of many of America's best-known writers, from Ray Bradbury to Raymond Chandler. Most of the pioneers of the comic book format were in some way associated with the pulp magazines. As pulp

FIGURE 2.3. Hully gee! Richard F. Outcault's comic strips featuring the Yellow Kid helped to sell newspapers and then other merchandise.

FIGURE 2.4. The Spider was the Master of Men—and the pulp magazines—well before Batman and other mystery men debuted in the comic books. © 1940 by Popular Publications, Inc. Copyright renewed © 1968 and assigned to Argosy Communications, Inc. All rights reserved. The Spider is a trademark of Argosy Communications, Inc.

magazine sales began to falter in the face of competition from comic books, a number of pulp publishers shifted their resources to comic book publishing. Many of the pulp writers (and a few of the artists) followed their publishers into the new medium.

The pulps had introduced heroes such as Tarzan (1912) and Zorro (1919), but sales peaked in the 1930s with the introduction of the "hero pulps." Each hero pulp featured a single recurring hero of remarkable appearance and extraordinary abilities. Both Tarzan and Zorro had appeared in various pulp magazines for years, but in 1931 the Shadow became the first character to appear in a magazine created specifically for his adventures and bearing his name: *The Shadow, A Detective Magazine*. A few years later, *Doc Savage*, *The Spider*, and other eponymous hero pulps appeared on the newsstands. With their costumes, secret identities, and abilities beyond those of ordinary mortals, it is easy to see that this new breed of pulp heroes had a direct influence on the superhero comic books that appeared in the late 1930s and 1940s. Ironically, the immense popularity of their progeny, such as Superman and Batman, is one of the factors that led to the rather precipitous decline of the pulp magazine industry.

The Modern Comic Book

The American comic book industry was born at Eastern Color Printing Company in New York. In 1929 Eastern Color printed *The Funnies*, the first product from George Delacorte's Dell Publishing Company. *The Funnies* was a sixteen-page tabloid-format collection of comic strips that came out on Saturdays and sold for 10 cents (it was later reduced to 5 cents). *The Funnies* lasted about a year and a half—thirty-six issues. *The Funnies* is significant for a number of reasons. It was the beginnings of Dell, a company that was destined to become one of the most prolific and successful comic book publishers. Also, while still consisting of one-page comic strips, it contained original material, not reprints of newspaper comic strips. And perhaps most importantly, it gave a couple of Eastern Color employees ideas.

Eastern Color also printed the color Sunday comics for most of the major newspapers in the northeast. Harry I. Wildenberg, the sales manager at Eastern

Color Printing, did not really care for comic strips, but he realized the powerful impact they could have on newspaper circulation. He reasoned that if the comics could sell newspapers, they could be used to sell other products as well. In 1933 Wildenberg sold the Gulf Oil Company on the idea of using comics as a gas station giveaway with a fill-up. In a direct imitation of the format of Dell's *The Funnies*, *Gulf Comic Weekly* was tabloid-sized and contained original, full-page comic strips. For Wildenberg, the motivation was simply to sell printing contracts that kept the Eastern Color presses rolling.

Wildenberg might not have cared for comics, but one of his salesmen, Maxwell Charles Gaines, seemed to have a true affinity for the medium. M.C. Gaines enthusiastically joined his boss in promoting comics in book form. In 1933 Wildenberg and Gaines produced *Funnies on Parade* as an advertising premium to be given away by Proctor & Gamble. This was the first of the comic strip reprint collections to have the look of a what came to be called a comic book: 7½ × 10½ with a paper cover.

Increasingly, Eastern Color's association with books of comics resulted from the efforts of M.C. Gaines. For the rest of 1933 Gaines and Wildenberg continued to promote advertising premium books, such as *A Century of Comics*, and print runs began to exceed 100,000 copies. Some editions with multiple sponsors ran to a million copies. Gaines' most famous efforts, and perhaps the true beginning of the comic book industry, were three books that confusingly bore the same name: *Famous Funnies*.

The first of these publications was issued in 1933 and titled *Famous Funnies: A Carnival of Comics*. This book of comic strip reprints was packaged and printed by Eastern Color for Kinney Shoe Store, Milk-O-Malt, and other clients as a give-away. Legend has it that Gaines stickered a 10 cent price on the covers of a few dozen of the books and talked some newsstands into participating in his experiment. They sold out over the weekend, and the news vendors wanted more. Gaines is often credited with being the first person to have the idea of selling a book of comics as a product in and of itself, but, of course, books of comic strip reprints, in one form or another, had been selling briskly for decades.

The second book, *Famous Funnies, Series One* #1 was issued by Eastern Color in partnership with George Delacorte in early 1934. It consisted of reprints, portions of which were from *Funnies on Parade* and *Famous Funnies: A Carnival of Comics*. To test the market for comic books as a product, approximately 40,000 copies were published to be sold in chain stores for 10 cents.

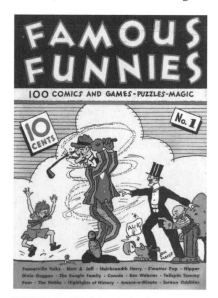

FIGURE 2.5. Third time's the charm: *Famous Funnies* makes its third debut. © 1934 Eastern Color Printing Company

Finally, in May 1934, the third *Famous Funnies* #1 debuted. With this book, Eastern Color Printing Company went beyond merely packaging and printing books of comics and established itself as the first major comic book publisher. When the second issue of *Famous Funnies* came out, it was the first product that looked like the modern comic book to be sold monthly on the newsstands. Newspaper comic strip reprints were the mainstay of the book, but original filler material began to appear after the first few issues. *Famous Funnies* lasted until 1955, for a total of 218 issues. Thusly, Gaines and Wildenberg had laid the foundations of the comic book industry.

New Fun

The colorful Major Malcolm Wheeler-Nicholson began the publishing company that would become the cornerstone of the new comic book industry. In 1934 he founded National Allied Publications, which later became National Periodical Publications and ultimately DC Comics. As a cavalry officer, Major Wheeler-Nicholson had had his share of adventures in exotic corners of the globe. After a forced retirement from the military, he made a living writing military adventures and historical swashbucklers for pulp magazines such as *Argosy* and *Adventure*. However, Wheeler-Nicholson took note of the new medium of comic books. He decided to try a different approach to publishing comic books by publishing all new content (he was probably unaware of Delacorte's failed attempt with *The Funnies* in 1929). Perhaps he reasoned that if reprints books could sell so well, a book with original material should do even better, or perhaps he published new material because he thought it would be cheaper than paying the licensing fees for comic strip reprints. Whatever his motivation, in early 1935 he published *New Fun Comics*, a regularly published comic book containing original material.

New Fun was far from an immediate success. Wheeler-Nicholson's Fourth Avenue office began to fill up with unsold copies of the book. Distributors were reluctant to give valuable rack space to an unproven commodity such as the comic book, and they were especially cautious with a book that had totally unknown characters. Despite the lack of sales and a lack of funds, late in 1935 Wheeler-Nicholson added another title, *New Comics*. By this time *New Fun* had been changed to *More Fun*, and the books were being edited by former contributors Vincent Sullivan and Whitney Ellsworth. Perhaps they were paid regularly, but the Major was so unreliable about paying the writers and artists that he had an almost constant turnover of staff. Of course, this meant there were plenty of opportunities for new talent. For instance, two youngsters from Cleveland, Jerry Siegel and Joe Shuster, did a number of features for the Major's comics, including "Dr. Occult," "Slam Bradley," and "Federal Men." However, the Major could not be convinced to publish their favorite feature, "Superman."

The flamboyant Major was more con man than businessman. Sales of his books remained shaky, and he was becoming further in debt to a man by the name of Harry Donenfeld. The Major's books were distributed by Independent News, which Harry Donenfeld and his partner Jack Liebowitz had formed in 1932. Independent News had advanced Wheeler-Nicholson funds which he had never paid back. Donenfeld also owned the printing plant that printed the covers for the Major's books, and the Major was behind on paying those print-ing bills. So when Wheeler-Nicholson wanted to add a third title, *Detective Comics*, to his line of comic books, he was forced to do so in partnership with Donenfeld and Liebowitz. In fact, when *Detective Comics* debuted in 1937, it was the product of a newly formed company—Detective Comics, Inc.—with Wheeler-Nicholson and Liebowitz listed as the owners. Harry Donenfeld was an energetic and aggressive entrepreneur. In addition to being a printer and distrib-utor, he published pulp magazines. Perhaps he saw his association with Wheeler-Nicholson as an easy way to move into the new comic book field. If so, he was correct. By the end of 1937, the Major had essentially turned National Allied Publications over to Donenfeld to cover his debts. The following year, he sold his interest in Detective Comics, Inc. to Donenfeld. After the Major's departure, Detective Comics, Inc.—commonly referred to as DC Comics—would go on to become the most enduring publisher of American comic books.

THE ERA OF PROLIFERATION

Wheeler-Nicholson returned to writing for the pulps, and almost immediately after his departure the fledgling comic book enterprise he had left behind began to blossom into an empire. Donenfeld and Liebowitz's three titles—*More Fun Comics, Adventure Comics,* and *Detective Comics*—were selling well enough to keep the presses running, but comic books did not become a big business until the introduction of their next title, *Action Comics*.

Of course, the first issue of *Action Comics* introduced Superman, a character who single-handedly established the identity of the American comic book. Writer Jerry Siegel was always a bundle of nervous energy, always wired. Artist Joe Shuster was very quiet. He was small, but worked out a lot to try to be more muscular. In 1933, while still high school students in Cleve-land, the boys produced a mimeographed fanzine, *Science Fiction.* For the third issue, Siegel wrote and Shus-ter illustrated a story titled "The Reign of the Super-man." The title character was a bald villain (who

FIGURE 2.6. Will Eisner rendered a character reminscent of the eccentric founder of DC Comics, Major Malcolm Wheeler-Nichol-son (alongside another resembling Jack Liebowitz), in *The Dreamer* by Will Eisner. © 1986 by Will Eisner. Used by permission of W. W. Norton & Company, Inc.

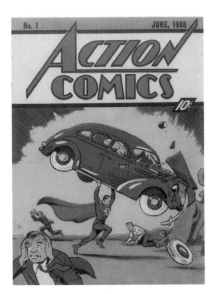

FIGURE 2.7. *Action Comics* #1 (1938) was arguably the most important comic book in the industry's history. © DC Comics

looked a lot like future arch-villain Lex Luthor). Later in the year they toyed with the idea of making their Superman villain into a hero. By 1936 Shuster had sketched various poses of the not-yet-published Superman with a couple of phrases, including "The Greatest Super-Hero of All Times." Shuster based the Superman costume on a trapeze artist outfit.

Siegel and Shuster's original goal was to do a newspaper strip, but they also tried comic book publishers. They got seventeen rejection letters. One said: "We are in the market only for strips likely to have the most extraordinary appeal, and we do not feel the Superman gets into that category" (Goulart, *Great* 85). Despite the lack of encouragement, Siegel and Shuster kept submitting their Superman strip. Ultimately, DC editor Vincent Sullivan decided to purchase the feature for *Action Comics*. The pair was paid ten dollars a page for that first thirteen-page story. So, for $130 to split between them, Siegel and Shuster sold all rights to Superman, who would go on to become one of the most lucrative merchandising properties of all time.

When Harry Donenfeld saw the first *Action Comics* cover, with Superman holding a car over his head, he thought is was just too wacky. Superman stories continued to appear, but for the next five issues the covers featured more conventional adventure heroes: aviators, mounties, and such. By the fourth issue of *Action Comics*, sales figures were impressive. Donenfeld did a newstand survey and found out that kids were not asking for *Action Comics*, but for "that magazine with Superman on it" (Goulart, *Over* 78). Starting with issue twelve, Superman's image or name graced every cover therafter.

Superman was both the triumph and the tragedy of the comic book medium. Within a few years, *Action Comics* and its spin-off title, *Superman*, were each selling over a million copies a month. Superman assured the financial success of the new industry. Unfortunately, he also assured that that the comic book medium would be forever (well, at least so far) associated with adolescent power fantasies of muscular men in tights. The legion of "long underwear" imitators that followed Superman cemented this image in the popular imagination.

Super-Imitators

Superman's first direct competitor had a very short career. Donenfeld's accountant, Victor Fox, probably saw the sales figures on *Action Comics* before anyone else in the company, realized Superman was a goldmine, and left DC to stake his own claim. Moving to a different floor in the same building that housed DC, he formed Fox Features Syndicate and commissioned the Eisner-Iger Shop to create a Superman imitation called Wonder Man. *Wonder Comics* #1 was cover-dated May 1939. *Wonder Comics* only lasted two issues, and Wonder Man himself didn't even make it past the first one: DC immediately sued Fox for infringement of copyright. Fox, however, did not go away. Over the next few years his company published plenty of less-Superman-like superheroes supplied by the Eisner-Iger Shop, including the Flame and the Blue Beetle.

Another superhero inspired by the success of Superman had a much longer career, probably because he was sponsored by Superman's publisher. In 1939 DC introduced its second major superhero—and comicdom's second most recognizable icon—the Bat-Man (the hyphen was dropped in short order). When twenty-two-year-old comics newcomer Bob Kane complained about the "big salaries" Siegel and Shuster were getting for the Superman feature, editor Vince Sullivan suggested Kane work up his own costumed character. The following Tuesday, Kane came back with a Batman story. The first Batman story was published in *Detective Comics* #27.

The story had been co-written, or perhaps totally written, by Kane's long-time friend and collaborator, Bill Finger, who wrote the first two Batman stories, and another gifted writer named Gardner Fox wrote the next five or six. Kane had assistants and ghosts from very early on (*Grand*). In fact, by 1948 Kane was doing very little of the actually drawing. The first two stories were credited to "Rob't Kane." Thereafter, every single Batman story was credited to "Bob Kane" until 1968. The early comic book publishers could not conceive that the kids reading the stories actually cared who had created them, so the majority of early comic books gave no writer or artists credits. In a few cases, as with Kane, they followed the model of the comic strips, where a single person, usually the artist, received sole credit. Publishers bought a product and they didn't care who assisted or ghosted for the artist they made the check out to. Everyone, including the assistants and ghosts, accepted the practice.

By the summer of 1941 comic books were selling at the rate of 10 million copies a month. There were more than twenty-nine comic book publishers, and over 150 different titles were being published (Stevenson). By 1943 the U.S. comic book market "totaled 18,000,000 monthly copies, constituting a third of total magazine sales, to a value of $72,000,000" (Ames and Kunzle 552). It was an incredible number of comic book pages to be produced each month, but a system had been developed to facilitate the growth of the industry.

The Shop System

The shop system, or studio system, was developed in the mid-thirties to meet the sudden and growing demand for original material to fill comic books. At first this was primarily Major Wheeler-Nicholson's books, but by the end of the decade there were more than a dozen publishers utilizing the services of the shops. Most of the early publishers had no in-house staff, so the shops usually packaged entire books for them. The usual setup was a large one-room studio with writers and artists working at rows of tables. In some shops an artist was responsible for an entire feature, but in other instances each artist did a particular aspect of a feature and it was passed along in an assembly-line fashion.

FIGURE 2.8. Will Eisner recalls the assembly-line production process practiced in shops in *The Dreamer* (1986). From *The Dreamer* by Will Eisner. © 1986 by Will Eisner. Used by permission of W.W. Norton & Company, Inc.

More than a dozen other small shops formed during the 1940s, including Funnies, Inc. (who had assembled the contents for *Marvel Comics* #1), C.C. Beck and Pete Costanza Studio (who did much of the Captain Marvel material for Fawcett Comics), and Harry "A" Chesler's Shop. Chesler's approach was a typical comic book factory that produced material quickly and cheaply with an assembly-line approach. Eight to ten artists worked at rows of drafting tables on the third floor of an old tenement building with creaky, dusty wooden floors and no air conditioning. The writers worked down the hall, or worked at home and brought the scripts in to Chesler. The shop produced stories for more than a dozen comic book publishers.

Gradually, however, the shop system gave way to writers and artists working directly for publishers, and that arrangement has given way to a freelance system for most creators. Just as the shop system grew to support the boom in superhero comic books, it is not coincidental that the shops began to close as superhero titles went into decline. The turning point year for the superheroes came in 1947.

Profile: Will Eisner

born: William Erwin Eisner
March 6, 1917
Brooklyn, New York

"To me, I write about living and the art of living. My villain is Life itself. Human beings are struggling to survive."

Cont'd

Career Highlights

1936   Goes into business with Jerry Iger to operate one of the first comics production shops.

1940   Begins *Weekly Comic Book* with *The Spirit* as the lead feature.

1975   Receives the Lifetime Achievement Award at the International Salon of Comic Books in Angoulême.

1978   Publishes what is regarded as the first prominent graphic novel, *A Contract with God*.

1985   Publishes *Comics and Sequential Art*, a how-to book for cartoonists and the rudimentary formalist theory of the comic book art form.

1988   The Oscars of the comics, the Eisner Awards, are named in Will's honor.

1995   Receives the Milton Caniff Lifetime Achievement award from the National Cartoonists Society.

2005   *The Plot*, Eisner's first nonfiction graphic novel and his last major work undertaken before his death, is published posthumously.

Growing up in the Jewish ghettos in Brooklyn and the Bronx, Will Eisner decided that art would be his means to a better life. While still a teenager, Eisner partnered with established editor Jerry Iger to form the Eisner-Iger Shop, a comic book shop that packaged comics for Fiction House, Fox Comics, and other publishers. A few years later Eisner dissolved his partnership with Iger when he was offered an opportunity unique in the history of comic books: *The Des Moines Register* and Tribune Syndicate wanted Eisner to create a supplement to be inserted into newspapers across the nation. The *Weekly Comic Book* supplement, later renamed *The Spirit Section*, contained three features—*Lady Luck*, *Mr. Mystic*, and *The Spirit*.

The syndicate wanted *The Spirit* to be a superhero comic. In early stories the character had a hidden crime lab and even a flying car, but soon Eisner was reshaping the malleable concept into stories of every imaginable genre, and the only remaining concessions to superhero conventions were a simple domino mask and a pair of gloves. Most of the stories began with a dazzling splash page that set the tone. On the pages that followed Eisner experimented with layout and composition. Comics historian Michael Barrier says, "Eisner was in those years the comic-book equivalent of Orson Welles: he was the first complete master of a young and

FIGURE 2.9. Will Eisner in his role as teacher from unpublished storyboards. © 2008 by Will Eisner Studios, Inc.

Cont'd

heretofore unformed medium" (197–198). For many of Eisner's contemporaries and generations of artists who followed him, *The Spirit* was the textbook from which they learned how to create comic books.

Eisner's experiments with *The Spirit* were interrupted in the spring of 1942 when he was drafted into the U.S. Army. While in the Army, Eisner worked in the Ordnance Department, where he produced comics about equipment maintenance. The experience convinced Eisner of the educational and business potential of comics. A few years after he was discharged, Eisner formed American Visuals Corporation to produce the educational and corporate comics that would become the focus of his career for the next twenty-five years.

In the mid-seventies, inspired by the independence and mature content he saw in underground comix and needing an expressive outlet for the tragic loss of his teenage daughter, Eisner created *A Contract with God and Other Tenement Stories* (1978), a collection of four short stories about the lives of New York tenement dwellers. Although not the first to create a long work in comic book form, nor even the first to use the term *graphic novel*, Eisner might deservedly be considered the father of the modern graphic novel because he showed the potential of the new format by using it to tell intimate human dramas. In his early sixties Will Eisner began blazing a new trail in the comics medium, and he followed *Contract* with more than two dozen graphic novels of heartbreak and perseverance. His final work, published after his death, was *The Plot* (2005), a nonfiction graphic novel that marked the beginning of what he had intended to be another new direction in his career.

Will Eisner influenced generations of cartoonists, entertained and moved thousands of fans, and worked tirelessly to champion comics as a valid form of artistic expression. When he passed away at age eighty-seven, Eisner was still an ambitious creative genius striving to break new ground in his chosen art form.

THE ERA OF DIVERSIFICATION

In 1946 only one new superhero character was introduced—Marvel's Blonde Phantom. By the end of 1947 circulation on almost all superhero titles began to falter. Even *Captain Marvel Adventures* was down nearly 2.5 million from its 1944 peak of 14 million copies (Benton, *Comic Book* 39 & 41). However, the comic book industry as a whole was still robust, and it was beginning to diversify. Over the next few years superheroes were overshadowed by a number of genres: funny animals, romance comics, westerns, crime comics, and horror comics.

The most consistently popular of these genres, funny animals, began in 1940 with Dell's *Walt Disney Comics and Stories*. The title "lasted for more than forty years and probably achieved the highest overall circulation of any comic book in history" (Benton, *Comic Book* 158). In 1941 Dell also licensed the Warner Brothers cartoon characters. Funny animal titles helped Dell grow into the largest comic book company in the world. The funny animal genre also contained some of the best work ever done in the comic book medium. In 1942

Carl Barks began a twenty-five-year stint writing and drawing hundreds of adventures of ducks (Donald, his nephews, and his his very stingy Uncle Scrooge McDuck). These are probably the most frequently reprinted and translated American-made comic book stories.

Romance comics got their start in 1947. Significantly, it was the team of Joe Simon and Jack Kirby, who had made their name with superhero comics such as Captain America, that produced *Young Romance* #1. It took a few years for romance comics to find an audience, but they reached a peak of popularity in 1950 when they accounted for more than a quarter of the entire comic book market.

A slight boom in western comics occurred in 1948. Western comics dated back to the late 1930s, when there had been a few short-lived western comic books, but the genre took off in the early 1940s, with books devoted to movie cowboys like Gene Autry and *Hopalong Cassidy*. By 1948, Fawcett's Hopalong Cassidy was selling over 8 million copies. Noting this success, other publishers began introducing their own cowboy characters. DC even converted the super-hero title *All-Star Comics* into *All-Star Western* to capitalize on the audience's newfound interest.

Yet the real comic book boom of 1948 occurred with crime comics. In 1942, Lev Gleason Publications had changed his flagship title, *Silver Streak Comics*, into the first monthly crime comic book, *Crime Does Not Pay*. Initially, the circulation was barely over 200,000 (a lackluster figure for the time) (Benton, *Comic Book* 125, 155). However, circulation climbed steadily until the book was selling over 1.5 million copies a month in 1948. Gleason's book had a slow and steady rise to success, but for the rest of the comic book industry, the crime comic burst onto the scene suddenly and with dramatic results. The ten crime comic book titles of 1947 were joined by twenty-three new crime titles—ten of them beginning with the word *crime* or *criminal*—in 1948 (Stevenson). Even family-friendly Dell attempted to tap into the trend with *Dick Tracy Comics*. Virtually every publisher had at least one crime comic book in 1948.

Crime comic books got a great deal of attention that year. In July, a medical symposium on "The Psychopathology of Comic Books" was presided over by Dr. Fredric Wertham, the senior psychiatrist for the New York Department of Hospitals. Citizens' groups formed to push for regulation or banning of comic books. Some towns even held comic book burnings in order to exorcise the threat of crime comics from their communities.

In response to these concerns, a few publishers, including William Gaines of EC, formed the Association of Comics Magazine Publishers (ACMP) in July 1948. They created a code of standards and an ACMP seal to be put on comic book covers. However, the majority of publishers simply ignored the ACMP, and it soon faded away. Most publishers were not worried about a bit of public outcry. After all, business was booming. A record 425 titles were published in 1948, and that shot up to 592 titles in 1949 and 696 in 1952 (Stevenson). But the media attention did not go away. ABC radio braodcast the program "What's Wrong with Comics?" The Cincinnati Committee on the Evaluation of Comic Books published the findings of their study in the February 1950

FIGURE 2.10. A crowd cheerfully burns stacks of comic books at a rally in Binghamton, NY, in 1948. St. Patrick's Academy yearbook, Vincent Hawley collection, courtesy of David Hajdu.

Parents Magazine. They concluded that 70 percent of comic books contained objectionable material.

EC Comics' "New Trend"

The concerned citizens in Cincinnati and elsewhere must have been appalled by the comic books that appeared later in 1950. William Gaines had inherited the newly renamed Entertaining Comics in 1947 when his father, M.C. Gaines, died in a boating accident. William began reshaping the small line of comics. Soon *Tiny Tot Comics* and *Animal Fables* were replaced by *Crime Patrol* and *Saddle Justice.* The new books seemed to have a bit more market appeal, but Gaines was still not satisfied. So he decided to shake things up. In 1950, with the help of editor-writer-artist Al Feldstein, Gaines launched the EC "New Trend" line of comic books: *The Vault of Horror, The Haunt of Fear, Weird Science, Weird Fantasy, Crime SuspenStories, Two-Fisted Tales,* and *Crypt of Terror* (which was later renamed *Tales from the Crypt*).

The EC line of comics were intelligently written, wonderfully drawn, and as gory as hell. EC historian E.B. Boatner says, "EC horror opened new vistas of death from sources previously unimagined by the reader. Victims were serial-sectioned by giant machines, eaten by ghouls, devoured by rats—from inside and out—pecked by pigeons, stuffed down disposals, skewered on swords, buried alive, dismembered and used as baseball equipment, hung as living clappers in huge bells, made into sausage and soap, dissolved, southern-fried, hacked by maniacs in Santa Claus suits, and offed in unusually high percentages by their wives or husbands" (qtd. in Slade). The readers, many of them older than the average reader of a few years before, seemed to love it. EC had the strongest fan following the industry had yet seen. Some of these self-styled "EC fan-addicts" started the first fan-produced magazines.

EC was helping to fuel the incredible growth of the comic book industry. By 1954, the presses were churning out 150 million books every month. At the beginning of the year there were over six hundred different titles being published (Benton, *Comic Book* 53). But 1954 was a turning point. The comic book industry had reached the peak, and was about to plummet downhill.

Backlash against Comic Books

It is doubtful the American public had ever confused comic books with literature, but at least for the first decade of its existence, the public did seem to be rather accepting of the new medium. That benign attitude began to erode in the late 1940s as articles about the pernicious effects of comic books began to appear in popular magazines such as *Collier's* (March 1948), *Reader's Digest* (August 1948), and *Ladies' Home Journal* (November 1953). The negative publicity came to a crescendo in 1954 with the publication of Fredric Wertham's book *Seduction of the Innocent: The Influence of Comic Books on Today's Youth*. Wertham's book fueled fears that comic books were one of the causes of juvenile delinquency. Actually, since not that many Americans read books, Wertham's message reached more people by way of an excerpt that appeared in *Ladies' Home Journal*.

In the spring of 1954, a Senate Subcommittee to Investigate Juvenile Delinquency in the United States held hearings on the effects of comic books, and Dr. Wertham was called as the star witness. They also called William Gaines. While most of the comics industry professionals who testified admitted that there had been excesses and declared that comic books had to be made more suitable for children, Gaines remained rather defiant. When confronted by Senator Estes Kefauver with a cover that showed a man with a bloody axe in one hand holding the severed head of a woman in the other, Gaines maintained that the cover would only be in bad taste if the man was "holding the head a little higher so that the blood could be seen dripping from it" (Goulart, *Over Fifty* 216). None of the senators seemed to agree with this aesthetic judgement. The Subcommittee concluded that American kids were being fed "a concentrated diet of crime, horror, and violence" that had to be eliminated (Kefavuer 32). While most parents did not read Wertham's pedantic book or watch the boring hearings, they could hardly avoid the basic message that filtered through the mass media: Comic books are bad for children.

FIGURE 2.11. The Seal of the Comics Code let parents know that a comic book had passed the censors, but its adoption meant that the entire industry began pandering to juvenile content.

In response to the rising criticism, comic book publishers established the self-regulatory Code of the Comics Magazine Association of America on October 25, 1954. This time most of the publishers joined the association.

According to the Code, "all scenes of horror, excessive bloodshed, gory or grue-some crimes, depravity, lust, sadism, [and] masochism shall not be permitted." The Code even prohibited using the words *horror* or *terror* in a title. The public outcry provided an opportunity for publishers like Dell, DC, and Archie, who were putting out relatively unobjectionalbe material, to eliminate some of their competitors who were specializing in crime and horror comics.

THE ERA OF RETRENCHMENT

The comic book industry fell on hard times in the latter half of the 1950s for a number of different reasons—some of them unrelated to the anti-comic book crusade. For one thing, it was during the fifties that television became the domi-nant mass medium. At the beginning of the decade, television sets were in barely 10 percent of the homes in America, but by the end of it, 90 percent of American homes had at least one television. Reading in general declined as people's fasci-nation with television grew. And certainly kids had less incentive to spend 10 cents of their allowance on a comic book when they could follow the televised adventures of Robin Hood and Zorro for free.

The thinning of the ranks of comic book publishers was due in part to a natural boom-and-bust cycle. The profits of the so-called "Golden Age" of comics had attracted more publishers than the market could support. Even though enthusiasm for superheroes had waned in the post-war years, publishers found other genres—romance and westerns, then crime and horror—to fill the void. The industry as a whole remained strong in 1954, with 625 comic book titles and an annual revenue of $90 million (Stevenson; Benton, *Comic Book 53*). New titles were still flooding the market, but sales of individual titles were down significantly from the previous decade, and new publishers came and went quickly. A number of publishers did fold after the imposition of the Code, but most of those were recent startups that had tried to capitalize on the very trends that the Code banned. The only major publisher that left the comic book busi-ness specifically due to the Code was EC. And although EC had to cancel all of its crime and horror titles, they managed to stay in business for a couple more years by switching to the so-called "New Direction" comics, such as *Aces High* and *Psychoanalysis*. However, comic circulation went down pretty much across the board. By 1957 there were 150 fewer titles on the stands than in 1954 (Stevenson). The comic book industry was definitely slowing down.

The most immediate impact on comic book sales in 1955 was that, with the implementation of the Comics Code, two of the bestselling genres, crime and horror, were suddenly banned. Publishers scrambled to discover "the next big thing." They found it for a time in TV-based comics, from *Gunsmoke* (Dell, 1956) to *The Many Loves of Dobie Gillis* (DC, 1960). Publishers not only hoped that such titles might lure TV viewers back to comic books, but saw that adapting material that had been created under a network produc-tion code meant it would easily qualify for the Comics Code Authority seal of approval.

The implementation of the Code did not immediately rehabilitate the industry's image. Wertham continued his criticism of the industry with an April 1955 *Saturday Review of Literature* article entitled "It's Still Murder." And some locales thought they needed to provide their children with stronger protection than that guaranteed by the Code. In 1955 the state of Washington passed the Comic Book Act, which required a license to sell comic books. Los Angeles County adopted an ordinance that made it illegal to sell or distribute a crime comic book to a child under eighteen. Both laws were challenged in court and found unconstitutional, but they were indicative of the pervasive anti-comic book sentiment of the time (Nyberg 132–133).

The forces at play in the 1950s not only reshaped the comic book industry, but took a financial and emotional toll on many of the comic book creators. After 1954 there was less work to be found, and that work often paid less. Citing bad publicity and declining sales, DC asked creators to take a rate reduction of two or three dollars per page (Infantino and Spurlock 38).

Comic book creators were painfully aware of the negative publicity generated by Wertham's crusade and the Senate Subcommittee hearings. Carmine Infantino speaks for many of the comic books creators of the day when he says, "We were ashamed to tell people what we did for a living" (Infantino and Spurlock 39). John Romita told people he was a commercial illustrator, and Stan Lee preferred just to say he was a writer, but when pressed on the issue, referred to himself as a writer of illustrated children's books. Some of the most talented creators left the field, at least for a time. John Buscema and Gene Colan went into advertising, and Bill Everett went to work for a greeting card company.

Dell: Above the Fray

If anything, the campaign against comic books improved Dell's position in the industry. To many, they were examples of what comic books should be. When other publishers attempted to regain public acceptance with the self-imposed regulation of the Comics Code Authority, Dell didn't bother to submit their books for the Code seal of approval. The public still approved of their books, and besides, Dell's internal standards

FIGURE 2.12. Dell's Pledge to Parents, courtesy of Dell Publishing.

had always been higher than those established by the Comic Code Authority.

While they refused to carry other comic books that didn't have the CCA seal of approval, American News Company still distributed Dell Comics. Perhaps this was because Dell not only had a wholesome reputation—unsullied by Wertham—but they had economic clout. According to comic book historian Mike Benton, "During the 1950s Dell was the largest publisher of comic books in the world. In these boom years, Dell sold over three hundred million comic books annually" (*Comic Book* 109).

Dell had never followed the horror and crime trends that swept through the rest of the industry. As other publishers had scrambled to outdo one another with gore and sex in the late forties and early fifties, Dell continued to maintain strong sales with innocuous comic books based on cartoons (*Looney Tunes*) and movie cowboys (*Roy Rogers Comics*). Next to funny animals, westerns were Dell's bestselling comic books. Dell gradually moved from movie cowboys to comics based on popular western television series. They began publishing *Gunsmoke* in 1956, the year before it became the nation's most popular television show, and then added *Maverick* in 1958 and *Bat Masterson* and *Rawhide* in 1959. It was a canny move on Dell's part because westerns ruled the airwaves in the late fifties. There were no westerns among the twenty most popular television shows of the 1955–1956 season, but by the 1958–1959 season, westerns accounted for eleven of the top twenty programs, and the four highest rated programs were westerns (Brooks and Marsh 1096–1097).

However, Dell's success would not last indefinitely. While *Walt Disney's Comics & Stories* had begun the fifties with over $4 million in sales per issue, they had slipped to around $2 million by 1960. Dell accelerated the decline in 1960 by raising cover prices from 10 cents to 15 cents, while their competitors remained at the 10 cent cover price for at least another year. By the end of the following year, per issue sales on *Walt Disney's Comics & Stories* were around half a million dollars (Beerbohm). Shifts in the public's genre preferences dealt Dell another blow: by the early sixties the popularity of the western was in decline, and so were Dell's sales.

DC Endures

As the competition dwindled, DC Comics solidified its position in the industry. In 1956, DC bought out Quality Comics and its stable of heroes, including Plastic Man, Blackhawk, and Uncle Sam. DC continued the *Blackhawk* series, picking up with #108, but most of the other heroes sat on the shelf for quite a while. DC Comics had a number of advantages that helped them weather the hard times. They were a large enough company that they had always maintained a fairly diverse line of titles. That meant they could see which genres caught the readers' imaginations, and then shift resources accordingly. DC also had top talent and the most recognizable characters.

One genre with which DC found success was movie- and television-based comic books. DC's *Movie Comics* (1939) was the first comic book based on popular movies. Their later successes, however, were not adaptations, but new adventures of movie and television personalities. *The Adventures of Bob Hope* began in 1950 and ran for eighteen years. *The Adventures of Dean Martin and Jerry Lewis* began in 1952 and ran for twenty years, although it was renamed *The Adventures of Jerry Lewis* in 1957 after the duo split up. In the post-Code years, DC added titles such as *Jackie Gleason and the Honeymooners* (1956), *Pat Boone* (1959), and *Sergeant Bilko* (1957), which had its own eleven-issue *Sgt. Bilko's Private Doberman* spin-off in 1958.

Even titles such as *The Adventures of Rex the Wonder Dog* were drawn by top-notch artists because DC was able to hang on to the best of the industry's remaining talent, including Gil Kane, Carmine Infantino, John Broome, John Severin, Bob Kanigher, and Joe Kubert. They took the pay cuts and felt lucky to be getting work. And there was some security in working for DC because, for almost a decade, DC was virtually closed to new talent. Working with the stable talent pool, the editors cultivated a house style—"The very clean, sleek appearance"—and artists who did not fit that style had no chance of working at DC (Infantino and Spurlock 60). While the approach worked well for a time, the insular and conservative DC was slow to respond to the innovative competition they had to face in the 1960s. As former DC editor Murray Boltinoff explains, "We were the top dog for so long, we became impervious to any criticism or new ideas" (qtd. in Duin and Richardson 119).

Even though most of DC's heroes lay dormant at the time, the superhero concept still provided the company's identity and enduring strength in the industry. DC had done superheroes first and, arguably, best. DC's three most iconic characters, Superman, Batman, and Wonder Woman, were the only superheroes appearing regularly in the 1950s. The books were still selling reasonably well, but the characters were going through some strange times.

In order to keep fans interested in DC's flagship character, editor Mort Weisinger continued to proliferate the Superman mythos. Supporting cast members were given their own comic books. *Superman's Pal Jimmy Olsen* appeared in 1954 and *Superman's Girlfriend Lois Lane* in 1958. Lois and Jimmy were spotlighted in these stories, but Superman appeared on virtually all of the covers and played an important role in most of the stories. In 1958 a younger version of Superman, Superboy, first encountered the Legion of Super-Heroes, a group of young interplanetary superheroes who were inspired by the heroic legacy of the Man of Tomorrow. 1959 saw the introduction of Supergirl, Superman's cousin; Krypto, the super dog; and red kryptonite, which could produce bizarre transformations in natives of Krypton. Writers used the red kryptonite plot device to place the normally invulnerable Superman in real jeopardy with a loss of memory or crucial powers, but they also used it to turn him into a midget, a fire-breathing dragon, and to give him a third eye in the back of his head. The core concept of Superman was becoming encrusted with a large supporting cast and outright silliness.

Batman fared much worse. As with Superman, Batman's supporting cast proliferated during the late 1950s. First there was Ace the Bat-Hound in 1955. Batwoman followed the next year. Bat-Mite was introduced in 1959 and the original Bat-Girl in 1961. Thankfully he never joined the supporting cast, but in 1958 Batman and Robin even had a run-in with the Bat-Ape. This was actually a fairly mild example of the bizarre science fiction adventures Batman had under the tenure of editor and sometimes writer Jack Schiff. If Batman was not visiting other planets, then aliens and giant creatures were visiting Gotham City. It was not until Julie Schwartz took over as editor in 1964 that Batman began a return to his roots as an "eerie figure of the night" (Kane and Fox 1).

Atlas: The Diminished Giant

Martin Goodman had been publishing comic books since 1939 under various corporate names. During the 1950s his comic books were distributed by Atlas Magazines, Inc., which he also owned. (Essentially, one of his corporations paid another to distribute his comic books.) Goodman's publishing companies seldom established a distinct corporate identity, but the Atlas logo appeared on the comic book covers, so Goodman's comic book line of this era is generally referred to as Atlas Comics. In 1957 "Atlas Comics" was one of the largest comic book companies that had ever existed (Duin and Richardson 32).

Owning both ends of the business seemed to be a profitable arrangement, but in 1956 Goodman's publication business manager, Monroe Froehlich, Jr., convinced him to contract with a national distributor for his growing line of comic books. Froehlich negotiated a five-year contract with American News Company, and Goodman dissolved his distribution company. Approximately six months after assuming distribution of Goodman's comic book line, American News Company went out of business. Desperate for a distributor, Goodman had to agree to the terms of the DC-owned Independent News Company (IND). Using the opportunity to hamstring one of DC's chief rivals, IND limited Goodman to eight titles per month. Goodman and his sole remaining full-time employee, editor Stan Lee, opted to publish sixteen bimonthly titles, mostly of the western, romance, and war variety.

At the beginning of 1957, Atlas Comics was publishing eighty-five different titles. By the end of the year, they were down to sixteen books published every other month (Stevenson). With so many titles canceled, editor Lee had a large enough inventory of completed stories that he was able to get through most of 1958 without having to hire freelance writers or artists. The once-mighty Atlas Comics (now essentially nameless) had one employee and a small line of bland, imitative comic books.

Retrenchment is an appropriate term for this era because, as with troops abandoning one line of defense and falling back to defend the next wall or trench, comic book publishers would focus their resources on briefly popular genres, only to abandon them as sales faltered and shift their resources to the next "hot" genre. After having to leave behind crime, horror, television comics, and other genres, the major publishers found a familiar last line of defense. By the early 1960s, most of the industry was making a gradual return to the concept that had spawned the Golden Age of comic books—the superhero.

THE ERA OF CONNECTION

The return to superheroes was tentative. Atlas had tried it first in 1954 with revivals of Sub-Mariner, the Human Torch, and Captain America. The Human Torch and Captain America comics only lasted for three issues each. Without the threat of the Axis powers, the characters needed a new raison d'être. And publisher Martin Goodman had never been timid about having his characters enter the fray of current events. On the cover of his own book, Cap was billed as

"Captain America . . . Commie Smasher." This attempt to revive superheroes and profit from the "red scare" was derailed by the "comic book scare" that was reaching a crescendo in 1954 with the Senate Subcommittee hearings.

It was, however, the industry's establishment of self-censorship that once more made superheroes an attractive genre for publishers. The sanitized violence and moral purity of superhero comic books might not have been as titillating as the sexy and gory books of the early fifties, but they were a good fit with the standards of the new Comics Code. In late 1955 DC introduced their first new superhero in years, the Martian Manhunter, as a backup feature in *Detective Comics*. While this visitor from Mars had plenty of superpowers, he operated more as a detective than a superhero in his early stories. It would take a new twist on an old hero to get the superhero revival going.

Schwartz and the Fans

The true flashpoint of the superhero revival was *Showcase* #4 in 1956, when DC attempted a revival of a character that had bowed out five years prior: the Flash. Unlike Marvel's earlier approach to reviving the same character, DC, under the editorial guidance of Julius "Julie" Schwartz, experimented with reviving the *concept* of the Flash. This Flash had similar powers to his predecessor, but a different identity and costume. By 1959, sales of the Flash's trial runs in *Showcase* warranted his continued adventures, and an emboldened Schwartz attempted a second revival, this time with a makeover of the Green Lantern. Spurred on by a second success, Schwartz pursued reviving the concept of the superhero team, first piloted by DC in the 1940s with the Justice Society of America in the pages of *All-Star Comics*. Schwartz opted to update both the team's name—changing "society" to "league"—and its roster. Along with his two new stars, the Flash and Green Lantern, Schwartz added the Martian Manhunter and stalwart characters Aquaman and Wonder Woman. Superman and Batman were also members, but they were largely consigned to cameo roles in the group's earliest adventures. In 1960 the Justice League of America debuted in the pages of *The Brave and the Bold* #28, and in 1961 *Justice League of America* became the bestselling new title of the year. There was no denying that the superhero revival was in full bloom.

In addition to his wizardry for revitalizing stale properties, Schwartz was also a supporter of the emerging comics fandom. **Fans** are audience members who express their devotion, and Schwartz understood them, as he himself had been an early organizer among science fiction fans. He took the time to respond to fan letters, to help fans connect with one another, and ultimately to support their gatherings at conventions. Doing so helped these fans feel a connection to each other and to the men who created the comic books they loved.

The Marvels

In the comic book industry, what works well for one publisher is usually soon copied by other publishers, and if there was ever a publisher who could follow a trend, it was Atlas Comics' Goodman. According to legend, Goodman was on a golf outing with DC's publisher, Jack Liebowitz, and Liebowitz happened to mention the sales success of *Justice League*, which got Goodman going. (Whether that legendary exchange happened or not, Goodman would hardly need such a tip, as most of the publishers kept an eye on what was working for the competition.) Goodman directed his lone editor, Stan Lee, to come up with a team of superheroes. For years, Lee had been putting out stories about huge monsters with names like Moomba and Fin Fang Foom, and after twenty years in the business he had grown tired of the routine. Since he was ready to quit anyway, his wife Joan encouraged Lee to write the kind of comic he *wanted* to write. And that's what inspired Lee, in collaboration with artist Jack Kirby, to try something different with the Fantastic Four.

Fantastic Four #1 debuted in 1961 and featured a take on superheroes that was very different from anything DC was putting out. Superficially, these superheroes had no secret identities, they (initially) wore no costumes, and one of their members was the grotesquely misshapen Thing. Upon closer inspection, readers would discover characters who bickered amongst themselves, struggled with self-esteem issues, and had financial woes. Lee explains, "The characters would be the kind of characters I could personally relate to: They'd be flesh and blood, they'd have their faults and foibles, they'd be fallible and feisty, and—most important of all—inside their colorful, costumed booties they'd have feet of clay" (17). This was a marked departure from DC's heroes. DC tended to focus on plot development at the expense of characterization, and as a result, the DC heroes all had "essentially the same personality" and spoke in "the same carefully measured sentences" (Bradford Wright 185). The appeal of Marvel was this more human approach to its heroes.

Lee and Kirby began to turn out flawed heroes one after another. In 1962 they unleashed scientist Bruce Banner's dark side in *The Incredible Hulk*. Then a frail doctor was transformed into the Mighty Thor in the pages of *Journey into Mystery*. But the seminal Marvel hero came from Lee in collaboration with another artist, Steve Ditko. Lee proposed making a teenager the lead instead of merely the sidekick, but publisher Goodman was lukewarm to the idea and it got relegated to the last issue of a series that was about to be cancelled. *Amazing Fantasy* #15 introduced the world to Peter Parker, a teen bookworm who gains the powers of a spider while at a science demonstration. Instead of using his powers to jump immediately into crime fighting, Peter launches into a career in showbiz as the Amazing Spider-Man. His initial pride in his newfound station is squelched, though, when an irresponsible act on his part leads to the death of his Uncle Ben. He then vows to use his abilities for good, and, despite his best intentions, begins a life complicated by an aunt in fragile health, difficulty in making ends meet, and the jealous wrath of a newspaper publisher out to defame him. The problems Peter Parker faced out of costume spoke to his audience, and, perhaps better than any superhero before him, they could identify with Spider-Man. (**Identification** occurs when audiences can see themselves in a character.) The "web-slinger" had problems with family, romance, and money, which seemed like the same problems many of his adolescent readers were facing. As one fan noted, "I *especially* liked Peter Parker being an average guy who is rejected by

FIGURE 2.13. Stan Lee's prose and Steve Ditko's pose capture the angst of a teenage superhero from *Amazing Spider-Man* #4 (1963). © 2008 Marvel Entertainment, Inc. and its subsidiaries.

the in-crowd at school because he had brains. Now here was a comic book character with whom I could identify! If this was Marvel, I wanted more" (Schelly, *Sense* 42).

And so did a lot of other fans. As Marvel's superheroes grew increasingly popular, Lee and his stable of artists—including Kirby, Ditko, Don Heck, and Bill Everett—soon introduced Iron Man, the Avengers, and a revived Captain America. Then came the X-Men, Doctor Strange, and Daredevil. Marvel Comics was gaining fans in part because of the connection readers were making with the characters inside the comics, and in part because they had a favorable conception of the people making those comics. "One reason for the success of the new Marvels, besides the generally high quality of the art and writing, was that Stan Lee created a personality cult around himself. Where DC comics were edited by a generally faceless lot of men whose names were unknown to the general public, Lee *was* Marvel" (Thompson, Don 129). Lee addressed the reader in his captions, he developed a "Bullpen Bulletins" page to highlight the goings-on in the Marvel offices, and he hit the college lecture circuit. "For the first ten to fifteen years of Marvel's existence, Lee and his company were selling more than just comic books. They were selling a participatory world for readers, a way of life for its true believers" (Pustz 56).

Marvel did not actually achieve dominance of the market until the early seventies. In the meantime, prompted perhaps by the phenomenon of the *Batman* television series (1966–1968), plenty of other competitors attempted to jump on the superhero bandwagon, but none of them quite captured either DC's inventiveness or Marvel's humanity. Archie attempted to revive some of its wartime characters like the Shield; Charlton unleashed its "Action Heroes" line, including *Captain Atom*; and Tower Comics introduced Wally Wood's *T.H.U.N.D.E.R. Agents*, which attempted to cross the spy craze in film and television with the superhero craze in comics. Dell, American Comics Group, and even Harvey Comics all jumped on the bandwagon as well, but to short-lived success. By the end of the decade, most of the competitors had moved on to other genres, leaving DC and Marvel the dominant publishers in superhero fare.

ANALYZING: ART VERSUS COMMERCE

Big changes were ahead for the medium, as we shall see in our next chapter. Those changes reflected a return to comics' artistic roots. A medium that had begun as a means of self-expression was about to return to that focus, thanks to the work of some independently minded artists. In this chapter, we have seen how self-expression was gradually subverted to the needs of a commercial culture as comic books became a mass-marketed commodity. As with other forms of expression, such as music, film, or literature, the more commercial a medium becomes, the less artistic merit it seems to hold for its critics. A seismic change from instrument of commerce to tool of self-expression would come upon the comic book industry in its next era.

Discussion Questions

1. Contrary to some claims, comic books are not a wholly American invention; however, Americans have contributed much to the modern conception of the comic book. What would you say are among the most significant American contributions to shaping the medium?

2. Careful readers may have noted a shift in tone from this chapter's discussion of the Era of Invention, which was largely focused on individual accomplishments, to the Era of Retrenchment, when the focus was more on corporate activities. What do you think such a shift indicates about the nature of publishing over the time elapsed through these periods?

3. What is it about the superhero genre that has made it so consistently linked to the comics medium? Or, taken from another perspective, what is it about the comics medium that makes it so favorable to the superhero genre?

Activities

1. Consult a historical source (like a textbook) that chronicles one of the eras profiled in this chapter. What additional socio-political influences of the times seem to have manifested in the comics medium? Be prepared to bring three talking points to class in order to share with your peers.
2. Compare and contrast comic book storytelling as conducted in one of the eras described in this chapter with more recent publications. Start by tracking down a reprint edition of earlier comics (e.g., Marvel's Essentials or DC's Showcase line) and reading a selection. Then pick up a recent comic magazine or graphic novel. Write a brief essay in which you explain at least two ways the storytelling is similar in the two examples and at least two ways the techniques are different.

Recommended Readings

Comics:

Siegel, Jerry, and Joe Shuster. *Superman: The Action Comics Archives* Vol. 1. New York: DC Comics, 1997.

> Many reprints of classic comics are available through DC Archive Editions, the EC Archives, and the Marvel Masterworks series. These hardcover volumes represent comics from the early eras of the medium, like, in this case, the debut of Superman, as chronicled by his co-creators Siegel and Shuster.

Van Lente, Fred, and Ryan Dunlavey. *Comic Books Comics*. Brooklyn, NY: Evil Twin Comics, 2008.

> Van Lente and Dunlavey, also known for their engaging *Action Philosophers* comic books, use a canny mix of historically accurate details and irreverent humor to chronicle the history of the American comic book industry.

Scholarly Sources:

Nyberg, Amy Kiste. *Seal of Approval: The History of the Comics Code.* Jackson, MS: University Press of Mississippi, 1998.

> Nyberg investigates the predecessors to, development of, and ramifications of the Comics Code in a thorough historical review of the fifties' campaign against the comic book industry.

Wright, Bradford W. *Comic Book Nation: The Transformation of Youth Culture in America.* Baltimore: John Hopkins University Press, 2001.

> While there are many fine histories of the comic books, this one stands out as one of the more scholarly attempts to explain the development of the medium.

The History of Comic Books,
Part II: The Maturation of the Medium

*"[B]oth the mainstream . . . and the artists and publishers outside it have retrenched and con-
centrated on what they do best. The result is that American comics . . . have become divided
into two very different schools, with almost no overlap between them—in fact, there's a
distance between the two of them that sometimes turns into outright mutual contempt."*

—Douglas Wolk, scholar, 2007

Harvey Pekar seems about as unlikely a celebrity as you're likely to find.

In 1976 Pekar, a file clerk in a veterans' hospital, decided to chronicle his daily
triumphs and frustrations in a comic book. In Pekar's case, the tribulations tend
to outnumber the triumphs, and the book's title, *American Splendor*, is meant to
be ironic. Pekar's idiosyncratic work might never have attracted an audience
had he not owned some old jazz records he could offer to acquaintance and
underground comix artist Robert Crumb as enticing payment to draw the initial
issues. In a typical issue of *American Splendor*, an episode or two from Harvey's
life would be accompanied by a number of short strips relating humorous inci-
dents he had observed. Pekar's work focuses on the "acts of heroism and great
comedy happening around us every day" (Pekar qtd. in O'Sullivan 182). Pekar
often addresses the reader directly in panel after panel of his intense visage as
he waxes philosophical (or rants) on a variety of topics, from relationships to
1920s music.

Since launching *American Splendor*, Pekar has gone on to produce a number
of autobiographical comic books and graphic novels in collaboration with a
host of artists, all while maintaining his modest lifestyle in Cleveland, Ohio. But
the quality and candor of Pekar's work has brought him to popular attention,
and he has been a recurring guest on *David Letterman* as well as the subject
of the 2003 Academy Award-nominated film, also titled *American Splendor*.
Pekar's repute is all the more impressive when one considers that the comic
books that propelled him to fame were published either independently or
through small, alternative presses. In Pekar and other creators, we see the
potential for comic books to be more than commodities sold by corporate
publishers to juveniles; we see them as artistic expression crafted by dedicated

FIGURE 3.1. Harvey Pekar, as seen through the eyes of artist Robert Crumb, talks directly to his audience in the pages of *American Splendor* #4 (1979). © Harvey Pekar

artisans with the potential to communicate sophisticated ideas. The rise of independent voices in the shadow of the mainstream producers and their influence upon one another is the focus of our second chapter on the history of the American comic book industry.

OBJECTIVES

In this chapter you will learn:

1. how the underground movement developed and spread its influence throughout the industry;
2. the ways in which mainstream publishers began to address more relevant topics;
3. about the proliferation of independent comics;
4. how ambitious projects increased the profile and prominence of the medium; and
5. about the familiar themes reiterated in recent comic books.

ERA OF INDEPENDENCE

The rise of other companies attempting to compete with DC and Marvel in the superhero market was not the only significant development for comic books in the 1960s. As we might expect for this fabled decade, something more radical began to happen to comic books as both a medium and an art form.

Spontaneously across America, creative and unconventional young people who had grown up reading the genre fantasies mass-produced by the traditional comic book publishers began to make their own comics. A number of these comics first appeared in college humor magazines and counterculture newspapers. Even when they were published in the familiar pamphlet format, they did not compete with traditional comic books on the newsstands, but developed a distribution system of alternative bookstores, record stores, and head shops. The content and even the style of the artwork were a conscious rebellion against the Comics Code restrictions, editorial policies, and genre formulas of traditional comic books. These convention-defying, politically charged, and independently produced comics became known as **underground comix**. As individuals and small presses began to produce alternatives to their products, the traditional, mostly New York-based publishers became known as the **mainstream**.

The underground comix movement has its roots in the crude little sex comics known as **eight-pagers** or **Tijuana Bibles**, although there is no proof any were actually produced in Tijuana. The creators of these wallet-sized sex romps had to be much more underground than the comix artist of the 1960s, because the eight-pagers were illegal due to both obscenity violations and copyright infringement. The Tijuana Bibles depicted—in graphic detail—celebrities, political figures, or fictional characters using obscene language and enjoying a wide variety of sex acts, most of which were illegal at the time. By far the favorite subjects were characters from the newspaper comic strips (e.g., Popeye finds himself in a threesome with Olive Oyl and Wimpy). If any of the creators of these eight-pagers had been found, surely they would have been both sued and jailed. Cartoonist Art Spiegelman believes that while the eight-pagers did not directly inspire his fellow underground comix artists in the 1960s, "the comics that galvanized my generation—the early *Mad*, the horror and science-fiction comics of the fifties—were mostly done by guys who had been in their turn warped by those little books" (*Those Dirty 5*).

While the underground comix were uninhibited and willfully shocking in the tradition of the sex comics that had existed on the fringes of society, at least a part of their financial success was due to a mainstream comics publisher, Marvel Comics. Underground comix found their most avid fans among college-age readers. Reading comics had been primarily an adolescent or pre-adolescent pastime for decades, but Marvel began to cultivate an older audience just a few years before the undergrounds made the scene. By the mid-sixties, the adventures of Spider-Man, the Hulk, and Doctor Strange were becoming popular on college campuses. In particular, Steve Ditko's "trippy," surrealistic illustrations of Doctor Strange's adventures in magical dimensions seemed evocative of the visions many young people were experiencing in their experiments with psychedelic drugs. "A 1965 psychedelic rock happening in San Francisco's Haight-Ashbury was called 'A Tribute to Doctor Strange'" (Houston), and author Tom Wolfe wrote of LSD guru Ken Kesey "absorbed in the plunging purple Steve Ditko shadows of Dr. Strange" as he traveled America's byways on his Magic Bus (93). A more direct attempt to identify with youth culture was Stan Lee's handling of the Silver Surfer character. The angst-ridden Surfer would often, after dispatching the villain with a blast of his power cosmic, moralize to the awed bystanders about peace and love. The Silver Surfer became a counterculture hero.

It is likely that the twenty-something comic book reader of the late sixties did not make a clear distinction between mainstream and underground comics. A college-age fan's stack of reading material might have included Marvel's *Doctor Strange* and DC's *Strange Adventures* (featuring Deadman), along with *Snatch Comics* and *Radical America Komiks*. If Marvel had not already made reading comics hip, there might not have been as many young people ready to go along for the ride when the undergrounds made reading comix rebellious.

The taproot of the undergrounds goes back to another New York-based, but somewhat less than traditional, mainstream publisher. Those science fiction and horror comics Spiegelman claimed galvanized his generation were mostly from William Gaines' infamous EC line that included *Vault of Horror*, *Crime Suspen-Stories*, and *Mad*. The gore, violence, sensuality, and occasional political commentary strained against and often violated the boundaries of what was considered good taste until EC became the primary target of the newly created Comics Code Authority (CCA). When most of Gaines' titles were denied Code approval and distributors refused to carry them, EC stayed afloat on the back of one title begun in 1952: *Mad*.

By the time the Comics Code had forced the horror and crime titles off the newsstands, *Mad* had been converted from comic book to magazine format. Magazines were not subject to CCA approval and were treated differently by distributors. Sales steadily increased, and by the early 1970s, *Mad* magazine was selling 2.5 million copies an issue (Sabin, *Adult* 167). However, it was *Mad* the comic book, in particular those early issues edited by Harvey Kurtzman, that planted the seeds from which the underground comix sprouted like wild cannabis. Underground comix historian Mark Estren says Kurtzman is the "person most often cited by the underground cartoonists as a major influence on their consciousness and their style" (294), and the underground's leading light, Robert Crumb, has referred to Kurtzman as his hero ("Twenty" 5). Kurtzman's satire in those first twenty-eight issues of *Mad* skewered pop culture icons from Tarzan to James Dean, and revealed the fundamental fallacies of our national myths. "Kurtzman is the man who decisively determined the style of humour and satire in the USA after 1950" (Reitberger and Fuchs 218).

After leaving EC in 1956 due to a dispute with Gaines over control of *Mad*, Kurtzman had a remarkable five-year run editing and doing much of the writing for *Help!*, a magazine with even more aggressive and risqué humor than *Mad*. Kurtzman not only foreshadowed the content of the soon-to-emerge underground comix, but he provided encouragement and a taste of publication to future comix superstars Robert Crumb, Jay Lynch, Gilbert Shelton, and Skip Williamson in the amateur section of *Help!*

The Underground Digs In

Humor magazines had been a tradition at larger universities for decades, but when the teenagers who had grown up reading *Mad* arrived at college in the late 1950s and early 1960s, they reinvigorated campus humor with biting satire and radical views that often led to clashes with university administrators. With a circulation of over 12,000, the *Texas Ranger* published at the University of Texas in Austin was among the most successful of the college humor magazines. It was also central to the genesis of the underground comix.

Gilbert Shelton graduated from the University of Texas in 1961, but when he received his pre-induction notice he decided he had better return to UT as a graduate student to get a draft deferment. With the September 1962 issue (vol. 77, no.1), Shelton took over as editor of the *Texas Ranger*. The comix revolution was underway. Multi-page comics featuring the adventures of Shelton's superhero parody, Wonder Wart-Hog, appeared in all but one of the *Texas Ranger* issues Shelton edited. Wonder Wart-Hog became the first underground comix "hit." Just weeks before his series debuted in the *Texas Ranger*, the "Hog of Steel" was presented to a national audience in the pages of *Help!* and a profile in *Mademoiselle* magazine.

After his one-year stint as editor, Shelton stayed with the *Texas Ranger* for another year as art director. Shelton and his friends must have felt a bit stifled under the new editor, who quickly phased out the Wart-Hog comics. In January 1964 Shelton, Jack Jackson, and Tony Bell published the first issue of *THE Austin Iconoclastic Newsletter* (known simply as *THE*). *THE* ran for five issues as a newsletter, then, starting in the summer of 1964, was a magazine for two issues. At only four pages, the first newsletter was sparse on content, but historically important for the inclusion of the one-page comic "The Adventures of J" by Frank Stack. Though never called by name, J is obviously Jesus; the characters are dressed in Biblical attire and J is popular at a wedding feast because he turns the water into wine. Shelton collected about a dozen of the Jesus strips, convinced another student to run off fifty sets on the Law School Library photocopier, and began passing out the stapled fourteen-page "comic book," *The Adventures of Jesus*. Stack, as editor of the *Texas Ranger* for the 1958–1959 academic year, had published a few of sophomore Gilbert Shelton's cartoons, and now Shelton was returning the favor by making Stack's creation into what many consider the first underground comic book.

1964 was also a landmark year for another former *Texas Ranger* staffer. In the fifth issue of *THE*, the following ad appeared: "Have you got your copy of *God Nose Adult Comix* yet? Available exclusively at The Id Coffee House—407 W. 24." *God Nose* was by Jack Jackson, with assistance from Pat Massey and Lieuen Adkins. In his job at the State Comptroller's office, Jackson often had coffee in the capitol cafeteria with some of the guys who ran the state government print shop down in the basement. Jackson supplied the paper, including purple construction paper for the cover, and between jobs and after hours his print shop buddies ran off a thousand copies of the forty-two-page *God Nose* comic book (Wheat 272). Because Jackson did not want to lose his government job, he signed the *God Nose* book Jaxon, the nickname Shelton had coined for the notes he left his friend around the *Ranger* office. The main character of the comic was a short, large-nosed supreme being who had misadventures in the world of the foolish humans he had created.

God Nose and *The Adventures of Jesus* are the two leading candidates for the "first" underground comic book, among other contenders. And if you consider work in formats other than a stand-alone booklet, the origins of the undergrounds are extremely murky. Underground comix in the standard comic book format, or at least resembling it, did not appear until near the end of the decade, but scores of edgy, obscene, and anti-authoritarian comics were published in college humor magazines and underground newspapers throughout the 1960s. A number of these papers formed the Underground Press Syndicate and shared features, giving aspiring cartoonists wider exposure.

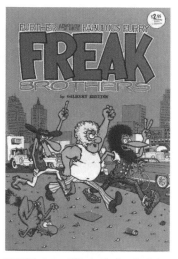

FIGURE 3.2. Gilbert Shelton's Fabulous Furry Freak Brothers would eventually become the best known and most widely marketed characters from the underground comix. © 1968, 2008 Gilbert Shelton

One such cartoonist, Robert Crumb, had been making comic books and fanzines since the age of eight, and saw the underground newspapers as a promising venue for his work. In 1967 he began taking LSD and filling sketchbooks in a feverish outpouring of bizarre ideas. Virtually all of the characters for which he became famous— Mr. Natural, the Vulture Demoness, Eggs Ackley, Angelfood McSpade— were conceived during this period. Even most of the underground press didn't know what to make of Crumb's bizarre visions, but the Philadelphia-based underground newspaper *Yarrowstalks* published a couple of his strips in its first two issues during the summer of 1967. *Yarrowstalks* editor Brian Zahn made the third issue an all-Crumb issue, and at about the same time, New York's *East Village Other* newspaper began to regularly publish Crumb's strips. Energized by the growing acceptance of his work (and quite a few drugs), Crumb produced another book's worth of strips, including "Whiteman" and a page of uncharacteristically lighthearted "Keep on Truckin'" images that were destined to make their way into mainstream culture. He just needed to find someone willing to publish the book.

Crumb's work was already beginning to garner him fans, and two of those fans, underground newspaper publisher Don Donahue and printer Charles Plymell, were anxious to publish Crumb's new work, which they did as *Zap Comix* #1 (1968). While Crumb and his wife Dana made their way through the streets of San Francisco selling copies of *Zap* out of a baby carriage, Donahue went and sold the majority of the print run to Third World Distribution. "From there they went all over the country," explained Donahue. "The hippie vendors from all over the Bay Area went there to pick up their stuff" (qtd. in Rosenkranz 71). Within a couple of months, Donahue had to do a second printing, and soon copies of *Zap* were showing up in head shops and record stores across the

FIGURE 3.3. Robert Crumb became the star of the underground movement thanks to images like the iconic "Keep on Truckin'" cartoon.

nation. By the fall of 1968 Robert Crumb was a minor celebrity, and the acclaim from *Zap* led to opportunities that made him a major celebrity. He turned down an offer to do a Rolling Stones album cover, but when Janis Joplin herself asked, he did a front and back cover for Big Brother and the Holding Company's *Cheap Thrills* album. Crumb was only paid $600 for the work, but it became one of the most collectible album covers of all time. Toward the end of the year, Viking Press published a slightly censored sampling of his work from 1965 to 1968 in *R. Crumb's Head Comix*. Crumb's growing fame fueled the growth of underground comix in general.

Much like the mainstream comic book industry had flourished following the success of Superman, within a few years of the appearance of *Zap*, undergrounds had developed into a strong alternate comics industry, complete with a Berkeley Comix Convention in 1973. At the peak of the underground phenomenon in 1973, there were over three hundred comix titles in print, with nearly as many people referring to themselves as underground cartoonists (Rosenkranz 4), and the average book sold 40,000 copies (Raeburn 35).

Comix Contents

It has become orthodox to consider underground comix as more sophisticated than mainstream comic books due to their critiques of politics, religion, and social norms. Yet they are also more primitive than their mainstream counterparts. Not only is the art often less refined and more visceral, but the content itself speaks directly to the id, to our repressed impulses. In just flipping through underground comix, the most obvious aspects of the content are explicit sexuality and graphic violence. In his study of the themes of the comix, researcher Paul Ling found that they deal in "immediate gratification of the instincts" and that "sublimations of sexuality—romantic love, tenderness, altruism—are, on the whole, lacking. Sexuality is manifested directly in terms of sexual pleasure and hedonism" (40). The violence in underground comix is often impulsive and brutal. It is not presented as a warning about the horrible consequences of violence, but as a gleeful release of aggressive impulses.

The strongest and most consistent element in underground comix is the anti-authoritarian theme. Part of defying authority was simply using all the words and depicting all the acts everyone knew mainstream censors would never allow. While the underground cartoonists might have been primarily thumbing their noses at conservative morality, they also occasionally violated liberal political correctness. Crumb's Angelfood McSpade, a voluptuous African tribeswoman who was often the object of white men's sexual desire, and Shelton's Watermelon Jones no doubt offended some readers, but others seemed to interpret such characters as commentary on the racist stereotypes in popular culture.

Comix not only defied the sources of authority in conventional society by breaking their taboos, but they also went on the direct attack. Authority figures are presented as inept or brutish and always corrupt. The structures of society, institutions and bureaucracies, are portrayed as soulless and oppressive. As German media critics Rheinhold Reitberger and Wolfgang Fuchs correctly observed from their outside perspective, "the underground cartoonists and their creations attack all that middle America holds dear" (219).

Underground publishers had a fierce commitment to freedom of expression that allowed the creators to be not only offensive, but also creative and experimental. As the creators matured there developed an impressive variety of work in the undergrounds. Once they got over the initial intoxication of all the "bad" things they *could* do, the best of the underground cartoonists gave more serious thought to what they *should*.

FIGURE 3.4. While men like Shelton and Crumb may have achieved recognition beyond the underground community, men were not the only pioneers in the movement. At a time when few females worked in mainstream comics, *Wimmen's Comix* debuted in 1972 and became a significant outlet for the creative expression of female cartoonists in the decades to follow. Cover of issue #14 (1989) by Trina Robbins and used with permission.

By the mid-seventies there were a number of forces pulling the undergrounds into the mainstream. The informal distribution system was disappearing and the audience for radical underground comics was dwindling. It became risky to sell underground comix in most parts of the country. In their 1973 ruling in *Miller vs. California*, the Supreme Court reaffirmed that obscenity was not protected by the First Amendment. The court established a three-pronged test for obscenity under which the vast majority of underground comix were certain to be declared obscene. Of course, there were some comix outlets where the owners relished defying authority. Many underground comix were sold in head shops, after all, alongside the pipes, bongs, and roach clips. However, the head shops were being forced out of business, or at least harassed, as states attempted to make it against the law to sell anything used for making, using, or concealing illegal drugs. Within a few years most drug paraphernalia shops had been legislated out of existence.

The audience for underground comix was also under siege from more subtle cultural forces. With the end of the conflict in Vietnam, youth subculture was no longer galvanized by the anti-war movement. The Summer of Love was a fading memory, and many of the "flower children" who dropped out of college at the end of sixties had by the mid-seventies finished degrees, taken jobs, and started paying mortgages. Even the cartoonists who had started the underground movement in their freewheeling teens or early twenties were starting to find themselves with families and responsibilities. Moreover, the hippies who had formed cooperatives to help get their work printed more cheaply and distributed more efficiently had evolved into the "establishment" in underground comix. The cartoonists who ran Rip Off Press, Kitchen Sink, and Last Gasp had become publishers and, much to their chagrin, businessmen. What started as a subculture had become an industry. That shift in perspective made it easier for many underground creators to overcome their revulsion when the mainstream attempted to co-opt their movement.

Marvel writer, editor, and publisher Stan Lee had spent most of his career copying the latest trends. It is doubtful Lee had seen many underground comix by the early seventies, but he knew they were generating a lot of buzz and he hoped to cash in on that energy. So he conceived of a magazine that would attract new readers by featuring work from leading underground cartoonists, but still protect the Marvel name by only accepting their milder material and displaying the logo of Marvel's parent company, Curtis Publishing, rather than the familiar Marvel logo. In 1973 Lee convinced underground publisher Denis Kitchen to edit an underground comix title for Marvel. *Comix Book* appeared in 1974 and featured work from top underground talents such as Art Spiegelman, Trina Robbins, Skip Williamson, and Kitchen himself. As Lee explains, "being Marvel, we couldn't get raunchy enough to be truly underground" (qtd. in Schreiner 38). In fact, *Comix Book* failed to find an audience and was cancelled after five issues, a seeming epitaph for the underground movement itself.

Relevance in the Mainstream

Change was upon the mainstream comics starting in the late sixties and on into the seventies, but the changes were not a reaction to the underground comix movement. The men who ran DC and Marvel knew very little—and cared even less—about the undergrounds, but they were deeply interest in relating to their audience.

Relating to the 1960s culture seemed to come most naturally for Marvel Comics. Perhaps underneath the hip persona he projected, editor and head writer Stan Lee really was pretty tuned in for a guy nearing fifty. One of Marvel's most obvious attempts to address issues of the day appeared in *Amazing Spider-Man* #68 in early 1969. The story "Crisis on Campus" was inspired by the student demonstrations that had occurred at Columbia University the previous year. Like most superheroes, Spider-Man maintained a centrist position, "rejecting the extreme and violent response of both the left and the right" as Marvel "struggled to stay hip to leftist trends in youth culture without alienating conservative readers" (Bradford Wright 235–237). Marvel's truest cultural barometer is Captain America, who as the symbol of America has reflected the mood of the nation, from jingoistic patriotism during World War II, to brooding about the generation gap in the early seventies. In 1973 through 1975, a storyline that developed as the Watergate scandal continued to unfold, Cap contended with the shadowy forces of a Secret Empire bent on undermining the nation's democratic principles. In the story's conclusion, after President Nixon's resignation in 1974, Cap discovers the head of the Secret Empire is the president of the United States. This revelation shakes Steve Rogers' faith in the nation he symbolizes, and for a time he abandons his Captain America persona, becoming Nomad, the man without a country.

In the fall of 1969, in an atmosphere of increasing demands of equality for blacks in American society and the exploits of real-life heroes such as Martin Luther King, Jr., Marvel introduced the Falcon, its first African American superhero. The first superhero of color, the Black Panther, had appeared in *The Fantastic Four* three years earlier, but he was an African native, not an African American. The Falcon, a reformed hoodlum turned social worker, became Captain America's partner, and his name was added to the book's masthead, but not to the official title. As scholar Jeffrey Brown points out, the Falcon functioned as more of a sidekick than a partner to Captain America, and "their unequal relationship was seen by some as an unintended metaphor for the black experience in white America" (*Black Superheroes* 20). The first African American superhero to have his own title was Luke Cage, the star of *Hero for Hire* (1972). Billy Graham, one of the first blacks working in comics, was inking the series, but writers Archie Goodwin, Steve Englehart, and Len Wein were all white. While Cage's black dialect and ghetto slang might have been laughable to most African Americans, he was clearly designed to cash in on the early-seventies phenomenon of blaxploitation films, which featured badass, highly sexualized protagonists with ghetto street smarts. By the mid-seventies, kung fu films were pushing blaxploitation off the movie screens. Luke Cage had already been made a more generic superhero by having his name, and the title of his book, changed to Power Man, but when sales continued to drop, Luke gained a kung fu partner and, in 1978, the title of the book was changed to *Power Man and Iron Fist*. DC added their African American superhero, backup Green Lantern John Stewart, in 1972.

DC's desire to connect with the sensibilities of teens and young adults in the late sixties and early seventies, and thus sell them more comic books, was aided by an influx of young talent being hired. This was partly due to management's search for fresh ideas, and was partly a matter of timing. Not only were most of the writers who had been carrying the workload at DC in their fifties, but in 1968 they had banded together in a failed attempt to unionize and demand a piece of the concepts they created, as well as some sort of benefits package. Just as management had reason to be easing out the old writers, there were a horde of young aspiring writers clamoring to get in the door. By the late sixties, many of those fans were old enough to try to break into the industry, and a handful of the most persistent and most talented succeeded. Newcomers such as Len Wein, Marv Wolfman, and Mike Friedrich, all of whom started at DC in 1968, might not have been San Francisco "flower children," but a few of them lived in the hip Greenwich Village, and all of them were more in touch with the spirit of the times than the mainstream old guard.

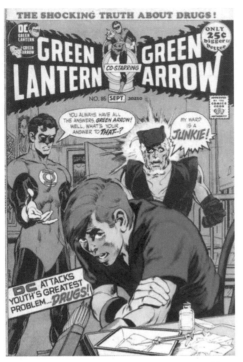

FIGURE 3.5. The mainstream's attempts to achieve relevance were seen as Green Arrow confronts his former sidekick, Speedy, on the cover of *Green Lantern* #85 (1971). Art by Neal Adams. © DC Comics

Young turks Denny O'Neil and Neal Adams, who were in the process of transforming the campy Batman into a dark avenger, were given a fairly free hand in revitalizing the *Green Lantern* series. With issue #76 in 1970, which had a masthead that read *Green Lantern co-starring Green Arrow*, there began an uneasy partnership between the blandly conservative Green Lantern and the radically liberal Green Arrow, a B-list DC character without his own title. O'Neil and Adams contrived a "journey across America" narrative structure that confronted their heroes with the emotional issues of the day, from racism to exploited workers to pollution. The *Green Lantern/Green Arrow* series was popular with the college audience.

Relevant comics were getting positive media attention and apparently being noticed in some unexpected quarters. In 1971 an official at the United States Department of Health, Education, and Welfare encouraged Stan Lee to use Marvel Comics, in particular their most popular character, Spider-Man, to educate young people about the dangers of drug use. However, the Comics Code Authority (CCA) specifically prohibited any depiction of drug use in comic books. Nonetheless, Lee penned a three-part story about Peter Parker pal Harry Osborn's improbably brief battle with drug addiction for *Amazing Spider-Man* #96–98 (1971). The CCA refused to give the issues its seal of approval. Lee convinced his publisher that the lack of the CCA seal would not hurt sales and the issues would garner Marvel some good press coverage. A decade earlier, no comic book without the CCA seal was likely to be allowed on the newsstands, but by 1971, few retailers noticed or cared. Seeing that Marvel had been able to defy them without consequence, the CCA immediately called a meeting of publishers and modified the Code to allow for the depiction of narcotic or drug use as long as the story met the CCA's new criteria for showing drug use to be "a vicious habit." The ink was still drying on the new policy when the CCA gave the seal of approval to a DC comic that showed a hero shooting up heroin on the cover. Although Neal Adams claims the concept had already been in the pipeline at DC for some time, it seemed a bit derivative and forced when a few months after the Spider-Man drug issues appeared it was revealed in *Green Lantern/Green Arrow* #85 that Green Arrow's sidekick Speedy was a heroin addict.

Teen hero Speedy with a drug syringe was a shocking image for comic book readers, but the true loss of innocence for superheroes and their fans occurred in *Amazing Spider-Man* #121 (1973), in a story penned by Gerry Conway and drawn by Gil Kane. Unlike the calculated attempts at relevance, this story was a more genuine, perhaps subconscious, emotional response to the fear created by the stream of violent images on the nightly news and the failure of American power in Vietnam. The Green Goblin had kidnapped Spider-Man's girlfriend Gwen Stacy, and was threatening to throw her off a bridge. Enacting one of the familiar and satisfying conventions of the genre, Spider-Man swings in at the last moment to save the girl. He manages to snag the plummeting Gwen's leg with a strand of webbing. In the panel in which Spider-Man exults "Did it!" there is also a small "SWIK!" sound effect next to Gwen. In the context of the story, neither Spider-Man nor the Green Goblin hear the snap and realize exactly how Gwen died. Only the readers know that by stopping her fall so suddenly, Peter snapped his girlfriend's neck. The readers were stunned and transformed. Scholar Arnold Blumberg contends, "The death of Gwen Stacy was the end of innocence for the series and the superhero genre in general—a time when a defeated hero could not save the girl, when fantasy merged uncomfortably with reality" ("The Night" 199).

The tone of the Marvel Universe seemed to change in the wake of Gwen's death. When DC and Marvel introduced darker themes it was no doubt partially a reflection of the times, but when these changes proved to be popular, the trend was fueled by the tendency of the mainstream to copy what sells. Indeed, the 1970s were a time when both Marvel and DC seemed to be throwing everything against the wall just to see what would stick.

Mainstream Searches for Direction

Marvel and DC entered the seventies with faltering superhero sales and a slight but growing competition from underground comix and the magazine-format horror comics that were unfettered by Code restrictions. This sent the Big Two scrambling to find the next big thing, and they often attempted to adapt to whatever current trend in popular culture was selling. For example, when interest

FIGURE 3.6. Part of mainstream comic books' innocence died along with Gwen Stacy in the pages of The *Amazing Spider-Man* #121 (1973), in a story penned by Gerry Conway with art by Gil Kane. © 2008 Marvel Entertainment, Inc. and its subsidiaries

in martial arts hit Hollywood, the comic book industry began to produce kung fu features like Marvel's *Master of Kung Fu* (debuting in 1973). As sword-and-sorcery books boomed, the comics industry experimented with adapting that genre, the most successful of which was unquestionably Roy Thomas and Barry Smith's interpretation of Robert E. Howard's *Conan the Barbarian* (1970). Following the lead of magazine publishers Warren and Skywald, who were publishing popular black-and-white magazines, the industry returned to publishing horror comics, revising the Comics Code in 1971 to allow for the inclusion of vampires, ghouls, and werewolves as long as they were "handled in the classic tradition" of "high calibre literary works." Marvel's entries included *The Tomb of Dracula* (1972) and *Werewolf by Night* (1972), but perhaps the most important new horror character developed at this time was DC Comics' Swamp Thing. Debuting in a short story by Len Wein and Bernie Wrightson in the horror anthology *House of Secrets* in 1972, Swamp Thing would return in his own ongoing series later in the seventies and again in the eighties. Under the guidance of British author Alan Moore, the character would headline one of the most influential titles of the 1980s, showcasing Moore's sophisticated approach to storytelling.

Despite a downturn in their popularity, superheroes still made up the bulk of comic book titles at this time, and several high points demonstrated that they were still a viable mode for storytelling. Jack Kirby had left Marvel Comics in 1970 for the chance to exercise greater editorial control over his stories at DC. His first project there was a magnum opus, a series of four interrelated ongoing comic book series: *New Gods, Forever People, Mister Miracle,* and *Superman's Pal, Jimmy Olsen.* The story focused on the clash of opposing gods of light and darkness whose ages-old conflict opens a new chapter on Earth. Kirby's "Fourth World" titles would be canceled or reassigned before he could finish the story the way he originally intended, but the New Gods would be integral players in the DC Universe in decades to come.

A more immediate, but no less enduring, success would debut in 1975, when Len Wein and Dave Cockrum attempted to re-launch Marvel's *X-Men* series, which had faltered and been canceled in 1970. This time around, though, the creative team didn't simply resurrect the same five Anglo-American teenagers in the lead roles, but instead recruited a cast of international characters, including an African woman, a Japanese man, and a Russian teen. Wein ended up stepping aside for another author, Chris Claremont, and Cockrum left thereafter to be replaced by artist John Byrne. Claremont and Byrne would form one of the most highly regarded collaborations in the field, and by decade's end *X-Men* was at the top of the sales charts, a position it has rarely relinquished in the more than thirty years since. The secret to the *X-Men* was both in its popular creative team and in the way it wove the flawed characters and soap opera elements that had been introduced by Marvel in the early sixties together with the attempts to relate fantasy to real world concerns of the late sixties and early seventies. The *X-Men*'s roster changed (with one member killed in the team's second adventure), the members were often in conflict with one another, and all the while they fought for a world "that feared and hated them" because of their genetic differences. The successful formula of matching realistic themes with a popular creative team was confirmed a few years later when writer Marv Wolfman and artist George Perez launched *The New Teen Titans* (1981) for DC and produced another sales-charting success.

As the competition between Marvel and DC continued into the late seventies, both publishers attempted to squeeze out one another—and their remaining competitors such as Archie, Charlton, and Harvey—by publishing more and more titles. DC promoted the expansion of its line with house ads heralding the "DC Explosion," and promised more diverse titles and increased page counts in each issue (which, consequently, came with a higher price). But severe winter storms in 1977 and 1978 disrupted distribution and prevented many comic books from ever making it to retail outlets. The combination of unsold stock, a general downturn in the U.S. economy, and the poor

FIGURE 3.7. *Giant-Size X-Men* #1 (1975) introduced an "all-new, all-different" team of mutant superheroes who would go on to dominate the sales charts for next several decades. Art by Gil Kane and Dave Cockrum © 2008 Marvel Entertainment, Inc. and its subsidiaries

quality of some of the new titles prompted DC's parent company to dictate a trimming of the line. By the end of 1978, the "DC Implosion" left more than two dozen titles, or about half its line, canceled. Although DC was forced to curtail the number of ongoing monthly titles it could commit to publishing, in 1979 it began experimenting with the concept of a limited series that would only last for a specified number of issues. The first one, *The World of Krypton*, was written by Paul Kupperberg, with art by Howard Chaykin and Murphy Anderson, and it retold the story of the last days of Superman's home planet. The limited series would become an important tool for publishers in the years to come because of the flexibility it offered to their lineups. But the shrinking market for comic books in general would need more than new formats to keep the industry afloat. It would also need a new business model, which would be introduced shortly in the form of the direct market, thanks to alternative comics.

Independent Alternatives

In the mid-seventies, the mainstream publishers were desperately seeking the right genre or approach to attract readers, and the underground comix were disappearing or changing into something else. Comic books, as both a medium and an art form, were evolving, and there was widespread uncertainty in the industry as to what they might become. In the latter half of the 1970s, there developed four often indistinguishable, frequently cross-pollinating varieties of non-mainstream but not quite underground comic books: Newave, Ground Level, Independent, and Alternative.

Newave

The term *newave* was coined to refer to a new phenomenon of even less visible and more independent comics that began in the mid-seventies and became a widespread movement in the eighties. Most newave comics were produced in a quarter-page or half-page format commonly referred to as **mini-comics**, or **mini-comix** for those that were considered to be in the underground tradition. The newave comic books were produced completely independent of publishers and editors, and there were no mandates about content or format. The small format was simply a matter of convenience and cost for newave creators, and the term *mini-comic* has come to mean any individually produced, "homemade" comic book, regardless of size (Spurgeon 133). Many of the newave books were from a new generation of underground cartoonists who could not find publishers once the underground industry went into a slump in 1973, but some were by mainstream fans, and a few were even done by established underground creators, such as Trina Robbins, Art Spiegelman, and Jay Kinney.

Many cartoonists—Jessica Abel, Craig Thompson, Julie Duocet, and Adrian Tomine among them—have launched alternative comics careers from their mini-comics work, and some continue to do mini-comics as a sideline. Although it is still possible to get mini-comics through mail order or in local comics shops, many have migrated to the internet, and mini-comics can now be found at online stores such as Bodega Distribution and the Poopsheet Shop.

Ground Level

The term *ground level* was first applied by *Star*Reach* publisher Mike Friedrich in 1974 "to denote overground genres being explored with an underground sensibility" (Sabin, *Adult* 270). To the readers of the comics anthology *Star*Reach* (1974), the underground sensibility might have been most evident in the topless females, but to the mainstream artists such as Jim Starlin and Howard Chaykin who contributed to *Star*Reach*, the important underground legacy was that Friedrich offered artists ownership of the characters they created and relative freedom from editorial restrictions. The stories in *Star*Reach* were science fiction and fantasy adventures aimed primarily at mainstream fans who were excited about seeing their favorite superhero artists doing a different sort of work. The U.S.–Soviet space race, especially once it culminated in humans landing on the moon in 1969, heightened interest in the science fiction genre. The fantasy genre was given a boost when J.R.R. Tolkien's trilogy, *Lord of the Rings*, became a cult favorite with mainstream geeks and counterculture hippies alike. Ground-level comics that told stories in these genres attracted both fans of superhero comics and readers of underground comix.

In 1974 former Skywald and Marvel artist Jack Katz began his fantasy epic *First Kingdom*. It took Katz twelve years and twenty-four issues to complete his tale. *First Kingdom* was a personal vision executed independent of editorial control. The underground sensibility was also manifest in Katz' lovingly rendered, long, lean women and muscular men who wear little or no clothing. Wendy and Richard Pini published their first stories of heroic elves in the underground anthology *Fantasy Quarterly* in 1978. Unsatisfied with the quality of that publication, the Pinis began self-publishing their *Elfquest* series in 1979. Like *First Kingdom*, *Elfquest* was an epic tale developing toward a planned conclusion. The original series ran for twenty-one issues and was followed by a number of sequels. At first *Elfquest* seemed like a mainstream adventure tale, but as the series progressed the violence became more intense and the omnisexual elves more frequently enacted the values of the sexual revolution.

FIGURE 3.8. Wendy and Richard Pini's *Elfquest* series (1978) began as a self-publishing venture. Art by Wendy Pini © 2009 Warp Graphics, Inc.

The ground-level comics phenomenon was a brief, transitional phase that gave way to creators of **independent** comics who aspired to mainstream success, and alternative comics creators who considered themselves part of the underground comix tradition and purposely maintained an artistic distance from the mainstream.

Independent

By the mid-seventies there were only six mainstream comic book publishers—Marvel, DC, Archie, Charlton, Gold Key, and Harvey—and to the majority of comic book fans only Marvel and DC mattered. The term **independent** came to refer to any new publisher that attempted to compete with the established publishers by offering genre fiction comic books intended for a mainstream audience.

A key example of independent publishing was Eclipse Enterprises. Founded in 1977 by brothers Jan and Dean Mullaney, Eclipse lasted for seventeen years and published 125 different titles, covering virtually every genre. The Mullaney brothers and editor cat yronwode were innovators, taking chances on new formats and daring material, some of which had a lasting impact on American comic books. In 1978 their initial publication was the first graphic novel intended for the emerging comics specialty store market: *Sabre: Slow Fade of an Endangered Species* by Don McGregor and Paul Gulacy. In partnership with Viz Communications, Eclipse brought English translations of Japanese manga to

FIGURE 3.9. Kevin Eastman and Peter Laird conceived of the *Teenage Mutant Ninja Turtles* as a parody of several popular comic book themes of the day (teenage super heroes, mutants, and ninjas), and doing business as Mirage Studios, they self-published the first comic in May 1984. The Turtles' popularity has transcended comic books as the characters have become a fixture in feature films, animated television programs, video games, toys, and countless licensed products. *Teenage Mutant Ninja Turtles* cover art by Kevin Eastman and Peter Laird. © 1984 Mirage Studios, Inc.

American readers in 1987. That same year, the company pioneered documentary-style comics with "graphic journalism," such as *Real War Stories*, created for the use of the Central Committee for Conscientious Objectors, and *Brought to Light*, a CIA exposé.

There were scores of other small publishers with comic books on the market, at least briefly, during the 1980s, like Pacific Comics, Comico, and First Comics, just to name a few. While the overcrowding of the comic book market led to some problems we will examine in a moment, there were also some benefits. The competition from the independent publishers had a positive impact on both the financial and creative practices at the Big Two. Most of these independent publishers paid royalties and allowed creators to retain ownership of their intellectual properties. It was not long before DC and Marvel had to offer royalties and at least negotiate ownership rights with the most influential creators. Eventually Marvel and DC created new imprints to publish the type of intelligent, mature material readers had been attracted to in independent offerings. Yet Marvel and DC also treated the independents like farm teams where new talents could prove themselves before trying to break into the majors, and most of the independent publishers and the newcomers who worked for them aspired to join the established mainstream. At the time, there were other cartoonists who were charting a course that took them far from the mainstream, and their efforts did more to revolutionize the art form.

Alternative

Alternative comic books are usually created by a single cartoonist and present a very personal vision. Many are autobiographical in nature and put more emphasis on the author than on characters. These are self-published or small press works that resist or even satirize the clichés of mainstream genre fiction and valorize their roots in the comix tradition.

Arcade: the Comics Revue (1975) was conceived by editors Art Spiegelman and Bill Griffith as a means to get comix material on the magazine racks alongside the black-and-white horror magazines (Rosenkranz 235). The magazine never got distribution beyond the usual underground outlets, and those were dwindling in number by the mid-seventies. After only seven issues, *Arcade* folded, and comics journalist Gary Groth sees *Arcade*'s end as signaling "the last whimper of the underground movement" (Groth, "Independent" 21). *Arcade* can also be seen not only as "a bridge between the underground and the more experimental approach of *Raw*," but also a transitional publication between underground comix and alternative comics (Sabin and Triggs 10).

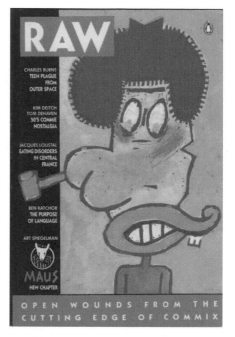

FIGURE 3.10. Art Spiegelman and Françoise Mouly produced the anthology *Raw* to showcase the work of alternative cartoonists. Art by Gary Panter. © 1980 Art Spiegelman, reprinted with permission of The Wylie Agency, Inc.

After the hard work and frustration of the *Arcade* experience, Spiegelman swore he would never get involved with producing another magazine, but when he met future wife Françoise Mouly and she suggested they start a comics anthology magazine, he found himself immediately acquiescing. When Spiegelman and Mouly published the first issue of *Raw* in 1981, they thought it might be a one-time venture. It had a print run of only 4,500 but sold out quickly, and both readers and artists who wanted to contribute began asking when the next issue would be published (Rosenkranz 253). Subsequent issues of *Raw* contained work by such underground stalwarts as S. Clay Wilson and Bill Griffith, as well as emerging alternative cartoonists like Gary Panter and Charles Burns, but the mostly historically significant aspect of *Raw* was Spiegelman's own contribution. For years Spiegelman had been working on a long-term and very personal project that began as a three-page story in *Funny Aminals* [*sic*] back in 1972. In *Raw* #2 Spiegelman began serializing *Maus* as a mini-comic insert. *Raw*'s bold experimentation with design was an indication that Spiegelman and Mouly aspired to bridge the considerable gap between comics and high art.

These new varieties of comic books were able to find a substantially different audience than the one that had supported the underground comix, due to a radical change in comic book distribution and marketing that allowed independents, alternatives, and even a few of the residual undergrounds to be sold side-by-side with mainstream comics in a new type of store.

Direct Market

For decades mainstream comic book publishers had taken it for granted that, aside from meager subscription sales, the newsstand distribution system was the only way to sell their product. It had always been an inefficient system, and by the 1970s newsstand sales had declined dramatically (Sabin, *Adult* 66). Bundles of mixed titles were distributed to newsstands, drugstores, and supermarkets, where they were displayed in a haphazard fashion, and each month a large number of unsold issues were returned to distributor warehouses where they were ground into pulp. The system also discouraged many readers from becoming fans because it was difficult to follow a character or storyline when one could not rely on particular titles to be available at the corner store from month to month. Phil Seuling, a Brooklyn high school teacher and comic book fan, had a better idea.

In 1973 Seuling approached all the major publishers with the same deal: If they would give him a 50 percent discount (they ended up giving him 60 percent), he would keep the unsold issues rather than returning them for reimbursement (Dean 51). Seuling had been selling comic books through mail order and at the New York Comic Art Convention, which he had been instrumental in starting. Unlike the distributors, who cared little and knew less about the comics in their trucks, Seuling knew that during the 1960s, comic book narrative had evolved from stand-alone stories to ongoing soap operas sustained through multiple subplots and crossovers between titles, and he realized most fans were frustrated about not being able to reliably follow the trials and tribulations of their favorite characters. That's why he felt confident he could make money with his scheme. He knew which new titles the fans he dealt with wanted to buy, and any issues not immediately sold would become back issue stock for the mail order business, which he could eventually sell to fans unable to find those issues at their hometown newsstands.

Seuling was not the only entrepreneurial comics fan in the early seventies. A growing number of teenagers and young adults were using their personal comics collections to set up comic book shops in cheap storefronts or storage sheds in their backyards. Chuck Rozanski, who opened his first store at nineteen and became a Seuling sub-distributor four years later, estimates that in 1974 "there were no more than 30 comics specialty shops throughout the United States and Canada, with another 100 stores that featured comics along with other wares such as books or records" (qtd. in Dean 51). Seuling, through his newly established Sea Gate Distribution company, offered these retailers a 40 percent discount on new comics—10 percent better than the newsstand distributors were giving them—and shipped them the precise mix and quantity of titles they needed. As the number of comics shops increased, Seuling set up sub-distributors throughout the country and established what became known as the **Direct Market** system. By the beginning of the 1980s, a number of fans turned retailers turned distributors had challenged Seuling's monopoly and energized the direct market. From fewer than two hundred stores in 1974, the comics specialty retail network grew to approximately three thousand stores by the mid-eighties (Dean 51–54).

FIGURE 3.11. Phil Seuling, who was instrumental in starting direct-market distribution and the New York Comic Art Convention, posed for this photograph at the 1976 convention. From left to right are DC Comics President Sol Harrison, inker Joe Sinnott, Seuling, and cartoonist Jim Steranko. Photography courtesy of Mark Sinnott.

Publishers embraced the system. They could take advance orders from retailers and print quantities that more precisely matched demand, and they didn't have to take returns from comic shops; issues that didn't sell within a month or two of their release went into the store's back-issue bins. Marvel created a book, *Dazzler*, to try out a direct-market-only offering. *Dazzler* #1 (1981) sold in excess of 400,000 copies (Sabin, *Adult* 66). DC followed with limited series, such as *Tales of the New Teen Titans* (1982) and *Camelot 3000* (1982), which were aimed at the fan market. Limited newsstand distribution and subscription sales continued, but Marvel and DC gradually shifted their marketing efforts to the direct market.

The Direct Market System encouraged other fans to try their hand at publishing, like Pacific Comics, which entered comic book publishing near the end of 1981 and released their first book exclusively for the comics specialty stores. New comic book publishers were not likely to get much rack space if they attempted to compete with the Big Two on the newsstands; those outlets were only interested in carrying proven titles. However, they stood a good chance of getting their product in the comics specialty stores. The fans who ran the comic shops got excited about new characters and concepts, and probably stocked more titles from the upstart publishers than was financially prudent.

It was also an environment that nurtured fans. Stores ordered books based on the tastes of their particular clientele, and fans were almost guaranteed not to miss an issue of their favorite books because retailers used pull lists to put aside each of their regulars' requests as the books arrived each week. On the other hand, the direct market isolated comic books and their readers from mainstream culture, and also isolated comic books from potential new readers. While at first the system seemed perfect for both publishers and fans, there quickly developed what retailer Chuck Rozanski has called "an economic micro-world" and others have referred to as "a superhero ghetto" (qtd. in Dean 59). The economic health of all segments of the industry—mainstream, independent, and even alternative—became dependent on the Direct Market System, and when the system faltered in the 1990s, the effects would be devastating. In the meantime, comic books would not only explore new markets, but also new merits.

The Rise of the Graphic Novel

In a 1960 lecture to the Bristol Literary Society, novelist John Updike speculated on new forms the novel might take and told the audience, "I see no intrinsic reason why a doubly talented artist might not arise and create a comic-strip novel masterpiece" (Gravett, *Great British* 8). Updike was not the only person considering the possibility of a more prestigious future for graphic storytelling. Richard Kyle, a prominent and outspoken member of the growing comic book fan community, was aware of the more mature work being produced in European comics and he expressed a desire for similar comics work in America. As early as 1964, Kyle advocated using the terms "graphic story" and "graphic novel" to distinguish serious works from run-of-the-mill newsstand comic books (Schelly, *Golden Age* 130). *Graphic novel* was the term that caught on. In 1976 five longer works aimed at adults were referred to on their covers or in their introductions as graphic novels. In 1978 Will Eisner's *A Contract with God*, distributed in both bookstore chains and direct market comic book shops, garnered wide attention and firmly established *graphic novel* as the term for a longer comics work with literary intent.

Over the past thirty years the number of graphic novels in comic books shops—and more recently in major bookstore chains—has steadily increased, due in part to a new generation of alternative cartoonists who, inspired by the work of their underground and independent predecessors, are creating ambitious long-form comics. However, the *graphic novel* section at Barnes & Noble would not be so extensive if not for more Japanese manga reprints being marketed in the United States, and a rather indiscriminate use of the term graphic novel. Any work longer than the standard comic book, from Howard Cruse's 210-page hardcover *Stuck Rubber Baby* to a trade paperback collecting seven issues of *Amazing Spider-Man*, might be labeled a "graphic novel" by eager marketers.

Some comics theorists and critics see the graphic novel label as a burden to the comic book art form. Cartoonist Scott McCloud claims that "in moving from periodical to book, an implicit claim of permanent worth was being made—a claim that had to be justified" (*Reinventing* 29). Scholar Charles Hatfield worries that the term "may encourage expectations, positive or negative, that are not borne out by the material itself" (5). The expectations were first raised as the term *graphic novel* was given widespread exposure in the mid-eighties with the appearance three influential graphic novels—*Maus, Batman: The Dark Knight Returns*, and *Watchmen*.

THE ERA OF AMBITION

The Era of Ambition was a period in which the comic book industry truly aspired to produce more than mere ephemera, objects that are here today and gone tomorrow. Lending credibility to this aspiration were works that advanced the art of comic books and won attention in the popular press. The three works that engendered the most hope for the future of the comic book all graced the shelves in what might be the medium's greatest year: 1986.

The Greatest Year

The publication of Art Spiegelman's *Maus: A Survivor's Tale* brought mainstream attention to the potential of comic books to tell stories other than those about superheroes. *Maus* is a memoir about Art trying to relate to his father, Vladek, a survivor of the Holocaust, whose experiences leading up to his internment in a concentration camp are told in flashbacks. The characters, however, are depicted as animals, with the predatory Nazis cast as cats and the persecuted Jews as mice. Spiegelman had actually begun to publish sections of his narrative in underground comix anthology *Funny Aminals* in 1972 and returned to the work in 1977, publishing installments serially in *Raw*. In 1986 he published the collected chapters to much acclaim. While numerous accounts of the Holocaust had been published in the decades since World War II, there had never been one quite like *Maus*, and critics took notice. Spiegelman would go on to produce a second volume of the memoir and publish it in 1992. That volume would win a Pulitzer Prize Special Award, the first and only comic book to earn one of publishing's most prestigious prizes.

Given that Spiegelman's work was emerging in the less restrictive confines of the underground movement, it might be expected that his accomplished works would be more artistically than commercially driven. Yet the two other major works of comic's greatest year were issued by a mainstream publisher, DC Comics. In 1986 they had two of the industry's most talented storytellers, Frank Miller and Alan Moore, on projects that took apart the very concept of the superhero.

Deconstructing Superheroes

Frank Miller had already earned a reputation for spinning gritty narratives with his run on Marvel's *Daredevil* series (1979–1983) and a miniseries he had done for DC called *Ronin* (1983) when he had the opportunity to create *Batman: The Dark Knight Returns*. The four-part limited series is set several years in the future, where a middle-aged Bruce Wayne find himself drawn back to his former life as a masked vigilante. His return to crime-fighting puts him in conflict with former foes like the Joker and friends like Superman, all in stunning visuals delivered by Miller's pencils, with inks provided by Klaus Janson and a color palette from Lynn Varley. DC even debuted a new square-bound binding for the limited series, calling it "Prestige Format." Miller's take on the Dark Knight drew more attention than the character had received since the campy TV show of the 1960s. Miller had brought Batman back to his violent roots and provided a grittier, less sanitized vision of vigilantism. As one critic noted, "the repercussions of this Miller story continue to affect even far less ambitious superhero tales a decade after its publication" (Mark Nevins 29). Miller would go on to write a number of special projects for Batman, but his first take on the hero would be his most influential, bearing considerable influence on the darker tone and direction of the film franchise that would debut with Tim Burton's *Batman* (1989).

Like Frank Miller, Alan Moore explores the real-world implications of people dressing up in colorful costumes and taking to the streets to dispense vigilante justice. In late 1986, DC Comics began to publish *Watchmen*, a twelve-issue limited series by Moore in collaboration with artist Dave Gibbons. *Watchmen* is regarded as quite possibly "the most complex and ambitious superhero series ever published" (Bradford Wright 272) due to its layered narrative of plots and subplots all weaving together and leading to an unanticipated climax. Unlike most previous superhero narratives where the protagonists defend the status quo, *Watchmen* features characters—including the Machiavellian Ozymandias and the anti-hero Rorschach—who take steps towards real social change, imposing their vision of what is right upon society, even though doing

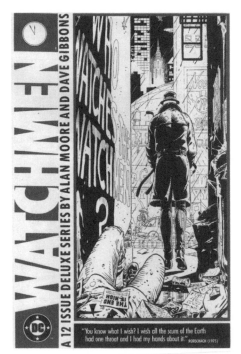

so comes through amoral means. Moore had previously explored the horrific side of superheroes run amuck in his *Marvelman* series for the British comics anthology *Warrior* beginning in 1982. (The series was reprinted stateside by Eclipse Comics as *Miracleman* in 1985.) Numerous superhero series would explore the trope further, from Mark Gruenwald's *Squadron Supreme* (1985) to Warren Ellis and Bryan Hitch's The Authority (1999). After completing its initial run as a serial, *Watchmen* was reprinted as a trade paperback and marketed as a graphic novel to much critical acclaim and academic analysis. In 2005 *Time* magazine named it one of "the 100 best novels from 1923 to present" alongside such literary luminaries as Harper Lee's *To Kill a Mockingbird* and William Faulker's *The Sound and the Fury*.

FIGURE 3.12. DC's house ad for Alan Moore and Dave Gibbons' masterpiece asks, "Who watches the watchmen?" in the aftermath of a violent attack from trenchcoated anti-hero Rorschach. Art by Dave Gibbons © DC Comics

The darker heroes of *Batman: The Dark Knight Returns* and *Watchmen* were at the forefront of a wave of anti-heroes who grew steadily more popular in the mainstream as the eighties ended and the nineties began. Cartoonist Mike Grell took DC's liberal loudmouth Green Arrow and turned him into an urban hunter, switching from his trademark trick arrows (e.g., the boxing glove arrow) to regular pointed shafts with which he maimed or impaled his criminal prey. Writer Chris Claremont and a number of collaborators (beginning with none other than Frank Miller) unleashed the feral mutant Wolverine from the X-Men ensemble and turned him into a comics superstar, well known for cutting and impaling his foes with his razor-sharp claws. And the Punisher, who had been created by Gerry Conway as an antagonist for Spider-Man, resurfaced as the lead in his own popular series. In fact, by the early 1990s the gun-toting, death-dealing vigilante starred in three monthly magazines of his own, making him almost as visible a property in the comics as Spider-Man, Superman, and Batman.

New Publishers

The proliferation of new comic book titles and of new comic book publishers was another significant development of the Era of Ambition. In 1986 a new independent publisher called Dark Horse Comics issued its first comic book and was on its way to becoming one of the mainstays of the industry into the twenty-first century. Dark Horse was the brainchild of Mike Richardson, a successful comics retailer out of Portland, Oregon. His initial foray into comics publishing, *Dark Horse Presents*, was a black-and-white anthology, featuring a rotating cast of creators and characters, including the debut of cartoonist Paul Chadwick's endearing everyman, Concrete. Dark Horse would go on to secure the **licensing** rights to a number of lucrative film properties, including *Aliens* (1988), *Predator* (1989), and *Star Wars* (1991). It would also welcome a number of the industry's top talents to develop creator-owned projects under its banner, among them Frank Miller (*Sin City*, 1991), Mike Mignola (*Hellboy*, 1993), and Bryan Talbot (*Tale of One Bad Rat*, 1994). Except for a brief flirtation with superheroes in its "Comics Greatest World" imprint in the mid-nineties, Dark Horse has largely steered clear of publishing them, choosing to make its fortunes in other genres. As a result, Dark Horse has outlasted many of the

FIGURE 3.13. Dark Horse published Paul Chadwick's *Concrete*, which often took on environmental issues, as in *Concrete Celebrates Earth Day 1990*. © Paul Chadwick

independent publishers that preceded it (e.g., Eclipse, First), as well as a number who came along after them.

A couple of these newer competitors, who would play a role in the expanding comics market within the Era of Ambition, deserve to be mentioned. The first is Valiant Comics, begun in 1991 by comics giant Jim Shooter. Shooter had begun writing comics in the sixties while he was still a teenager, doing scripts for DC's "Legion of Super-Heroes" series in *Adventure Comics*. He eventually went on to become the editor-in-chief at Marvel Comics, wielding tight control over the Marvel Universe during his tenure (1978–1987). Shooter returned to comic books in 1991, using Valiant to reintroduce *Magnus, Robot Fighter* and *Solar, Man of the Atom*, based on characters introduced by Gold Key Comics in the sixties. Valiant quickly expanded to a stable of titles featuring its own original characters (e.g., *Shadowman, Harbinger, X-O Manowar*), and early issues of its titles' runs commanded high prices in back issue trade. For a time, Valiant was even nipping at Marvel and DC's heels as the third-largest comic book publisher. But in 1993 the expanding comics market began a downturn, and video game maker Acclaim bought out Valiant the following year. Despite efforts to re-launch the line under the Acclaim Comics imprint, publication folded altogether by 1999.

Another victim of the mid-nineties downturn was Malibu Comics, which began producing comics in 1987 backed by comic book distributor Scott Rosenberg. Malibu published a modest variety of genres in its run, including creator-owned properties (Will Jacobs and Gerard Jones' *The Trouble with Girls*) and licensed properties (*Tarzan*), but it became more of a market force when it launched its own superhero universe in 1993 with titles such as *Prime, Mantra*, and *Ultraforce*. Marvel Comics bought out Malibu in 1994, and after a half-hearted re-launch of a handful of their superhero titles, let the line fade into oblivion in 1997. Indeed, Malibu might have been just another minor publisher competing in the comics boom of the early nineties, except for one very significant step it took that changed the face of the industry: In 1992 it had offered to assist another fledgling publisher make use of its distribution network. That new publisher was Image Comics.

Image emerged when a group of artists sought to win for themselves a larger share of the profit that their talents were generating for America's largest comic book publisher. No company profited more from the expansion of the comics market in the early 1990s than Marvel, and while Marvel long held that it was its stable of attractive characters that drew its audience, it certainly owed a portion of its market share to the talents of the creators who breathed life into those characters. Marvel recognized these creators' influence and capitalized on their appeal. In 1990, they gave artist Todd McFarlane his own *Spider-Man* #1, which sold almost 3 million copies. Another artist, Rob Liefeld, helped sell 5 million copies of *X-Force* #1 in 1991. A few months after that, the Jim Lee-drawn *X-Men* #1 set new industry records by selling 8 million copies. Such massive sales, coupled with lucrative licensing of the original artwork, generated a lot of profit for Marvel, but only a modest percentage of it came back to the artists. Frustrated by Marvel's compensation, the lack of creator ownership over what they were producing, and various creative differences, McFarlane, Liefeld, and

FIGURE 3.14. The Image Comics founders reunited in 2008. In the front row, left to right, are Jim Valentino, Jim Lee, and Whilce Portacio; back row, Marc Silvestri, Erik Larsen, Rob Liefeld, and Todd McFarlane. Photo courtesy of *Wizard*: The Comics Magazine/wizarduniverse.com.

Lee joined with four other rising stars, Erik Larsen, Marc Silvestri, Jim Valentino, and Whilce Portacio, to establish their own publishing house.

The seven Image founders discovered an eager audience for their initial offerings. Nearly a million copies of Liefeld's *Youngblood* #1 were pre-ordered by retailers. McFarlane's *Spawn* #1 would sell 1.7 million copies. The sales were unprecedented for independent publishing, and so were the profits for the creators, who reaped financial rewards many times greater than they had drawing for Marvel on work-for-hire contracts. The seven were hailed as superstars by the fans, who made Image products so hot that even the venerable DC Comics, the number-two seller in the marketplace, felt the heat. But Image was not without its critics. Given that artists ran the company, its comic books emphasized visual spectacle over story structure or dialogue. Moreover, many of the titles came to rely on stereotypes of hyper-masculine heroes and impossibly proportioned heroines. Finally, as time went by, more and more Image comic books were delivered later and later, frustrating retailers and fans alike. Internal disputes would eventually fracture the alliance among the Image founders, and Image would settle into a distant third, well behind Marvel and DC, in the marketplace. However, Image had proven that creator-owned publishing was not only practical but could be profitable. Other publishers scrambled to create imprints friendly to creator-owned properties such as Dark Horse's Legends and Malibu's Bravura, but their development was ill-timed. The boom that the industry had enjoyed for several years was about to go bust.

Rise and Fall of the Speculators' Market

The Era of Ambition had begun to draw to a close by 1993, when the expansion of the comics market reached its most dizzying heights and then came crashing down, taking publishers, distributors, and retailers down with it. For several years, all three sectors of the comic book industry had profited from the increased attention that had been directed to the fact that older, collectible comic books had been increasing in value, with some of the most desirable having grown to be worth hundreds of thousands of dollars. This spurred a speculative response from some investors who bought up multiple copies of new comics, hoping that their freshly minted comic books would in short order increase in value. Publishers responded to the growing collectors' market by offering numerous gimmicks to entice these buyers' attention, from covers with special effects like hologram enhancements to copies sealed in polybags. Collectively, they also produced more comic book titles than ever before. Marvel Comics alone was putting out about one hundred titles a month at the height of the boom. At the same time, comics were selling more copies than ever, and the launch of the Marvel's new *X-Men* in 1991 set an all-time sales record with its 8 million copies sold. Yet the flood of comics would contribute to the expansion's undoing.

The decline in the comic buyers market came, in part, from the realization among speculators that scarcity is what inflates the price of collectibles. An issue of *Wolverine* published in 1990, whose press run was nearing a million issues,

could increase only modestly in value over time. The reason that 1940's *Batman* #1 was worth hundreds of thousands of dollars was because there were so few copies still in existence. Rozanski cites the 1992 "Death of Superman" storyline as the moment of epiphany for many speculators. DC had hyped the story—in which the Man of Steel dies while stopping an Image-inspired muscle-bound monster named Doomsday—in the popular press, resulting in the sale of millions of copies of the story's climax in *Superman* #75. Yet those who bought the issue as an investment would be disappointed in short order: "When these new comics consumers/investors tried to sell their copies of *Superman* #75 for a profit a few months later, however, and discovered that they could only recover their purchase price if they had a first printing, their bitter disillusionment did much to cause the comics investing bubble to begin bursting" (Rozanski).

,FIGURE 3.15. The death of Superman garnered national media attention but may have contributed to the end of the speculators' market. Art by Dan Jurgens and Brett Breeding © DC Comics

As speculators began to walk away from the industry, they left retailers with tons of unwanted back stock, forcing many to close up shop. By 1996, the number of comics retailers shrank from an estimated 10,000 shops to just 4,000 nationwide (Jones and Jacobs 363). Other woes beset the publishers. With fewer buyers and increased competition for those who remained, many of the publishers went out of business. Distributors also began to feel the bite of a shrinking industry. When Marvel Comics made a bid at vertical integration by setting up an exclusive distribution deal using its own recently acquired distributor, Heroes World, the move spurred other publishers to seek out exclusive deals of their own with competing distributors. Marvel soon abandoned its scheme, and in the aftermath most distributors were driven out of business, except for Diamond Comic Distributors, who emerged from the fracas with a virtual monopoly over comic book distribution in 1994. The mismanagement at Marvel continued until 1996, when the company was forced to declare bankruptcy and reorganize its business. Marvel successfully emerged from the proceedings and even maintained its sales dominance over the industry, but by the time it did, it was clear that it was going to be a smaller industry than ever before.

The comic book industry has yet to return to the commercial success of the early nineties. Case in point, the most popular comic book in January 2008, a re-launch of the *Hulk*, printed about 133,000 copies. The most popular comic from the same month in 1998, an issue of *Uncanny X-Men*, sold approximately 154,000 copies. This is a decrease of 14 percent in a decade. A generation earlier, *Superman* reported a circulation of 636,000 copies per issue! Ironically, this decline in interest comes even as more and more comic book characters are recognized for their influence in other media. Sam Raimi's *Spider-Man* film (2002) is one of the top ten box office hits of all time, but sales for Spider-Man comic books have not enjoyed a bump from the character's higher profile. Retailers have attempted to draw attention to the industry with promotions like "Free Comic Book Day" in 2002 to try to cultivate press attention and bring the public into retail comics specialty shops. But on a whole, the industry's efforts seem to be more insular than inclusive, with most marketing going to promoting particular comic books among existing readership, rather than attempting to reach out and encourage new readers to join in. By largely catering to existing readers, many of whom eventually move on to other pastimes, the number of overall consumers of comic books continues to dwindle.

The Era of Ambition gave the comic book a larger sense of what it could aspire to, both in terms of achieving artistic merit and attracting a large audience once again. While credibility in the comic book's artistic merits has continued to find affirmation in the latest era, it remains to be seen if such sizable audiences will ever return again.

THE ERA OF REITERATION

Without sufficient distance from the most recent events in the history of the American comic book, it is difficult to accurately discern the characteristics of the present era; however, in the course of the last two decades, comic books appear to have entered into an Era of Reiteration. In this era, superheroes continue to be the dominant genre sold by the mainstream publishers, and among the most frequently told stories have been periodic reinterpretations of these familiar characters. Doing so has tapped into the mythic qualities of the genre, demonstrating the vitality of heroic mythology for generating stories. It has also meant that mainstream publishing has been fixated on the genre, leaving much of the most progressive and experimental storytelling to independent publishers who have attempted to push the boundaries of the medium well beyond the limitations of just one type of story.

Reconstructing Superheroes

In 1985 DC Comics celebrated its fiftieth anniversary by presenting a twelve-issue limited series called *Crisis on Infinite Earths*. The intent of the series was to tidy up the continuity—the inter-relationships among previously published stories—and ideally make DC titles more accessible to new readers. On the heels of *Crisis*, DC revamped a number of its most high-profile characters, beginning with Superman in 1986. Cartoonist John Byrne, who had become a fan favorite on Marvel titles like *X-Men* and *Fantastic Four*, re-introduced Superman in a six-issue limited series, *The Man of Steel*, before taking over monthly duties on the continuing *Action Comics* and a newly numbered *Superman* series. In short order, DC introduced reinterpretations of Batman, Wonder Woman, and many other characters in their line. DC's efforts to revitalize well-worn characters for a new generation were, by the late 1980s, hardly innovative. Stan Lee had attempted to revive Captain America, the Human Torch, and the Sub-Mariner under the Atlas banner in the mid-1950s and failed. Julius Schwartz had succeeded in revitalizing Flash, Green Lantern, and other Golden Age heroes thereafter, and spawned the great superhero revival of the late fifties and early sixties. But by the mid-nineties something had changed. An era filled with **nostalgia**, the longing for things of old, seemed to take hold of creators and led to an increasing number of "Year One" flashback projects that revisited and re-envisioned the roots of popular superheroes more frequently than just once in a generation.

The flashpoint for such nostalgia came in 1994, when Kurt Busiek and Alex Ross teamed to create the four-issue limited series *Marvels*. The series retold many of the most famous events in Marvel's chronology, but this time from the perspective of an everyman, a newspaper photographer who followed the exploits of the marvelous superheroes who inhabited his world. The series was blessed with Ross's photo-realistic painted artwork and Busiek's keen recollection of Marvel lore. Busiek would go on to produce other works that were reminiscent of the characters of earlier eras. His critically-acclaimed, creator-owned *Astro City* series featured a collection of original characters in the mold of some of the most familiar heroes from Marvel and DC's stables (e.g., his Samaritan was a Superman imitation). Other authors would also tap into the preference for nostalgia, including the highly regarded Alan Moore, who would pay homage to early Marvel Comics in his *1963* limited series, honor the Silver Age Superman in a run on Image's *Supreme*, and resurrect several all-but-forgotten Golden Age superheroes originally published by Nedor Comics. Revivals of nostalgic heroes are still going strong with Dynamite Entertainment's *Project Superpowers* (2008), which features over a dozen Golden Age heroes from publishers Fox, Crestwood, and Nedor, along with Marvel's resurrection of a dozen of its own obscure superheroes from the Timely era, for the limited series *The Twelve* (2008).

The desire to return to less complicated continuities has become not only a creator-driven but also an editorially dictated direction in the Era of Reiteration. For instance, Marvel had long prided itself on building an expansive, interconnected saga when it hired several talents from Image Comics to re-imagine some of its most prominent titles in the separate imprint Heroes Reborn in 1996. After more than thirty years of continuous publication, the ongoing titles for the *Fantastic Four, Captain America, Iron Man,* and the *Avengers* were canceled and restarted with number one issues. The substitution in talent and continuity lasted for just over a year before Marvel reintegrated those characters with the rest of its line. But then in 2000 it launched an entirely separate line of comics under its Ultimate imprint. The Ultimate line attempted to be much hipper and much more accessible to a new generation of readers, and it met with considerable success. *Ultimate Spider-Man* was joined in short order by *Ultimate X-Men* and several other hit titles, many of which consistently placed at the top of the sales charts in the first decade of the new millennium.

The Era of Reiteration has thus come to be characterized not only by the reintroduction of superheroes with updated backgrounds and appearances, but also by the coexistence of multiple versions of the same character coming forth from its publisher simultaneously. For example, Marvel Comics is, as of this writing, publishing at least three distinct versions of Spider-Man on a monthly basis: the first is the "Marvel Universe" version whose adventures exist in relationship to other Spider-Man stories that began in 1962; the second is the "Ultimate Universe" version who debuted in a series of separately interrelated stories in 2000; and the third is a children-friendly version appearing under the banner of "Marvel Adventures" which launched in 2003. Though nothing can replicate the experience of having been on hand for a classic superhero's debut, publishers have certainly attempted to give new readers an opportunity to get in on the ground floor of a character's revitalized adventures by either rebooting or revisiting their origins time and again in recent years. One result of this emphasis has been fewer and fewer original superheroes being introduced, and more and more reiteration of those that are already proven commodities.

Alternative Comics Achieve Recognition

While the industry's superhero mainstream continues to present more and more of the same material, a number of independent publishers have tackled a diversity of genres and even non-genre works. There are dozens of independent publishers, collectively sharing less than 30 percent of the American comics market. Yet, arguably, their contributions do more to advance comics as an art form than anything put out by the mainstream publishers throughout this era.

While the industry's third-largest publisher, Image Comics, got its start competing directly with DC and Marvel in the superhero genre, it has in recent years increasingly gravitated to other genres. In 1998 Image began to publish Eric Shanower's *Age of Bronze*, a retelling of the siege of ancient Troy based on historical sources. Image also achieved critical acclaim with Brian Michael Bendis and Michael Avon Oeming's *Powers* series (2000), which deftly revitalized detective fiction by setting it in the world of superheroics. Likewise, Robert Kirkman's *The Walking Dead* (2003) scored with audiences in telling the ongoing saga of survivors coping in a world of homicidal zombies. Despite a foundation firmly rooted in superheroics, Image has grown to be among the industry leaders in marketing other genres for the medium.

The fourth-largest publisher, Dark Horse Comics, has also enjoyed commercial success in offering comic books from other genres. Its most high-profile projects have been works by Frank Miller, including the gritty *Sin City* crime comics, which began in 1991, and the historical drama *300* in 1998. Both properties went on to be highly profitable film adaptations. Another recognizable creation, Mike Mignola's *Hellboy*, which first appeared in 1993, has also gone on to enjoy two major Hollywood film adaptations.

Other publishers have been less commercially successful than Image or Dark Horse, but have produced works held in high esteem by critics. Fantagraphics has promoted the work of a number of reputable and influential cartoonists, including Chris Ware (*Acme Novelty Library*, 1993), Peter Bagge (*Hate*, 1990), Daniel Clowes (*Eightball*, 1989), and Los Bros Hernandez (*Love and Rockets*, 1982). Many of these cartoonists tell slice-of-life stories far removed from the fantasies offered by mainstream comic book publishers. Another publisher, Top Shelf, has offered everything from memoirs (Craig Thompson's *Blankets*, 2003) to pornography (Alan Moore and Melinda Gebbie's *Lost Girls*, 2006). From established independent publishers like Drawn & Quarterly to recent start-ups like IDW, independent publishers have set a precedent for the diversity of stories to which the medium can be applied.

In fairness, one must acknowledge that many of the independent publishers have financed their more artistic endeavors by relying on the production of more marketable comic books based on popular licensed properties. Dark Horse has published scores of books based on George Lucas's *Star Wars* film series, Top Cow adapted the *Tomb Raider* video games, Fantagraphics has produced books reprinting Charles Schultz's *Peanuts* strips, and IDW has acquired the rights to the *Star Trek* franchise, a lucrative property that has been published by everyone from Gold Key in the sixties to Malibu in the nineties. At least in this regard, the independent publishers have been in sync with the two major publishers in the Era of Reiteration, reproducing familiar narratives in comic book form.

Yet the artistic impact of the independents still resonates, even among the major publishers. In order to attract talent interested in exploring mature themes and retaining ownership of their creative properties, both DC and Marvel have moved towards creating imprints to publish creator-owned content separate from their main lines. DC launched Vertigo in 1993 under the editorial guidance of Karen Berger (see profile in Chapter Eleven), building on its edgier titles like *Swamp Thing* and *Sandman* before going on to release a number of successful creator-owned series, from Garth Ennis and Steve Dillon's *Preacher* (1995) to

Brian K. Vaughan and Pia Guerra's Y: *The Last Man* (2002). Marvel, which first experimented with creator-owned properties in its Epic Comics line in the eighties and nineties, now publishes such material under its Icon imprint, which began in 2004 to take over the *Powers* series from Image Comics.

Perhaps the most visible effect of the growth of the independent market upon the mainstream publishers is the abandonment of censoring review by the Comics Magazine Association of America (CMAA). Since 1954 most mainstream publishers have submitted their comic books for review by the CMAA, particularly if they hoped to sell their magazines on newsstands. However, as the market for comic books shifted from newsstands to specialty shops and new publishers bypassed the association entirely, its seal of approval became less and less significant. In 2001 Marvel abandoned the review process entirely, electing to begin its own self-assessed rating system on its covers. DC continues to submit only a few of its titles for review, mostly those in its Johnny DC children's imprint. Consistent with its squeaky-clean image, Archie Comics continues to be a staunch subscriber, but for most publishers the Code has little remaining relevance. Its waning influence is a testimony to its stifling reputation as a censor. Marvel's editor-in-chief Joe Quesada notes, "In retrospect, thinking about the Code and the CMAA, let me just put this bluntly, I just think the CMAA did a very poor job with respect to letting people in the general public know that there were comics other than the ones for kids, thus I think in a lot of ways perpetuating the CMAA, and Marvel was a very big part of that." (qtd. in Alls).

ANALYZING: GRAPHIC NOVELS IN THE MAINSTREAM MARKET

While the fate of the comic book as a periodical for sale in a comic book specialty shop seems to be in decline according to recent sales trends, the art form itself is nimbly adapting to the wider retail market of traditional book outlets. According to ICv2, a publication that tracks sales figures in the industry, sales of graphic novels have climbed in recent years. In 2007 sales rose more than 19 percent from the previous year alone, with more than 3,300 titles released that year ("Over").

A number of factors have contributed to the growing popularity of the graphic novel. One is the support that graphic novels have been given by professional librarians. Ever since *Maus* won recognition from the Pulitzer committee in 1992, more and more libraries have been adding graphic novels and trade paperbacks to their collections, driven by patron demand that has made comics among the fastest growing materials that the libraries circulate. This interest came to a flashpoint in 2002, when the American Library Association invited creators Jeff Smith (*Bone*), Neil Gaiman (*Sandman*), Art Spiegleman (*Maus*), and Colleen Doran (*A Distant Soil*) to speak at its annual convention. Since then, libraries have demonstrated even more enthusiasm for graphic storytelling.

Another factor is the surge in popularity for Japanese comics, or manga, in the American market. While the indigenous Japanese comic book industry had operated successfully for decades (see Chapter Thirteen), it was only in the late eighties, with the translation of manga series like *Akira* (1988), that American audiences began to take note of the comics. Viz Communications began to reprint a range of manga titles for the English-speaking American audience in 1987, but the market for manga grew slowly. Yet by 1997 the market had grown, and Viz was joined by competitor Tokyopop. In the first decade of the new century, manga has been the fastest growing segment of comic book publishing, with dozens of publishers offering translated manga or American-made comics imitating its distinctive style. In 2007 estimates place sales of manga at $210 million in the United States alone ("Over"). The largest retailer for manga is actually the Borders chain of bookstores, not the comics specialty stores' direct market, which further suggests that their appeal stretches beyond traditional comics readers.

FIGURE 3.16. The changing face of American comic book sales is characterized by the increasing popularity of Japanese manga such as Viz Communications' *Shonen Jump* magazine (2007). © VIZ Media

As comic books continue into the twenty-first century, the quest for wider acceptance comes at a time when the medium's core audience finds itself distracted by more and more competing media messages. Ever since television offered up an inexpensive alternative to graphic storytelling in the 1950s, the comics audience has spent less time—and money—on reading comic books. The widespread acceptance of video games in the 1980s, and then the adoption of the internet in the 1990s, have only increased competition among media for attentive eyeballs. Still, comic books establish an intimacy between storytellers and readers that is unlike the communication occurring in television, video games, or most websites. Successfully inviting people to experience that connection will be an ongoing challenge sure to help define the next era of the comics medium's history.

Discussion Questions

1. What do you find to be the most enduring repercussions of the underground comix movement on contemporary comic books?
2. Aside from those reviewed in this chapter, are there other factors that have contributed to the gradual decline of the comic book market? Why else do you think fewer people, especially young people, read comic books now than they did before?
3. Can you forecast the future of comic books based on recent trends in the industry? What do you think will be the defining characteristics of the next era of comic book history?

Activities

1. There are many important contributors to comic book history whom we barely had space to mention in this chapter, each of them interesting characters in their own right. Research one of these other figures on your own and provide a biography highlighting that person's contributions to the medium. Some suggestions of people to investigate are Gary Arlington, Clay Geerdes, and Jim Steranko, among many, many others.
2. The hallmark of the Era of Reiteration is the way familiar stories in comics culture are retold. Identify a familiar story outside of comic books and aside from superheroes that has been retold across time. Some possible examples include a fairy tale like Cinderella or even a religious story like a virgin birth. Do a little research into this story to come up with three to five versions of it. Be prepared to explain how each version is similar and yet different from the others: What essential elements remain part of each version? What liberties can be taken? Does the medium of storytelling (moving, say, from text to film) alter the story in significant ways?

Recommended Readings

Comics:

Busiek, Kurt, and Brent E. Anderson. *Kurt Busiek's Astro City: Life in the Big City*. La Jolla, CA: Homage Comics, 1996.

> Like Metropolis or Gotham City, Astro City is an imaginary place filled with superhuman adventurers, misfit villains, and everyday people trying to cope with the craziness produced by the interaction among them. Busiek's stories reverently explore the human side of these larger-than-life figures who are fresh yet familiar to anyone conversant with the superhero genre.

Crumb, Robert. *The Complete Crumb Comics*. 17 vols. Seattle, WA: Fantagraphics, 2001–2005.

Fantagraphics Books has set out to reprint the entirety of Robert Crumb's unorthodox career. At this writing, the volumes in this series re-present Crumb's comix and other artwork from some of his earliest efforts as a teenager in the late fifties in its first volume to material published in the early nineties in the latest volume.

Scholarly Sources:

Hatfield, Charles. *Alternative Comics: An Emerging Literature*. Jackson, MS: University Press of Mississippi, 2005.

Hatfield traces the development of alternative comics from its roots in the underground comics movement of the late sixties through to its most gifted practitioners of recent years. Along the way, he provides analysis of the trends and tropes in the literary comics published outside of the industry's mainstream.

Jones, Gerard, and Will Jacobs. *The Comic Book Heroes*. Rocklin, CA: Prima Publishing, 1997.

Jones and Jacobs provide an effective history of the development of American comic book publishing from the dawn of the Silver Age innovations of Julius Schwartz and Stan Lee through to the mid-nineties.

The Comic Book
Industry

"The idea that comics stores, distributors and publishers simply 'give the customers what they want' is nonsense. What the customers wanted they didn't get—and they left."

—Scott McCloud, cartoonist and comics theorist, 2000

Wednesdays are the busiest days of the week at Super-Fly Comics in Yellow Springs, Ohio. A brisk flow of customers stream in from the streets and line up in one of two queues. One forms shoulder-to-shoulder along the right-hand side of the store as the patrons study a floor-to-ceiling display of new comic books, reprinted collections, and graphic novels for sale. The other starts at the cash register as regular clients wait eagerly for their weekly stack of comics from a "pull file" that the management has prepared at their request. Across America, Wednesdays are "new comics" days at specialty shops like Super-Fly. Walk into the store or any of its competitors and you are sure to see for sale many of the items that have attracted these consumers. In addition to the draw of new comics, there are often long boxes of older comics for sale. Super-Fly has rows of such comics going back to the 1970s set up in one back room. Many stores also sell collecting supplies like tailored plastic bags for the storage and preservation of large comics collections. There are comics-inspired action figures, statues, and clothing for sale. Many of these stores also sell trading cards and gaming supplies. At certain times of the week, they may even have a special area set aside just for gaming activities, but this generally doesn't take place on Wednesdays. Wednesdays are for comic books—new comic books, to be exact. As the faithful fans make their weekly pilgrimage to the Super-Fly and every other comics specialty shop around America, they help to finance this media industry. Some of them spend a few dollars on the latest comic books, while others put down hundreds for comics and accompanying paraphernalia. The comics bring the customers reading pleasure and the customers, through their dollars, bring the industry its lifeblood.

FIGURE 4.1. The comic book specialty shop becomes a hub of activity on Wednesday afternoons, as eager fans descend to purchase newly released comic books. Photo courtesy of Thacher E. Cleveland and Super-Fly Comics.

OBJECTIVES

In this chapter you will learn:

1. how the traditional comics publishing industry operates through production, distribution, and exhibition stages;

2. why a limited number of producers control most of the comics market and the influence that has on the industry;

3. how two different forms of distribution have shaped the business of comics;

4. how the exhibitors in comic book specialty shops have built a business for themselves by appealing to collectors' sensibilities; and

5. which market players beyond the current dominant marketing stream are exerting influence over the medium.

The comic book is fundamentally a medium through which any number of people could potentially communicate, but the comics that are most recognized are those that reach large audiences through mass distribution. Thus, while any aspiring cartoonist might craft a perfectly enjoyable example of the art form, it is those comic books that have appeared through mass distribution that have typically had the most far-reaching impact on culture. Traditionally, the power to make mass-produced comics has been centralized in the hands of a select few corporate entities—those with the capital to hire the talent, pay to subcontract the printing presses, arrange for widespread distribution of their publications, advertise their sales, etc. Certainly electronic forms of distribution like the internet have challenged the traditional methods of publishing and distribution that have characterized comics for the last several decades, and we will consider those challenges later in this chapter. First, though, this chapter traces modes of making mass-marketed comics by explaining who has made, delivered, and sold comics over the past several decades.

Traditionally, media industries have been composed of three interacting stages: production, distribution, and exhibition. **Production** refers to those entities that make the media messages. In comic books, production is associated with the publishers, from the major corporate professionals in New York City publishing houses on down to the guys making comics with pen and ink on their dining room tables. **Distribution** deals with those in the business of transporting the comics from the printing presses to the various outlets that sell them. We will look at how comics have moved from traditional newsstand delivery, where they competed with every other kind of magazine for sale, to a Direct Market System that brought them into specialty stores. Finally, **exhibition** includes all the retail outlets where comics are for sale. We will take a close

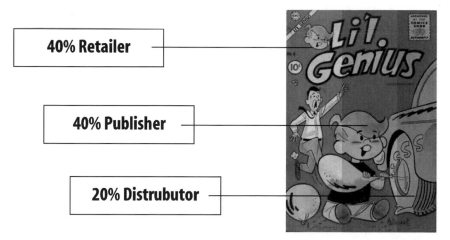

FIGURE 4.2. Where does your comics dollar go? Industry insiders estimate that 40 percent of the cover price goes to retailers, which they use to pay overhead expenses such as personnel and rent (and still hope to turn a profit). Another 20 percent of the price goes to the distributor, Diamond Comics, who delivers the comic books from the publisher to the retailer. The remaining 40 percent goes to the publisher, who must divide it among all the creative and administrative talent, as well as the publishing and advertising costs. *Li'l Genius* © 1955 Charlton Comics Group

look at the comics specialty shops that have become the principle vendors for most comics-related materials today.

PRODUCTION

The first stage to consider in mass media industries is that of production. This refers to the entities who craft a media product for public consumption. Today, a producer of comics could be found in as intimate a setting as an independent cartoonist uploading completed comics to the internet; traditionally, however, commercial comics have been produced by organizations with many contributors to the process, and they have been a print rather than an electronic form of communication. We will discuss online comics later in this chapter, but for now we will focus on print-based comics publishing.

Processes of Production

When it comes to making comics, two principal processes of production characterize the medium: the industrial process and the artisan process. According to Mark Rogers ("Beyond"), the **industrial process** refers to those places where comics are created as a collaborative product, with the task of developing comics divided among writer, artist, inker, letterer, and colorist, and supervised by an editor. In some less flattering characterizations, this process is labeled an *assembly line*, in which a product is put together in the service of commercial rather than creative priorities. Of course, some of the earliest comics were drafted in this fashion. From the early Eisner-Iger Shop (see Chapter 2) to today's Marvel Bullpen, the production formula of the industrial process still makes most of the profitable comics for sale.

On the other hand, the **artisan process** describes those comics created by the individual cartoonist who typically does most of the creative work of producing the finished story. Most of the artisan comics published today come from smaller, so-called independent publishers rather than large commercial ones. Unlike the commercial publishers, who often emphasize the sale of the character featured in a comic rather than the creators behind it, independent publishers are less likely to prioritize regular monthly titles. Unencumbered by the strict production schedules that such periodicals demand, artisan cartoonists can craft a small series of comic books or an entire graphic novel that they can exert full creative control over, rather than relying on an editor to assign portions of the production to other specialists. As Rogers notes, "artisan production has tended to produce comics more varied in scope and more interesting aesthetically. Industrialized production is limiting in and of itself" ("Beyond" 88–89). Just what limits industrialized production imposes on creativity is often a function of the constraints put upon it by owners who tend to be more focused on profitability than creativity.

Discovering: Publishers of Repute

In addition to the Big Two (DC and Marvel), literally hundreds of publishers have impacted the American comic book industry. Here is a brief sampling of some of the key names in the last three-quarters of a century of publishing:

Archie Comics (1939–present)—originally called MLJ Comics (the initials of its founders), the company went on to define the teenage humor genre with Archie Andrews and his pals Betty, Veronica, and Jughead

Charlton Comics (1935–1991)—originally a publisher of song lyrics, Charlton ventured into publishing second-rate comics, the most enduring of which was the Blue Beetle and the most influential was its 1960s "Action Heroes" line, which was later absorbed by DC

Dark Horse Comics (1986–present)—publisher with particular skill in managing licensed properties such as *Star Wars* and forefronting creator-owned properties that go on to feature film development (e.g., Frank Miller's *Sin City*)

Dell Comics (1929–1973)—licensor of Walt Disney's and other famous animation characters; at one point Dell outsold every other publisher

Eastern Color Printing Company (1933–1955)—developed the first modern comic book magazine, *Famous Funnies*, using reprinted material from newspaper strips

Dark Horse Comics® & the Dark Horse logo are registered trademarks of Dark Horse Comics, Inc.

Eclipse Comics (1978–1993)—broke ground as an independent comics publisher catering to the direct market, and also published one of the earliest graphic novels, *Sabre*

Entertaining Comics/E.C. (1946–1955)—originally the E.C. stood for Educational Comics, but William Gaines changed the name and tone of the company when he turned to crime comics and developed the first horror comics (e.g., *Tales from the Crypt*); he later launched *Mad*

Fawcett Publications (1940–1953)—published the most successful rival for Superman's popularity, Captain Marvel, who along with the rest of the Marvel Family gifted pop culture with the magic word "Shazam!"

Harvey Comics (1940–1994)—noted for kid-friendly fare like *Richie Rich* and *Caspar the Friendly Ghost*

Image Comics (1992–present)—formed by a group of popular artists in order to advance creative control over their own comic book properties; at one point their sales rivaled those of Marvel and DC

Ownership Concentration

When it comes to printed comics that have been marketed in mass quantities, large corporate entities have led the industry. As we reviewed in Chapters 2 and 3, there have been many comics publishers over the past eight decades, though through time the market has been increasingly consolidated into a limited number of leading ones. In the American comics scene, production is characterized as an **oligopoly**, a climate in which a few competitors control most of the field. In comics the few is actually two, with the majority of sales concentrated in a pair of major publishers, Marvel Comics and DC Comics. Together the so-called "Big Two" command more than 70 percent of the comics market, leaving the remaining portion to be divided among all the other publishers. Such competing presses are significantly smaller, with Marvel and DC's nearest competitors, Dark Horse Comics and Image Comics, each commanding less than 5 percent of the market (Mishler "Overall"). Both Marvel and DC are not stand-alone comics publishers, but are part of much larger conglomerates that also create other media.

Marvel Comics is the publishing division of Marvel Entertainment, Inc., a publicly traded corporation engaged in movie production (Marvel Studios), toy

manufacturing (Toybiz), and licensing of its characters on virtually every consumer product imaginable. Marvel began in 1939 under publisher Martin Goodman and published comics under a number of names, including Timely in the 1940s and Atlas in the 1950s, until finally settling on Marvel Comics in the 1960s. The wave of creativity that spawned the Marvel Universe

© 2008 Marvel Entertainment, Inc. and its subsidiaries

of superheroes also earned the company the nickname "The House of Ideas." Since that time, Marvel has attempted to expand beyond publishing and transform itself into more of a multimedia conglomerate, with the aspiration of being another Walt Disney Company. Its rapid expansion in this regard in the 1990s famously led it to become the target of corporate raiders. This struggle for control over Marvel is chronicled in Dan Raviv's *Comic Wars* (2002), and it ended with Marvel's declaration of bankruptcy and ultimate reorganization. Marvel's recent, more deliberate attempts to expand its properties into feature films and other media in the dawning years of the twenty-first century have proven successful in transforming Marvel into more of a licensing company than just a comics publisher per se.

Marvel's chief competitor is DC Comics, a subsidiary of Warner Brothers Entertainment, which is itself a part of Time Warner Company—the largest media con-

glomerate in the world. Warner Brothers is famous for its presence in film, animation, television, and home video production. The media conglomerate acquired DC Comics in the late 1960s, while it was still known as National Periodical Publications, the name under which it began publishing comics back in 1935. The "DC" seal had appeared on covers from the line for decades, in homage to the company's *Detective Comics* series, the first comic book magazine to have a dedicated theme. DC is comicdom's most enduring publisher and one of

© DC Comics

its most successful: It was at the top of the sales market when Marvel displaced it in the early 1970s, and it has stayed comfortably in the number-two spot for over three decades. Because DC has been embedded within a larger media conglomerate for some time, its properties like Superman and Batman frequently find themselves marketed by different divisions of the Time Warner family. For example, *Smallville*, a teen drama about Superman's youth, is based on the DC Comics character, produced by Warner Brothers Television, and originally aired on the WB and CW networks. While its properties have gone on to successful venues in other media, DC itself has remained focused on publishing, creating imprints: like its Vertigo and CMX lines to expand into new markets.

Because the Big Two command so much of the comics readers' attentions, they are often referred to as forming the **mainstream,** which is both a concession to their preeminence in the field and a critique of their conservative publishing practices. Such large publishers have the burden of having to return large profits. As a result, much of what they sell is what is popular, rather than being cutting edge or pertinent to smaller interest groups. The mainstream publishers then become caught up in a bit of a conundrum, as they are leading the industry in terms of reach but also subservient to the demands of appealing to a mass of readers. This results in a market that is largely homogeneous and imitative. For example, the majority of comic books made by the Big Two are from one genre, superheroes, and the two compete head-to-head using the conventions of that genre. Other genres of storytelling are relegated to other publishers or, in some cases, to imprints of the mainstream publishers. DC gave horror comics a venue when it launched its Vertigo imprint, and Marvel attempted more adult themes in its MAX line. Many critics, however, contend that the truly experimental work in comics is not done by the major publishers, constrained as they are by the demands of sales, but by smaller presses which enjoy the freedom to experiment—and fail—by attempting new things. These smaller publishers are often referred to as **independent** publishers because they are not obliging the demands of the masses or the high financial expectations of corporate stockholders.

Still, the profitability of the Big Two makes them undeniable forces in the medium and key players in the larger cultural industry to which all media contribute. Part of the success that both Marvel and DC have enjoyed has been in their copyright and corporate ownership of the properties they have in their respective catalogs. Most work done in mainstream comics is on a **work-for-hire** or freelance basis, meaning that the creators are commissioned to design characters and stories for the publishing corporation. As part of this arrangement, the corporation—not the cartoonist—copyrights the characters featured and the stories told in their publications. On one hand, such an arrangement raises ethical questions about creators' rights (which we will take up in Chapter 5). On the other hand, it has ensured the corporations' long-term financial rewards, as the corporate owners can print and reprint successful stories time and again. Even more lucrative is the licensing of comic book characters to other vendors for the marketing of consumer products. Characters like Superman and Spider-Man bring in far more money via their licenses than they make from sales of their publishing endeavors in comics. Consider, for example, that *Spider-Man 3* brought Marvel a hefty $70 million licensing fee from Hasbro, Inc., just to make the toys marketed in conjunction with the film (Bloomberg D8).

DISTRIBUTION

Getting media products from their point of manufacture to the retailers is the business of the distributor. Comics have found their way from the printing presses into the hands of eager readers through two systems of distribution. One system, **mass-market distribution**, predates the industry, and the other, **Direct-Market Distribution**, is an offshoot of the medium's popularity.

Mass-Market Distribution

Early comic books, as discussed in Chapter 1, were composed of reprinted comic strips that had originally appeared in newspapers. Like their newspaper forbearers, comic book magazines found their initial outlet on newsstands. Newsstands once dotted street corners across America, selling all manner of periodicals, including comic books. For newsstands, the system of distribution that came to dominate the relationship they had with comic book publishers was one that involved little risk for the retailer and proved lucrative for the distributors. Dealers would take receipt of a bundle of comic books from a distributor and display them for a given period of time. Ongoing comic book titles were typically published on monthly, bi-monthly, or quarterly schedules. When new issues of a title or competing titles crowded it out, an older magazine was removed from the stands. The retailer would then remove the cover of the older magazine and dispose of the interior in order to save on hauling expenses. The cover would serve as a receipt for the retailer, who would return the detached covers to the distributor for credit. The retailer would only owe for the total number of magazines that were actually sold, payable to the distributor. And the retailer only owed a percentage of the cover price, since a considerable chunk of the cost was pocketed directly by the retailer. Thus, from a retailer's perspective, comic books represented a low-risk commodity for them to stock. The producers took nearly all of the risk in electing to publish a certain title, since, if the magazine did not sell, they would have taken on the expense of publishing a dud.

This meant that publishers had to print far more copies of a given comic book than would ever be sold. For example, in the waning days of mass-market distribution's dominance in the early 1970s, DC might print 675,000 copies of *Superman* but only sell around 400,000 (Beerbohm 81). Again, this placed the risk of making comics squarely on the shoulders of publishers, not the distributors or retailers.

Publishers were also at risk through their association with independent distributors. As vulnerable businesses themselves, distributors could go under just as easily as any other enterprise, leaving publishers without a way to get their comics to the market. This happened to Martin Goodman's Atlas group in the late 1950s. After closing down his own distribution business, he turned over his comics line to the American News Company. Shortly thereafter, American went under, leaving Goodman with little choice but to ask rival DC Comics to help distribute the line. It agreed to do so, but would only allow eight titles a month. Goodman was forced to cancel numerous titles and fire most of his staff as a result.

Though the risk-taking of a mass-market distribution system had turned a profit for comic book publishers since its inception, by the early 1970s the comics industry was in jeopardy of collapsing because of it. This threat was due in part to the disappearance of traditional retail outlets where comics had been sold during the previous three decades. The number of drug stores, grocers, and newsstands were dwindling, meaning fewer and fewer outlets for comic books. Also, an alteration in the return system had imperiled the profitability of making comics. Distributors had switched to a system of "affidavit receipts," where

FIGURE 4.3. The spinner rack at the local drug store hailed children with a clarion call: "Hey, kids, comics!" Photograph courtesy of Denis Kitchen.

retailers would simply sign a form reporting the number of unsold copies of a comic book, rather than returning the detached cover. Unsurprisingly, such an "honor" system was rife with the potential for abuse. Without having to produce any evidence that the unsold copies had been destroyed, dishonest retailers could sell the magazines and pocket the entire purchase price of a comic instead of splitting it with a distributor or publisher.

Mass-market distribution was also a source of frustration for comic book fans. Distributors were not always mindful to provide each retailer with each new title, and they would often simply drop off a mixed bundle of comics to an outlet, one of which might be heavy on Archie Comics while lacking the latest Marvel Comics. To such distributors, one comic book was indistinguishable from the next, and they were unaware that there was an audience who actively collected series of comic books. Even if they had known about the growing collector's market, the relatively small scale of that audience for a distributor handling hundreds of other magazines probably would not have motivated them to exercise greater care in allotting comics. Such carelessness spurred an alternative distribution system to emerge.

Today, estimates state that only about 10 percent of new comic books are being distributed through the venerable mass-market system and placed on to shelves and spinner racks at traditional retailers. However, this estimate does not take into account the distribution of trade paperback and hardcover editions, many of which go through separate book distribution channels (Beard 21). Still, the delivery of as many as 90 percent of new comics in periodical format today relies on an alternate system: direct-market distribution.

Direct-Market Distribution

We discussed the origins of the direct market in Chapter 3. But to briefly summarize, the direct market was rooted in the development of the informal system of trading out-of-print comic books among fans and preceded by the distribution of underground comix in head shops. The actions of comic specialty shop owners like Phil Seuling to work around the traditional newsagents who distributed comic books to newsstands introduced the alternative distribution system now known as the direct market.

According to researcher Charles Hatfield, the direct market essentially works like a subscription. Comics publishers solicit orders on soon-to-be printed comics. The shop owners then place orders with the publishers before the publisher takes the solicited book to print. This allows the publisher to print enough copies to meet the anticipated demand for new comics, without having to print far more copies than are needed to satisfy the newsstand system of distribution. With fewer wasted copies, publishers make smaller press runs and save a lot of money on production costs. That works well for the publishers. The risk, however, is simply shifted from the publisher to the retailer. The direct-market arrangement is such that the subscribing retailer buys inventory outright on a non-returnable basis. Now if a comic doesn't sell, it is the retailer who is stuck with the unsold copies. Although the direct market gives these retailers significant discounted pricing on copies of new comics, it does demand that the retailer deal with the financial consequences if the retailer does not sell everything ordered.

Another party affected by the emergence of the direct market was the creators. As the direct market emerged, more and more independent publishers used the direct market exclusively to try their hands at publishing comics. New companies, led by Pacific Comics and then joined by Eclipse, Comico, First, and others, could solicit new comics, print the number of copies demanded by comics specialty shop retailers, and thus avoid the risk of large print runs and messy returns associated with newsstand distribution. As these new companies competed for talent, they helped increase the amount of royalties and gave some copyright control to the creators. In order to compete, DC and Marvel followed suit, advancing the creator's rights.

According to scholar Roger Sabin (*Adult*), another consequence for the creators was the creation of a star system within the comics industry. Historically, comics were marketed based on their characters, not their creators. This system was in opposition to the marketing trend that dominates traditional book marketing, where the author's name is the key selling point. However, independent publishers often relied on the reputations of their creators to attract orders for their comics. Eventually, mainstream comics caught on to this idea. For instance, DC Comics recognized that the fan-favorite combination of writer

Marv Wolfman and artist George Perez was worth granting cover credit to in the January 1984 issue of the *New Teen Titans*, and within a few years DC was giving writers, artists, and inkers credit on all their covers. Industry top-seller Marvel would not follow suit, though, until well into the 1990s.

The initial success of the direct market attracted—and benefited from the financial support of—a good number of **speculators**, investors who would buy several copies of new comics in the hopes that they could cash in on the comics' anticipated increase in value. These speculators had noted how valuable certain out-of-print comic books had become, and they wanted to cash in on the next wave of profitable comics. Speculators would buy multiple copies of new comics, especially those starting a new series or featuring a marketing gimmick. Comics producers fed this demand with all manner of strange enhancements, ranging from the inclusion of trading cards packaged with a comic to glow-in-the-dark covers, and even variant editions of the same comic book, each with a different cover. Unfortunately, for reasons discussed below, the speculators did not see a quick return on their investment and abandoned the market, contributing to an overall downturn that led many comics specialty shops to close.

After the mid-nineties downturn, comics publishers and distributors began to enter into a number of complicated exclusive deals with one another, which has led to a practical monopoly in the distribution of comics to specialty shops. The process began when Marvel Comics announced that it would purchase the nation's third-largest distributor, Heroes World, and sell its comics exclusively through this newly acquired arm of the corporation. This prompted DC Comics and others to turn to the largest distributor, Diamond, and establish exclusive deals for their products through them. These arrangements left the number-two distributor, Capital City, along with all of the smaller distributors, without the products that comics specialty shops demanded. In the end, Marvel folded Heroes World and joined ranks with Diamond, but not before nearly all of the smaller distributors had been co-opted for their resources and market areas. Today, Diamond operates as a virtual monopoly, effectively controlling all distribution of new comics, with only a smattering of competition through small distributors who specialize in reordered stock (e.g., Cold Cut and Last Gasp). However, a 1997 U.S. Department of Justice investigation determined that since Diamond had not cornered the market on all published materials (e.g., other magazines or books), it still had competition and was not a legally defined monopoly. A trickle of independent comics do flow into comics specialty shops through other distributors, reports Professor David Beard, but Diamond's exclusive contracts with leading publishers like Marvel, DC, Dark Horse, and Image to deliver comics to specialty shops has afforded the company considerable power over the medium. Indeed, a publisher whose products do not appear in Diamond's *Previews* magazine—a catalog soliciting orders from retailers for upcoming comic books that publishers intend to publish—is not realistically able to compete in the direct market.

While the intervention of the direct market system may well have saved the comic book industry from extinction as newsstands disappeared, the system is not without its criticisms. For one, the direct market has focused on making sales to a limited and shrinking audience. Comics writer Kurt Busiek has said that reliance on an insulated fan base means that there are fewer ways to reach the next generation of new readers (qtd. in Duin and Richardson 130). Where once casual readers may have picked up a comic as a side purchase at a retail outlet, the lack of exposure to those unfamiliar with the medium has disadvantaged comic books in a field of media competing for people's attention. Busiek acknowledges the value of what the direct market did for the industry, but indicates that this should have only been a temporary retreat, and an alternative plan for recapturing market space should have been devised.

Discovering: Comic Book Advertising

Like that of most mass-market periodicals, the price of comic book magazines is subsidized by advertising. By selling space to paying advertisers who run their commercial messages, magazine publishers have a source of revenue that helps them to keep the cost of individual issues lower than if the entire magazine were filled with editorially selected material. In many modern magazines, advertising can consume as much as half of the content of the publication; recent comic books have a slightly more modest allotment of only about a third of their content consisting of advertisements. Because the costs of placing advertisements in mass media is considerable, most advertisers are rather strategic about where they place their ads and consequently target specific audiences in each venue. Since the majority of comic book readers are reportedly adolescent males, a great deal of advertising is tailored to them.

No ads better illustrate this target than those sponsored by Charles Atlas for his bodybuilding system. For nearly eight decades, Atlas has promised to help any mousy teen bulk up his body and gain a muscular physique by using a system of resistance training. The ads typically featured a photograph of Atlas himself, once proclaimed "The World's Most Perfectly Developed Man," in leopard-print trunks and bearing his toned body as testimony to the effectiveness of his approach. In keeping with their placement in comic books, the ads also featured a comic strip, "The Insult that Made a Man Out of 'Mac,'" a seven-frame story of a scrawny guy who goes from getting sand kicked in his face to becoming "The Hero of the Beach," thanks to the Atlas system. The Atlas ads were especially well suited to comics of the superhero genre, as Atlas himself personified for growing boys the wish fulfillment of physical strength often associated with fictional supermen (Brown, "Comic Book"). Indeed, according to scholar Gene Kannenberg, Jr. ("The Ad"), the advertisement's longevity and success can be attributed to its comic strip's narrative structure, which is reminiscent of the superhero origin, with "Mac" undergoing a metamorphosis from stringy weakling to buff hero (paralleling Spider-Man's origin, for instance). Charles Atlas sold boys not only the promise of a muscular body like that of their heroes, but also the accompanying respect and social position that came with such a form of masculinity.

Cont'd

FIGURE 4.4. The masculine conventions of the Charles Atlas ad became so familiar to comic book readers that they could be handily parodied in Marvel Comics' *What The—?!* #8 (1990). Words by Barry Dutter and art by Chris Eliopoulos. © 2008 Marvel Entertainment, Inc. and its subsidiaries

Other recurring ads have also addressed masculine wish fulfillment. Products like toy firearms (e.g., Daisy BB Guns) and athletic shoes (e.g., O.J. Simpson selling Spot-bilt "Juicemobiles") have long been staples of comics advertising. The collective, repeated messages of these ads present their young, impressionable audiences with a construction of what manhood should be like. In due course, Charles Atlas and his kin helped shape the expectations of generations of comic book readers.

Before moving on to consider the exhibition phase of the industry, we should note that fans can actually buy comic books from the publisher even more directly than the so-called direct market allows. For instance, the Big Two major publishers maintain subscription departments that offer fans the opportunity to have their favorite ongoing title shipped to their home in exchange for advance payment, sometimes at a discounted rate. Also, some publishers offer to sell products directly to consumers through their own retail websites and mail-order catalogs. GoComics, for instance, will deliver electronic versions of some comic books, in addition to comic strips and puzzles, to your cell phone for a monthly subscription fee. The profits generated by such alternatives, though, are quite modest in comparison to the sales transactions carried out by those retailers in the exhibition phase of the industry.

EXHIBITION

In media studies, **exhibition** refers to the stage where we find those organizations that engage the consumer in the sale of media products. In times past, the primary exhibitors were newsstand vendors. Today, retailers running comics specialty shops, who sell both new and out-of-print comics, are vital to the industry as points of sale. However, the increasing popularity of more durably bound materials has led to increased shelf space and attention for comics among bookstore chains. We next explore these competing exhibitors in greater detail.

Specialty Shops

The direct market discussed in our previous section serves comic book specialty shops. Thousands of these shops nationwide sell new comics materials and comics-related merchandise, such as action figures. Many also sell older, collectible comics, and many are involved in other areas of popular culture, including the fantasy role-playing game industry, sports cards, and so forth. Such shops can be found in strip malls, storefronts, and even people's converted basements. They tend to be owned by independent, small business proprietors, and most shops reflect the eclectic tastes of their owners. Comic specialty shop owners are lampooned most notably in popular culture by the character of Comic Book Guy on Fox's long-running television series *The Simpsons*, and the misconceptions that stereotype fosters may be all that many know about such retailers.

In order to draw more positive attention to their stores, owners began sponsoring Free Comic Book Day (FCBD) in 2002. In each of the FCBDs since, thousands of retailers have given away millions of specially printed comic books on one Saturday each May. While the giveaway is a promotion that garners the shops a lot of charitable publicity and increased foot traffic, the real challenge is for them to draw paying customers in the rest of the year. Essential for our consideration is how they do so through the sale of new comics and back issues.

New Comics

Specialty stores sell newly published comics in two distinct formats: periodicals and bound editions. The two primary distinctions between the formats lie in the type of cover binding used to assemble the products and the intended shelf life of the publications. **Periodicals** are what are thought of as traditional comic book magazines. Their covers are typically a glossy paper stock, and they are bound by a series of staples down their spine. Periodicals have an intentionally short shelf life, and most are only expected to be for sale until the next issue is available. In comics this can be monthly, bi-monthly, quarterly, or even annually for some titles. Issues appear as numbered series and usually contain aspects of serialization, such as recurring characters and continuing plots and subplots from issue to issue. In addition, most periodicals are relatively short on page count, with standard comics today containing thirty-two pages of material (nearly a third of which is advertising). As of this writing, a thirty-two-page comic book sells for $2.99. With some variations in size and printing quality over time, periodicals have always been the backbone of the American comic book industry.

The periodical products of the comics industry present both opportunities and challenges for retailers. On the one hand, the serialized stories in most comic books draw consumers back to the shops month after month. On the other hand, new readers may be discouraged from purchasing an issue in the middle of a series or spending the cumulative money it will take to collect an entire story run in serialized format. The attraction of bound editions, then, is in addressing these problems. **Bound editions** tend to feature stand-alone, finite storylines. Often these stand-alone storylines are a collection of a number of issues that have previously been serialized in periodical publication, much like the way a season's worth of television episodes might be bundled in a DVD collection. Thus, a bound edition is substantially larger than a periodical, running from around one hundred pages up to thousands of pages. The cost for a trade paperback might start around $9.99 and run well beyond $75 for a high-quality hardcover edition. Though these prices are considerably higher than the cost of the latest periodical, it is almost always less expensive for the consumer to purchase a collection than a series from the retailer, especially if the original periodicals are long out of print.

In contrast to a periodical, a bound edition uses more durable materials for its binding (at the very least a glossy, cardstock cover) and is intended to have an indeterminate shelf life, so that it may be "on sale" for years to come. In the publishing industry, booksellers classify a book by its binding. Bound editions of comics may be found in a format known as the **trade paperback** (TPB), characterized by a less rigid, less durable cover (usually cardstock), or **hardcover**, characterized by, well, you guessed it—a firmer, more durable cover. At present, TPBs are the preferred method for reprinting material that has previously been serialized in comic magazines. Both of the leading comics publishers in America, Marvel and DC, regularly collect and republish runs of their monthly titles in TPB form. For instance, Marvel will republish a storyline running across multiple issues of *Amazing Spider-Man* a few months later in a TPB. With increasing frequency, some publishers are reprinting material in the more expensive hardcover format, too, though this practice seems reserved for high-profile or critically acclaimed series. For instance, DC Comics has re-released the comics of *New York Times* bestselling author Brad Metzer in hardcover printings such as his *Identity Crisis* limited series and his run on *Justice League of America*. Of course, it is entirely possible for new material to appear in these more prestigious formats as well. Bound editions have been an important innovation in the last few decades of the industry, as the more durable, lengthy formats have made comics appearing in this packaging more attractive to bookstores and libraries. These important repositories have made room on their shelves for TPB and hardcover comics.

Back Issues

In addition to the sale of newly published comics, specialty shops will often stock back issues of previously published periodicals. The back issue market can be a lucrative one, as rare and in-demand comic books can draw collectors' dollars well in excess of the prices printed on the covers. Some comics that sold for 10 cents on the newsstands in the 1940s now garner hundreds of thousands of dollars. However, such values are rare and largely dependent on two factors: scarcity and condition. **Scarcity** refers to the availability of a given back issue. Although original runs of some comic books from the 1940s ranked in the millions of copies printed, only a comparative few were preserved. Magazines then, as now, were often trashed or recycled. Because there are fewer copies of such comic books available today, the price demanded for these copies on the market is driven up. For example, in January 1960 DC reportedly circulated over 800,000 copies of its *Superman* (#134) comic book magazine, retailing for 10 cents a copy; a perfect copy of that run would grow in value to $155 some forty-five years later (Miller et al. 1318). Conversely, more recent comics have much smaller print runs, but fans are much more diligent about retaining and preserving perfect copies, making those comics less valuable. For instance, Marvel Comics released nearly 8 million copies of *X-Men* #1 in October 1991, for $1.50 each. Today, in a market saturated by copies of that comic book, collectors can only expect about $3 on a well-preserved copy.

Of course, comic books are made of materials that deteriorate over time, and so the comparative **condition** of a comic book also factors into its value. The highest values are assigned to comic books that have the least damage. Borrowing from the terminology of coin collectors, an ideal copy of a given comic book would be in **mint condition**. Coins, of course, are made at a mint, which is why a single coin that is in as good condition as the day it was made is said to be in *mint condition*. Comics are not "minted," of course, but the analogy to "as good as it gets" provides a starting point for an elaborate system of grading the condition of comics. Collectors' publications from the *Official Overstreet Comic Book Price Guide* to *The Comics Buyer's Guide* report on the values of different grades of popular comics (see Figure 4.5).

FIGURE 4.5. The Comics Buyer's Guide provides its readers with an explanation of grading comics in its "Do-It-Yourself Grading" guide. Courtesy of the Comics Buyer's Guide *www.cbgxtra.com*

While grading is a highly subjective process, often resulting in much dickering between seller and buyer, the back issue market embraced a system of third-party grading beginning in 2000 with the establishment of the Comics Guaranty, LLC, or CGC. For a fee, the trained CGC staff grade comics according to a set of objective standards and then apply a numerical value to the condition of the comic ranging from 1.0 to 10.0, where 10.0 is mint condition. The book and an identifying label are then sealed within two sheets of transparent plastic, or **slabbed,** to ensure that the condition is preserved after it has left the evaluator's hands. This system was first practiced by CGC's parent company with collectors of coins and sports cards. However, while both coins and cards can be enjoyed by looking at them through a plastic sheet, comics are meant to be read, and in order to see the interior pages of a slabbed comic, one must break the seal of the CGC package and thus invalidate its grading. Still, collectors have not seemed to mind this irony and have reportedly embraced the corporation, with prices of slabbed back issues routinely outselling unslabbed ones in online markets.

Profile: Chuck Rozanski

born: Charles Rozanski
       March 11, 1955
       Goldbach, Germany

"Comic book retailing is the last refuge of the iconoclast and individuals who are unwilling to conform."

Career Highlights

1969   Working from his parents' Colorado basement, thirteen-year-old Rozanski delves into the business of selling back issues of comic books by running mail order ads in *Rocket's Blast Comics Collector* magazine.

1970   Begins promoting comics as the youngest seller to ever exhibit at the Colorado Springs Antiques Market.

1971   Founds Colorado Springs Comics Club.

1972   Attends first national comics convention, Multicon in Oklahoma City, and while there sells $1,800 in comics in three days, thus realizing that comics retailing could become a career.

1974   Opens first store in Boulder, Colorado with $800 in cash and 10,000 comics.

1977   With four stores in the greater Denver area, Rozanski purchases the Edgar Church Collection, the largest and highest-quality "Golden Age" comics collection ever discovered, which helps the company expand its influence nationwide.

1979   Purchases Richard Alf Comics' mail order division and thus gains systems and methods for greatly expanding mail order sales.

Cont'd

1980	Publishes a first-of-its-kind, double-page ad in mainstream (Marvel) comic books, listing prices for back issues that he has for sale and affirming the commodity nature of the collector's market.
1983	Mile High Comics buys out the New Issue Comics Express (N.I.C.E.) Subscription Club, which takes advantage of direct market discounts to offer collectors new comics at prices below what they would pay at newsstands.
1991	Opens the first comics mega-store (11,000 square feet) in Denver.
1992	Expands into Southern California with second mega-store.
1997	Mile High Comics begins to list its inventory online, offering collectors even easier access to the largest dealer of back issue comics in the world.
2002	Begins to author the "Tales from the Database" column in *The Comics Buyer's Guide*.

FIGURE 4.6. Chuck Rozanski has spent four decades in the comics retailing business. Photo courtesy of Mile High Comics.

Mile High Comics is among the nation's most successful comics specialty shops, in part because it has branded itself as a reliable dealer with a wide selection. Named for its location in Denver, the Mile High City, the influence of Mile High Comics has spread much farther than the Colorado Rocky Mountains. This is due in no small part to the imagination and good fortune of its founder, fan turned franchiser Chuck Rozanski.

The imagination came into play from Rozanski's vision of a comic book specialty store, a vision that led him from selling comics in his parents' basement to owning eight retail stores. "I wanted to be my own boss," he says. "Still, I'm a much harder taskmaster on myself. As a consequence, I've been a success." Rozanski still drives all over the country visiting local comics shops to stock Mile High's tremendous back issue inventory.

The good fortune came into play in the late 1970s when Rozanski got a call from the family of Edgar Church, a collector who had purchased and safely stored nearly every comic book published between 1939 and 1950. The Church family sold the collection, the most pristine ever seen, to Rozanski, who used the profits generated from sales of the collection to build his local enterprise into a national one. In particular, Rozanski facilitated a seismic shift in the collecting industry when Mile High ran a double-page advertisement in mainstream comics in 1980, breaking with the advertising practice of the time by actually listing the prices for his back issues. "It was a way to educate non-collectors to the value of their collections," he explains. Rozanski's mail order business boomed thereafter, as did the entire market for back issue sales, as comics moved more and more from consumable to collectible.

Cont'd

Success, of course, breeds competition, and now that buyers can find back issues in consumer-to-consumer venues like eBay, Mile High relies on a business model that emphasizes service more than product. "We don't sell comics; we sell convenience. Mile High is a premium brand: We offer all brands, all titles, all the time." And discerning collectors seem to respond favorably to the brand as Mile High continues to hold its own. More than just his business, though, the comics industry is a personal passion for Rozanski. After four decades, he says, "I still get excited about this industry. Maybe the comics that interest me today are different than those when I started out, but I continue believing in, sharing through, and working for this industry." As a prominent retailer, he cites a special responsibility to give something back. In part, he does this by sharing his experiences and advice in a monthly column in *The Comics Buyer's Guide*. He is also a frequent attendee of comic book conventions across the country, experiences which never seem complete to him until he has had a chance to encourage a fellow retailer or meet a fellow fan.

Additional Outlets

The majority of sales for new comics may be conducted in specialty shops today, but the growing interest in graphic storytelling is opening other retail outlets wider for sales. A number of reasons have contributed to this growth. One factor is the change in publishing format by the publishers themselves. More durable formats like the TPB and hardcover editions have helped to make comics more attractive to both readers and merchants. Another factor contributing to a renewed interest in comics is a recent growth in international influence. The expanding interest in manga, a style of comics originating in Japan, has garnered the attention of many readers who might not otherwise read American comics. Manga includes various genres, many of them appealing to audiences that mainstream publishers long ago abandoned. (We will explore more about the impact of manga in Chapter 13.) A third factor is the recognition that comics have received by libraries, both those that serve schools and those that serve the larger community. Comics are some of the most widely circulating items in libraries across the country, and the access to comics materials that libraries afford helps to draw new readers—who may become new customers—into the medium.

One market that is increasingly open to comics is bookstore chains. America's largest chains, like Barnes & Noble, Borders, and Books-A-Million, all have set aside valuable shelf space for designated graphic novel sections in their stores. In early 2007 "[Milton] Griepp reported that general bookstores sell the most graphic novels and continue to show the fastest growth. General bookstores were responsible for about $220 million in sales and the comics shop market reported about $110 million in sales" (Reid). In addition to shelf space in brick-and-mortar stores, online bookstores like Amazon.com have offered TPB and hardcover comics for sale for some time.

As an alternative to selling printed comics, some cartoonists are experimenting with online sales of their comics. Online sites offer previously unexposed and unaffiliated cartoonists the opportunity to reach an audience, and according to researcher Todd Allen, they can offer readers a larger archive of materials to select from, as they do not compete for shelf space like printed comics must. However, there is a challenge in convincing website visitors to pay for content, which makes it difficult for the cartoonist and any sponsors to make money. However, Scott McCloud says that cartoonists may find that they can attract audiences if they charge small amounts for installments of their stories (qtd. in Boxer E1). Given the savings in production and distribution costs, online comics are a financially viable alternative to paper-based comic books.

ANALYZING: COMIC BOOKS AS CULTURAL COMMODITIES

Comics have been a consumer item since they debuted, including those comics given away as corporate premiums. "It could be said that without the concept of the giveaway comic or the marketing push behind it, there would be no comic book industry as we have it today," says historian Arnold T. Blumberg ("Promotional" 286). In 1933 the Eastern Color Printing Company produced *Funnies on Parade*, the first modern comic book, as a premium to be given away by Proctor & Gamble. Ever since that initial success, comic books have been used as promotional items to help sell other products and ideas. For instance, both Superman and Batman advocated the sale of war bonds on the covers of their respective magazines during World War II. In matters as diverse as commerce (e.g., marketing the Atari Game system in the 1980s) to campaigns (e.g., *Oral Roberts' True Stories*), comic books have been employed as a medium for marketing.

Comic book characters have also become highly marketable themselves. Long before comic books came on the scene, comic strip characters like Buster Brown were being used to entice children to buy, or influence their parents to buy, products and services. The idea of licensing comic book characters for use in other media has gained increased momentum, as revenue recouped from licensing has far outstripped the money made by publishing (McAllister, "Ownership"). Though characters have generated big returns on everything from toy lines to peanut butter, the visibility afforded by translation into feature films is particularly lucrative. While the commercial success of famous characters like Spider-Man and Batman are bankable assets for Hollywood filmmakers, what has proven surprising is the adaptation of even supporting characters into box office gold. The poster child for this kind of unanticipated success was 1998's *Blade*, a supporting character that Marv Wolfman created in the pages of *Tomb of Dracula* in the 1970s. The feature film garnered $133 million in box office sales worldwide, and spawned two sequels (Leonard).

Like other media producers, the people who own comic book properties increasingly employ synergy to help market and sell media products. **Synergy** is a type of carefully planned cross-pollination, where the timing of the release of one media product is coordinated with the release of other products related to it. For example, Time Warner carefully coordinates the release of its latest Warner Brothers Studio *Batman* movie with a CD soundtrack, licensed toy line and T-shirts, and, of course, a comic book adaptation from DC Comics. In this way, the film product is marketed more broadly than through traditional advertising messages alone, plus the anticipated popularity of the film increases the likely sale of the tie-in products like the toy line and T-shirts. Synergy can net a return in the millions of dollars for a media conglomerate, and for that reason consumers can expect to see more of it as future comic book properties migrate to other media outlets.

While comics aspire to and are capable of being valued as artistic achievements, one cannot dismiss the fact that the roots of the medium are firmly entrenched in commercialism. Likewise, the mainstream of comics continue to be dominated by market concerns that shape not only who gets to tell stories, but even what stories are allowed to be told. Those schooled in the medium must note that market forces have played and continue to play an influential role in shaping this form of communication.

Discussion Questions

1. What implications does the concentration of ownership have for diverse genres and new ideas to take hold in the mainstream of the industry? What alternatives exist for creators and consumers who want something other than what the mainstream producers are offering?
2. What advantages did direct-market distribution offer that mass-market distribution did not? What sacrifices has the industry made in moving almost completely away from newsstand reliance?
3. What factors have led comics to become collectible?

Activities

1. Visit both a local bookstore and a comics specialty shop (addresses can be found in your phonebook's yellow pages under "Comic Book Dealers" or at *www.comicshoplocator.com*). Note the placement of materials published by the Big Two publishers, Marvel and DC, and compare to those of all other publishers at each outlet. What share of the market do the Big Two publishers seem to command in terms of shelf space? Is there any noteworthy difference in how the bookstore and specialty shop treat the Big Two and all other publishers? Using these observations as a reference, write an essay in which you reflect on the competition afforded by the exhibition branch of the comic book industry.

2. Purchase a recently published comic book magazine and conduct an audience analysis on the advertisements. Begin by charting the advertisers and what products or services they are selling. Next, identify the principal characters depicted in each advertisement (e.g., young boys, cartoon characters, etc.) and the actions in which they are engaged. Then, identify whom you believe the advertisers are targeting. Finally, review all your findings and answer the following questions: What ads (if any) target you, and what makes them appealing or unappealing? Have the advertisers overlooked other potential audiences with their techniques? If the advertising is targeted to one group, what hurdles does this create in accessing a larger, more diverse audience for the medium?

Recommended Readings

Comics:

Clowes, Daniel. *Pussey!* Seattle, WA: Fantagraphics, 1995.

Dan Pussey (which he insists is pronounced "Pooh-say") is a comic book artist loosely based on cartoonist Daniel Clowes' own experiences with the industry. *Pussey!* critiques the comic book business from its obsession with superheroes to its struggles with art and commerce in this collection of stories from the acclaimed author of *Ghost World*.

McCloud, Scott. *Reinventing Comics: How Imagination and Technology are Revolutionizing an Art Form*. New York: Perennial, 2000.

In this sequel to *Understanding Comics*, McCloud goes into elements of the production, distribution, and exhibition of comic books. McCloud is critical of the choices mainstream publishers have made in the past but offers alternative conceptions for how comics might be distributed henceforth.

Scholarly sources:

Overstreet, Robert. M. *Official Overstreet Comic Book Price Guide*. 38th ed. New York: Gemstone Publishing, 2008.

For nearly four decades, Overstreet's guide has been the bible for comics' collectors, cataloging the definitive record of American comics publishing. In addition to being the authoritative price guide for the back issues, it also publishes articles tracing the ups and downs of the collectors' market and features on the medium's history.

Rhoades, Shirrel. *Comic Books: How the Industry Works*. New York: Peter Lang, 2008.

A former Marvel executive, Rhoades examines the production processes and markets for comics and comic-based properties in an extended examination of their operations. Topics include intellectual property issues and tracing trends such as the manga invasion.

	Advertiser	Product/Service	Characters	Actions	Targets
1.					
2.					
3.					
4.					
5.					
6,					
7.					
8.					
9.					

Comic Book Creators

"There are three things that define someone who works regularly in comics: they're a good talent, they do their work on time, and they're nice people. You need two out of those three to get steady work."

—MIKE FRIEDRICH, COMIC BOOK WRITER, 1994

Few of the people who grew up desperate to make ends meet during the Great Depression would have ever predicted that the story of their struggle would become fodder for a popular novel, much less one as honored as *The Amazing Adventures of Kavalier and Clay*. But author Michael Chabon crafted a story about the trials of some of the earliest comic book creators in a book that not only hit the *New York Times* Bestseller List, but was also honored with the Pulitzer Prize "for distinguished fiction by an American author" in 2001. The novel recounts the professional and personal development of two cousins, Joe Kavalier and Sam Clay, as they come of age in the late 1930s and early 1940s. The two Jewish boys create a comic book superhero known as the Escapist in the wake of the successful debut of Superman. Over the course of the novel, the Escapist becomes a popular character and moneymaker for his publisher, but the profits from this lucrative creation are not fairly shared with its creators. Though fictional characters themselves, Kavalier and Clay are based on Chabon's research into the lives of comic book greats like Jerry Siegel and Joe Shuster, who lost control over Superman, and Jack Kirby

FIGURE 5.1. Dark Horse Comics went on to publish actual comics about Kavalier and Clay's *Escapist* after the success of Michael Chabon's novel *The Amazing Adventures of Kavalier and Clay*. Art by Jae Lee. "The Escapist" and the likeness of the Escapist are trademarks of Michael Chabon. Published by Dark Horse Comics, Inc.

and Joe Simon, who lost control over Captain America. Chabon's novel was not only entertaining, it drew attention to the treatment of these creators at the hands of greedy publishers. Most importantly, it showed audiences who had never thought about the origins of their favorite comic heroes that there were writers and artists behind them.

OBJECTIVES

In this chapter you will learn:

1. about the qualities of three generations of comic book creators and the relationships they have had to their employers;
2. how the industrial and artisan processes of creating comics differ;
3. the characteristics of an auteur, or great creator, and how such esteem factors into the business of comics; and
4. how novice creators begin to build careers within the industry.

Although the characters that populate America's favorite comics are household names, the men and women who created them are far less famous. Yet despite not being as well known to the general public as a film director like Stephen Spielberg or a novelist like Stephen King, there is certainly an artistic community that creates comics. This chapter introduces you to that community by presenting an overview of the last several generations of comic book creators, a primer on the production process, and a discussion of the elements that contribute to a claim of greatness among those working in the medium.

THE GENERATIONS OF CREATORS

The first wave of commercial American comic book creators that entered the field in the thirties and forties were, by and large, very young, teenagers in many cases. Many of these writers had grown up on the science fiction or adventure tales of the pulp magazines. They yearned to spin their own fantastic tales in the pulps, or, better yet, in novels. Some of the artists were striving for the "brass ring" of a syndicated newspaper comic strip. Others were ecstatic that the new medium provided an outlet for their imagination and talent. Much of the work was raw and undisciplined, but bursting with the vitality of youth. Quite a few of those youngsters stayed in the field to become the creative establishment, the "old guard" of the fifties and sixties.

Will Eisner—for whom the industry's major awards are now named—was a teenager when he had his first comics work published. He was barely out of his teens when he teamed up with Jerry Iger to form one of the major comic book production shops. Subsequently, a number of well-known comic book creators got their start at the Eisner-Iger Shop. When he joined the staff in 1936, Bob

Kane (the creator of Batman) was twenty-one years old. Jacob Kurtzberg (who later changed his name to Jack Kirby and became the most influential artist in the history of the medium) was about the same age when he began producing work for Eisner-Iger. Joe Simon (Kirby's future creative partner) was a nearly ancient twenty-three years old when he first got involved with creating comic books at Funnies Incorporated. And when Eisner left to do *The Spirit*, Jerry Iger's shop continued to be a proving ground for young talent. Dick Giordano (who became editor-in-chief first at Charlton Comics and then at DC) was about twenty when he did his first work for Iger. Joe Kubert (a popular comics artist who founded the Joe Kubert School of Cartoon and Graphic Art) was still in high school when he began doing work for Harry Chesler's shop. The best-known figure in the comics industry was in his mid-teens when he began sharpening pencils and getting donuts as an assistant editor at Timely Comics. However, it was less than a year later that young Stanley Lieber began doing some writing, and less than two years after that he became the editor-in-chief. Lieber eventually had his name legally changed to the nom de plume he used for his comic book work—Stan Lee.

In addition to being young and eager, many of the comics' earliest creators had another characteristic in common: being of Jewish descent. Eisner, Kirby, Simon, Kubert, and Lee, as well as Superman creators Jerry Siegel and Joe Shuster and Batman creator Bob Kane, were all Jews. Many of these men were second-generation Americans, poor and struggling to break into the creative fields. Given the low regard in which most professional artists held comic books in those early years, more established, reputable talent was hard to come by. But people of many classes, races, and ethnicities struggled for recognition during the Great Depression, and so editor Danny Fingeroth argues that there is an additional dimension that makes displaced Jews particularly capable of adapting to and then articulating the ideals of another culture. He writes, "Even in situations where there is little or no hope for immediate financial reward, or even for an audience, there seems to be some kind of perhaps historically driven impetus for Jews to absorb, reflect, and express idiosyncratic visions of the world around them" (*Disguised* 19). That significant numbers of people from the Jewish tradition are involved in other storytelling media as well, including film, television, and theater, testifies to this drive. In comics, their skills have produced many of medium's most enduring icons.

The work done by these comic book pioneers was popular with the vast majority of American youngsters during the forties and early fifties. However, a handful of these young readers not only loved the thrilling stories, they also loved the medium. They wanted nothing more than to grow up to be comic book writers or artists. By the mid-sixties virtually every new writer or artist to enter the field was a comic book fan weaned on the work of these predecessors. This generation of fan-creators moved comic book storytelling to new levels of complexity and sophistication. For one thing, they had studied the medium and had learned from the "old masters" such as Eisner, Kirby, and Harvey Kurtzman (whose work for EC Comics and *Mad* magazine was groundbreaking). For another, they still loved comic books, so they wanted to tell tales that they and other adult fans could enjoy. They were writing for their peers rather than for the hypothetical eleven-year-old boy that had been the target audience of the industry for decades. Early fans turned pro include creators like Roy Thomas (who was Stan Lee's immediate successor as editor at Marvel), Marv Wolfman, Mike Friedrich, and Len Wein.

However, their reverence for the characters and their history also proved problematic. The fan-creators' attention to "historical detail" and adherence to continuity within fictional universes often results in stories that are nearly inaccessible to anyone who has not been a longtime fan. Perhaps there has also been a degree of "in-breeding" that results in "obsessive recapitulation of the same fantasies" and limits innovation in the art form (Spiegelman qtd. in *Masters*). As *Maus* creator Art Spiegelman articulates it, what the art form needs are "people whose background is not so solely drawn from comic books that all that can be spit back is more comic books" (*Masters*).

Spiegelman must be at least somewhat gratified by the creative voices that have emerged since he made that statement in 1987. The new breed of writer-artist such as Dan Clowes, Seth, and Chester Brown probably read their share of Marvel superhero comics, but they were also influenced by the independent spirit of the underground comix and inspired by the serious, non-genre work produced by Eisner, Spiegleman himself, and others. These artists, who produce very personal work that they self-publish or publish through small presses, are referred to as "alternative" or "independent" creators, but in fact, the vast majority of comic book creators have always been independent.

The people who work in the comic book field in America are, generally, either staffers or freelancers. And, of course, some individuals move back and forth between these categories during their careers. A staffer is an employee of the publisher with a set salary, regular paychecks, and fringe benefits. Editors, assistant editors, art directors, and production managers comprise the core of

FIGURE 5.2. Staffers engage in a blur of activity in the Marvel Comics post-production "Bullpen." Photograph by Elliot R. Brown. © 2008 Marvel Entertainment, Inc. and its subsidiaries

the creative staff at most publishers. There are also staff artists who work in post-production doing minor art corrections, pasting logos and indicia, and whatever else the art director or production manager deems necessary to create a polished product.

Most of the writers and artists who create comic books are freelancers, independent contractors who work on assignments for a specified page rate. Most freelancers still do work-for-hire. That is, they contract to do work for a specific issue with the understanding that the publisher will own the work they produce. A few of the most popular writers, and particularly artists, might negotiate some sort of royalty arrangement, usually under a special imprint of the publisher, such as Vertigo at DC.

Some writers or artists worked for the same publisher for decades. To fans they might be perceived as a "DC writer" or a "Marvel artist," but, in most cases, they were simply freelancers, working from assignment to assignment. Even when a writer or artist is "assigned" to a monthly title and has some expectation of working on that book long term, the assignment can be changed at the whim of the editor or his supervisors. The only security these creators have is their ability to produce work that the publishers value. And work is not always valued solely for its quality. For editors who have to get books to the printer on schedule each month, speed and reliability can be just as important as talent.

While traditionally most creators have risen out of obscurity or fandom, in recent years a trend has emerged where talent from publishing and Hollywood have contributed work to regular comic book series and special projects. Although some comics creators have gone on to work in other media—*Sandman* creator turned novelist Neil Gaiman is one of the most successful examples— historically people who have achieved success in other media have rarely turned to comics. However, best-selling authors like Brad Meltzer (*Justice League of America*), Jodi Picoult (*Wonder Woman*), and the aforementioned Michael Chabon (*The Escapist*) have now written for comics. In fact, some of today's top writing talents started out in Hollywood, including J. Michael Straczynski (*Amazing Spider-Man*), Jeph Loeb (*Batman: Hush*), Geoff Johns (*Green Lantern*), and Allan Heinberg (*Young Avengers*). Many of these creators move easily between storytelling platforms, but the clout they bring to their comics projects has certainly raised the profile of an industry some have uncharitably considered the gutter of popular culture.

THE PRODUCTION PROCESS

Comics scholar Mark C. Rogers uses the terms *industrial process* and *artisan process* to delineate the two broad categories of production that occur in the American comic book industry ("Understanding"). The **industrial process** involves a number of collaborators performing specialized tasks in the creation of a comic book and is generally associated with publishers such as Marvel, DC, and Archie.

Industrial Process

Comic books are often a collaborative art. The average monthly comic book is probably the result of the effort of seven or more creative individuals: editor, writer, penciller, letterer, inker, colorist, and cover artist. In the early production houses, such as the Eisner-Iger Shop, all of these individuals worked in one room in a virtual assembly-line process. Even if they did not work in one of the shops, nearly all of the Golden Age creators worked in New York City. Now, much of the work is produced by freelance collaborators who might well live in different states, or even on different continents.

This system of fragmenting the creation of comic books began in the 1940s because it got work turned out faster and it made the publishers less dependent on any one creator. Any "cog in the machine" could be replaced easily, and each comic book was the product of the company, not a creator. Although most of the creative personnel dislike the system, it still continues, and most mainstream comic books are produced by a team of creators.

The so-called **Marvel Method** is the predominant production model among large publishers. Historically, most comic writers developed full scripts (not unlike screenplays) with detailed instructions for the artist to follow in depicting the action of the scene. But in the 1960s Stan Lee was writing and editing most of the books at Marvel Comics himself. There was no time for him to write full scripts for each of these books. He developed the method of giving the artist a plot summary from which to work. These summaries were not even always written down; sometimes Stan described the story over the phone or while carpooling. The artist later drew the story, and then Stan wrote dialogue and captions to match what the artist had drawn. It got the work done faster and it kept the emphasis on the visual element—where most comic books publishers thought it belonged. Marvel's competitors soon adopted this method.

The virtue of the Marvel Method, as pointed out by veteran writer Peter David, is that "with the Marvel style, the artist has greater freedom to bring elements in terms of visualization that might not have occurred to me" (qtd. in Coale, 30). On the other hand, writer Mike Baron counters, "A script should be a complete operating diagram for a comic. It's essential to include the dialogue up front so the artist has a cue how to cast the character" (qtd. in Coale 12). The issue seems to be centered around who has control over the storytelling and who is willing to relinquish it, or as William Messner-Loebs, who has been both a writer and artist, says, "When I'm the artist, I like Marvel style. When I'm the writer, I like full scripts. Control, that's my bag!" (qtd. in Coale 70).

While some elements of comic book storytelling can be strengthened by a full script, other aspects might be weakened. A full script allows for more narrative complexity and depth. Yet one of the (probably) unforeseen benefits of the Marvel Method is that it often results in a blending of the verbal and the visual that more effectively utilizes the comic book form than a word-heavy script that relies too much on a prose aesthetic.

There is more to the creation of a finished comic book than just the determination of who controls the visuals of the story. Here is a brief summary of the industrial process, forefronted with the Marvel Method of interaction among the editor, writer, and artist:

Step One: Editorial Conference. The editor and the writer (and, sometimes, the artist) discuss ideas. Established writers are more independent of this step. However, even with established or "star" writers, the editor has to make sure that the product is in accordance with company policy and coordinates with other events in the company's "universe."

Step Two: Plot Summary. The writer creates a plot summary that can be very brief or very detailed, depending on their working relationship with the artist and their own inclinations. Occasionally, the writer who does the plot summary is not the same writer who does the final script. A few "star" writers refuse to do plot summaries, and do full scripts instead.

Step Three: Penciling. The artist does the breakdown of the story into panels, the layout of the panels on the page, the composition within the panels, and the pacing of the story. This job requires not only drawing skill, but storytelling ability as well.

Step Four: Scripting. Looking at the rendered pages, the writer creates a script, indicating what dialogue, narration, or sound effect goes in each panel.

Step Five: Lettering. The letterer uses the writer's script as a guide for where to place word balloons, captions, and sound effects.

Step Six: Inking. Sometimes the penciller also does the inking, but it is usually two different artists. In either case, drawings done in ink are overlaid on the pencil sketches.

Step Seven: Coloring. Colorists use software like Adobe Photoshop to apply colors to scans of the inked artwork.

Step Eight: Post-Production. The art director oversees staff artists and production technicians' touch-ups, corrections, and paste-ups of the **splash page** and cover.

Step Nine: Printing. After printing and binding the books, the printer ships them to the distributors. They are usually shipped about two months before the date printed on the cover.

Step Ten: Distribution. The distributor sends some books to grocery stores, bookstores, and newsstands, but most go to fill orders from comic book specialty shops.

Step Eleven: Retailers and Other Outlets. On the average, it takes about six months for a comic book to go from an idea to a product that is available to consumers.

Artisan Process

Even though the major publishers have always preferred the team approach to comic book creation, throughout the history of the medium there have been scores of **cartoonists,** people who fulfill the roles of both writer and artist—and

FIGURE 5.3. *Star*Reach* #1 (1974) broke new ground by giving mainstream comics creators who had only done work-for-hire an opportunity to retain ownership of their creations. Cover by Howard Chaykin and used with permission.

maybe other jobs as well—in the production of the finished comics. For example, in the nineteenth century Rodolphe Töpffer produced comic books without collaborators. Also, in the early days of the Eisner-Iger Shop, Will Eisner often produced stories for which he was writer, artist, letterer, etc. In the studio where he produced *The Spirit*, Eisner closely supervised his staff in all aspects of the production (at least in the early days of the feature). However, cartoonists were, and still are, the exception rather than the rule in mainstream comic book production.

The first major deviation from the industrial process came from the underground comix of the sixties and seventies. Artists like Frank Stack, Robert Crumb, Jack Jackson, and Art Spiegelman wrote, drew, lettered, and even self-published their own comic books. Most of the underground artists had never worked in mainstream comics. Some had been fans of comics (primarily comic strips and EC comic books), but, to some extent, they turned to the comics medium because it was accessible in terms of the money and talent required to produce and distribute a counterculture message.

The underground comix demonstrated that comic books could be created and find an audience outside the established system of production and distribution. The very existence of the underground comic books inspired some mainstream creators to produce independent work.

The alternative comics scene of small presses and self-publishers began with the undergrounds but became more visible to the average fan in the mid-seventies with Mike Friedrich's *Star*Reach*, which featured creator-owned work by Steve Englehart, Walt Simonson, and other popular mainstream writers and artists. Many of the so-called alternative comic books were simply poorly executed and cheaply produced rehashings of familiar mainstream genres and themes. And there have been cycles of boom and bust in the self-publishing, black-and-white comic book market (some fueled by the desire to strike it rich in the manner of the creators of the *Teenage Mutant Ninja Turtles*). During the boom times there is a glut on the market of titles that last no more than a few issues. Yet amidst the "vast wasteland" of comic book publishing, there have emerged a growing number of serious artists—Dave Sim, Eddie Campbell, Donna Barr, Peter Bagge, Mary Fleener, and Seth, just to name a few—who found an outlet for their distinctive voices in alternative comic books. Even the best of these alternative comic books usually have fewer than 50,000 readers, and often far less. These are relatively small runs when compared with the mainstream publishers (whose leading titles are in excess of 100,000 copies), but for many of those publishing in the alternative press, their interest lies in telling their own stories more than using the forum as a stepping stone to the mainstream publishers. There are probably more of these cartoonists working in the artisan process now than at any other time.

In comparing the artisan with the industrial process, Rogers noted:

> While I do not wish to suggest that the artisan method is inherently artistically superior to the industrial method, artisan production has tended to produce comics more varied in scope and more interesting aesthetically. Industrialized production is limiting in and of itself; the fact that it is used to produce comics mostly in the superhero genre makes it even more limiting. There are, of course, plenty of exceptions to this. There are many examples of creators who work well within the context of the specialization of labor caused by the industrial process and many examples of cartoonists who work alone and produce bad comics. ("Understanding" 7)

The best of these creations have led to the idea that there are particularly gifted creators, the auteurs, whose works represent the very best of the medium.

COMIC BOOK AUTEURS

Will Eisner believed that because words and pictures should combine as a seamless whole, "the ideal writing process occurs where the writer and artist are the same person" (*Graphic Storytelling* 111). It is certainly widely held that much of the outstanding work in the comics medium has been produced by a single and personal artistic vision, whether that of a cartoonist or a writer. This same tendency has been recognized in film. The creation of a film requires the collaboration of hundreds (sometimes thousands) of individuals. During the 1950s, French film critics like François Truffaut developed the **auteur theory** to explain how out of this very collaborative art a single artistic vision could sometimes emerge. These film critics believed that some directors—though certainly not all—were the artistic driving force, or "author," of the film. The auteur theory identifies certain characteristics of auteurs.

One quality that is often studied about an auteur is one's technical *competence* in using the art form. In the comics medium this means that one must demonstrate an understanding of how to use encapsulation, layout, and composition to effectively tell a story. Frank Miller, creator of *Sin City* and *300*, is known for his ability to depict moments of powerful action using stark contrasts of shadow and light.

A second characteristic that distinguishes the works of the auteur is the recurrence of certain *themes* across works. For decades cartoonist Jim Starlin has been weaving epic tales of cosmic forces, from his early work on Marvel's *Warlock*, to his creator-owned *Dreadstar*, to more recent work on DC's *Death of the New Gods*.

A third mark of distinction is the auteur's *stylistic traits*. This may be manifest in a particular writing style, drawing particular layouts, etc. One of Will Eisner's signature effects in *The Spirit* was to make the series title a part of the splash page art, so that a city skyline or old newspapers blowing in the wind spelled out "The Spirit."

The fourth consideration is *collaboration*, as auteurs tend to work with the same co-creators time and again. Jeph Loeb and Tim Sale have repeatedly teamed up to produce special projects for DC (*Batman: The Long Halloween*) and Marvel (*Daredevil: Yellow*).

Finally, auteurs often *borrow* ideas and styles from other outstanding creators, evidencing outside influences but reworking them to make them their own. This borrowing may manifest itself in the mimicking of well-known images, phrases, or approaches from other works in the medium, perhaps even their own previous work. For instance, Erik Larsen draws his *Savage Dragon* in a bombastic style reminiscent of the artwork of Jack Kirby.

Identifying exactly who might be among the auteurs of comics began with the bibliographic work of Jerry Bails and Hames Ware in their multivolume *The Who's Who of American Comic Books*, published in the 1970s. This project took a first crucial step in acknowledging the works of comics creators by giving names and bibliographies to the often uncredited creators of the Golden Age. Since that time, a steady stream of biographies produced by devoted fans have expanded our understanding of the creators and their contributions to the art form. There is currently no comics **canon**, or definitive collection of auteurs, but cartoonists like Harvey Kurtzman and writers like Alan Moore are widely regarded as being among the finest. Creators such as these have mastered the essentials of effective storytelling and managed the limitations of the form.

Working within Constraints

The vast majority of comic books that have been produced are simply not very good. This leads many people to conclude that comic books are an inferior art form, incapable of supporting literate and artistic content. But while most of the content has been inferior, this does not mean that the medium itself is inherently limited. In *Understanding Comics*, cartoonist Scott McCloud encourages us to separate form and content in order to recognize that "the art form—the medium—known as comics is a vessel which can hold any number of ideas and images" (*Understanding* 6). Comic books are words and pictures. There is simply no limit to how great the words can be or how wonderfully rendered the pictures can be.

This is not to say that comic books, like any other art form, do not have constraints of form. In fact, one criterion for judging the greatness of art is how well the creator works within the constraints of the medium. What are the particular limitation/constraints of the comic book form? Here are a few suggestions to consider:

1. *Space limitations* such as the number of pages or the page size. Creators of monthly comic books find themselves working with only twenty-two pages of story, but a graphic novel can be of any page length. Books such as Chris Ware's *Acme Novelty Library* have shown that a comic book can be any size or shape, not just the modern standard.

2. *Reproduction technologies.* Paper quality has come a long way from the pulpy newsprint of yesteryear and now includes high quality, glossary papers that enhance the artwork.

3. *Unrealistic images.* Comics are two-dimensional and lack the photo-realistic qualities of other visual storytelling media (film, theatre, television, video gaming, etc.). Yet McCloud (*Understanding*) claims that the simplified drawing actual enhances identification with the characters.

4. *Limited control of the reader.* The artist's use of layout can influence, but not control, reading behavior. A reader can view panels and pages in any order and for any duration.

5. *The page as a unit of composition.* The page as a unit does allow some control over the reader, and so successful use of the page is part of the art of the comic book. Eisner says: "Pages are the constant in comic book narration. . . . Keep in mind that when the reader turns the page a pause occurs. This permits a change of time, a shift of scene, an opportunity to control the reader's focus. Here one deals with retention as well as attention" (*Graphic Storytelling* 63).

6. *Selected moments.* Comics creators have to make more precise choices than have to be made in film, as they can only show frozen fragments of the action. The story can be successfully told if the "moments of prime action" are selected (Duncan).

7. *Interdependence of words and pictures.* According to cartoonist Robert Harvey, the success of the verbal-visual blend is the most important aesthetic criteria for judging a comic book. The limitation here is that for visually oriented readers, the art tends to dominate the initial attention, whereas prose readers not accustomed to the comic book form tend to move from one block of text (balloon or caption) to the next, and often miss important visual cues in the pictures.

8. *Artistic skill.* Often what can be depicted is limited by the skill of the artists.

9. *The serial aesthetic.* Most mainstream comic books are published as episodes in an ongoing saga rather than "done-in-one" complete stories. This can lead to repetitive situations among a cast of recurring characters, which can discourage growth for the characters. Even when radical change is introduced (e.g., "The Death of Superman"), it is almost always changed back in short order.

It is in managing, if not transcending, these constraints that the best creators distinguish themselves. For some gifted creators, this can lead to "star" status within the industry.

Creator Star Power

In 1970 DC Comics negotiated the unthinkable: Jack Kirby, the artist who had been Stan Lee's chief collaborator in the creation of the Marvel Universe, was leaving "The House of Ideas" to produce comics for rival DC. The venerable publisher could hardly contain its enthusiasm, featuring house ads proclaiming that "The Magic of Kirby!" was on its way in advance of Kirby's new assignment. But advertising Kirby's defection was something of an anomaly. Mainstream comics have traditionally relied on character-driven marketing based on the readers' recognition of the property more than the creative personnel who produced it. Publishers have long reasoned that marquee characters like Superman and Spider-Man sold comics more than artists like Joe Shuster or Steve Ditko. Thus, house ads proclaiming the arrival of Kirby at DC represented a progressive step in the recognition of creator star power in selling comics.

FIGURE 5.5. DC Comics announces Kirby's arrival in house ads appearing in 1970. © DC Comics

It would be some time before mainstream publishers would once again overtly tap into the marketing power of their creators' names. The largely understated way in which creators were used to market comics stands in stark contrast to the way in which most fiction is marketed. Just visit any bookstore and examine the covers of the latest bestselling novels: The author's name is probably far more prominent than the title of the book. While comics creators had been and continue to be credited for their contributions on the splash page of each issue, their names were not even a part of the cover presentation. After more than four decades in the business, DC finally began to credit their creative teams on selected projects in 1983 (such as Frank Miller's *Ronin* limited series), and gradually expanded to include cover credits on most of the line until by 1987 they became a standard feature. Marvel would not follow suit for nearly a decade, until the late 1990s. Yet even so, publishers still emphasize the title of comic book series over the creators' credits, with only rare exceptions, perpetuating the notion that the principal appeal is in the properties.

In the meantime, of course, publishers had tapped into creators' star power in less overt ways. As comics shifted to the direct-market distribution system, advance solicitations of upcoming comics would almost always credit the creative team as an asset for marketing the forthcoming comics, particularly if a fan favorite like Walter Simonson (*Mighty Thor*) or Michael Turner (*Witchblade*) was attached to the project. Publishers also made their creators accessible through personal appearances at comic book conventions. This practice had evolved thanks to early fan interest in meeting creators, which originated as informal occurrences of comics writers and artists showing up to meet fans at these events. Eventually, though, publishers began to stage these interactions with more elaborate promotion and settings. Today, at the largest comic book conventions, most publishers sponsor grand booths that showcase their talent pools.

The flashpoint in the development of the comics star system came when seven artists left Marvel to form their own company, Image Comics, in 1992. These artists had quite a fan following at the time, and Marvel had even launched titles specifically to cash in on their popularity. The defecting-artists-turned-Image founders were Erik Larsen, Jim Lee, Rob Liefeld, Todd McFarlane, Whilce Portacio, Marc Silvestri, and Jim Valentino. For a time, Image managed to become one of the three largest comic book publishers, nipping at the heels of industry leaders Marvel and DC. In short order, the fans had demonstrated that they would follow their favorite creators and were no longer solely driven to buying books for the characters. In fact McFarlane, creator of *Spawn*, became one of the wealthiest cartoonists to ever produce comic books. The success of Image inspired a number of other creator-owned imprints to come into being. Dark Horse distributed the Legends imprint featuring creator-owned works by fan-favorites Frank Miller (Sin City), John Byrne (*Next Men*), and Mike Mignola (*Hellboy*). Similarly, Malibu Comics launched creator-owned series under the Bravura imprint, including contributions from Jim Starlin (*Dreadstar*) and Howard Chaykin (*Power & Glory*). All of these efforts played a role in extending both creators' rights and control over their properties, though not all of them lasted very long. Many of these imprints suffered in the downturn in the comics market in the mid-nineties, and Image endured a number of in-house conflicts. One of the studios to splinter from Image and enjoy success thereafter was Jim Lee's WildStorm Productions (now owned by DC), which introduced a number of well-received creator-owned properties in the late 1990s, including Warren Ellis and Bryan Hitch's *The Authority* and Alan Moore and Kevin O'Neill's *League of Extraordinary Gentlemen*.

Certainly one of the most positive outcomes in the wake of the star system has been the adoption of several measures to increase creators' rights over their creative properties. Major publishers have long considered the characters and stories developed by the creative talent to be corporate property, and have been hesitant to share in the profitability of these properties. Siegel and Shuster were so eager to get their Superman creation into print that they signed over the rights to the character himself to their publisher, who went on to make millions merchandising the character in comics and other venues. It was not until the 1970s, when star artist Neal Adams (see profile below) used his clout within the industry, that Superman's owners finally gave Superman's creators a small share of the profits the character was generating. It was also in the 1970s that DC and Marvel finally made it a routine practice to return original artwork to their artists. Original artwork is a highly prized commodity in today's collectors' market, and artists can generate a good deal of money from selling the original pages of their published comics. Today comics creators have more opportunities for ownership of their properties and can enjoy more of the profits that their work can generate.

A relatively recent phenomenon that both exploits and feeds the star system is the use of exclusive contracts to secure the products of certain creators for finite periods of time. Having a commitment from a popular talent ideally delivers that person's fan base to a publisher, enhancing both the publisher's sales and prestige as dedicated comics buyers follow their favorites. Exclusive contracts also benefit the freelance talent, though, guaranteeing them steady assignments instead of relying on piecemeal jobs. These arrangements are of limited duration, usually around three years, giving both parties the flexibility to walk away from the arrangement should it no longer be advantageous to them. For the publishers this means not having an indefinite commitment to a talent whose popularity may wane, and for the creators it means being able to negotiate better deals down the road or get out from under unfavorable editorial control. Although exclusive contracts are a potential boon to the publishers and the creators who are offered them, they are still rare in the industry, meaning that most rising comics creators must struggle until their popularity warrants the presentation of such security.

While creators have long struggled for recognition and rights with mainstream publishers, the star status of many of comics' finest creators was never in doubt with the fans. As we will explore more fully in Chapter 8, fans are dedicated consumers of comics. At the dawn of organized fandom in the 1960s, it was the fans who began to recognize favorite comics creators with praise in their fanzines and even with fan awards. Fans would organize conventions to talk comics, trade back issues, and eventually invite their favorite creators in to meet in order to shower adulation upon them. Without the commitment of fans, who are dedicated to following the works of their favorite creators, no star system would have emerged. In recent years, the adulation of fans has been complemented by other authorities. The works of comics creators have been acknowledged with recognition (e.g., Alan Moore and Dave Gibbon's *Watchmen* named to *Time* magazine's list of the 100 best English language novels from 1923 to present) and awards (e.g., Neil Gamain's *Sandman* winning a World Fantasy Award and Art Spiegelman's *Maus* winning a Pulitzer Prize). Creators have also found themselves the subject of documentary films (e.g., Stan Lee was profiled in an hour-long episode of the popular A&E series *Biography*) and television appearances (e.g., Harvey Pekar was a repeat guest on *Late Night with David Letterman*). Although these significant, albeit infrequent, acknowledgements from mainstream culture help to enhance the status of those who practice the art form, the source of star power lies more squarely with the fans than those outside the reading community.

Profile: Neal Adams

born: Neal Adams
June 15, 1941
Governor's Island, New York

"I don't think of myself as an artist; I think of myself as a storyteller. The art is the facility I learned along the way in order to tell a story."

Career Highlights

1959   First professional work published: *Archie's Jokebook Magazine* #41.

1967   Deadman stories in *Strange Adventures* bring hyper-realism and bold experiments in page layout to mainstream comic books.

1970   Collaborated with writer Dennis O'Neil to give the campy Batman of the late 1960s a darker look and grimmer tone; then the duo tackled comic book relevance in *Green Lantern/Green Arrow*.

1971   Founded Continuity Graphics Associates with Dick Giordano.

1978   *Superman vs. Muhammad Ali* tabloid-sized comic released

1982   *Ms. Mystic* published by Pacific Comics

1984   Begins publishing his own line through Continuity Comics.

1998   Inducted into the Eisner Awards' Hall of Fame.

1999   Inducted into the Harvey Awards' Jack Kirby Hall of Fame.

Neal Adams' influence on comic book art has been second only to Jack Kirby. Adams took the dynamic visual vocabulary of Kirby—the poses and angles—and heightened their effect with a realistic rendering style. Adams' work spawned countless imitators and transformed the look of mainstream comic books. The simply rendered, stiff figures that populated the comic book pages for so long became hyper-realistically rendered figures displaying kinetic body language. The simple cartoonish faces were transformed into expressive faces contorted with emotion. "Adams, more than anyone else, revolutionized comic book art by bold experimentation, near technical

FIGURE 5.6. Adams' rendering of Batman shows his talent for capturing hyper-realistic figures in motion. From *Batman* #251 (1973). © DC Comics

Cont'd

FIGURE 5.7. Neal Adams as seen by Neal Adams! Courtesy of Continuity Studios.

perfection and a cinematically realistic style that has spawned countless imitators" (Young and Foltin 4).

Adams has also helped change the way the comic book industry does business. He was one of the first and most outspoken advocates of creator rights. He almost single-handedly stopped the practice of original artwork being destroyed, and he campaigned for it to be returned to the artist. He devoted four months of his life to championing the cause of Superman creators Siegel and Shuster, and ultimately helped them secure an annuity from DC Comics.

ANALYZING: BREAKING IN

For those hopefuls aspiring to a career in comics, there is no single route to success. Indeed, even traveling down some of the well-worn paths does not necessarily lead to achieving professional status. Still, the experiences of those who have made it suggest some methods for breaking into this highly competitive industry.

For artists, a combination of training and networking with other artists can help. Several high-profile artists started out as assistants to already established professionals in the field. George Perez, Terry Austin, and Bob Layton all apprenticed before making their own mark in the field. Also, attending one of the formal training programs for comics art, such as the Joe Kubert School of Cartoon and Graphic Art or the Center for Cartoon Studies, can be like attending a top film school for aspiring movie makers. The schools not only provide technical training, but they also facilitate making connections, as many established professionals are either on the faculty or regular visitors to such programs.

For writers, previous writing experience seems to be an important qualification in pursuing a career as an author. Some writers, like Mark Waid, earned experience by first writing or editing for magazines about the industry. Of course, formal education is also an important credential in opening doors. Though there are currently few courses explicitly dedicated to comics writing, the skills taught in creative writing courses in general or screenwriting courses in particular are certainly transferable to this medium.

For artists, writers, and other comics artisans such as letterers or colorists, there are additional strategies for getting one's foot in the door of the industry. One of these approaches is to work one's way up within a publishing company, starting with a position in the production or sales departments, for example. Fan favorites like Peter David and Kurt Busiek broke into the field this way. One can also demonstrate what one can do by actually producing work in the form of mini-comics, online comics, or small press comics. This helps to build a portfolio that can then be used to submit samples to publishers. Whenever samples are ready for outside review, care should be exercised in researching and targeting materials to the right publisher and editor. Otherwise the submission is likely to be simply dismissed. All the major comics publishers post submission guidelines on their websites that specify what to send and how to send it. One other strategy is to sign on with an agent, who might be able to help place you with a publisher.

Whatever else professionals in the field have in terms of training, talent, or connections, the one trait that they all seem to possess is a passion for the art form that drives them forward.

Discussion Questions

1. How have different storytelling traditions influenced each generation of comic book creators?
2. Since monthly comic books have more limitations of form than other comics, can you argue for any auteurs emerging from that format ? Can you cite a particular writer, artist, or cartoonist working in serial comics who transcends those limitations?
3. Given the difficulty in breaking into, much less achieving success in, the comics industry, what do you suppose still attracts people to pursue careers in a competitive field like comics?

Activities

1. Identify a comic book writer, artist, or cartoonist you believe qualifies as an auteur, other than someone appearing in one of the "Profile" boxes in this book. Write a one- or two-page explanation of how the selected person meets all (or most) of the characteristics of an auteur listed in this chapter.
2. Read a copy of "A Bill of Rights for Comics Creators" (available on our website at *www.powerofcomics.com* and elsewhere) and prepare answers to the following questions:
   - How would the history of the comic book industry have been different if these rights had been granted to creators from the very beginning?
   - What factors (e.g., size of publisher, popularity of creator) influence the degree to which these rights can be exercised by a contemporary comic book creator?
   - The document advocates "prompt and complete return of our artwork in its original condition." Is the artwork the property of the penciller and the inker? What about the writer who might have conceived and described the majority of images that someone else drew?

Recommended Readings

Comics:

Cooke, Jon B., and John Morrow, eds. *Streetwise: Autobiographical Stories by Comic Book Professionals*. Raleigh, NC: TwoMorrows Publishing, 2000.

The men behind mainstream comic books tell of their upbringing, influences, and entrée into the world of graphic storytelling. Sergio Aragonés won an Eisner Award for Best Short Story for his contribution to this anthology, which also features memoirs from two dozen professionals.

Eisner, Will. *The Dreamer*. Princeton, WI: Kitchen Sink Press, 1986.

This graphic novella (i.e., shorter than most graphic novels) tells of the career of a young artist struggling to make it big in the burgeoning comic book industry in the 1930s. Although a fictional account, the story is nonetheless based upon experiences Eisner himself had at the dawn of the industry.

Scholarly Sources:

Dooley, Michael, and Steven Heller, eds. *The Education of a Comics Artist: Visual Narrative in Cartoons, Graphic Novels, and Beyond*. New York: Allworth, 2005.

More than sixty professionals from the fields of comics publishing, animation, and education contribute essays and interviews about the craft of graphic storytelling in this anthology.

Jones, Gerard. *Men of Tomorrow: Geeks, Gangsters, and the Birth of the Comic Book*. New York: Basic Books, 2004.

Historian and comics writer Jones retells the stories of the actual men who created the Golden Age. This account is the perfect companion to Michael Chabon's fictional *The Amazing Adventures of Kavalier and Clay*.

Creating the Story

"Immobile images separated by gutters: how do we tell a story with these things?"

—THIERRY GROENSTEEN, COMICS THEORIST, 2007

"Sequential art is the act of weaving a fabric."

—WILL EISNER, COMIC BOOK PIONEER, 1985

Not only have self-avowed pop culture geeks such as Kevin Smith, J. Michael Straczynski and Joss Whedon taken time from their screenwriting careers to pen the adventures of some of their favorite superheroes, but in recent years novelists such as Brad Meltzer, Jonathan Lethem, and Jodi Picoult have tried their hand at the medium. While they came to the venture accomplished story-tellers and wordsmiths, they soon discovered that the comic book art form required a different skill set than what they had developed as novelists.

Lethem, who wrote the *Omega the Unknown* limited series for Marvel Comics, characterized the project as "a learning experience." He explained, "I needed to

FIGURE 6.1. Writing the "fictional" comic book that was woven through her novel *The Tenth Circle* (2006) led Jodi Picoult to write Wonder Woman (2007). *The Tenth Circle* © 2006 by Jodi Picoult. Used by permission of the author. *Wonder Woman* © DC Comics.

127

feel my way into the form. One of the reasons why I've been slow has been that I really have to do this job of storyboarding and visualization in my head, in order to make my storytelling work in the medium's terms" (Lethem qtd. in Zack Smith). Perhaps it was because part of her prose novel *The Tenth Circle* was written in the form of a comic book (drawn by artist Dustin Weaver) that DC editors approached Picoult about writing a *Wonder Woman* story arc. Unlike Lethem, Picoult was not a comics fan, and she struggled even more with the "visualization of how the words are going to play out on the page and where. . . . That was really foreign to me," says Picoult (qtd. in Ridley).

OBJECTIVES

In this chapter you will learn:

1. some of the narrative structures commonly found in comic books;
2. the types and techniques of encapsulation;
3. the nature of the relationship between the pictorial and linguistic elements of comic books;
4. the decisions that have to be made in creating the layout of the comic book page; and
5. the choices and techniques of composing individual comic book panels.

In 1957 Marshall McLuhan noted that "today we are just beginning to realize the new media are not just mechanical gimmicks for creating worlds of illusion, but new languages with new and unique powers of expression" (119). While McLuhan would have had no problem recognizing the techniques and devices of comic books as a "new language," most comics theorists speak of a comics language merely as an analogy, because the visual aspects of comic books have no definite lexicon and no concrete rules of grammar. However, Neil Cohn (*www.emaki.net*) is doing some fascinating and challenging work applying theories of linguistics and cognitive science to understand how sequences of images in comics literally operate as a language. In this book we do not attempt to explain comic book communication as a type of language, but any serious student of the comic book medium should consider Cohn's work as a supplement and occasionally a counterpoint to the concepts presented in this text.

As illustrated by the model of comic book communication presented in Chapter 1, creating (encoding) a message in comic book form is a process occurring on four levels: story, encapsulation, layout, and composition. The comic book creator often considers a number of these levels simultaneously rather than in a strict sequence.

ENCODING: STORY

On the broadest level of comic book communication there is the story or narrative—what happens. In the basic model of narrative there is a conflict or series of conflicts that build in rising action to a climactic moment in which the conflict is resolved. Rather than ending abruptly, the story is often rounded out with a denouement that might show the consequences of the resolution, resonate the theme of the story, or simply reemphasize the tone or mood of the tale.

A **simple narrative** structure that revolves around a problem and ends with the resolution of that problem (often followed by a punch-line denouement) was the standard form for funny animal comics, romance comics, humor comics (e.g., *Sugar and Spike*, *The Adventures of Jerry Lewis*), and self-contained adventure stories (e.g., *Uncle Scrooge*, the early superhero stories). While simple narratives still exist in the comic book medium, it is now more common for writers to construct **complex narratives** in which the main plot line is expanded by back story, character development, and ongoing subplots. Relatively rare in what is normally a storytelling medium are avant-garde comic books that could be labeled **antinarrative**. While they might contain narrative elements such as setting, characters, and actions, these elements do not fit together to form a comprehensible story. The purpose of such antinarrative works is not to tell a story, but rather to evoke a mood or elicit an aesthetic response.

It might seem that any comic book or graphic novel would fit into one of these three categories: simple narrative, complex narrative, or antinarrative. However, the conventional concept of narrativity assumes that events build toward some ultimate resolution of conflict and an ending of the narrative, whereas many comic books are serialized, continuing stories that have no ultimate resolution and never come to an end as long as there are enough readers willing to purchase the next issue. Even a cancelled series is usually left open-ended in anticipation of being revived at some later date.

Literary scholar Marie-Laure Ryan has proposed a number of new modes of narrativity she feels can more accurately describe the various ways in which narrative structures are realized in texts. Two of Ryan's modes—braided narrativity and proliferating narrativity—seem particularly applicable to comic books:

> **Braided narrativity:** This type of narrative follows the intertwined destinies of a large cast of characters. The text presents no global plot, but a number of parallel and successive subplots developing along the destiny line of characters. . . . Since this mode of narrativity presents no macro structure, it does not end in an event motivated by the demands of narrative closure, but may be continued ad infinitum by stringing new episodes along destiny lines. (Ryan 374)

It might seem that Ryan's concept of braided narrativity would apply to most mainstream comic books. This is certainly the narrative mode of the television soap opera, and many mainstream comic book series seem to be nothing more than soap operas with colorful costumes and frequent fisticuffs. However, in braided narrativity characters and events have an internal consistency and develop along a strict linearity that is not manifest in most mainstream, particularly superhero, comic books. Braided narrativity best describes a single title that is creator-owned and tells stories about characters that are not part of a larger fictional universe. *Strangers in Paradise*, *Hate*, and *Cerebus* are good examples.

The popular mainstream superhero comic books are part of a sprawling fictional universe, with shaky continuity among the events in all of the titles that comprise the universe. Within these complex fictional structures (where editorial decisions are often driven by commerce), neither characters nor plots are stable concepts. There are often inconsistent, even contradicting narratives across titles and across years. In an effort to appeal to new readers and bring a contemporary feel to characters whose adventures have been published for half a century or more, there are occasional **reboots** that begin a new version of a character or team, with an alternate telling of events already chronicled in previous issues. For example, Superman's origin has been retold and retooled many times since his first appearance in 1938. While longtime readers can be annoyed or even alienated by radical changes to beloved characters, they can also take pleasure in being able to identify how elements from the previous version(s) are modified and integrated into the new "reality."

These continuity-conscious, serialized comic books seem to fit what Ryan calls a **proliferating narrativity**:

> In these works, the main plot functions mostly as support for the telling of adventures and anecdotes. The focus of interest does not reside in the building and resolution of dramatic suspense spanning the entire text, but in the narrative verve displayed in the accumulation of little stories. The macro structure that holds the micro narratives together is of the most primitive kind; the life of the hero, a family saga, a love affair stretching over a lifetime. (Ryan 373)

A proliferating narrative is not so much a story as it is a mythos. With the most recognizable and exploitable corporate commodities (e.g., X-Men, Superman, Batman, Spider-Man), the proliferation of the mythos occurs across multiple titles of their own, numerous guest appearances in other titles, novels,

FIGURE 6.2. The Legion of Super-Heroes have been rebooted more than most comic book characters. Here are three of their new beginnings: *Adventure Comics* #247 (1958), *Legion of Super-Heroes* #0 (1994), and *Legion of Super-Heroes* #1 (2005). © DC Comics

television series, motion pictures, merchandise, and even theme parks. Thus, readers/consumers come to know a character through encountering many varied forms of the "character concept." Because a number of these forms are significantly more profitable for the corporation than the publication of comic books, the comic book narrative must sometimes conform to the mythos proliferated in the more popular media.

Speaking in a roundtable discussion with Steve Bissette and Tom Veitch, writer Neil Gaiman has speculated that it is not the superhero character's story that persists in the culture, but rather the character's **state of grace**, a set of powers, appearance, supporting characters, and behaviors that are preserved in a recognizable form for the economic interests of the corporation that owns the character. The colorful costumes, dramatic displays of power, and familiar character traits that constitute this state of grace provide much of the narrative verve that makes reading comics enjoyable.

The never-ending, intricately interlinking, periodically reconstructed stories of mainstream comic books constitute a unique form of narrativity. They also communicate their narratives in ways unique to the medium. The process of encoding a comic book story further consists of encapsulation, layout, and composition.

ENCODING: ENCAPSULATION

A comic book does not present each moment of action in the narrative; the writer and/or artist must decide which images (pictures and words) to show in order to tell the story. The process of **encapsulation** involves selecting certain moments of prime action from the imagined story and encapsulating, or enclosing, renderings of those moments in a discrete space (a unit of comic book communication that is called a **panel**, irrespective of whether or not there are actual panel borders). As cartoonist Megan Kelso explains about the comics she loves best, "it's very clear to me that the cartoonist saw the entire world that was represented in the comic, and then carefully chose what to show me" (229).

While the term *encapsulation* is generally used to refer to the act of creating panels, it is also true that there is encapsulation, a deciding of what to show, at the levels of scene, sequence, and even story. Telling a story always entails choices about where to begin and where to end. The major building blocks of the story are **sequences**. A sequence is comprised of related and usually consecutive **scenes**. Scenes are imprecise units of the story that usually, but not necessarily, have unity of time and space and portray a continuous action. Scenes are unified by a central concern, be it a location, an incident, or a stream of thought.

The page is, by necessity of the form, a unit of encapsulation. There must be a conscious decision about which panels will appear together on a page. The same is also true of any two facing pages of the story. Cartoonist and educator Will Eisner, in *Comics and Sequential Art*, comments on the importance of encapsulation at the page level:

Keep in mind that when the reader turns the page a pause occurs. This permits a change of time, shift of scene, and opportunity to control the reader's focus. Here one deals with retention as well as attention. The page as well as the panel must therefore be addressed as a unit of containment although it too is merely a part of the whole comprised by the story itself. (63)

Within each page, though, we find moments of encapsulation with each panel. The panel itself is the most central and vital level of encapsulation. The majority of comic book panels are presented in an orderly progression of framed rectangles, usually separated by a white space known as the **gutter.** However, borders and gutters are not necessary or defining elements of the panel. The unit of comic book communication known as a panel occupies a finite space on the page and encapsulates a finite, if sometimes indeterminate, span of time. Yet, because innovative artists such as Bernie Krigstein, Art Spiegelman, Joe Quesada, and David Mack are constantly finding new ways to use the very elastic form of the comic book, it is not always easy to recognize or define a panel. Not all comic book panels are enclosed by a border, and not all pictures enclosed by a border function as a panel (see Figure 6.3).

FIGURE 6.3. Just because a picture or a word is enclosed by a frame does not mean it functions as an independent panel. How many panels are there on this page from *Blankets* (2003)? © Craig Thompson and courtesy of Top Shelf.

The Process of Encapsulation

The decision of which moments of the story to present to the reader is the primary concern of encapsulation. Comics theorist Robert Harvey writes that "the selection of what is to be pictured is greatly influenced by the quantity of story material (how much exposition is required, how much action, what must be depicted in order to prepare for subsequent events, and so on) and by the available space" (178). There is also a constant dynamic between what *is* shown and what *could* be shown.

One aspect of this dynamic is the **syntagmatic choice,** the process of selecting which panels to present from the possible progression of story images that could occur. This process is analogous to selecting the word order to create a sentence. The images of syntagmatic choice are arranged along the horizontal axis to form scenes and sequences of the overall story. While images not selected might well be imagined by the reader as he or she mentally constructs a narrative flow from the discrete moments of encapsulation, as Harvey points out, "what is chosen to be pictured necessarily acquires more dramatic emphasis than what is left out"

(178). Because the syntagmatic axis involves not only selection but sequencing and combining, it will be discussed in more detail in the upcoming section on layout.

At each panel and at each image in a panel, the syntagmatic intersects with the vertical axis of the **paradigmatic choice,** the chosen images and all the images that could have made sense or communicated nearly the same meaning at the same point in the panel. According to film scholar James Monaco, a paradigmatic connotation results from comparing, not necessarily consciously, the image shown with "its unrealized companions in the paradigm" (131). Or, as media scholar Jonathan Bignell explains it, "every sign present has meaning by virtue of the other signs which have been excluded and are not present in the text" (14). For both the syntagmatic and the paradigmatic choices, meaning is created by a combination of the present and the absent.

FIGURE 6.4. The panel can be an elastic and even elusive concept. This page from a Jim Starlin *Warlock* story contains four disjointed panels in which the words and pictures that constitute each panel are not contiguous. The figure and the thought balloons on the left function not as a panel, but as captions for the four panels to the right. © 2008 Marvel Entertainment, Inc. and its subsidiaries

The Reductive Nature of Encapsulation

Comics are reductive in creation and additive in reading. That is, creators reduce the story to moments on a page by encapsulation, and readers expand the isolated moments into a story by a process called *closure.* We will look more closely at the process of closure in the following chapter on experiencing the story.

The most prevalent reductive device in comics is **synecdoche,** using a part to represent the whole or vice versa. For example, in the majority of panels, only a portion of a character's body is drawn to represent the reality of the entire body (see Figure 6.5). This is true even more often for objects (cars, building, etc.). In the static medium of comic books, the frozen moments of prime action stand for the entire action. If this reduction is done with thought and skill, readers understand the whole from the parts presented.

FIGURE 6.5. Eisner demonstrates a type of synecdoche in which a panel showing only a portion of a character actually communicates an impression of the character's entire body. From *Comics and Sequential Art* by Will Eisner. © 1985 by Will Eisner. © 2008 by Will Eisner Studios, Inc. Used by permission of W. W. Norton & Company, Inc.

Metonymy, the use of an associated detail to represent the whole, is another useful reductive device in comics. The most common metonymy used is the depiction of part of the physical manifestation of an emotion. In his study of the language of film, director Vsevolod Pudovkin noted that "there is a law in psychology that says if an emotion gives birth to a certain movement, by imitation of this movement the corresponding emotion can be called forth" (193). In comics as well the gestures, postures, and facial expressions associated with an emotion can be used to represent that emotion. Chapter two of cartoonist Scott McCloud's *Making Comics* provides a detailed examination of how emotions are conveyed by facial expressions and body language (see Figure 6.6).

A detail can also represent a whole through a less direct, more indexical relationship based on common usage or conventions. One of the conventions established early on in film and picked up by comic books was that tattered clothes indicate that someone has been in a fight. In the first issue of Superman there is an extreme example of this. In a series of six panels, Superman deals with a wife-beater. The man, wearing a long-sleeve shirt and tie, is thrown against the wall by Superman and then breaks a knife on Superman's "tough skin." Superman never does anything to rip the man's clothes, but by the fifth panel the man's sleeves are completely torn from his shirt (see Figure 6.7).

Symbols are another means of economy of expression in comics. Symbols can manifest as a **sequence metaphor**, two juxtaposed images that together create a meaning not present in either image alone. For example, in the first issue of *Aces High* (1955), an image of a medieval knight appears in the sky behind the image of a World War I aviator in his plane. The co-presence of these two images is the vehicle that creates the **tenor** (underlying meaning) that the aviator is a modern-day knight. Common-lore metaphors are based on a relationship that has become conventionalized by repeated association. Because the moon has repeatedly been depicted as romantic in poetry, song, and film, an image of the moon in a love comic is going to symbolize romance for most readers. Yet visual metaphors are very dependent on context, and a similar drawing of the moon in *Tomb of Dracula* would symbolize lurking terror.

FIGURE 6.6. Scott McCloud says there are six pure expressions (anger, disgust, fear, joy, sadness, and surprise) which can be modified and combined to create thousands of other recognizable expressions. Page 85 from *Making Comics* © 2006 by Scott McCloud. Reprinted by permission of of HarperCollins Publishers.

Since everything in comic books, including character, is reduced to two-dimensional images, the use of **stereotypes** is prevalent. A stereotype is a recognizable generalization of a type. Especially when the art style moves away from realism and into caricature, generalizations about characters can be quickly established. The generalizations can be based on physique, hair, posture, clothing and other artifacts, and especially on facial features. For instance, comics veteran Will Eisner often employed what was already a venerable technique in caricature—character renderings based on animals (See Figure 6.8).

FIGURE 6.7. The convention of torn clothing is used to show the ferocity of a fight in *Superman* #1 (1939), script by Jerry Siegel and art by Joe Shuster. © DC Comics

Encapsulation of Actions and Motions

Cartoonists have developed a number of techniques to give a sense of movement to the flat, static images on the comics page. The most common technique is simply the posture of the characters. Another frequent technique, used in conjunction with posture, is thin lines (called *speed lines*) or puffs of "smoke" drawn behind a character or object to indicate the direction and rapidity of movement (see Figure 6.9). It is generally the case that the more blurred the image, the faster the speed depicted. A third method of communicating movement is drawing, next to the completed figure, a partial outline of a figure in its previous position(s). In the fourth method the artist makes multiple full drawings of the character in action with only slight differences in the character's position each time (see Figure 6.9). With the fifth technique motion is implied to have happened between panels because a figure or object is occupying a different space or assuming a different posture than in the previous panel. A less frequently used variation on this technique, but one that can imply a sudden departure, is the absence of a figure or object from a panel that otherwise has all the elements of the preceding panel (see Figure 6.11). In still another variation, a meta-panel composed of a number of smaller panels can establish a stationary setting that stretches across all the panels, while in each of the smaller panels the same characters or object can be shown at a different place in the setting, thus giving a sense of the figure moving within the frame of the meta-panel.

FIGURE 6.8. Visual stereotyping examples from *Graphic Storytelling and Visual Narrative* by Will Eisner. © 1996 by Will Eisner. © 2008 by Will Eisner Studios, Inc. Used by permission of W. W. Norton & Company, Inc.

FIGURE 6.9. Speed lines, posture, and a puff of smoke convey motion from Walt Disney's *José Carioca* (1980). © Disney Enterprises, Inc.

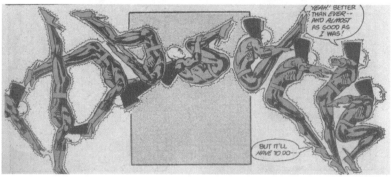

FIGURE 6.10. In the top panel, speed lines are drawn in to convey motion. In the middle panel, a path of motion is indicated by a combination of speed lines and repeated figures. In the bottom panel, repeated figures aim for the same effect but without the use of speed lines. From *DC Comics Presents* #24 (1980) with words by Len Wein and art by José Luis García-López. © DC Comics

FIGURE 6.11. Motion implied by a change in the second panel in *Cerebus* #46 (1983), art by Dave Sim. © Aardvark-Vanaheim

Encapsulation of Time

A panel seldom encapsulates a single instant, but rather a span of time. The amount of time encapsulated in a panel can be an instant, a moment, or even a sequence of events. Both an action and the reactions to that action are often contained in the same panel.

Panel size and panel content can be used to indicate the passage of time in a comic book narrative. While there are many exceptions, it is often true that the larger the panel, the longer the time span depicted in it. Yet a sequence of events can also be crammed into a small panel, while a splash page can depict a single instant of time. While McCloud's generalization that in comics "time and space are one and the same" dramatically highlights the spatial nature of comic book time, as he points out, "there's no conversion chart" (*Understanding* 100). There is no exact formula for how space equals time.

When constructing panel content, a creator has to be aware that a reader senses the amount of time elapsed based on his or her own experience of how long it takes to perform the action depicted. This includes both physical actions and saying or thinking words. Generally, words that appear in captions do not affect the time span of a panel unless they can be attributed to a character in a story or they describe the passage of time.

The manner in which time is encapsulated controls the duration of attention and affects the pacing of the story. In general, the more words in a panel, the slower the reading pace. Thus, effective action scenes usually contain fewer words as the action becomes more intense so that the tempo picks up as the reader moves rapidly from panel to panel.

Interdependence of Pictorial and Linguistic Elements

Perhaps the most significant and elusive element of comic book encapsulation is the unique blend of words and pictures that must occur for the art form to communicate effectively. An important consideration of how language and picture are encapsulated is the correspondence of the words to the action/scene. Balloons or captions can be **synchronous**, occurring at the same time as the action, or **asynchronous** with the picture. The relationship between the words and the static image can never be absolutely synchronous, but skillful comics creators make an effort to create panels in which the words correspond to the duration of the action. However, when there are many speech balloons in a panel with a single image, "the picture is appropriate to only some of the conversation—and the remainder of the speeches lose dramatic force because they lack the narrative reinforcement of suitable accompanying visuals" (Harvey 188). Eisner claims that "a protracted exchange of dialogue cannot be realistically supported by unmoving static images," and that, ideally, "the dialogue terminates the endurance of the image" (*Graphic*, 60). Comics theorist

FIGURE 6.12. The bartender in *Scalped* #5 (2007) would have to speak very rapidly to say all of these words while performing the action pictured. Words by Jason Aaron and art by R.M. Guéra. Used with permission.

FIGURE 6.13. In this incident from David Lapham's *Stray Bullets* #8 (1996), the words are spread out over a number of panels in order to better fit with the action pictured. © David Lapham

Thierry Groensteen believes the images of characters engaged in conversation are always desynchronized because each character is "living the moment of their word balloon" (133). Scholars Rheinhold Reitberger and Wolfgang Fuchs offer a general rule for the combination of words and images in comic books: "the text must be contained within the picture" (25); in other words, the dialogue must fit with the action shown. The means by which the linguistic and the visual work together will be discussed further in the section on composition.

It might seem that composition would be the next level of encoding to consider, since panels must exist before they can be positioned or sequenced. However, in the typical process of comic book creation, the panels are arranged on a page while they exist in only a rudimentary form—as thumbnails or roughs. Relationships of panels are established before the details of composition in individual panels are selected and rendered.

ENCODING: LAYOUT

Layout concerns the relationship of a single panel to the succession of panels, to the totality of the page, and to totality of the story. A cartoonist or writer-artist team constructing a comic book page must consider how the meaning of each panel is affected by the variables of size, sequence, and juxtaposition.

The relative size of a panel does not necessarily indicate the relative significance of the panel. A **splash page** is a full-page panel, usually at or near the beginning of a comics narrative and used to establish the situation in which the story begins. A splash page seldom depicts the climax of the story or a turning point in a character's life. Many splash pages, and most double-page spreads, simply operate as pinups of the hero leaping into action, a use of narrative space

FIGURE 6.14. Unnecessarily confusing page layout by Neal Adams in *Strange Adventures* #208 (1968). © DC Comics

FIGURE 6.15. Brilliant page layout by José Luis García-López in *Deadman* #1 (1986). © DC Comics

that Eisner dismissed as "pretty wallpaper, but poor storytelling" (Conversation). However, on occasion, a full page or even two pages are warranted to convey the scope of a huge battle or the grandeur of a setting.

In order to link up with the larger narrative structures of scenes, sequences, and story, panels must be presented in a sequence that follows a discernable narrative path. While readers can, and usually do, scan an entire page as they turn to it, an artist can design a page so as to influence how a reader moves through the space.

In the early years of the comic book medium, the application of both size and sequence was standardized. The first American comic books consisted of newspaper strips cut and re-pasted for a page format. Because most newspaper strips had a standard vertical dimension, it was easy to arrange them in three or four rows across the page. Even after comic books began publishing original material, the three-tier or four-tier format was the standard layout for most comic books of the forties and fifties (Evanier "POV"). In the late sixties and early seventies, more and more artists began to break free of the strict grid layout. Veteran pencillers such as Carmine Infantino and Gil Kane began to experiment with layout, and they were soon followed by a wave of innovative young artists such as Jim Steranko, Neal Adams, Barry Smith, Bernie Wrightson, Mike Kaluta, Jim Starlin, Mike Ploog, and Howard Chaykin. Page layout can be inventive and complex, but it should not be confusing. Cartoonist Harvey

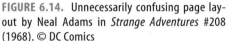

Kurtzman warned that "experimenting with a comics page's layout is a tricky business. Unless you respect the importance of each panel—the panels are the vital building blocks of the art form—you can wreck the narrative flow" (81).

As the reader follows the sequencing of panels and moves from one panel to the next, the element of juxtaposition comes into play. The reader performs an ongoing construction of meaning by considering each panel in direct relationship to the one immediately before it, as well as in the context of all previous panels. The understanding of the next panel can also be influenced by a number of the panels yet to come because, as Groensteen points out, "the focal vision never ceases to be enriched by peripheral visions," and the reader can scan ahead to other panels on a page or even on the facing page (*System* 19). And each next panel has the potential to provide new information that creates a "retroactive determination" of the meaning of one or more previous panels (Groensteen *System* 110).

Occasionally pages will be primarily decorative in nature, and the layout decisions (panel size, sequence, and position) are more influenced by aesthetic principles than they are by service to the narrative.

ENCODING: COMPOSITION

The third act of encoding the comic book message is composing the individual panels. While most readers superficially take in the overall panel for a sense of what is happening, there are techniques of composition that artists can use to direct attention and movement through the panel once the reader becomes immersed in it.

A symmetrical composition tends to give every character and object in the panel equal importance and can be visually boring. The conventional wisdom for mainstream comic books, with their emphasis on action and adventure genres, is that figures in a panel must be arranged asymmetrically to make both the characters and their actions seem more dynamic (Alcala qtd. in MacDonald and Yeh). Kurtzman claims that most composition in early comic books "was static, pale, anemic," until Joe Simon and Jack Kirby's work on *Captain America* created dynamic composition "through opposing lines that clashed and exploded all over the panels" (20). However, for alternative comic books, in which the narrative contains less physical action and more conversation and emotion, the dynamism of Simon and Kirby's style composition can be inappropriate.

Film borrowed from theater the concept of mise-en-scène, or "putting in the scene." Most of the mise-en-scène elements present on stage or screen can be depicted in a comic book panel: background details, color, "lighting," distance, angle, and "movement." Comic books also have some unique elements of composition: visualized sound, the blending of the pictorial and the linguistic, and art style.

Background Detail

In most comic books, figures (visual representations of characters) are the focus of the story and the reader's attention. However, the details depicted behind and around those characters are essential for establishing setting and mood. Once setting is established by background details, a vague sense of that setting persists in the reader's imagination, and details tend to become sparse or drop out altogether. In fact, there are times when continued depiction of a detailed setting can be counterproductive to the author's purpose. "When you've got a lot of background detail," warns artist Richard Corben, "it can slow down the pacing of the story and may even detract from what the story is saying." However, Corben goes on to say that "sometimes it may be an important part of the story, such as the setting and the ambiance" (qtd. in Van Hise 53). In genres such as science fiction and western, background details can be as crucial to the narrative as any of the characters.

Color

Most mainstream comic books have traditionally been ablaze with the bright primary colors (red, blue, and yellow) thought to appeal to adolescent males. Certainly the colorful costumes are part of the appeal of superheroes. How would the concept of the Batman be altered if his costume was a pastel color? Would the Flash seem as fast if he wore gray instead of red? In recent decades, however, coloring techniques have become more sophisticated and the color palette has become more varied, since skillful use of color can give a character dramatic impact in a given panel. "As long as the colorist is aware of providing a contrasting background for [the] sake of clarity," advises colorist Bob Sharen, "the costume colors don't matter that much. Hue and value contrast will make almost any character 'pop' in a given panel."

Color can serve a number of narrative functions. Most mainstream comic book characters, from superheroes to cowboys to ducks, have a recognizable and unvarying color scheme. As European comics scholar Ann Miller points out, color can make the story easier to follow "by allowing characters to be rapidly recognizable from one panel to the next" (95). Color can also create or amplify the emotion in a story. "Generally, anger, violence or any impact panel will have a hot color like red, yellow, or orange. Cool colors like blue and purple are used when the mood is sad and depressed" (Oliver).

Using black and white instead of color can also affect the meaning of a story. Because many of the most ambitious and critically acclaimed comics works have told their stories without using primary colors, black and white, or at least subtle color (sepia tones, green ink, etc.), has become emblematic of serious comic books. McCloud believes "colors objectify their subjects" and emphasize form rather than meaning, while "in black and white, the ideas behind the art are communicated more directly" (*Understanding* 189, 192).

Lighting

With skillful use of shading and color, a comic book artist can simulate many of the lighting techniques employed on stage or in film. Will Eisner, drawing on his knowledge of theater lighting, was a pioneer in using lighting effects in comic books. According to Eisner, "an enormous amount of visual storytelling, and enormous amount of environment can be suggested by clever lighting" (qtd. in Viola). Eisner was one of the first artists to bring the mood and the danger of the big city at night to the comic book page by simulating the low-key lighting of the film noir genre.

A comic book artist can use **chiaroscuro**, a stark contrast of light and dark, to funnel attention to a particular point in a panel. When the panel is mostly light, dark objects stand out, and when the panel is mostly dark, light objects stand out. According to comics art collector Kenneth K. Kirste, "when evenly balanced, the lighter parts of a work tend to stand out while darker ones recede" (14).

Distance

The distance from which readers perceive themselves viewing the scenery or action in a panel can influence attention and interpretation. One of the primary functions of the **extreme long view** is to create a context or sense of place. The **long view** can also be used to establish setting at the beginning of the story or scene. Repeated use of long views in a story (especially when not motivated by a

FIGURE 6.16. A striking example of chiaroscuro from *Daredevil* #189 (1982) from writer Frank Miller and artist Klaus Janson. © 2008 Marvel Entertainment, Inc. and its subsidiaries

scene change) tends to stress setting over character. The medium view creates a balance between character and setting. A specific form of **medium view** is known in film as the **two shot**. The two shot frames multiple characters interacting so that their reactions to one another can be viewed simultaneously. The **close-up view** emphasizes character over setting because very little of the setting is visible and the character's **affect displays** (emotions indicated by facial expressions) are more in evidence. The **extreme close-up** view is often used to emphasize some detail (e.g., a ring, a scar, a signature) that is important to the plot.

Angle

Linguist Mario Saraceni reminds us that "the point of view from which each individual panel is drawn is a major aspect of the way in which meaning is conveyed in comics" (84). The **extreme high angle**, or bird's-eye view, can be used to present a subjective experience, suggest relationships, or make the reader an omniscient viewer. The **high-angle view** can be used to make something or someone seem small and weak, or make the reader feel detached from the action. Panels that present an **eye-level view** tend to create identification with the characters and a sense of involvement in the action. A **low angle** can make the person or object being viewed seem powerful or menacing. The **extreme low angle**, or worm's-eye view, can make whatever is shown seem towering and powerful, but it can also make the reader feel omniscient by taking a vantage point usually unavailable to humans.

Movement

While it is true that the images on the printed page are static, there are two types of "movement" that can be implied in comic books: **primary movement** (of people or objects in the frame) and **secondary movement** (of the frame itself). Comic book artists have developed certain techniques to convey a sense of movement, and they have to rely on the reader's imagination to perceive those techniques as actual movement. The five basic techniques for communicating primary movement in a comic book were detailed earlier in this chapter in the encapsulation section.

Secondary movement, or implied movement of the frame, can be used to direct reader attention, control mood and tempo, suggest relationships, and make the reader feel involved in the action. The changing view in successive panels can mimic the five basic movements of the frame in film: panning (moving sideways), tilting (moving up or down), rolling (tilting to the side or even completely around), tracking or dollying (following a moving subject), and craning (can combine any or all of the other types of movement; a freedom of movement made possible in film by attaching a camera to a crane).

Visualized Sound

In comic books, any sound that is introduced into the story has to be visual, and is, therefore, an element of composition. Voice, sound effects, and music represented in comic books lack the realism found in an auditory medium, but they can be a great deal more expressive than they are in non-illustrated prose.

FIGURE 6.17. The bold and distinctive sound effects lettering created by Howard Chaykin and Ken Bruzenak make sounds a tangible part of the environment in *Time²: The Epiphany* (1986) and *American Flagg!* #8 (1984). © 2008 Howard Chaykin

FIGURE 6.18. Even though the musical notes in these two panels from Peter Kuper's *The System* (1997) are identical, readers will understand the notes to represent different music—the type of music to which a stripper might perform and the type of music a young skateboarder might enjoy. © Peter Kuper

Comic book dialogue and narration is usually presented in neat, clearly printed lettering. Such lettering is easy to read, but it does little to convey the **paralanguage** (volume, emphasis, rate, vocal quality, etc.) of human speech. Less tidy, but more expressive lettering comes closer to representing qualites of the spoken word. Aspects of paralanguage can be suggested visually by varying the size, thickness, and shape of both the words and the balloons or boxes that contain them.

Because of the "ZAP," "POW," and "ZOWIE" of the sixties *Batman* television series, onomatopoeic sound effects are probably one of the best-known features of the comic book. While such sound effects add the element of "sound" to the action, they also clutter the artwork, and often, probably also due in good measure to the *Batman* television show, seem juvenile. Yet some artists, particularly Walter Simonson, Howard Chaykin, and Ken Bruzenak, have created imaginative sound effects which, rather than impeding the artwork, become part of the page design and could even narrate a sequence of actions that we do not actually see in the panel. For example, in the second image in Figure 6.17, the sound effects communicate that Luther made a heavy belly flop into the snow with a *"splongksh"* sound, grabbed a car bumper that popped of with a *"poinck,"* and then the car sped away with a *"vrooom."*

Of the three types of sound, music is the one least effectively represented in comic books. The words of a song, and even the musical score, can be placed in a comic book panel, but for those who are not familiar with the song or do not read music, it is merely text. However, the pictures can give clues as to the type of music and the readers can fill in sounds from their own experiences.

Pictorial-Linguistic Blend

One of the most intriguing elements of comic book composition is the combination of the pictorial and the linguistic. It is the blend of pictures and printed words that make comic books a unique form of communication. However, this blend is not always an exact balance between the two components. Traditionally, the artwork has received the greatest emphasis. Reitberger and Fuchs make the generalization that a comic "is bad—that is it lacks effect—if it is too wordy where a picture would be more striking" (230). However, a comic book that tackles weighty moral or philosophical issues is likely to rely on words to carry most of the meaning. There are even times when duplication between words and pictures can be effective.

It is the proper emphasis and interaction of pictorial and linguistic that is the basis of effective comic book communication. In *Understanding Comics*, McCloud details categories of word and picture combination. In *word-specific* combinations, the pictures illustrate, but do not significantly add to, a largely complete text. In *picture-specific* combinations, words do little more than add a soundtrack to a sequence told with pictures. Words and pictures communicate essentially the same message in the *duo-specific* combination. Cartoonist Art Spiegelman says he used to believe that "repeating what's in a picture in the words is bad comics by definition," but he has come to realize that overlap of the visual and linguistic "can create a strong mood, stronger than when you're given the information only one way or the other" (qtd. in Van Hise 81). In *additive combinations*, words amplify or elaborate on a picture or vice versa. In rare instances the pictures and the words seem to follow very different, non-intersecting narrative paths in *parallel* combinations. A *montage* combination uses words as integral parts of the picture. The comic book form is at its most powerful when words and pictures go hand-in-hand to convey an idea that neither could convey alone in an *interdependent* combination.

Art Style

Encapsulation, layout, and composition are what comic book creators do; style is how it is done. According to Eisner, "the reality is that art style tells the story" (*Graphic* 155). The very manner in which an artist draws a line has expressive power. An artist can communicate emotional tone by varying width, direction, curve, or even number of lines.

Style is difficult to reduce to categories and rules. Harvey believes that style is too elusive and individualistic to be fully described by the theorist or evaluated by the critic. Perhaps style is impossible to capture in concrete, referential language and must be described with expressive language. For instance, artist Neal Adams described the style of fellow artist Joe Kubert as coming "from a very primitive place," a "gut-level powerful style" full of "gristle," while artist Wally Wood's style has been described as "cool, clean lines and careful balance of light and shade" (Garriock 90). Jack Kirby's style is distinctive for what critic Thomas Durwood characterizes as "the unprecedented libidinous energy that surges through the main characters as they fight one another in violent scenes of really primal fear and intensity" (3). In the following chapter on experiencing the story, we will consider more of the emotional impact that can be created by art style.

The use of language in a comic book can also have a distinctive style. Certainly writer Stan Lee's captions and dialogue in early Marvel Comics had a distinctive style that was alternately operatic and breezy. Another writer, Brian Michael Bendis, became popular partly due to his ability to write dialogue that mimics the fragments and disfluencies of actual conversation. Brian Azzerello, in his crime comics such as *100 Bullets*, convincingly captures the vernacular of the streets. Alan Moore, perhaps the most lauded of comic book writers, is known for intricately devised plots and beautifully crafted sentences. Yet even with Moore, in whose detailed scripts the description of a single panel might go on for pages, the writing process is fragmented because Moore must rely on an artist to make manifest his concepts.

Eisner believes the best comic books are produced when the artistic style and the linguistic style are unified by a single person creating both the words and the pictures. In fact, Eisner sees comic book "writing" as a creative act done with both words and pictures wherein "the images are employed as a language" (*Graphic 5*).

ANALYZING: CHOICES AND TECHNIQUES

Frank Miller's run on *Daredevil* from 1979 to the mid-1980s contained a level of formal experimentation that had not been seen since Will Eisner's work on *The Spirit* in the 1940s. That is why we have chosen to demonstrate how encapsulation, layout, and composition choices can be analyzed using an interesting page from a 1982 story Miller drew and co-wrote with Roger McKenzie (see Figure 6.19).

Miller and McKenzie's paradigmatic choices on this page must be considered in the context of the preceding pages. On the two previous pages, Mary, a twelve-year-old girl who has taken angel dust, begins hallucinating and foaming at the mouth during a civics class in which guest Matt Murdock is lecturing about the Constitution. In the final panel of the previous page, Mary is leaping toward the window.

The page we are examining depicts Mary's leap from the window, and, in response, Murdock's transformation into Daredevil. There are only two pictures of Mary, but their placement on the page involves us in her death. If we follow the natural reading path from left to right, we experience/imagine Mary's path through the window. The composition of the panel makes the incident even more horrific. The orientation of Mary's body and the shards of shattered glass radiating from her head indicate that she crashed through the window face-first. Normally, after we have taken in all the information in a panel, there is a slight break in our reading as we move to the next encapsulated moment. However, in this instance we experience no break; our reading flows into a new space because there are elements of the panel, the glass shards, that lead us across the

FIGURE 6.19. "Child's Play" *Daredevil* #183 (1982) by Frank Miller and Roger McKenzie. © 2008 Marvel Entertainment, Inc. and its subsidiaries

panel border and down the page. In following the shards from the top of the page down to the bottom, we participate in Mary's plunge to the pavement until our eyes stop abruptly, as if on impact, at her crumpled body. That small body, in the midst of a white space, lacking a panel border or background details, invites us to linger on the tragedy longer than we would if there were an immediately adjacent panel demanding our attention.

We have been led to the bottom right of the page, a point from which we would normally proceed to the next page. However, there are four panels on this page to which we have given only peripheral attention. A page layout that requires the reader to go back up and to the left is certainly unconventional, and neophyte comic book readers might be confused by the reading path. Most experienced comic book readers would have no problem deciphering the reading path, though, and might not even have to give focused attention to the remaining four panels. Readers tend to take in a page at a glance before engaging with its reading path, and experienced comic book readers would likely glean enough information in that glance to know that the four remaining panels depict a typical transformation from civilian to superhero identity.

Of course, relying on that mere glance, readers might miss some of the subtleties of the composition in these four panels. For example, the third panel in this scene, showing Murdoch in silhouette behind the storeroom door, is an intertextual reference to an often-repeated image of Clark Kent ripping open his shirt to reveal his Superman costume. This image appeared occasionally in the comic books, but is best known from the 1950s television series in which Kent would routinely duck into a storeroom at the Daily Planet when Superman was needed.

The four panels showing Murdoch's reaction are a good example of the sort of synecdoche used in portraying actions. We do not see every action Murdoch performs between leaving the classroom and emerging from the storeroom as Daredevil, but the four pictures presented in these panels give us enough information to understand what has happened. They also demonstrate how movement can be suggested by static images. Daredevil's posture indicates vigorous running, and the way the picture laps over the panel border creates a sense of depth, as if the superhero is coming off the page toward us. Even though it is in the middle of the page, this panel acts as the cliffhanger panel (what is Daredevil going to do?), and his bursting forth from the page creates a sense of energy that propels us to the next page.

We have written this analysis of Miller and McKenzie's creative choices in terms of how those choices direct and affect us as readers. In the next chapter we will undertake a more detailed examination of the interactive nature of the comic book form and how we create our own meanings from the reading experience.

Discussion Questions

1. Do you agree with Eisner's assessment that unified writing (words and pictures created by the same person) is inherently superior to fragmented writing (one person writing the words and another drawing the pictures)? If you agree, can you explain why the unified process is better? If you disagree, can you give some examples of successful collaborations you consider to be just as good as any unified writing?

2. The authors characterize Figure 6.14 as confusing and 6.15 as brilliant. Do you agree with these assessments? If so, what do you find confusing about Figure 6.14? What do you find most effective about Figure 6.15?
3. In the analysis of Figure 6.19 at the end of the chapter, we discussed how the shards of falling glass lead the reader from Mary at the top of the page to her fallen body at the bottom of the page. This layout is a good example of the flexibility of the panel concept. Is Mary's leap and fall depicted in two panels or three panels? If it is only two panels, where is the border between the panels?

Activities

1. On the following pages you will find a short comics story, "Our Block," by Will Eisner. Use the concepts discussed in this chapter to analyze how Eisner uses the comic book form to tell this story. Pay particular attention to his paradigmatic choices, how background detail helps tell the story, and how visual depiction of sound (or lack of sound) contributes to the story. Decide if the final page of the story is a single panel or contains a number of panels.
2. Adapt a short prose story into a comic book. Ernest Hemingway's "Hills Like White Elephants" works well for this assignment, but your instructor might assign a different story. You can do this assignment as thumbnail sketches with word balloons and captions included or as a full script. As you plan and write your story, think about a) what important moments from the visualized story you want to encapsulate in panels, b) what moments need to go together on the page, c) how best to arrange the panels on the page, and d) how best to compose the elements within each panel. Even if you can't draw, it is probably useful to sketch out thumbnails of each page to help you with the problem-solving process.

Recommended Readings

Comics:

Eisner, Will. *New York: The Big City*. New York: DC Comics, 2000.

> The vignettes that comprise this collection are not only poignant glimpses of Eisner's beloved New York City, but they are also experiments in storytelling technique.

Lutes, Jason. *Jar of Fools*. Montreal, Quebec: Drawn and Quarterly, 2003.

> On the surface there is nothing flashy about this sparsely told tale of loss and redemption, but a careful reading of Lutes' masterful choices of encapsulation, composition, and layout reveal a rich subtext that make this a work of literature.

Scholarly Sources:

Groensteen, Thierry. *The System of Comics*. Translated by Bart Beaty and Nick Nguyen. Jackson, MS: University Press of Mississippi, 2007.

> This ambitious attempt to build a comprehensive theory of comics as a sign system was first published in France in 1999. It provides and excellent introduction to the European comics scholarship that was flourishing decades before serious study of the art form was undertaken by American scholars.

McCloud, Scott. *Making Comics: Storytelling Secrets of Comics, Manga and Graphic Novels*. New York: Harper, 2006.

Among the dozens of how-to books in the marketplace, McCloud's stands out as more genuinely theoretical and entertaining than the rest.

"Our Block" from New York: Life in the Big City (1986)

FIGURE 6.20   Will Eisner's "The Block" from *New York: Life in the Big City* (1986). Copyright © 1981, 1982, 1983, 1986 by Will Eisner. Copyright © 2006 by the Estate of Will Eisner. From Will Eisner's *New York: Life in the Big City* by Will Eisner. Used by permission of W. W. Norton & Company, Inc.

"Our Block" from New York: Life in the Big City (1986) *continued*

"Our Block" from New York: Life in the Big City (1986) *continued*

Experiencing the Story

"The whole brain activity that is activated by reading comic books is what provides the 'comic book experience'; a fulfilling fantasy involvement with the printed page that one gets from no other media."

—Rick Veitch, cartoonist, 1986

Years ago, one of the authors of this book conducted research on the comic book reading experience. As part of the study, subjects read a short story in an anthology comic book and one hour later answered questions about the story. The story included a swordfight depicted simply in just a few panels. When asked to describe the swordfight, subjects often provided details of dramatic actions and gory wounds that did not actually appear on the printed pages of the comic book. No two descriptions of the swordfight were exactly the same. Subjects were using their imaginations to not only make the static images in the panels come to life, but also to fill in actions between the panels. Each subject's creation of the swordfight was influenced by his or her unique background knowledge. Perhaps some of the subjects had taken fencing lessons. Perhaps some were fans of swashbuckling movies. The comic book reading experience is the result of the interactionbetween what is on the page and the life experience and even the emotional state of each reader.

FIGURE 7.1. McCloud explaining how readers insert their own experiences amongst static images in order to create a narrative flow. Page 67 from *Understanding Comics* © 1993, 1994 by Scott McCloud. Reprinted by permission of HarperCollins Publishers.

OBJECTIVES

In this chapter you will learn:

1. about diegetic images that show the world of the story;
2. about interpretive images that comment on the story;
3. the impact art style has on the emotional reactions of the reader; and
4. how the meaning of each image is affected by the relationship to other images in that particular book, in other texts, and in the reader's personal experience.

In the previous chapter we examined the decisions creators make in the process of encoding a story or idea in the comic book art form. As stated, for comic books, the creative process is reductive, but the reading process is additive. Comic book creators reduce an imagined story to encapsulated fragments (pages and panels), and readers add those fragments together, along with their own background knowledge, to create a story. In this chapter we will explore the active role the reader must take in turning those static fragments into a comprehensible and perhaps compelling narrative.

When fully engaged with a work in the comic book form, the reader has both a **cognitive response**—perceiving, organizing, and interpreting the images on the page in order to construct meaning—and an **affective response**, emotional reactions (e.g., excitement, pity, fear) that arise without conscious effort. The readers' understanding of and reactions to the work are the result of a series of inferences about functions of the images in panels and the relationships between and among panels. In general, the comic book reader begins building meaning from the images within a panel and moves outward to the panel as a whole, panels in relation to other panels, the page, the story, and how the story, in some cases, fits into an ongoing narrative continuity.

DECODING: IMAGES

Comic book reading is an integrated perceptual experience that involves not only the decoding of linguistic and pictorial symbols, but an understanding of the **interanimation of meaning** between the words and the pictures. That is, the reader must understand how text and pictures in the same panel each affect the meaning of the other, and together create a meaning beyond what is communicated by word or picture alone. Because we cannot simultaneously gaze at pictures and read words, there is not an instantaneous unity of perception, but an integration of two different ways of perceiving information. While never truly blending together, words and pictures in a comic book do tend to become more like one another. Jessica Abel and Matt Madden's cleverly titled textbook on creating comics, *Drawing Words & Writing Pictures*, reflects the reality that words are rendered as images on the page and pictures become textualized to the extent they can be read to produce meaning.

Pictures and words have different characteristics and functions, but they both appear on the comic book page as images. In this chapter when we use the term *image*, it refers to not only the pictures of characters and objects, but also to the words that represent dialogue and thoughts (usually in balloons), the words that represent narration (usually in captions), and the words that represent nonlinguistic sounds in the world of the story.

In order to understand comic book communication, readers must make inferences about the functions of images, both pictures and words as images on the page (Hatfield 40–41). Most of these images are used to depict the world of the story, or what is often referred to as the *diegesis*. Readers must distinguish between **sensory diegetic images**, which depict the characters, objects, and sensory environment of the world of the story; **non-sensory diegetic images**, which depict specific memories, emotions, or sensations occurring within characters in the world of the story but undetectable by the senses; and **hermeneutic images**, which are not part of the world of the story, but instead comment on the story and influence how readers interpret it.

Sensory Diegetic Images

We experience the world through our five senses (seeing, hearing, tasting, smelling, touching). Yet, aside from the tactile sensation of holding and turning the pages of a printed volume, reading a comic book is almost totally a visual experience. And, in fact, the vast majority of pictures in a comic book represent visual experience: the people and objects we would see if we lived in the world of the story. Much of what we see in the real world is in motion. A reader can easily imagine similar motion in the world of the story if the artist has successfully employed a combination of the techniques of communicating movement explained in the previous chapter.

Non-visual sensory experiences have to be suggested by visual imagery, and the readers have to "participate in the acting out of the story" in order to "feel" the sensory experiences suggested by author's encapsulation and composition choices (Eisner, *Graphic* 57). In the following section we will briefly consider how each of the other four senses can be stimulated and simulated in the readers' imagination by the comic book creators' use of images.

Readers seem to vary in how they experience the sound elements of a comic book. Some are actively engaged in imagining the sound effects and distinct voices of each character, while others understand the content of the dialogue without "hearing" the voices. How a reader responds to the sound images of a comic can be influenced by the skill with which the words are lettered. The expressive lettering of a cartoonist such as Dave Sim or a letterer such as Todd Klein can communicate volume, rate, inflection, and other vocal aspects of human (or Inhuman, gorilla, etc.) speech. Some "artists with a strong personality, like Robert Crumb, have a style of lettering—and a matching tone—that is unmistakenly [*sic*] theirs" (Pollman 17). In other words, we can "hear" an author's distinctive voice telling us a story.

As comics scholar Gene Kannenberg, Jr. points out in his study of graphic text, even the shape of the balloon in which the text appears can communicate something about the nature of the sound:

> For *thought*, the balloon's edge is scalloped and the tail is replaced by a series of small circles or bubbles. *Whispering* is indicated either by forming the balloon with a dashed line or by using smaller-than-normal text. To convey *shouting*, a balloon's edge is spiked, or the text is made relatively larger than that used for normal speech. Similarly, *electronic speech* can be simulated by a jagged-edge or geometrically shaped balloon. *Sarcasm* has even been awarded its own iconic representation, the "dripping" word balloon ("Graphic" 174).

Nearly all comic book lettering is now digitally applied. While computer lettering might lack the spontaneity of hand lettering, it can still be distinctive. Todd Klein has developed over a hundred computer fonts that he sees as "an extension of my personal style."

Dialogue is the type of sound most commonly represented in comic books, but the most dramatically presented sound images are the inventive and often boldly lettered words that represent non-vocal sounds, from the faint impact of a single drop of sweat to the shattering force of a super-powered punch. Such sound effects are **onomatopoeia**—invented words that mimic sounds—and due to the infamous "Pow!" and "Zowie!" of the *Batman* television show, they are one of the elements the general public most associates with comic books. Those sound effects that were campy fun in the 1960s have grown clichéd and puerile,

FIGURE 7.2. Letterer Todd Klein creates a distinctive font and balloon—and, thus, a distinct "sound"—for each character in this panel from *Sandman* #47 (1993) © DC Comics

but, as evidenced by the Chaykin sound effects shown in Chapter 6, comics creators are constantly developing new means, both subtle and outrageous, to communicate sound.

The sensation of taste is conveyed by both verbal and nonverbal reactions. Words such as "yum" or "yuck" can broadly indicate a positive or negative sensation of taste, but flavors are more precisely communicated by facial expressions. If in one panel a character puts something in his or her mouth and in the next panel is smiling, we take that as an indication of a pleasant taste, whereas we take a contorted face to mean a sour or bitter taste. A smell can be abstractly represented by graphic conventions, often first established in comic strips, such as lines wafting off a freshly baked apple pie. Odor can be implied by showing phenomena commonly associated with strong smells, such as flies buzzing around a garbage can or exaggerated but stereotypical character reactions such as a man holding his nose. In *Fun Home* (2007) Alison Bechdel uses a few scent lines, but also takes the unconventional approach of labeling the smells of summer in the city. Bechdel's drawing of a busy New York street is accompanied by seven captions with arrows. One caption pointing down the subway says "urine and electricity," and one pointing at a pedestrian says "Brut" (a cologne popular in the time period depicted).

Subtleties of touch are not easily communicated in the comics form. Generally, only the most extreme tactile sensations, such as punching and blasting, are depicted in comic books. However, when more familiar touch encounters, such as handshakes and embraces, are pictured, they are "felt" in terms of a reader's own experiences of touch. Similarly, a sense of weight or pressure can be conveyed by postures associated with effort and facial expressions associated with strain.

Non-Sensory Diegetic Images

So far we have only been dealing with those aspects of the world that can be perceived with the senses. There are also aspects of existence—like thoughts, emotions, and psychological states—that must be perceived by other means. While they cannot actually be seen in the real world, in a comic book narrative these non-sensory aspects of the diegesis have to be represented visually. Sometimes the communication is direct, as with thoughts written out in scalloped thought balloons. Occasionally artists employ pictorial representations of thoughts or feelings (see Figure 7.3). For instance, one of the conventions established in comic strips is to use dotted lines and a dagger that seem to be emanating from a character's eyes to indicate the anger behind a look.

FIGURE 7.3. In *Jar of Fools* (1994–1997) Jason Lutes uses pictures rather than words in a thought balloon to communicate a hungry man imagining pigeons as a piping-hot meal. © Jason Lutes

FIGURE 7.4. Craig Thompson masterfully portrays a confused state of mind in his autobiographical graphic novel *Blankets* (2003). © Craig Thompson and Courtesy of Top Shelf

Other times, characters' internal states are represented by implication. For instance, in the graphic novel *Blankets* (2003), when Craig awakens the first morning in a strange house and does not remember where he is for a few moments, his confusion is represented by ellipses in the balloon above his head and, in the background, blank panels are interspersed with panels depicting fragments of memory (see Figure 7.4).

The comic book form cannot truly show the world of the story, but can only suggest it by employing the device of **synecdoche**, using a part of something to represent the whole of the thing. All images on the comic book page stand for more reality than they can depict. First, the images are, by necessity, an abstraction from the real. Comic book drawings are often highly exaggerated or simplified, but even the most detailed drawings or paintings fall far short of reproducing reality. Second, because panels occupy a finite and often small space, the images in them usually show only a portion of objects and beings. Readers use their background knowledge to understand what is not shown. Figure 7.5 illustrates how the process of synecdoche works on an individual figure or on an entire city.

Hermeneutic Images

Hermeneutic images, whether linguistic or pictorial, are not meant to represent sounds or objects that exist in the world of the story; instead they comment on the story itself. Words that serve a hermeneutic function are not embedded in the story; no one in the world of the story is speaking or thinking these words. Instead, these words are commentary on the story, and are addressed directly to the reader. While these words by necessity exist on the page as images, they are bland images, lacking the expressiveness of dialogue or sound effects. They are presented in a straightforward manner so that the focus is on the linguistic content. Readers are not expected to "hear" these words. Of course, there are always exceptions, such as the captions in which Stan Lee, a distinct personality to most Marvel Comics readers of the sixties and seventies, chatted with readers, many of whom imagined his voice.

Lee's quips to readers are clearly hermeneutic (they are not words that exist in the world of the story), but they do little to influence interpretation of the story. On the other hand, the words of first person narrators, especially in memoir comics, can be very directive as to how readers should feel about the events depicted, but they are not clearly hermeneutic. Such narration is not heard by other characters in world of the story, but it is at least partially diegetic because it is the words of the chief character in the world of the story. Purely hermeneutic text that is separated from the world of the story is rare in comic books.

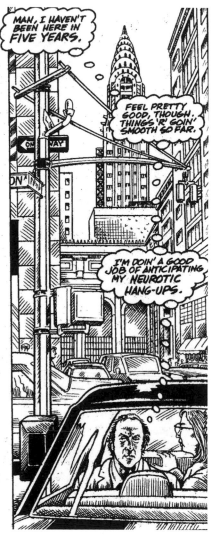

FIGURE 7.5. This panel from *American Splendor Special* (1994) presents enough elements (tall buildings, traffic, light pole, etc.) to connote a big city, and the familiar Chrysler Building is emblematic of New York City. Readers can infer the rest of Harvey Pekar's body from the picture of his head and shoulders. © Harvey Pekar

Commentary on the narrative occurs primarily in hermeneutic pictures that can be very rich in meaning. Such images do not simply represent something that exists in or is occurring in the world of the story. Hermeneutic pictures imply more than what is literally shown. Three common types of hermeneutic pictures are psychological images, visual metaphors, and intertextual references.

FIGURE 7.6. In the autobiographical *Bitchy's College Daze* (1997), Roberta Gregory provides a commentary on the personalities of her parents by the way in which she draws them. Courtesy of Fantagraphics Books

A **psychological image** represents some aspect of a character's personality or state of mind. It operates much like the sort of non-sensory diegetic image illustrated in Figure 7.3. However, diegetic images portraying a state of mind are usually objective, an attempt to portray a "reality" of the world of the story, while hermeneutic images tend to be subjective, reflecting a particular narrative point-of-view. Consequently, psychological images serving a hermeneutic function are generally more exaggerated than non-sensory diegetic images. For example, the way cartoonist Roberta Gregory draws her parents (Figure 7.6) is not a realistic depiction—the reader is not meant to believe Gregory's mother is so vacuous that her face consists of only a smile and big eyelashes, or that her father has a mouth full of long fangs and squiggly lines emanating from his body—it is an insight into her attitude toward them and the constant embarrassment she feels.

This is an appropriate instance in which to note that in most cases hermeneutic images are layered over diegetic images. Gregory's drawings comment on her parents (hermeneutic) but also indicate the presence of her parents in the car (diegetic).

Visual metaphors use a picture of one thing to evoke the idea of something else. For example, in *Fun Home* Bechdel uses a visual metaphor to communicate the depth of her father's obsession with the historical restoration of their old home. Bechdel draws her father struggling under the weight of a pillar he carries on his shoulder in a manner sure to evoke Jesus staggering under the weight of the cross, particularly when considered in conjunction with the text in the accompanying captions: "It was his passion. And I mean passion in every sense of the word. Libidinal. Manic. Martyred" (7). In this example, the picture and the text collaborate to carry off the metaphor. What we are terming *visual metaphors* are not always strictly pictorial in nature, because picture images and text images in a panel often work together to create the association.

It is also usually true that the reader must understand broader contexts than just the information on the page in order to understand the metaphor.

The publication of *Maus* brought Art Spiegelman a degree of fame and fortune to which he had not been accustomed. As he worked on *Maus II*, Spiegelman had qualms about his success. On the opening page of the second chapter of *Maus II*, these doubts are not clearly expressed in words, but are cleverly suggested by visual metaphors (Figure 7.7). One of the visual conceits of *Maus* is that all of the Jews, including Spiegelman himself, are drawn as mice. The image of a human head behind the mouse mask seems to indicate that Spiegelman feels he is hiding behind or even defined by his own autobiographical persona from the graphic novel. In the third panel of Figure 7.7 we see Spiegelman's drawing table atop a mound of naked corpses (as indicated by the flies). To read this image as representing Spiegelman's misgivings that he has built his career on the

FIGURE 7.7. *In Maus: A Survivor's Tale II* (1991), Art Spiegelman uses two visual metaphors: depicting himself as a human wearing a mouse mask and showing his drawing table perched atop the bodies of Holocaust victims. From *Maus II: A Survivor's Tale/And Here My Trouble Began* by Art Spiegelman, copyright © 1986, 1989, 1990, 1991 by Art Spiegelman. Used by permission of Pantheon Books, a division of Random House, Inc.

suffering of others, Holocaust victims in general and his own family in particular, the reader must understand the context of Spiegelman's earlier work, the arc of his career, and even aspects of his personality established in his earlier work. It is not uncommon for visual metaphors to derive their meaning from reference to other texts or events—that is, they are intertextual.

Intertextual images remind the reader of something he or she has encountered in other media (movies, books, paintings, TV shows, etc.). Some intertextual pictures refer to real-life events, but of course, most of us only see those events indirectly, as reports in newspapers or on television. A writer or artist might intend for a picture to be an intertextual reference, but whether the picture has the intended meaning for a particular reader depends on that reader's background knowledge. For instance, most Americans over fifty would immediately recognize the panel in Figure 7.8 as a reference to the Oswald assassination, but the image might have no intertextual meaning for many adolescent and young adult readers.

Even the pencil lines with which a picture is drawn and the brush strokes with which it is inked can have a hermeneutic function. For example, in Figure 7.6 Roberta Gregory's commentary on her parents is communicated primarily by the clean and simple lines for the mother she considers to be simple-minded, and a jagged, cluttered style for her always-angry father. Gregory's drawings

FIGURE 7.8. This drawing of Speedball being shot in *Civil War: Front Line* #7 (2006) is an intertextual picture that will remind many readers of the famous photo or news footage of Jack Ruby shooting Lee Harvey Oswald. © 2008 Marvel Entertainment, Inc. and its subsidiaries

of her parents, while not pure examples of the styles, tend toward two very different approaches to comics art often referred to as the *clear line style* and *ugly* (or brut) *art*.

Readers can develop expectations about story content and tone from the style of art before they even read the first panel. A clear line style is usually associated with a lighthearted adventure in which the heroes are sure to triumph over the bad guys (e.g., *Tintin, Legion of Super-Heroes in the 31st Century*). An ugly (brut) art style is more likely to depict a pessimistic worldview in which triumph is not an option and the best the protagonist can hope for is survival (e.g., Ben Templesmith's cartoon-noir pencils and moody coloring in *Fell*; Keith Giffin's José Muñoz–inspired style in the "Five Years Later" storyline of *Legion of Super-Heroes* volume 4). These are, of course, generalizations, and plenty of exceptions can be found. For example, in *Jimmy Corrigan: The Smartest Kid on Earth*, Chris Ware tells a pessimistic story in a clean line style, but the reader soon understands that, like the title of the work, the art style is a commentary on the main character's delusions.

Mixing the clean line and brut art styles in the same story can encourage certain responses from readers, particularly when there is a stark contrast in how characters are depicted. In one of a series of "Waiting" vignettes (Figure 7.9) by Linda Perkins and Dean Haspiel, the waitress is drawn in a clear line style that makes her attractive, while customers who ask annoying questions are drawn in an ugly art style that makes them unattractive, if not repulsive. The art makes a hermeneutic comment on the characters—nice waitress, exasperating customers—and the natural affective response of most readers is likely to be to side with the waitress.

Of course, reaction to the "Waiting" vignette is not solely dependent on the art style. The drawings of the characters have clearer meaning and more emotional impact when considered in relation to the accompanying text, which shows that the customers are asking a question answered in the very menu they hold.

FIGURE 7.9. The use of ugly art directs the reader's sympathy in "Waiting" in *Keyhole* #1 (1996). Story by Linda Perkins and art by Dean Haspiel.

Comic book readers have to make inferences not only about the function of images, but also about the contexts and relationships in which those images appear. Images in a comic book do not exist in isolation; they are encapsulated in a panel. And each panel exists within larger units of meaning—the page, the sequence, and the story.

DECODING: PANELS

The meaning of each image is affected by its relationship with other images, whether those in the same panel, in other panels, or in other texts. The interpretation of an image is also likely to be affected by the reality, the individual experience, of each reader.

Other Images in the Panel

The comprehension of what each picture image represents and what each text image means can be a virtually instantaneous and barely noticeable operation, but after that first glance, readers immediately begin modifying their understanding of the image by considering it in the context of the other images around it.

Cognitive (comprehension) and **affective** (emotional) reactions to an image are often influenced by reactions to other images in the same panel. For instance, a car shown with speed lines behind it out-distancing another car makes readers think about the speed at which a car can travel. Readers did not necessarily think about the weight of a car until they encountered that cover of *Action Comics* #1, with Superman holding a car over his head. The relationship between the images of the car and the man made the weight the most significant characteristic of the car for that particular drawing. In panels depicting a battle, Jack Kirby often drew

flying debris that had no clear source, but it effectively conveyed the impact of a blast or a punch.

Quieter and more complex inter-animation of meaning can occur in simple conversations (see Figure 7.10). In one of his autobiographical comic books, Seth depicts a visit with his brother. Seth, neat and trim in his coat and tie, is frowning. Stephen, overweight and sloppy in his Bayfield T-shirt, is grinning. Seth holds a pen and Stephen holds a television remote. The assumptions readers make about each character are heightened by the contrast between the images. Understanding the relationship between the images in this panel leads to inferences about the relationship between the brothers. Of course, this panel is just one of a series of panels presenting the conversation, and each panel in the series adds more information and potentially alters the reader's assessment of the characters.

Inferences about the relationships between images create a synthesis of those images, an understanding of the panel as a totality. And it is not merely an understanding of the panel as a frozen tableau of related images, but as an event, or most often a segment of an event, spanning a certain period of time. A reader actively engaged with the story incorporates each panel, each segment of time, into the narrative that has been encountered up to that point and into the narrative that has been anticipated based on a scanning or peripheral awareness of yet-to-be-read panels on the page or the adjoining page. The process of incorporation and the flow of the narrative in the reader's imagination is facilitated by repetition and change from panel to panel.

Images in Other Panels

European comics scholar Ann Miller claims comic books are "an art of both iteration and transformation" in which the narrative is moved forward in consecutive panels by "the conservation of certain elements and the modification of others" (88). There is, of course, always some iteration, or repetition, because the principal characters of the story appear in the majority of panels. There is also the need for the characters to be identifiable from panel to panel so the reader can follow who is doing what. Especially in the days when even the best of artists, such as Jack Kirby, drew generic and virtually indistinguishable faces, superhero costumes served this function: You could always tell which character was Captain America. This device was often used in other genres as well: cowboys, detectives, and even jungle queens were pictured in the same distinctive clothing, panel after panel and issue after issue.

The story is advanced when repetition of key elements (e.g., characters, setting) are combined with some degree of change. Differences in or the transformation of images advance the narrative with new information about location or character actions and emotions. A portion of a page from David Lapham's *Stray Bullets* demonstrates the power of repetition and difference to convey information even with the aid of text (see Figure 7.11). The first three panels show preparation for and anticipation of a romantic encounter. Some of these images, and even the point of view from which the reader sees the images, are repeated later on the page. However, the narrative is advanced primarily by the transformation of images. Panels four and five communicate a passage of time. In panel four it is obviously dark outside and so late at night the candles have burned all the way down. In panel five the singing birds and the angle of the sun's rays indicate early morning. In panels three and six the man is sitting in almost the same position on the couch, but aspects of panel three have been significantly transformed in panel six—the music has stopped, the previously clean-shaven man has stubble, the look of anticipation has turned to a scowl, and the **emanata** above his head indicates he is "steaming" mad. The reader's understanding of the images in this panel is dependent not only on the contrast with the previous images of the character, but also upon the intervening panels that stress just how long he has been sitting and waiting.

Belgian comics scholar Thierry Groenstcen cautions that, while repetition and difference are often used to advance the narrative, comic books can employ "all sorts of narrative strategies" and "redundancy is far from being an obligatory bridge between two consecutive panels of a narrative sequence" (*System* 117). Some comics theorists believe the static images in panels become a narrative flow primarily due to the work readers do in blending panels together.

The Panel in Relation to Other Panels

The chief task of comic book creators is to reduce the imagined story to images encapsulated in panels. The reader must

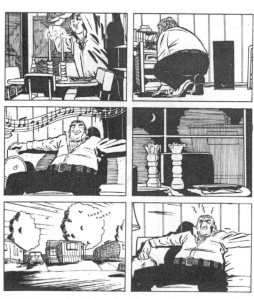

FIGURE 7.11. In this portion of a page from *Stray Bullets* #9 (1996), the narrative is advanced by repetition and difference. Art by and © David Lapham.

FIGURE 7.12. Even though these two panels from *Carnet de Voyage* (2004) have no borders and no gutter between them, we understand they are two distinct panels due to the captions, the repeated figure of the main character, and the different settings. © Craig Thompson and Courtesy of Top Shelf.

then work at blending those static panels into a narrative experience. In order to explain the work the reader performs between and among the panels, Scott McCloud adapted from gestalt psychology the concept of **closure**—creating a whole from fragments. As it has been applied to comics, closure refers to the reader applying background knowledge and an understanding of the relationships between encapsulated images to synthesize (or blend) sequences of panels into events, and those sequences of events into an overall story.

The comic book reader performs closure within each panel, between panels, and among panels. Earlier in the chapter we examined the inferences a reader makes to create meaning from the fragmentary images within a panel. We now turn our attention to closure between and among panels, the filling in or blending together of panels that transforms the encapsulated static moments into a continuous flow of narrative.

As a number of comics scholars have noted, panels do not have to be surrounded by a box, and there does not have to be a white space (referred to as a *gutter*) between panels (see Figure 7.12). As Mario Saraceni points out, the gutter is conceptual (55). Similarly, Jeffery Miller believes that when McCloud speaks of filling in the gap of the gutter, "we cannot take this to be anything but a metaphor." For Miller, the "sense-making...occurs in the interaction between text, reader, and culture." Robert O'Nale proposes that readers progress through a series of panels not by adding information between panels, but by adding the panels to the background knowledge they already possess, including expectations created by the comic book form itself and that particular book's cover and genre.

Closure, or the construction of meaning from fragments, does not occur only between two panels at a time because, as Groensteen points out, "every panel exists, potentially if not actually, in relation with each of the others" (*System* 146). The reader performs an ongoing construction of meaning by considering each panel in direct relationship to the immediately previous panel and in the context of all previous panels. The understanding of the next panel can also be influenced by a number of the panels yet to come because "the focal vision never ceases to be enriched by peripheral visions," and the reader can scan ahead to other panels on a page or even on the facing page (Groensteen, *System* 19). And each next panel has the potential to provide new information that creates a "retroactive determination" of the meaning of one or more previous panels (Groensteen, *System* 110) (see Figure 7.13).

Readers also engage in a sort of closure among the panels on a particular page, considering them in relation to the totality of the page. Each panel is both an element of encapsulated action (perceived as time) and an element in the design of the page layout (perceived as space). Each page is experienced as both **linear** (a sequence of events encapsulated in panels) and **holistic** (a designed object). The linear, narrative function of

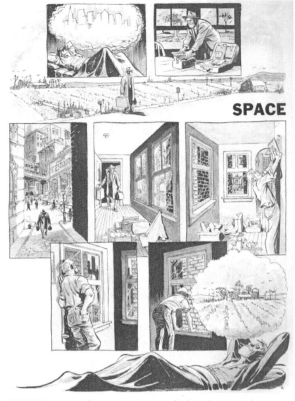

FIGURE 7.13. In this one-page story, the last three panels retroactively change the meaning of the first three panels. "Space" © 1981, 1982, 1983, 1986 by Will Eisner. © 2006 by the Estate of Will Eisner. From Will Eisner's *New York: Life in the Big City* by Will Eisner. Used by Permission of W. W. Norton & Company, Inc.

the page usually dominates the reader's attention, and, in fact, pages often encapsulate a full scene or otherwise meaningful segment of the narrative. Yet on rare occasions pages are so highly designed that their function is more lyrical than narrative.

ANALYZING: THE FUNCTIONS OF IMAGES

Three panels from Craig Thompson's memoir graphic novel *Blankets* (2003) illustrate the three functions (sensory diegetic, non-sensory diegetic, and hermeneutic) of comic book images (see Figure 7.14). The multiple pictures of the two brothers, Craig and Phil, are clearly sensory diegetic images; they are fairly realistically rendered representations of the brothers as we would see them if we were in the world of the story. The word images in balloons are also part of the sensory diegesis; they represent the spoken words we would hear if we

were in the world of the story. Our analysis will focus on the background details, or lack thereof, on this page.

The pictures of the landscape in panel one are sensory diegetic images giving us enough details that we can infer a woodland setting. The drawings of the trees are not hyper-realistic, but they clearly provide the idea of trees so we can, through the process of synecdoche, rely on our own experiences of the woods to complete the setting in our imaginations.

The background details in panel two demonstrate that images can operate in multiple modes. The pictures here do not represent a setting, but two internal faculties not accessible to the senses. They function as non-sensory diegetic images illustrating a blending of Craig's memory and imagination. Yet the exaggerated nature of the images—a winged lizard and angels—give a clue that they are doing more than accurately rep-

FIGURE 7.14. *Blankets* by Craig Thompson (2003). © Craig Thompson and Courtesy of Top Shelf.

resenting an internal state. The images also serve a hermeneutic function, because Thompson uses them to alert the reader that he is an unreliable narrator whose fertile imagination cannot always be trusted. The meaning of these images is only fully understood as a commentary on Craig's fanciful imagination when we consider them in relation to the background in panel three.

It is not unusual for a comic book artist to drop out the background details and focus on characters once a setting has been established. However, in panel three the choice to use no image is clearly hermeneutic when considered in the context of the previous two panels and Phil's dialogue in the panel: The blank background is a visual metaphor for Phil's lack of imagination. This metaphor is reinforced by Phil's matter-of-fact dialogue and the contrast to Craig's vivid imagination represented in the background details of panel two.

It is not possible for a reader to passively receive meaning from a comic book. Even comprehending what each picture represents and what each word means requires some effort, and moving beyond image comprehension to understanding the panel as a whole and how it fits into the overall narrative requires comic book readers to make inferences about the functions of images and the relationships between images.

Artist Brent Anderson believes that for a comic book to be effective, the reader has to be actively involved in creating meaning. The comic book creators facilitate this process with their decisions about what to show and how to show it. If too little information is given then the story is incomprehensible, but if the artist provides too much information then the reading experience is boring. Says Anderson, "I try to give them just enough communication to be stimulating."

Discussion Questions

1. Many carefully selected and crafted details that might give nuance to the meaning of a story can be overlooked as readers are impelled through the story from action to action. This is particularly true for young readers, but even mature readers often do a rapid and superficial first reading, to experience the reading rush, and then go back through the book to appreciate elements of craft. Take another, more careful look at a comic book or graphic novel you read recently. Do you find significant diegetic or hermeneutic images your overlooked on your first reading? Does taking these images into account alter your interpretation of the story?

2. Look again at Figure 7.10. What inferences can you make about the personality of each character? What inferences can you make about the relationship between these two characters? Explain how the cartoonist's image choices influenced your inferences.

3. In this chapter we argued that you cannot be a passive consumer of comics. How would you compare the amount of activity you have to engage in with comics with that of other media? Is the activity more active or less so than media such as television, books, video games, etc.? Why is this so in each case?

Activities

1. Design experiments to test one or more of the following hypotheses:

   - H1: Language-oriented readers move through a comic book from one grouping of words (balloons, captions, etc.) to another, taking in pictures as secondary information.
   - H2: Visual-oriented readers move through a comic book from picture to picture, taking in words as secondary information.
   - H3: Visual-oriented readers are more aware of words as images (lettering technique, color, etc.).

   First, devise a way to measure the language or visual orientation. You might do this with a questionnaire to determine the amount of time each subject spends on reading activities (books, newspapers, etc.) and viewing activities (television, movies, YouTube, etc.). Another approach is to determine each subject's learning style using the free tests which are available at a number of sites, including: *www.ldpride.net/learning-style-test.html* and *www.learning-styles-online.com/inventory*.

Next, devise a method for determining how each subject goes about reading a comic book. Will you observe them while they read? Will you rely on some form of self-reporting (questionnaire or interview) immediately after the reading? You might want to use a combination of these methods, or devise your own approach.

2. Take another look at Figure 6.3 and describe the diegetic and hermeneutic images in these panels from Craig Thompson's *Blankets*.

Recommended Readings

Comics:

Kuper, Peter. *The System*. New York: DC Comics, 1997.

A virtually "silent" comic book that, even more than a comic with text, requires the reader to actively engage in making inferences in order to construct a narrative.

Thompson, Craig. *Blankets*. Marietta, GA: Top Shelf, 2003.

In this multiple award–winning graphic novel, Thompson blends well-chosen diegetic images that create the world of the story with clever hermeneutic images that create a poignant subtext.

Scholarly Sources:

McCloud, Scott. *Understanding Comics*. Northhampton, MA: Tundra Publishing, 1993.

The first formal theory of comics undertaken in the English language. Since 1993 all American comic scholars have explained their theories of comic books in terms of how they agree with or differ from McCloud.

Varnum, Robin, and Christina T. Gibbons, eds. *The Language of Comics: Word and Image*. Jackson, MS: University Press of Mississippi, 2001.

A collection of insightful essays on how pictures and text interact to create meaning in comic books and strips.

The Comic Book Readers

"I've always wondered: Are these normal people who have been turned strange by comic books? Or were they strange already and comic books just attracted them?"

—Steve Fischler, retailer, 1998

The architect of the so-called "Silver Age" of superhero comic books, Julius Schwartz, began his career as a fan. Back in 1931—three years before the "official" birth of the comic book—fifteen-year-old Julie Schwartz met fellow teen Mort Weisinger at a gathering of science fiction enthusiasts known as the Scienceers. The next year the two young men gave the fledgling science fiction fan movement momentum when they published *The Time Traveler*, the first nationally distributed fan magazine, or **fanzine**, devoted to science fiction. Two years later, Schwartz and Weisinger turned their avocation into their vocation when they formed Solar Sales Service, the first literary agency for science fiction writers. Their clients included soon-to-be notables such as Ray Bradbury, Otto Binder, H.P. Lovecraft, and Edmond Hamilton.

After Superman was introduced in *Action Comics* in 1938, comic books began attracting both fans and writers of fantastic literature. A number of the Solar Sales Service stable of writers, notably Otto Binder and Alfred Bester, made the transition from pulp magazines to comic books. Starting in 1944, Schwartz also ended up working at National Periodical Publications—later DC Comics— editing a wide range of titles over the next forty-five years. As a DC editor, Schwartz not only reshaped the comic book medium, but also stimulated the great explosion of comics fandom that occurred in the 1960s.

During the 1940s, while Schwartz was guiding the adventures of Flash, Green Lantern, and the Justice Society of America, some of his fellow science fiction fans were exhibiting the first behaviors of comics fandom: They started saving their old comic books. While the average comic book reader of the time was an eleven- or twelve-year-old who treated the books as disposable entertainment, the science fiction fans tended to be in their teens or twenties (some even older). For years, they had been filling closets and footlockers with pulp magazines and pocket paperbacks, so it was only natural to do the same with this new form of fantastic literature. And it was only a matter of time before they found one another, thanks in part to Schwartz. In 1961 he began printing the

171

FIGURE 8.1. Julius "Julie" Schwartz had one of the longest and most illustrious careers in the comic book industry, editing such series as *Superman,* and it all started while he was a fan. Art from a tribute issue, *Superman* #411 (1985) by Elliot S! Maggin (words) and Curt Swan and Murphy Anderson (art). © DC Comics

addresses of those who wrote letters to the editor. Rather than relying on chance encounters, now the fans had a way to reach one another and begin to build a community of their own.

OBJECTIVES

In this chapter you will learn:

1. how to define fans and recognize them as creators of a culture;
2. the ways in which fandom emerged as a virtual culture through the use of print media;
3. about how conventions and fan publications helped further develop fan culture;
4. how intertextual relationships become a major focus of fan conversations; and
5. to recognize the potential conflict that emerges between participatory culture and the cultural industries.

Julius Scwartz was one of the lucky few fans who managed to make the transition to professional. But crucially, he not only got to work in a medium he loved, he also remembered his roots and helped support fellow fans in their efforts to express their own enthusiasm for comic books. Comic book fans constitute a fascinating and understudied culture. They exert influence over the industry and those who make comic books through their engagement with the industry. In this chapter we will explore the culture of the comic book fan to better appreciate that influence. We will begin by defining some common terms used to label fans and exploring the roots of the organized fan movement, from its origins in science fiction fandom through to its expression in "Marvel Mania" and beyond. We will examine some of the activities that are manifestations of fan culture, including comic book conventions and periodicals about comic books. We will also explore one of the topics fans talk about most often, continuity, and analyze how certain forms of participation with fan culture can come into conflict with laws that protect the properties of the cultural industry. But first we define just what a fan is.

DEFINING FANS AND FANDOM

Fans do more than just read and collect comic books. They are more than just casual readers and consumers. Our definition of a **fan** is someone who wants to take part in the dialogue about the medium. Truthfully, many fans want to work in the comic book industry, but for those who don't make it, thinking, talking, and writing about comics is the next best thing. This dialogue takes place in comic book letter columns, in fanzines, on the internet, at comic book conventions, and even at some academic conferences. The content could be anything from an adolescent debate about whether the Hulk could beat up Superman, to a discussion of the psycho-sexual dynamics in Chris Ware's *Acme Novelty Library*, to a pure and simple appreciation of good storytelling and well-rendered artwork.

Scholar Jeffrey Brown reports that industry insiders estimate that only 10 to 20 percent of their audience is made up of hardcore fans, with the remaining sales coming from casual readers (*Black Superheroes*). And yet, what they lack in numbers, fans more than make up for in fervor. Fans make considerable investments in terms of their finances, time, and emotional involvement because of their love for the medium, its characters, and their creators. So much so, in fact, that to people outside of fandom, their behavior may seem strange. The term *fan* is, in fact, an abbreviated form of *fanatic*, and for many people fandom carries with it the same connotation of mania. Unsurprisingly, then, fans have been characterized in much of the popular press as oddly fixated and thus deservedly marginalized individuals. Media critic Joli Jensen observes that reports characterizing fans as being obsessed or frenzied in their actions contributes to a social construction of them that separates them from societal norms. Yet the devotion displayed by fans actually is little different than that put forth by other experts in society, such as a literature professor who knows every detail of the works of British poet John Milton, for example. The difference is that society puts a value on the cultural product of such (e.g., Milton), yet does not value the focus of the fans' attention, such as comic books.

In recent years, the term **fanboy** has been applied to comic book fans. Initially it was used as a term of derision, meant to demean a person who was "anal retentive, adolescent and emotionally arrested" (Sabin, *Adult* 68). The

FIGURE 8.2. Comic Book Guy has come to embody every unflattering stereotype of the fanboy. Words by Evan Dorkin and art by James Lloyd and Andrew Pepoy. Reprinted from *Simpsons Comics Presents Bart Simpson* #31. © 2006 Bongo Entertainment, Inc. The Simpsons © & ™ Twentieth Century Fox Film Corporation. All rights reserved.

most widely recognized manifestation of this insult in popular culture is Comic Book Guy, an overweight, rude know-it-all who runs the comics specialty shop on the television program *The Simpsons*. According to researcher Matthew Pustz, the term *fanboy* first appeared in reference to comics fans on the 1982 cover for *The Official Underground and Newave Comix Price Guide* by cartoonist Bill Griffith, but its use has grown to be contested in recent years. In the fashion of many epithets, the use of *fanboy* has since been co-opted by the fans themselves and is sometimes used as self-deprecating humor. To identify oneself as a fanboy, rather than being labeled as one by others, may be to express one's status as someone who is deeply immersed in comics culture.

What is clearly not taken in stride, though, is the fans' attitudes towards another group of collectors, the speculators. **Speculators** are people who purchase comics as investments in the hopes that they will increase in value over time. Speculators ran rampant in the early 1990s, when high-profile events like the "Death of Superman" storyline were bringing more and more buyers off the streets. Although fans may tout the value of their collections as one defense for their retaining them, most of them collect for the joy that they derive from the medium. To purchase comics as a profit-seeking venture—and to never even read the stories—runs counter to the fans' devotion to the narrative form. And while it is true that many comics have appreciated in value over the years, with copies of *Action Comics* #1 now worth well over $200,000, the market is essentially driven by scarcity: The more common a comic book, the less likely it will increase in value. Many speculators who rushed in to buy multiple copies of number one issues in the 1990s have been left with handfuls of comics that have increased very little in value since their publication. Unlike the comic books from the Golden Age, which are now worth tens if not hundreds of thousands of dollars, a lot of these more recent magazines have been carefully protected and stored, leaving them plentiful, not scarce, and leaving speculators rather confounded.

As we have thus far discussed, a fan is more than just a strident consumer of comic books. If a fan chooses to engage in the dialogue about comic books, that is almost assuredly being done in concert with others. This interaction initiates one into a community called **fandom**. By no means is fandom a highly centralized community, rather it is a good example of an "imagined" or **virtual community** where people are joined by bonds of mutual interest rather than geographic proximity to one another. Still, there are times when members of the community do convene, most visibly in the event of comic book conventions.

How did this movement begin? How did so many diverse and disparate individuals come to form a virtual community, even before the advent of the internet? At one level, it began spontaneously and chaotically, with thousands of readers across the globe who developed a devotion to the medium. Yet only a handful of these fans took the initiative to reach out and begin the dialogue. We will turn our attention next to those early efforts to reach out to one another and establish connections among those fans.

Discovering: Milestones in the Growth of Comic Book Fandom

The following chronology recognizes only a few of the many events in the development of American comic book fandom.

1936	David Kyle creates the earliest known comics-oriented fanzine, *Fantasy World*.
1947	Malcolm Willits and Jim Bradley publish *The Comic Collector's News*, another early comics-focused fanzine.
1953	Bhob Stewart publishes *The EC Fan Bulletin*, which launches EC fandom.
1961	Following the lead of other editors, DC Comics editor Julius Schwartz popularizes publishing the addresses of people who write letters to the editor, allowing these people to build fan networks by writing directly to one another.
1961	College professor Jerry Bails and teenager Roy Thomas publish the first fanzine devoted to comic book superheroes, *Alter Ego*. At almost the same time, Don and Maggie Thompson launch another influential comics-focused fanzine, *Comic Art*.
1961	Jerry Bails' *Comicollector* and Gordon Love's *Rocket's Blast* debut among the earliest ad-zines, where fans buy, sell, and trade back issues.
1962	Stan Lee begins to inflame "Marvel Mania" by directly addressing the fans in the letters pages and story text of Marvel Comics.
1964	Bernie Bubnis and Ron Fradkin organize the first fully realized comic book convention, the New York Comicon.

Cont'd

1964	*Capa-Alpha* begins to circulate, on its way to becoming one of the most influential comic book–focused amateur press associations.
1965	Roy Thomas leads a new generation of fans to cross over to professional status when a story he writes for Charlton Comics' *Son of Vulcan* is published.
1965	Full-page ads invite fans to join the Merry Marvel Marching Society (M.M.M.S.).
1965	The Argosy Book Shop publishes the first comic book price guide.
1968	Two California retailers set up business as among the first comic book specialty shops: Seven Sons Comic Shop in San Jose and the San Francisco Comic Book Company.
1970	Robert Overstreet publishes the first edition of the *Comic Book Price Guide*, which becomes the "bible" for collecting.
1970	San Diego's Golden State Comic-Con is held for the first time, beginning its journey to becoming Comic-Con International, the nation's premier comic book convention.
1971	Alan Light launches *The Buyer's Guide for Comic Fandom*, which will eventually become the industry's first weekly trade publication, *The Comic Buyer's Guide*.
1973	Fan turned dealer Phil Seuling inagurates the Direct Market System of comic book sales: from publishers to comic book specialty shop dealers.
1974	The first issue of the *The Nostalgia Journal* appears, on its way to becoming the industry's most outspoken press outlet, *The Comics Journal*.
1981	*Amazing Heroes* debuts, the first among a wave of eighties magazines profiling the industry.
1982	Jay Kennedy publishes the *Official Underground and Newave Comix Price Guide*.
1991	Gareb Shamus begins to produce *Wizard*, a slick glossy comic magazine whose monthly price guide becomes a new standard for collectors.
1992	The fan community begins to migrate its conversations to online bulletin board systems, including forums on CompuServe, America Online, and Usenet.
1994	The Grand Comic-Book Database begins the ambitious project of fans recording the creator credits of every comic book ever published.
1996	Jonah Weiland's *Kingdom Come Message Board* begins to evolve into *Comic Book Resources*, one of fandom's favorite online destinations.
2002	The first Free Comic Book Day attempts to lure a new generation of fans back into America's comic book specialty shops.

FANDOM COMES OF AGE

The reality is that most comic book readers never become comic book fans. In the 1940s and 1950s the average comic book reader kicked the habit by mid-teens. Even though the average age at which readers give up comic books has been steadily increasing, there still comes a point at which most comic book readers go cold turkey because comics are considered "uncool" or "childish" within their peer group. But the fans keep reading anyway. Perhaps it was more than just a pun when avid readers of the EC line of comics in the 1950s called themselves "fan-addicts."

The EC Fan-Addicts

During the 1950s, while Julie Schwartz was overseeing the creation of some exciting space opera titles such as *Mystery in Space* and *Strange Adventures*, comic book readers with a science fiction bent were getting more excited about what was going on over at Entertaining Comics (EC). In 1950, EC began its infamous horror and fantasy line, which included titles like *Weird Fantasy*, *Weird Science*, *The Haunt of Fear*, *Vault of Horror*, and *Tales From the Crypt*. These comics were well written, exquisitely drawn, and often extremely gory. By 1953, a handful of the older EC "fan-addicts" were producing mimeographed fanzines. By 1955, it was all over. A Senate subcommittee investigated the supposed corrupting influence of comic books, and a besieged industry reacted with a self-regulatory Comics Code that prohibited not only the content, but even some of the titles of the innovative EC line (e.g., the word *weird* was forbidden in a title). What might have been the first great movement of comics fandom never got the chance to grow beyond sporadic and isolated outbursts of enthusiasm.

The Silver Age of Comics/The Golden Age of Fandom

Even as the last embers of EC fandom were dying out, another group of fans, who were more excited about superheroes than science fiction or horror, just needed a spark to ignite their movement. It was, of course, Julie Schwartz who provided that spark. *Showcase* #4 (1956), edited by Schwartz, introduced a new version of one of the heroes he had overseen during the Golden Age of comics: Flash. This issue kicked off the great superhero revival and marked the beginning of what became known among fans as the Silver Age of comic books.

The appearance of Flash also galvanized the older readers who fondly remembered the original superheroes of the 1940s. What these fans remembered most fondly was *All-Star Comics*, the title that brought the DC heroes together in the Justice Society of America (JSA), the first superhero team. A mathematics graduate student by the name of Jerry Bails began writing to Schwartz, lobbying for the return of the Justice Society. Another fan, Larry Ivie, pitched an idea for a JSA-style team called Justice Legion of the World. Before Schwartz answered these dreams, he whetted appetites a bit more with the introduction of a new Green Lantern in 1959.

But 1960 was the year that comic book fandom really gained momentum. Early that year *The Brave and the Bold* #28 brought the "mightiest heroes of our time . . . together as the Justice League of America" (Jones and Jacobs 35). Few comic books have been so anticipated, and perhaps no other single comic book did more to create the excitement that fueled the fan movement. In September, Dick and Pat Lupoff published *Xero*, a science fiction fanzine with the first of a series of articles, "All in Color for a Dime," devoted to Golden Age comic books. Also that year, a college student named Roy Thomas wrote to DC asking how he could complete his *All-Star Comics* collection. Gardner Fox, who was scripting the adventures of the new Justice League, told Thomas how to get in touch with Bails. The fans were beginning to find each other.

A similar, though less immediate experience has characterized the comic book letter column. Since the 1950s publishers have printed letters that they have received from readers. Writing a letter to the editor offers fans a way to express their thorough reading of the material. It has also enabled them to connect with others in their imagined community by either producing an ongoing dialogue among them (albeit one printed quite slowly over a period of months) or facilitating a means for them to make one another's acquaintance and pursue a relationship beyond the printed page. (Future *ElfQuest* creators Richard and Wendi Pini famously "met" through an exchange in a letter column and later married.) Though these letter columns offered the fan community an opportunity for interaction in the era before the internet, they had to be viewed with a measure of awareness that they served the publisher's agenda as much as the fans. They were, after all, controlled by the gate-keeping decisions of the editor, who could only run a handful of the volume of letters received each month and probably screened out the most extreme comments. Today, many of the functions of the traditional letter columns have been superseded by the internet, with discussion boards provided by publishers and independent fan-created sites providing fans with even quicker, more voluminous, and unedited commentary. Still, they serve the same social function as the letter column, offering fans an opportunity to express themselves and connect with their peers.

More and more connections emerged in 1961. In *The Brave and the Bold* #35, Schwartz made it much easier for the widely scattered fans to form a fellowship. Including the complete addresses of letter writers seemed like a minor change, but it was a major catalyst for the fandom dialogue. Letters pages had already been a regular feature in comics magazines, a place to print the letters mailed in to praise creators or ask questions about the contents of their favorite stories, but the addition of addresses changed them from merely a marketing device for the publishers to a community-building tool for the fan community. Bails, for instance, began contacting his fellow letter writers about Thomas and his ideas for forming an Academy of Comic Art Fans and Collectors. Earlier in the year, Bails had visited New York and met with Schwartz and Fox. Schwartz regaled him with stories about the good old days of science fiction fanzines. The next month, Bails and Thomas published *Alter-Ego*, the first comic book fanzine devoted to superheroes. *Comic Art*, the fanzine Don and Maggie Thompson had been working on for nearly a year, came out the following month. Toward the end of the year, two additional Bails-edited fanzines appeared: *The Comicollector* and *On the Drawing Board*, the official newsletter of his newly formed Academy of Comic Art Fans and Collectors. And in December 1961, G.B. Love published *The Rocket's Blast*. The fandom dialogue had begun in earnest.

Marvel Mania

Schwartz's editorial decisions excited not only fans but competitors as well. The success of the Justice League of America prompted imitation. Martin Goodman owned a tattered but plucky comic book company that had been jumping on bandwagons and following trends since 1939. One version of what

FIGURE 8.3. A teenage Roy Thomas drew the cover and Jerry Bails edited the first issue of comic fandom's premiere fanzine, *Alter-Ego* (1961). Courtesy of Roy Thomas

happened next is that Goodman directed Stan Lee (who was his editor-in-chief, his chief writer, and his wife's nephew) to create a superhero team. Another version is that artist Jack Kirby, wanting to save Goodman's failing comic book enterprise, and thus his own livelihood, conceived a new approach to superheroes and presented it to Stan Lee. Whatever their working relationship, the team of Lee and Kirby put a raw energy and imagination between the comic book covers that captured the attention of fans and eventually transformed the industry. When their superhero comic, *Fantastic Four* #1, hit the stands in 1961, it was the beginning of the end of Schwartz's reign and the dawn of the Marvel Age of Comics.

Stan Lee realized that a thriving comic book fandom meant a steady market for his product, and he orchestrated a Marvel Mania that rivaled any comics fandom movement before or since. Contemporary caricatures of Lee often depict him as a carnival barker, and, in many ways, this is an apt metaphor. Lee himself has admitted, "as much as I may have contributed to Marvel's success with any stories, editing, creating characters, I think equally as valuable was the advertising, promotion, publicity, and huckstering that I did" (qtd. in Roy Thomas, "Stan the Man" 11).

The characters and the stories themselves were enough to get fans excited. In contrast to the perfect but dull characters of what Lee called the *Distinguished Competition* (DC Comics), Marvel heroes had insecurities, they lost their tempers, and when they were not fighting supervillains, they had to deal with all the

FIGURE 8.4. Even Marvel comic books parody Stan Lee as a carnival barker. From *Generation X* #17 (1996). Words by Scott Lobdell and Stan Lee, art by Chris Bachalo and Mark Buckingham. © 2008 Marvel Entertainment, Inc. and its subsidiaries

frustrations of daily living. Fans were also fascinated by the guest appearances, cross-references, and continuing subplots that wove the increasingly complex tapestry. Every issue of a Marvel comic book became a chapter in an ongoing, integrated saga of a fictional realm knows as the Marvel Universe. Lee's major collaborators, Kirby and Steve Ditko, seemed to be raising the bar for visually dynamic storytelling with each new issue. Yet Lee was not content to let the work speak for itself.

Lee himself spoke directly to the reader in cover blurbs and captions. Because Lee, using what became known as the **Marvel Method**, was writing and editing virtually all of the books in those early days, Marvel publications had a consistent tone. The most in-your-face aspect was the tongue-in-cheek hyperbole that permeated the covers, the ads, and even the credits. But the tone was also very direct and personal. Readers felt that they got to know Lee and, through him, the other members of the creative team, which he referred to as the Marvel Bullpen. However, Lee always remained the star of the show. He became the comic book medium's first, and most enduring, celebrity.

Even so, it took Lee a couple of years to find his voice. The development of the Stan Lee/Marvel persona (they became one and the same) can be charted in these early Marvel publications:

Direct and Personal	
March 1962	In *Fantastic Four* #3 Lee institutes a letter column called "The Fantastic 4 Fan Page." Later that year Lee writes, "Look—enough with that 'Dear Editor' jazz," and asks fans to use the salutation "'Dear Stan and Jack.'"
Aug. 1962	In *Amazing Fantasy* #15 Lee breaks the barrier between writer and reader when he writes, "Like costumed heroes? Confidentially, we in the comic mag business refer to them as 'long underwear characters'! And, as you know, they're a dime a dozen! But, we think you may find our Spider-Man just a bit . . . different!"
Dec. 1962	Beginning in *Fantastic Four* #9, Lee expands the credits to include inker and letterer (colorists were not yet credited), growing the notion of the Marvel Bullpen. *Cont'd*

Jan. 1963	In *Fantastic Four* #10 Lee and Kirby actually appear in the story and interact with their creations.
Feb. 1963	The splash page to *Fantastic Four* #11 reads, "Special Bonus to our readers! Presenting: The type of story most requested by your letters and post cards . . . A Visit With the Fantastic Four."
March 1964	Nicknames begin to be used in the credits in *Amazing Spider-Man* #10: Smiling Stan Lee, Swinging Steve Ditko, and Sparkling Sam Rosen.

By 1963 it did indeed seem that the Marvel Age of Comics had arrived. In that year's Alley Awards—given by the Academy of Comic-Book Arts and Sciences and named for the comic strip character Alley Oop—Marvel won ten of the fifteen professional categories. Lee won in the Best Writer and Best Editor categories, and *Amazing Spider-Man* won for Best Comic Book. Encouraged by the initial fan response, Lee turned up the hype. By 1965 the covers of Marvel Comics bore the label "Marvel Pop Art Productions," and even the credits were mock-dramatic:

> Let Marveldom cheer! Let humanity shout! Stan (the Man) Lee and Jack (King) Kirby have bestowed another masterpiece upon mankind. Exotically embellished by Joe Sinnott. Laconically lettered by Artie Simek. (*Fantastic Four* #73, 1968)

Comics scholar Robert C. Harvey notes that "Lee's was no small accomplishment: his extravagant verbal gyrations gave the books a tongue-in-cheek tone, and this attracted a new readership. Kirby created the visual excitement—the characters and the adventures; Lee created the marching minions of Marvel fandom" (47).

No comic book company had ever done more to connect with its fans, but Stan Lee continued to seek new channels of communication. In January 1965 Lee instituted the Merry Marvel Marching Society (M.M.M.S.)—"an honest-to-gosh far-out fan club in the mixed-up Marvel manner" (Daniels, *Marvel* 106). Historian Les Daniels claims that "Lee never presented the M.M.M.S.

FIGURE 8.5. The Merry Marvel Marching Society began to solicit membership in 1965. © 2008 Marvel Entertainment, Inc. and its subsidiaries

as anything more than a lot of foolishness, but apparently this very quality made it a big success" (*Marvel* 106). The office was soon flooded with membership applications.

Around the same time, Lee instituted a "Bullpen Bulletins" page in the comic books that provided teasers for forthcoming Marvel comic books and chatty behind-the-scenes news about the writers and artists. The Bulletins page eventually included a little yellow box entitled "Stan's Soapbox." This monthly column is where he most fully developed the Stan Lee persona and most directly connected with his fans: "I tried to write as if the readers were friends of mine and I was talking specifically to them" (qtd. in Daniels, *Marvel* 107). The column was a true soapbox, where Lee often preached his brand of optimism and tolerance, but without ever seeming preachy. Somehow Lee managed to get away with using hip phrases that would have seemed downright silly coming from any other Jewish guy in his mid-forties. His columns were peppered with admonitions for his "True Believers" to "Face Front!" and "Hang Loose!" His pronouncements on the social issues of the day were concluded with " 'Nuff Said," and he signed off each column with a resounding "Excelsior!"

The printed word was not Lee's only means of communicating with the "minions of Marveldom." His growing celebrity led to personal appearances on the college lecture circuit, television shows, and, of course, comic book conventions.

COMIC BOOK CONVENTIONS

Spurred on by the efforts of Schwartz and Lee, comic book fans yearned for a more fully realized fandom, such as many of them had experienced in science fiction fandom, which had been holding conventions since 1939. Because there was a good deal of overlap between science fiction and comic book readers, many members of the comics fan movement were familiar with the convention experience. In fact, science fiction conventions provided a venue for comic book fans to meet and express their enthusiasms. Dick and Pat Lupoff, who included a column about comic books in their science fiction fanzine *Xero*, wore Captain Marvel and Mary Marvel costumes for the masquerade at the 1960 World Science Fiction Convention in Pittsburgh. At the banquet of the same convention, Don Thompson and Maggie Curtis, without being aware of what the Lupoffs were doing with *Xero*, decided to do a fanzine devoted to comics and cartoons.

Four years later, Don and Maggie Thompson (now married) were there when comic book fans assembled for the first event that resembled a convention. In March 1964 Jerry Bails, the chief instigator of comic book fan activity in the 1960s, hosted a proto-con at his home in a suburb of Detroit. A few years earlier, Bails and nineteen other prominent fans had formed the Academy of Comic-Book Arts and Sciences and instituted annual awards, for both pros and fans, which Roy Thomas had suggested they name the Alley Awards.

As Executive Secretary of the Academy, Bails would be the one to receive the completed ballots. When he received over two hundred and fifty of them, each with twenty-eight categories, he made an open invitation to any member of the academy to come spend the weekend at his house and help count the votes. Dubbed the "Alley Tally" by Maggie Thompson, this gathering of about twenty fans had many of the characteristics of later comic book conventions: There was trading and selling of comic books, pages of original comic book art were on display, and there was even a one-man masquerade when Ronn Foss made his dramatic appearance as Rocketman. Of course, the Alley Tally is not considered a true con because it was not openly advertised to all of fandom.

However, a few months later, in nearby Detroit, most of the Alley Talliers and about fifty other fans attended a true convention that was at least partially dedicated to comic books. The Detroit Triple Fan Fair was held at the Hotel Tuller on May 24, 1964. The one-day celebration of fantasy, film, and comics was organized by seventeen-year-old Dave Szurek and fifteen-year-old Bob Brosch. There were no science fiction or comic book professionals in attendance, but fans gave brief talks on film and comics. The highlight for comic book fans was probably Bails' lecture "Comicdom—Past, Present and Future." Shel Dorf, who would take over organization of the con the following year, recalls that "It was little more than a swap meet. Bob's sister made a big bowl of punch, and there were a lot of card tables with cartons of books" (Schelly, *Golden Age* 78).

It took another few months before comicdom had its own convention. According to fandom historian Bill Schelly, "the New York Comicon has traditionally been considered the first real comicon" (*Golden Age* 81). Organized by Bernie Bubnis and Ron Fradkin and held in the Workman's Circle Building on Monday, July 27, 1964, the New York Comicon attracted only about fifty fans, but some of the region's leading dealers (Howard Rogofsky and Phil Seuling among them) and even a few comic book professionals were in attendence. Representing Marvel were Spider-Man artist Steve Ditko and office manager Flo Steinberg. Artist Tom Gill was there representing Gold Key. No one from DC attended, but editors Murray Boltinoff and Julie Schwartz donated some pages of original art for door prizes. This first attempt at a convention was not an unqualified success: It was not well publicized, the room was hard to find and far too hot, and the Monday date was inconvenient for many fans. Bubnis admits that he really had no idea how to organize a convention, but "I just did it because I thought someone should" (Schelly, *Golden Age* 81).

Being held near the heart of comic book production, the New York convention grew quickly. By the second year, there were nearly two hundred fans in attendance. Organizer Dave Kaler, with the help of a network of local fans (such as future comic book writers Len Wein and Marv Wolfman), made use of industry contacts and arranged for an impressive lineup of professional guests. This time DC was well represented, including editors Mort Weisinger and Gardner Fox, as well as writers Otto Binder and Bill Finger. By the time Phil Seuling, a high school English teacher and prominent comic book dealer, took over running the con in 1968, the attendance was over seven hundred, and it grew steadily thereafter. Seuling ran the renamed Comic Art Convention until it faded out of existence in the 1980s.

In the late 1960s Shel Dorf moved from Detroit to New York to San Diego and soon fell in with a group of area fans that included future cartoonist Scott

Shaw!, Richard Alf, one of the first mail-order comics dealers, and Ken Krueger, a longtime science fiction fan (Shaw 94–95). It was not long before Dorf was taking groups of fans to visit Jack and Roz Kirby at their home in Thousand Oaks, California. (Like Dorf, the Kirbys had recently moved to California from New York.) This whetted the group's appetite for more pro contact, and in 1969 they began seriously planning a comic book convention. Alf provided the seed money, Krueger provided the know-how from his science fiction fan experiences, Dorf provided the professional contacts, and the rest of the group provided tons of enthusiasm. After a March 1970 one-day con to help raise funds, the first official San Diego's Golden State Comic-Con was held August 1–3, 1970 at the U.S. Grant Hotel in downtown San Diego. Over three hundred fans showed up to see comic book artists Jack Kirby and Mike Royer, science fiction authors Ray Bradbury and A.E. Van Vogt, editorial cartoonist Bob Stevens, and, probably the biggest name on the ticket, monster maven Forrest J. Ackerman. By 1982 the renamed San Diego Comic-Con had left hotel venues for a new home in the massive San Diego Convention Center and was attracting five thousand fans. By the end of the decade, the San Diego Comic-Con was the premier comic book convention in the United States and the site of the industry's answer to the Oscars, the Eisner Awards Ceremony. Officially renamed Comic-Con International: San Diego in 1995, the event now attracts over 100,000 attendees a year.

At the core of the modern convention is commerce, with dealers and collectors engaged in the sale and trade of comic books and associated paraphernalia. Artists and independent publishers are also on hand to sell sketches, autographs, and signed copies of their publications. Many larger publishers take advantage of the crowds assembled at conventions to market their latest products and announce forthcoming products in spectacles akin to the unveiling of a new model of car at an auto show. Conventions also present opportunities for aspiring talents to market themselves to editors and try to win the opportunity for a career in the industry.

But more than just a marketplace, conventions are venues for the expression of community. Comic book conventions have a long-standing tradition of making creators accessible to their fans, allowing them to meet face-to-face. They also permit fans to network with one another, strengthening peer-to-peer relationships. Conventions often feature programming that further enhances the fans'

FIGURE 8.6. Comic-Con International draws fans of all ages and apparel and is just one of a number of professionally run conventions that are sponsored around the country and throughout the calendar year. Photo by Karen Stover.

experience or expertise. Panel presentations offered by creators, publishers, academics, and fellow fans allow those attending to engage in close readings of their favorite texts, express their dis/satisfaction with creative directions, and participate in ritualistic ceremonies honoring their favorite creators, among many, many other topics. In between pilgrimages to these events, though, fans rely on mediated encounters, including the kinds that take place in the fan press.

PUBLICATIONS FOR FANS BY FANS

What fan historian Bill Schelly calls the Golden Age of Comic Fandom ended sometime in the early 1970s. Crude mimeographed fanzines were replaced by polished photo-offset magazines full of professional artwork. Much of the wide-eyed wonder was gone, and many of the leading fans were leaving behind their amateur pursuits and taking a more businesslike approach to comic books as scholars, as dealers, as writers and artists, or as members of the emerging industry press.

A sea change in comicdom was evident in 1970. The Academy of Comic Book Fans and Collectors had dissipated and the Alley Awards had been given for the last time in 1969. Certainly no one realized it in 1970, but that the first convention in San Diego heralded the coming of the convention as a professional institution. However, it was the publications that appeared (or were at least advertised) that year that signaled the greatest change in the nature of fandom. *All in Color for a Dime*, edited by Dick Lupoff and Don Thompson, collected eleven of the best essays that had run in the "All in Color for a Dime" feature of the Lupoff's science fiction fanzine *Xero*. Artist Jim Steranko self-published an exciting, if not always accurate, exploration of comic book history modestly entitled *The Steranko History of Comics*. A second volume appeared in 1972, but Steranko never published the rest of the projected six volumes, and his history of the medium never made it past the 1940s. These publications were the first serious attempts to preserve the history of the comic book medium, and they mark the first time that the comics scholarship of the fanzines was available to a wider audience.

The Overstreet *Comic Book Price Guide*

The most significant fan publication of 1970 was Robert Overstreet's first *Comic Book Price Guide*. Overstreet started with the indexing work that had been done by other fans, primarily Jerry Bails (who served as associate editor for the first edition), and the price lists of practically every comics dealer operating in the 1960s. The first *Guide* had plenty of errors and omissions, but it was a monumental undertaking that no other fan had been willing to tackle. The intention of the *Price Guide* was stated in the introduction: "Everyone connected with the publication of this book advocates the collecting of comic books for fun and pleasure, as well as nostalgia, art, and cultural values. Second to this is investment . . ." (Overstreet, "Introduction"). Whatever his intentions, Overstreet's *Guide* soon turned from a hobby into a business. Bails eventually had

some regrets about his involvement, for he saw that the *Guide* "meant a loss of innocence for fandom" (Schelly, *Golden Age* 146).

Once collectors and dealers had partaken of the book of knowledge, there no was turning back. Because of the *Guide*, "even 'the little kid down the block' would have a way to assign a value to the stack of comics that his parents had saved through the years. Opportunities for windfall profits began to evaporate" (Schelly, *Golden Age* 144). While many early collectors had a love-hate relationship with the *Guide*, Overstreet expressed that "Sharing the knowledge with the mass market saved a lot of comic books that would have been thrown away" (Duin and Richardson 344). Overstreet only sold about 1,800 copies of the first *Guide*, but by the late 1970s sales reached 41,000. The *Guide*'s role as the bible for dealers and collectors has been at least partially supplanted by *Wizard*, a slick monthly magazine in the style of *People* magazine which features a price guide section. Still, the *Guide* has become a venerable institution of comicdom that is not likely to disappear anytime soon.

Comics Buyer's Guide

Another eventual institution was first introduced to fandom when Alan Light ran an ad for a free fanzine in the December 1970 issue of the popular fanzine *Rocket's Blast-Comicollector*. Teenager Alan Light had been cranking out small fanzines for a few years, but once he saved some money from his summer job he set his sights on something more ambitious. By 1970 Don and Maggie Thompson were wearying of writing, editing, and publishing their monthly fandom newsletter, *Newfangles*, which they'd begun in March 1967. Alan Light volunteered to take care of the printing and circulation management for them if they would just continue gathering the news, but the Thompsons were content to let two teenagers from New York, Paul Levitz and Paul Kupperberg, take over some of the functions of *Newfangles* in their fanzine *Etcetera*, which came out in February 1971. The same month, an unduanted Alan Light, with the help of his mom, dad, sister, and grandmother, mailed out some three thousand copies of the zine he had advertised in December, *The Buyer's Guide for Comic Fandom*.

Light's *Buyer's Guide* soon attracted the bulk of the advertising revenue available in comicdom, and hastened the demise of a number of fanzines, including, ironically, *Rocket's Blast-Comicollector*, where it had first been advertised. In the years that followed, Light began charging for subscriptions and providng editorial content as well as ads. The inclusion of editorial content meant that he could circulate copies via second-class mail for a huge savings in distribution costs, and that content eventually included Don and Maggie Thompson's "Beautiful Balloons" column and cat yronwode's news column, "Fit to Print." When Krause Publications bought the *Buyer's Guide* from Light in 1982 with the intention of turning it into a collectors' newspaper, Light suggested that the Thompsons had the experience to oversee the project. Since the *Cleveland Press*, for which Don had worked since 1960, had recently folded, they weren't reluctant to relocate to Wisconsin. The Thompsons took over as editors of the renamed *Comics Buyer's Guide* in 1983. The hobby publication thrived under the Thompsons, who took it weekly. Don Thompson died of heart failure in 1994, and today Maggie Thompson continues as senior editor of *Comics Buyer's Guide*, which returned to monthly publication and changed to magazine format in August 2004.

Profile: Don and Maggie Thompson

born: Donald Arthur Thompson   Margaret Judson Curtis
      Oct. 30, 1935   Nov. 29, 1942
      Youngsville, PA   Ithaca, NY

"The true 'Golden Age' is twelve."

Career Highlights

1957	Don Thompson and Maggie Curtis meet on June 8 at a science fiction picnic.
1960	They mail *Harbinger* in October, soliciting articles and information about comics.
1961	Distribution of *Comic Art* #1 introduces the first comics fanzine devoted to all aspects of the medium.
1962	Maggie and Don marry on June 23.
1967	They begin *Newfangles*, a newsletter for fandom, in March.
1970	Don co-edits *All in Color for a Dime* with Dick Lupoff.
1972	"Beautiful Balloons" column begins in *The Buyer's Guide for Comic Fandom* #19.

Cont'd

1976	The couple receives the San Diego Comic-Con Inkpot Award for services to fandom.
1982	Don and Maggie create *The Golden Age of Comics* #1.
1983	As editors, they transform the *Comics Buyer's Guide* into a full-fledged newspaper.
1990	The couple receives the Diamond Comic Distributors Gem Lifetime Fandom Award.
1994	Don dies of congestive heart failure on May 23.
1995	Maggie receives the Bob Clampett Humanitarian Award.
2004	Maggie receives the first Friends of Lulu Women of Distinction Award.

FIGURE 8.8. Don and Maggie Thompson shortly after taking over the editorship of *The Comics Buyer's Guide*. Photo by Alan Light.

Involvement in fandom was natural to Maggie Curtis. Her mother, Betsy, not only wrote for the science fiction pulps, but in the early 1950s Betsy and Ed Curtis published a science fiction fanzine, *The Cricket*. Accompanying her mother to a science fiction picnic in 1957, fourteen-year-old Maggie met Penn State college student and science fiction fan Don Thompson. Despite their age difference, Don and Maggie discovered a wealth of common interests. They spent the entire day rapt in conversation.

Maggie's first World Science-Fiction Convention was in Cleveland in 1955, and Thompson and the Curtises separately attended two World Science-Fiction Conventions: in Detroit in 1959 and in Pittsburgh in 1960. It was in Pittsburgh that Ed, Betsy, Maggie, and Mary Curtis and Don Thompson won the "Best Group" prize at the masquerade as "The Five Fannish Senses." The concept and costumes (by Betsy) consisted of Ed as "The Sense of Science," Betsy as "Extra Sense," Maggie as "Sense of Wonder," Mary as "Sense of Humor," and Don (wearing a tabard decorated with SF magazine covers and shiny discs) as "35–50¢, The Cost of SF Magazines." At that event, Don and Maggie saw Dick and Pat Lupoff dressed as Captain and Mary Marvel. Perhaps that is why their conversation at the convention banquet turned to comics. According to Maggie:

> We looked around the banquet room at all the people sitting there with that common interest in a common field learning about that field and sharing that enjoyment. We said, wouldn't it be neat if there were something like this about comics?

There soon was. The first issue of their fanzine, *Comic Art*, appeared in 1961, and it was published irregularly until 1968. Little interested in being limited to coverage

Cont'd

of the ongoing superhero revival of the Silver Age, Don and Maggie included articles on old and new newspaper strips, a series on *Mad* staffers, and the first major focus on the work of Uncle Scrooge McDuck creator Carl Barks. They also produced fanzines itemizing the titles in Dell's *Four Color* series (1968), listing fan award winners (1971), and even suggesting fannish etiquette (1969).

In 1972, more than a year after discontinuing their own fandom newsletter, *Newfangles*, the Thompsons began writing the "Beautiful Balloons" column for *The Buyer's Guide for Comic Fandom*. Don and Maggie had found a home. In 1983, they took over as editors of the renamed *Comics Buyer's Guide*. For over three decades they reigned as the first couple of comics fandom. Don Thompson died of heart failure in 1994. Maggie Thompson, as senior editor of *CBG*, continues to be a keen observer and enthusiastic promoter of the comic book medium.

The Comics Journal

Another significant industry publication and a competitor, or at least a counterpart, to the *Comics Buyer's Guide* was the result of another young fan segueing from fanzine publishing to professional publishing. In the late 1960s Gary Groth began *Fantastic Fanzine* as just another typical Marvel fanzine, but he soon distinguished the publication from the pack with excellent production values and plenty of artwork from professionals and talented amateurs. *Fantastic Fanzine* was also notable for being one of the few fanzines to discuss the business aspects of comics. Groth had to discontinue the publication when he went to college, but after leaving college he began looking for a way to combine his interests in journalism, criticism, and publishing. In 1976 he formed Fantagraphics with Mike Catron and took over the ad-zine *The Nostalgia Journal*, which was losing the battle for ad revenue to Light's *Buyer's Guide*.

Groth's first issue set the tone for things to come. Inside was an editorial with a "stinging attack on Alan Light's business practices," and on the cover was a blurb that proclaimed "Beginning a New Era in Adzines! (Watch out, TBG!)" (Schelly, *Golden Age* 156). However, Groth soon realized that he could not compete head-on with *The Buyer's Guide*, so he changed the emphasis of his publication to editorial content and the name to *The Comics Journal*. Groth's publication remains a vital part of comics fandom as the the leading journal of insightful criticism and sometimes vitriolic attack.

Wizard

A number of professionally produced fanzines have come and gone since *The Comics Buyer's Guide* and *The Comics Journal* raised the bar in terms of production values for the fan press in the 1970s. Fondly remembered titles such as Fantagraphics' *Amazing Heroes* and Starlog's *Comics Scene* in the 1980s were among the many additional outlets for news, reviews, and features about the comics medium. So when Gareb Shamus attempted to take his comic shop's newsletter and turn it into another contender, the fan press was already a crowded field. But several factor helped to set his magazine, *Wizard*, apart, contributing to its becoming the most widely circulated magazine about comics in the medium's history. One distinction was the emphasis *Wizard* put on collecting "hot" comic books of the moment, whereas most traditional zines—if they attended to the market side of the industry at all—focused on investing in older back issues. This accent was codified in *Wizard*'s monthly price guide, which tracked the rise and fall in values of comics as recent as just a month old. In many comic shops and at many conventions, *Wizard*'s price guide came to supplant Overstreet's venerable *Comic Book Price Guide* as the authority on the collectible comics market.

Wizard was also an unabashed promoter of new publishers and thus established many exclusive relationships in the industry, giving it an edge in terms of access and coverage. Shamus' relationship with Image co-founder Todd McFarlane helped establish this precedent, and *Wizard* became a major promotor of Image Comics in the early 1990s, then Valiant Comics in the mid-nineties, and others that followed. In this way *Wizard* did more to create interest in certain comic book titles than it did to simply report on them. In addition, the magazine had an adolescent sense of humor that helped it connect with its target audience, and its glossy, full-color pages were a cut above the general production values of the modest black-and-white pages used throughout most of the fan press. In short, *Wizard* was hip, slick, and quickly crushed imitators like *Heroes Illustrated*.

Today, *Wizard* continues to the rule the roost in terms of circulation among the fan press, with numbers approaching 200,000 copies per issue, though it has attempted to broaden its appeal by doing more stories about Hollywood and other entertainment producers. Still, the magazine has remarkable influence within the industry. According to Marvel editor-in-chief Joe Quesada, the "buzz" that comes from a title being profiled in *Wizard* can really boost a book's sales: "It's always been a great selling tool for us" (qtd. in Gustines). Additionally, Shamus' success with *Wizard* has allowed him to establish an entertainment company that has gone on to publish magazines for other collecting communities (e.g., *ToyFare* for toy collectors and *Anime Insider* for fans of Japanese animation). Wizard Entertainment also sells a number of fan-related products, including exclusive comic books, statues, and action figures. It sponsors more than half a dozen comic book conventions around the country under the banner of "Wizard World," where the fan conversation about comics moves from the printed page to the convention hall floor.

CONTINUITY: THE PREOCCUPATION OF FANDOM

So just what is it that fans talk about when they talk to one another? Any number of topics can arise, from the personalities and performances of favorite creative teams, to the editorial decisions to change a character's likeness or alter his destiny. But one of the more distinctive topics of fan conversations is the fixation with the way in which separately published comics narratives relate to one another. Individual comic books are often published as installments in a larger, ongoing saga, and as such can possess the serial nature of other episodic narratives, such as television soap operas. The interrelationship between one published comic book and another in the same series (or from the same publisher) results in the development of elements of continuity understood by the creators and readers. **Continuity** is a term used to express the intertextual links among separately published comics narratives. As more and more comics are added to a series, and as the series of one publisher are more and more expressly related to one another, continuity continues to grow in complexity. Indeed, whole "universes" of characters can interrelate to one another, as Stan Lee did with the Marvel Universe discussed earlier in this chapter. This can make accessing titles within such continuities daunting to new readers; however, for fans, familiarity with a given continuity "forms the most crucial aspect of enjoyment for the committed reader" (Reynolds 38).

What makes continuity so rewarding is, in part, its value as a commodity for the exchange of meaning among fans. "Information based on continuity becomes the source of discussion, jokes, and arguments, making it the raw material for the interactive glue that holds comic book culture together" (Pustz 134). Fans take great delight in knowing the history and interrelationships of characters, and also in watching the characters grow over time. Such evolution allows for comic book characters to develop a depth that might not seem possible in only twenty-two monthly pages of story. The leads in *Love and Rockets, Bone*, and *Cerebus* may have appeared in short monthly comic books, but over several years of publications, their exploits became the lengthy narratives of developed, and consequently beloved, characters.

While the use of continuity may be found in all genres of comics, certainly modern superhero comics are flush with its invocation. Early superhero comics were comparatively mild about relating one issue to another or one series to another within a publisher's stable of titles. But when Marvel Comics began to cross over its lead characters and cross-reference previous issues in its series, it set about building a narrative universe of enormous complexity. In due course, fans became the guardians for continuity gaffes, writing in to express their dismay when events in one story contradicted details in an earlier one. Stan Lee actually encouraged this behavior by awarding a "No-Prize" to any loyal reader who could not only spot a continuity error but offer an explanation for the inconsistency. (The "No-Prize," cleverly enough, was an empty envelope which read, "Congratulations this envelope contains a genuine Marvel Comics No-Prize.") For some fans, a given character's continuity can become a sacrosant matter. Marvel Comics editor-in-chief Joe Quesada stirred up a controversy over his 2008 "One More Day" storyline, which retroactivated Spider-Man's continuity by erasing Peter Parker's 1987 marriage to Mary Jane Watson. Fans cried out that such "retconning" insulted their patronage of the series for the past twenty years; however, Quesada insisted that a single Spider-Man would have more storytelling potential, and that he would be more accessible to younger readers without a wife.

The characters' continuities are such familiar fodder for superhero fans that publishers even publish well-received comics that intentionally violate a canonical

FIGURE 8.9 Editors' notes such as the caption in this panel from *Avengers* #151 (1976) reinforce the intertextual nature of comic books. The caption references another comic book in the same series published in 1964. Words by Gerry Conway, Jim Shooter, and Steve Englehart and art by George Perez and John Tartag. © 2008 Marvel Entertainment, Inc. and its subsidiaries

continuity in order to explore alternate continuities for some of their favorite characters. DC began this trend in the 1960s with "imaginary tales," such as exploring the fate of Superman if Krypton had never exploded. Marvel went on to have several series with the title *What If?*, which examined critical plot turns such as "What if Spider-Man had stopped the burglar who killed his uncle?" DC later launched a series of "Elseworlds"—limited series and one-shot specials putting their characters in unfamiliar settings, such as casting Batman as a late-nineteenth-century crime fighter on the trail of Jack the Ripper. Fans enjoy these departures from the canonical continuity partially because they are playful. Because such stories are labeled as non-canonical, they do not contradict the fans' accumulated knowledge of the mythology or violate their emotional investment in the characters. Yet, as Alan Moore observed in the overture to "Whatever Happened to the Man of Tomorrow" in *Superman* #423 (1986), "This is an imaginary story . . . about a perfect man who came from the sky and did only good. . . . This is an imaginary story . . . aren't they all?"

ANALYZING: COMIC BOOK FANDOM AS PARTICIPATORY CULTURE

Comic book fans enact a culture, but many of the raw materials of that culture—the characters, plots, images, and lines pulled from the comics—are almost always the property of other people. Copyright and trademark laws guarantee that the creators of comic book properties own the rights to control and profit from the use of them. (Of course, when a creator makes a comic in a work-for-hire arrangement, it is the publisher who holds the copyright.) Without first securing the permission of the copyright holder, fans who want to produce and publish their own comics, paint a mural with their favorite character, or even design their own costumes in the likeness of their favorite comic book personality are technically infringing on those rights. The framers of the United States Constitution thought that copyright was so important that they enshrined it in that fundamental document with the belief that people who create **intellectual property**—such as books and artwork—should be granted a measure of protection from others profiting from their creativity. The belief is that talented writers, artists, and intellectuals should be able to profit directly from the products of their labor. If someone could simply reprint a novel without its author benefiting from the arrangement, there would be a disincentive for the best and brightest to continue creating new works.

While many people might agree that it is a good idea to have such incentives in place for the creative and intellectual community, few are fully aware of how far copyright protection extends. Fans, in particular, often view the materials put out by the major publishers and independent publishers as contributions to the larger cultural mosaic from which they often sample or poach ideas. "Fans reject the idea of a definitive version produced, authorized, and regulated by some media conglomerate. Instead, fans envision a world where all of us can participate in the creation and circulation of central cultural myths" (Jenkins, 289). Media scholar Henry Jenkins has observed how fans engage in a participatory culture where they borrow characters, plots, images, and other elements from their favorite narratives (e.g., *Star Wars*) to produce their own stories. As you can start to see, though, the rights of copyright holder and the desires of fans can come into conflict with one another.

One infamous case of copyright infringement involving comics took place in the 1970s when the Air Pirates, a studio of underground cartoonists under the direction of Dan O'Neill, parodied the works of Walt Disney. *Air Pirates Funnies* featured a mouse named Mickey and his friends, drawn in the familiar Disney house style but engaged in adult activities like drug consumption and sexual intercourse. Aghast at such an antithetical depiction of their stars, the Disney corporation sued, and the subsequent legal wrangles went all the way to the Supreme Court. While O'Neill's motives for pursuing the case to that level were complex, the situation underscores the seriousness with which copyright holders are willing to defend their ownership.

While the Air Pirates might have been audacious in their parodies, the reality is that people regularly violate copyrighted material every day. For example, many fans produce their own original **fan fiction** using characters, situations, and images that are under copyright protection. Some of these stories are innocuous amateur attempts at creating additional narratives for a familiar mythology. Other fan fiction might delve into areas left unexplored in the copyright holder's canon, such as the notorious **slash fiction**, in which sexual situations might be probed in depth. While such unauthorized uses of their material may upset copyright holders, doing so is a means for fans to embrace the products of mass culture as their own. Fans can thus be both ally and adversary in the business of producing comics, with the delicate balance between copyright holder and audience member's ownership of the material always needing to find a necessary equilibrium.

Discussion Questions

1. Are comic book fans really any more obsessive about the object of their attention than other fans, like music groupies or television's coach potatoes? Are these groups treated with more or less respect than "fanboys"?
2. How does Stan Lee's communication with his "Marvel minions" exhibit the qualities of feedforward and feedback discussed in the model of comic book communication introduced in Chapter 1?
3. Why can't fans profit from their own original comics based on their favorite comic book characters? Does it make it fairer if fans are creating for love of the character and are not out for profit?

Activities

1. Conduct an in-depth interview with a comic book fan. Below are a few starter questions, but you will also need to devise additional questions of your own:
   - When did you begin reading comic books?
   - Did you stop reading comic books at any point? If so, why? What prompted you to start again?
   - What do you like about the comic book medium?
   - How have you benefited from reading comic books?
   - Besides reading comic books, do you take part in any other fan activities like attending conventions, collecting related merchandise, posting to a website, etc.? What do you gain from those activities?

   Be prepared to share what you learned about comic book fandom with your classmates.
2. Make plans to attend a comic book convention with your classmates or by yourself. While you are there, observe fan behaviors, paying particular attention to how fans exchange meaning with one another. You may even want to experiment by engaging in some of the fun yourself! A number of conventions, some large and many small, are sponsored each weekend across the United States. Magazines like *Wizard* and *Comic Buyer's Guide* print schedules for upcoming conventions, and numerous web sites document them as well.

Recommended Readings

Comics:

Evanier, Mark, and Sergio Aragonés. *Fanboy*. New York: DC Comics, 2001.

Evanier (former assistant to Jack Kirby) and Aragonés (*Mad*) are no strangers to the peculiar behaviors of the fan community. In this humorous take on fandom, they introduce Finster, a fan who takes flights of fantasy to interact with his favorite comic book characters (co-illustrated by some of comicdom's finest artists), even while living out his own misadventures.

Innes, Mark, ed. *The Comic Eye: Comics about Comics*. Hamilton, Ontario: Blind Bat Press, 2007.

Several dozen cartoonists present short pieces commenting on their love of and relationship to the comic book medium. Some of this anthology's contributions are biographical, relating how fans became professionals, while others offer amusing insights into the perceptions of fans and the culture of comics that they are immersed within.

Scholarly Sources:

Brown, Jeffrey A. *Black Superheroes, Milestone Comics, and Their Fans*. Jackson, MS: University Press of Mississippi, 2001.

Brown investigates how fans interpreted issues of race and masculinity in Milestone Comics, the short-lived DC Comics imprint that featured characters of diverse racial and ethnic backgrounds.

Pustz, Matthew. *Comic Book Culture: Fanboys and True Believers*. Jackson, MS: University Press of Mississippi, 1999.

Pustz provides perspective into the cultural practices of comic book fans by investigating their language, rituals, and habitat (i.e., the comic book specialty shop). This ethnography approaches the fans and their co-culture respectfully, revealing the complexity of meaning-making processes going on among those who immerse themselves in this culture.

Comic Book Genres:
Classifying Comics

"Bunglers and pedants judge art according to genre; they approve of this and dismiss that genre, but instead of genres, the open-minded connoisseur appreciates only individual works."

—FRANZ GRILLPARZER, NINETEENTH-CENTURY AUSTRIAN POET, 1820

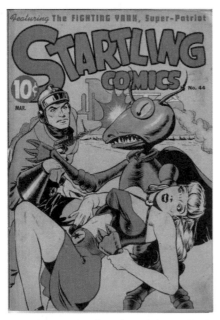

FIGURE 9.1. *Startling Comics'* Lance Lewis demonstrates some conventions of a good cover for a science fiction comic. © 1947 Nedor Comics

Absent from the cover of *Startling Comics* #44 (1947) is any wording about its lead feature, Lance Lewis. Yet even without a caption or dialogue offering any further explanation, the imagery alone provides regular consumers of popular culture with enough cues that they can quickly discern the type of story in which Lance Lewis stars. Certainly the unusual attire he and his female companion are dressed in offers some guidance. And then there is the man-sized bug attempting to kidnap her, not to mention the rather obvious ray gun Lance is firing at the creature's snout. Either alone or in combination, these cues suggest that this is a story belonging to a particular group of stories called *science fiction*. By 1947, many of the visual conventions associated with science fiction stories had already evolved and become standard, including expectations about the kinds of dress, characters, and technologies one might expect to find in such stories. Science fiction stories had become a staple of American fiction, having found popularity through novels, films, radio broadcasts, comic strips, pulp magazines, and, in time, comic books. Fans of science fiction, like fans of other types of stories, are often motivated to pick up one story after another in that group, giving the producers of media products incentive to return to these types of stories time and again. Thus fans of series like *Buck Rogers in the 25th Century A.D.* and *Flash Gordon* might eagerly purchase this issue of *Startling Comics*, with artwork by comics great Graham Ingels, because its imagery calls to mind those other tales. This is the basis for genre studies, which tries to identify what characteristics make up the kinds of stories that are most often told by our cultural industries, and also how the conventions of those media are used to market these types of stories to their audiences.

OBJECTIVES

In this chapter you will learn:

1. the definition of *genre* and the role it plays in shaping the creation of comics products;

2. the characteristics of genres, including character types, narrative patterns, themes, and other conventions;

3. how the example genres of teen humor, romance, funny animals, horror, and memoir developed in comics, and what characterizes each; and

4. how the hybridization of genres helps experimentation and expansion of narrative possibilities.

As a means for studying and better understanding narratives in various media, critics and scholars have identified genres for typing works according to similarities with other works. A genre is a way to classify similar types of stories. Genre comes from the same root as *genus*, a term you may recall from biology, which denotes the classification of organisms into groups. Genre studies look for groupings in media such as television, novels, film, and, of course, comics, and provide us with a shorthand for discussing trends and motifs that characterize a given narrative. For instance, film genres include categories for musicals, film noir, and romantic comedy. In comics, genres include teen humor, horror, and superheroes.

The conventions of the superhero genre in particular have been so richly analyzed that we've set aside treatment of them in their own chapter (Chapter 10). The superhero genre is arguably the comics' most significant contribution to popular culture, as it has gone on to achieve success in many other mass media, from radio, to television, to feature films. But the superhero genre got its start in comic books and continues to dominate the medium. Not to be overlooked, though, are the imported genres, adapted to comics only after popular exposure in other media. For instance, the detective genre has appeared in comics since the medium's inception, but it had already seized the popular imagination through novels, pulp magazines, films, and radio programs before modern comics began to publish stories within the genre in the 1930s. Although comics have often adapted already known and popular genres for their use, they have still placed an imprint on them, influenced by the unique conventions of graphic storytelling.

While genres may enable critics and scholars to talk about the elements that help construct a story, they also help the people who publish comics to find appealing products for particular audiences. From the artistic or creative viewpoint, tapping into a genre allows creators to use known and accepted elements as shorthand for less creative elements in a story. This frees mental energy and storytelling space to concentrate on the original elements of the narrative that the creators want to introduce. For instance, superhero comics usually don't spend much effort explaining the tailoring of their protagonists' spandex uniforms; the heroes simply seem to be able to come up with their costumes as though they were bought off the rack at a department store. From an economic standpoint, invoking genre is a helpful way to market a story. When the kung fu craze hit American audiences in the 1970s, it didn't take long for all the major comics publishers to mass-produce kung fu comics. Among other series, Marvel Comics launched *Master of Kung Fu* (1974–1983) and DC Comics responded with *Richard Dragon, Kung Fu Fighter* (1975–1977); they each wanted to cash in on the popular trend.

In order to appeal to an audience, though, producers have to walk a fine line between copying what someone else has published and neglecting to fulfill the expectations that an audience brings to the genre. In satisfying these expectations, an entry in a genre must attend to **standardization** to match the conventions of the genre closely enough to be recognized as belonging to the genre. In the sword-and-sorcery comics, which also became popular in the 1970s, this means a story featuring a stalwart sword-wielding hero who roams an exotic

FIGURE 9.2. Two very distinct genres emerged in 1970s comics: kung fu comics as represented by *Marvel Special Collector's Edition* with art by Gil Kane and John Romita, and sword-and-sorcery comics represented by DC's *Claw the Unconquered* with art by Ernie Chua, both from 1975. © 2008 Marvel Entertainment, Inc. and its subsidiaries; © DC Comics

land and confronts opposing warriors and mythical creatures. Balanced against standardization, though, must be **differentiation,** or the innovations brought to the individual narrative or series (Campbell, Martin and Fabos 2006). In our sword-and-sorcery example, Marvel Comics' popular *Conan the Barbarian* is set in the ancient "Hyperborean Age," a time described as occurring between the fall of mythical Atlantis and the beginning of recorded history. As a matter of distinction, in DC Comics' *Warlord* series, contemporary pilot Travis Morgan crash-lands into Skartaris, a world which exists below the earth and is populated by sorcerers and dinosaurs. These two settings are similar in some regards—both have sorcerers and fantastic beasts roaming about—but different enough to distinguish the two series (among other considerations). As a matter of practice, striking a balance between fulfilling a genre's conventions and introducing innovations allows new series to carve out a niche in a crowded marketplace.

This chapter takes a look at some of the most influential genres adapted to comics. We'll begin by reviewing some of the characteristics common to all genres, and looking at them through the lens of one long-running genre, the western. Next we'll review five other influential genres in comics: teen humor, romance, funny animals, horror, and memoir. Finally, we'll look at the ways some strips and series break through the artificial boundaries of genre and blend to create hybrid forms. By the end of this chapter, you should have a greater appreciation for the versatility of the comics medium and its ability to create narrative experiences.

GENRE CONVENTIONS

Genres evolve over time, such that the historic first entry might look markedly different from more contemporary entries. Yet despite such differences, genre studies attempt to identify a set of common characteristics. These characteristics can include the types of characters in such narratives, the way stories are structured, themes the stories revisit time and again, and other conventions. Let us look at each of these characteristics, using the western genre to help illustrate them.

Westerns were popular storytelling vehicles for much of the twentieth century. One of the first narrative films, *The Great Train Robbery* (1903), was a western. Many of radio's most successful programs were westerns, including *The Lone Ranger* (1933–1955). The longest-running dramatic primetime television series, *Gunsmoke* (1955–1975), was a western. And since the turn of the twentieth century, newspaper strips have featured western themes and western characters, many of which were reprinted in the early comic book magazines of the late 1930s. Eventually, titles like *Western Picture Stories* and *Star Ranger* (both February 1937) would debut—whole publications devoted exclusively to featuring the genre. Westerns would go on to achieve their greatest popularity in the late 1940s and early 1950s. The biggest sellers of this era were comic books featuring licensed characters, most of them movie and TV cowboys like Gene Autry, Hopalong Cassidy, and Roy Rogers (Horn, *American West*). Publishers who didn't want to pay expensive licensing fees tried their hand with their own original creations, like Marvel's *Two-Gun Kid* (1948) or DC's *Tomahawk* (1947). Comics historian Michelle Nolan ("Collecting") estimates that as many as five thousand western comics were published. Although long a staple in most comics publishers' lines, westerns steadily declined in popularity until the last monthly western comic, DC's *Jonah Hex*, ended in 1985. There are periodic revivals of western comics (*Jonah Hex* made a comeback in 2006), and a number of the original series are offered in hardbound reprint editions (such as the 2006 *Marvel Masterworks: Rawhide Kid*) to entertain new generations. We now examine what many of them had in common.

Character Types

One of the hallmarks of a genre is the familiar kinds of people who populate it. Certain character types return time and again, creating a recognizable familiarity with the situation for the reader. In the western genre, for instance, we have a number of familiar character types:

- the sturdy and reliable lawman, embodied by the town sheriff, a U.S. Marshall, or a cavalry officer, who has an unflinching moral code;
- the grizzled sidekick, whose main function is to provide comic relief;
- the respectable, beautiful woman, whose prim and proper demeanor make her a socially acceptable love interest for the virtuous hero; and
- the villainous outlaw who disrupts the social order in pursuit of self-serving ends and does so without a moral code or compass.

Obviously, some variation on these types (and others) appears from story to story, and series to series, but the recurrence of them in so many instances makes their presence a recognizable part of the genre's formula.

FIGURE 9.3. The cover of *Two-Gun Kid* #19 displays some of the conventions of the western, including the heroic individual and gunplay. Cover art by Chuck Miller. © 2008 Marvel Entertainment, Inc. and its subsidiaries.

Narrative Patterns

The narrative pattern refers to the structure of storytelling. Most stories in the western tradition follow the Aristotelian model of a beginning, middle, and end, but beyond that overarching structure, genre studies examine what additional patterns are laid upon the framework. For instance, in the western genre one recurring narrative pattern has the hero encountering a group of townsfolk who are ready to hang an innocent man. The hero must stop the hanging by not only finding the truly guilty party, but also bringing him to justice. While in pursuit of the villain, some sort of gunplay ensues, perhaps in the form of a shoot-out. In the end, the hero is almost always proven right, the falsely accused man is freed, and the guilty man is hauled off to the hoosegow. Again, within certain variations (the guilty party turns out to be a woman instead of a man in one variation), this pattern is recognized as belonging to the genre because its basic structure has been told so many times.

Themes

In addition to character types and narrative patterns, another major convention involves the repetition of themes. A **theme** is a recurring message either within a narrative or across a series of narratives. A given theme might be included in a narrative either intentionally or unconsciously, but either way it is given special attention by critics, as its repetition is interpreted to mean that the message is significant. A familiar theme in western comics is that of individualism. In the example above, where the hero confronts the townsfolk about hanging the wrong man, we see a message about the virtue of individual thought and action over collective thought and action. If the hero is right about the innocence of the falsely accused man and captures the actual criminal, we see that the message of individuality is reinforced as a theme in this particular story. As other stories about individuality come forth from the genre (e.g., the cavalry scout who notifies his comrades about an ambush, the lone marshal who confronts the villain on Main Street for a shoot-out), the strength of the theme, and its relevance to the genre, only increases.

Other Conventions

Finally, there are other storytelling elements which are recognizable within a genre. These conventions include, but are not limited to, the setting of the story, the use of certain tools or techniques, and the styles typically characteristic of the place or time. Each of these conventions is familiar to the producers and readers of western comics. For instance, almost all westerns are set in frontier territories of the United States in an era following the Civil War, a time when much of the continental U.S. was not yet fully tamed by civilization. Nearly all western heroes use a handgun or rifle (although a few used bows and arrows) with almost superhuman precision. And all are dressed in period clothing—complete with a cowboy hat, of course—and they often appear in the same outfit in issue after issue, almost as if in a superhero costume. Such conventions can make a given genre recognizable almost immediately. In fact, because conventions are so often taken for granted, they are often only noticed when they are absent! (The western hero without a hat would be the one who stands out.)

In the next section we'll look at some additional genres and introduce some of the different character types, narrative patterns, themes, and other conventions that characterize each. As you review them, keep in mind that not every convention has to be present for a story to fit into a genre. But chances are that such conventions have appeared in enough instances that they have become representative of the genre's distinct personality.

GENRE CATEGORIES

There have been numerous popular genres in the last seven decades of American comics, and to cover even a modest number in depth is beyond the scope of this introductory book. However, reviewing a few of the varied genres should shed some light on the versatility of comics to tell different kinds of stories that appeal to diverse audiences. The following are some of the most influential genres in terms of longevity, popularity, and impact on the medium. We will discuss them in terms of their development and several key elements which characterize each.

Teen Humor

Other than the ubiquitous superhero, teen humor is the only genre to be continuously published since it began in comics' Golden Age. And within the genre, the only character to be in continuous publication is the one who defined it: red-headed, tic-tac-toe templed Archie Andrews. Archie debuted as a backup feature to superhero lead-in *The Shield* in *Pep Comics* #22 (1941). Archie and his pals were the brainchild of MLJ Publishing co-founder John Goldwater, who asked, "Why does every book have to be Superman?" (Robbins, *From Girls* 8). Though the superhero genre was in full bloom at the time, Goldwater charged writer Vic Bloom and artist Bob Montana with the task of producing a feature that used the comics medium to exploit the humorous potential of coming-of-age trials and tribulations. Goldwater already had ample evidence of teenage characters' appeal from other media: Teenagers had begun to emerge as a separate social group in the 1930s, and by the time Archie came along in the 1940s the humorous misadventures of teenage protagonists had found an audience among filmgoers (particularly Mickey Rooney portraying Andy Hardy in a series of films begun in 1937) and radio listeners (notably the character of Henry Aldrich in *The Aldrich Family*, which began airing in 1939).

Archie's success was immediate, enduring, and oft-imitated. The year following his debut, he was awarded his own title—the first of many—and in due course his pals Jughead, Betty, Veronica, and Reggie all had titles of their own. By 1946 MLJ embraced its star feature by changing its name to Archie Publications. Numerous competitors attempted to imitate Archie's success. Within the company, characters like Bill Woggon's brunette actress Katy Keene achieved popularity, while over at Timely/Atlas/Marvel, another redhead, Patsy Walker, began a decades-long run under the guidance of Stan Lee. Archie Publications, though, ever the leader in the genre, would go on to further success with the introduction of *Sabrina the Teen-Age Witch* and *Josie and the Pussycats* in the 1960s. Even into the 1970s, there were competing teen comics such as *Binky* and *Millie the Model*, but ultimately it has been only Archie who has managed to perpetuate the genre he helped spawn.

Conventions within the genre quickly settled around the "Archie style," driven no doubt by Archie Comics' sales success. The features focus on an ensemble of idealized teenage characters, usually in a high school setting. Although the characters might embody some stereotype such as the vain prom queen, the clueless schmuck, or the unintelligent jock, most prove to have hearts of gold in the denouement of each story. Stories tend to focus on the most humorous aspects of coming of age, including dating, earning money, and getting access to an automobile. "In a teen comic book all the tensions of dating, of popularity, and of young love are winked at and laughed away" (Benton, *Comic Book* 182). The stories are rounded out with a healthy dash of **slapstick**—physical comedy such as a character taking a fall or tearing his pants. The artwork has followed a style which depicts the characters with realistically proportioned bodies but some caricatured facial features (such as Archie's enlarged eyes). At times, female leads like Cheryl Blossom have been criticized as being almost *too* realistic because of their curvaceous figures.

FIGURE 9.4. America's Typical Teen, Archie Andrews, is forever torn between his attraction to both Veronica and Betty. ™ & © 2008 Archie Comic Publications, Inc. Used with permission.

Unlike the superhero genre, teen humor comics have traditionally appealed to female rather than male readers, with estimates that as many as 60 percent of Archie's readers are girls, typically ages six to thirteen (Robbins, *Girls* 12). Part of the appeal seems to be the window that teen humor opens to preteen audiences who think they are finding out about what it is like to be a teenager. As historian Bradford Wright (2001) points out, this is a sanitized perception of the teenage years: "America's 'typical teenager' never uses teen slang, never fights, never smokes or drinks alcohol, always obeys his parents in the end, and betrays only the vaguest hint of his libido. In other words, he is typical only of the kind of teenager that most adults want to have around. Archie offered young readers a safe glimpse into teen life, while carefully observing the rules of adult society" (73). Not surprisingly, teen humor comics are not made by actual teenagers, but by reasonably mature, reasonably established men like Goldwater, Bloom, and Montana, whose works support a light, humorous interpretation of a period of life that can be otherwise fraught with troubling issues.

Romance

Unlike comics in the teen humor tradition that preceded them, romance comics took maturing very seriously, producing a distinct genre that spoke to an overwhelmingly female readership. Romance comics were concerned with dating, but were decidedly serious about the topic. Typically they were melodramatic in their treatment of young people's struggles with mature romantic relationships. The genre developed right after World War II ended, when many Americans were settling back into domestic roles. For the next thirty years, romance comics would be a vital part of the comics industry.

The first ongoing title to introduce romance to comics readers was *Young Romance* (1947) from Prize Publications, produced by Joe Simon and Jack Kirby, the same creative team who had created Captain America earlier that decade. The cover of the first issue of *Young Romance* proudly announced that this title was "Designed for the more *adult* readers of *comics*," and that audience, particularly the underserved audience of women readers, responded favorably. *Young Romance* soon had a circulation of over a million copies an issue, and other publishers followed in its wake with titles like *Girls' Romances, Heart Throbs*, and *Falling in Love*, producing over 120 imitators by 1949.

Romance comics were usually published in anthology format, featuring a collection of three or four stories of a few pages in length, each with a new cast of love-struck characters. Most of the tales were narrated as first-person confessionals, usually with a young woman admitting the burden of some guilt to the reader (e.g., having kissed an older man). Although each of these tales concluded with a happy ending and the destined couple together, a **narrative problematic** frustrated their union for six to eight pages. A narrative problematic is the challenge that must be overcome or resolved before a happy ending can be reached in a story. Oftentimes the path to true happiness was blocked by a female rival for a boy's affections, or an overprotective parent or town gossip could serve as villainous opposition on the pathway to true love. Story conflict could also come from within the principal characters, such as a girl who is already involved with a somewhat superficial boyfriend and needs to recognize her true place beside a less articulate but more genuine suitor. Though the titles of the stories could be lurid (e.g., "I Was a Pick-Up" or "You're Not the First"), the books were typically quite tame, especially after the Comics Code came into being in 1954. Although the pairings pointed towards physical relationships, the stories almost never depicted physical intimacy. As comics historian Maurice Horn put it, "It was all titillation and no satisfaction" (*Sex* 73).

The depictions of heroines and heroes in the romance comics were fairly realistic, as readers were meant to identify with the protagonists. However, these depictions could certainly be said to err on the side of idealism, with beautifully coiffed, shapely young women and handsome, well-built young men in the leading roles. Occasionally the portrayals might indulge in a stereotype, like having the blonde lead be the good girl while her brunette rival is the bad girl. More consistently, realities like braces, acne, and excessive weight were rarely depicted among the principal characters. These comics were meant to be fantasy fulfillment, and they depicted their characters accordingly. In due course, "They satisfied a kid's need to know what was ahead, to know that dreams could come true and that life was a simple matter once you found your man" (Scott 12).

Although romance comics may have given women an entertaining product, they did not give them role models who veered far from the societal norms of the mid-twentieth century. Female characters may have narrated the stories, but those characters typically fell into traditional gender roles within the stories themselves. This is not all that surprising when one considers that nearly all romance comics were created by men. Many of these men were talented story-tellers, but they were nevertheless portraying their conception of romantic courtship through their own worldview. Even the advice columns featured in many of these magazines were written by men under feminine pen names (e.g., "Julia Roberts") responding to their readers' inquiries.

American society underwent a shift in attitudes towards sexuality and gender roles in the 1960s, and although romance comics attempted to remain in tune with the changes, the creators labored under the restrictions of the Comics Code. Soon romance audiences could find more lurid content in television soap operas and Harlequin paperback novels. Romance comics may have also been undermined by their anthology format, largely lacking a continuing cast of characters with whom readers could establish and pursue **parasocial relationships.** Parasocial relationships develop when people perceive emotional connections to fictional characters or media personalities whom they have never met. These feelings of familiarity may be experienced as intensely as connections to people with whom we have shared relationships. Marvel Comics stopped producing romance comics in 1976 and DC Comics cancelled *Young Love*, its last title in the genre, in 1977.

The legacy of romance comics, however, extends well beyond the demise of their leading titles in the late 1970s. Writer John Lustig suggests that the angst-ridden characterization of Marvel Comics revolutionary superhero characters is indebted to the genre. After all, Stan Lee, Jack Kirby, and many of their fellow collaborators had been working exhaustively on romance comics in the decade prior to the birth of the Marvel Universe. Marvel superheroes often find themselves in challenging relationships, such as the forbidden love between the mutant Scarlet Witch and the android Vision, or the divine Thor's unfulfilled desire to marry his mortal sweetheart Jane Foster. Romance has remained a vital part of the mainstream comics scene.

Of late, the increasing attention directed at a female audience by manga has meant a return to prominence for romance comics within the American comics marketplace. Comics classified as *shôjo* ("little girl") manga are directed at a female audience and feature melodramatic treatments of maturing and relationships. Their central themes often

FIGURE 9.5. Two's company but three's a crowd on the cover of *Girls' Love Stories* #36 (1955). © DC Comics

focus on "getting the boy" but also increasingly on "finding oneself" in coming-of-age settings (Thorn 48). Even mainstream publishers like Marvel and DC have recently experimented with similarly focused titles like *Spider-Man Loves Mary Jane*, which tell stories from teenager Mary Jane Watson's perspective and are illustrated in the manga style. As they did a generation ago, such romance comics prove that comics are not just for boys.

Funny Animals

The concept of **anthropomorphism**—endowing animals with human qualities—is as old as recorded literature, reaching all the way back to Aesop's fables from ancient Greece (e.g., "The Tortoise and the Hare"). As a literary device, anthropomorphism acts as a mirror, allowing the storyteller to reflect human characteristics—more often than not, the less flattering ones—back upon the readers in order to enlighten them about the human condition. Encountering animals who speak eloquently, socialize according to human customs, and meet their just desserts when tripped up by their own pride, avarice, or ignorance makes for an entertaining story. Such imagined creatures have fascinated people throughout history and across cultures. It's little wonder then that these "funny animals" would find a home in early comic books.

Early comic strips had already embraced animal protagonists by the time comic books came to print. Most notably, George Herriman's strip *Krazy Kat*, launched in 1913, had captured a national audience in the pages of America's newspapers. Yet the fledgling comic book industry did not turn to its newspaper forerunners for funny animal material to fill its pages, but to the popular animated film shorts of the day. The first film studio to lend its characters to comic books was Walt Disney, who licensed stars like Mickey Mouse and Donald Duck to Dell Publishing. In 1940 Dell launched the first funny animal comic book with *Walt Disney's Comics and Stories*. Dell quickly followed up its successful relationship with Disney by establishing contracts with Warner Brothers Studios to use characters like Porky Pig and Bugs Bunny, beginning with *Looney Tunes and Merrie Melodies* (1941), and then enrolled MGM's Walter Lantz creations like Andy Panda and Woody Woodpecker for the first issue of *New Funnies* (1942). Other publishers tried to catch up to Dell's initiative, with first Timely and then St. John Publishing taking on 20th Century Fox's Paul Terry creations like Mighty Mouse in *Terry-Toons* (1942). National Periodicals got into the contest late with Columbia Pictures' the Fox and the Crow in *Real Screen Comics* (1945).

While such adaptations may have been popular with audiences, particularly young children, the translation did not always fare well when moving from one medium to another. For instance, part of the thrill of a Bugs Bunny animated romp is the pacing of the slapstick comedy and masterful vocalizations by voice actor Mel Blanc, but comics cannot convey these qualities. Indeed, the best remembered of the original spate of funny animal comics ultimately proved to be characters that emerged indigenous to the medium. To that end, two creators became synonymous with the genre: Walt Kelly and Carl Barks.

FIGURE 9.6. Walt Kelly's *Pogo* comments on the sad state of the swamp on Earth Day 1971. © Okefenokee Glee & Perloo, Inc. Used by permission.

Walt Kelly is highly regarded for the creation of Pogo Possum, an original character who debuted in Dell's *Animal Comics* #1 (1942). Pogo became highly successful in comic books and, beginning in 1949, migrated into a syndicated newspaper strip as well. In fact, while Pogo's comic book career came to end by 1954, his newspaper strip ran nationwide until 1975. Part of the strip's appeal was the genuine satire that Kelly introduced into the Okefenokee Swamp that Pogo inhabited, particularly as he skewered political figures of his day. For instance, Pogo took on Senator Joseph McCarthy during his infamous communist witch-hunts by parodying the senator and his crusade through the character of Simple J. Malarkey. Kelly's savvy satire made Pogo popular enough over the decades that the publishing house of Simon & Shuster issued dozens of collected editions reprinting his adventures.

Another cartoonist who had an enduring impact on the funny animal genre was Carl Barks, whose work for Dell's Disney line of comics earned him the title of "the good artist" from fans. Disney policy left artists' contributions uncredited—except for Walt himself—in their initial printings. But as fans learned to distinguish the care and style of Barks' work over time, he earned fan recognition despite his anonymity. Between 1942 and 1967 Barks drew hundreds of Donald Duck features and, in December 1947, he introduced fan favorite character Uncle Scrooge McDuck. To this day, Barks' work is still appearing in reprinted editions of his comics.

FIGURE 9.7. Carl Barks at his drawing board. Photograph courtesy of Tom Andrae.

The earliest funny animal comics, like the fables that preceded them, often focused on some moral lesson: be kind to one's neighbors, always tell the truth, etc. But the appeal for the audience might have been more utilitarian than moralistic. According to historian Les Daniels, "At an age when children had little on their side except the ability to dissemble and a repertoire of alternate fantasy identities, and were surrounded by dumb adults or neighborhood bullies, these images released, quite simply, the power to do infinite things with minimal resources" (*Comix* 53). Funny animals thus became equipment for the imagination, allowing readers to break free of an otherwise confining life. In regards to their quality of wish fulfillment, then, they may not have been all that different from the superhero comics with which they competed.

The popularity of funny animal comics reached its highest levels during the 1940s and 1950s, though their influence continued throughout the ensuing decades, particularly as subsequent artists began to use the juxtaposition of talking animals interacting with the idiosyncrasies of human society. A new generation of cartoonists tapped into this satirical vein, including Steve Gerber's *Howard the Duck* for Marvel Comics (beginning in 1973) and Dave Sim's epic *Cerebus* (1977–2004), which featured a talking aardvark who held vocations as varied as barbarian warrior and pope. Funny animals continue to allow cartoonists the freedom to explore the human condition, and later examples such as Reed Waller and Kate Worley's sexy soap opera *Ohama the Cat Dancer*, Jim Woodring's anthropomorphic creature Frank, and Jeff Smith's adventurous *Bone* have found a forum among comics' independent publishers.

Profile: Jeff Smith

born: Jeffrey Adams Smith
       February 27, 1960
       McKees Rocks, Pennsylvania

"I saw comics as books, and I wanted them to be treated like books. The majority of the comic book industry, however, saw them as magazines or collectibles."

Career Highlights

1980s   While attending Ohio State University, Smith creates the cartoon series *Thorn* for the student newspaper *The Lantern*.

1991   Smith and his wife, Vijaya Iyer, establish Cartoon Books and begin to publish the monthly *Bone* comic book.

1993   *Bone* wins its first of many Eisner Awards.

1994   Fellow self-publisher Dave Sim sets off a public feud with Smith after Sim writes an unflattering portrayal of Smith and his wife into his *Cerebus* series.

Cont'd

FIGURE 9.8. Bone and his creator, Jeff Smith. Courtesy of Cartoon Books.

1999   Smith collaborates with artist Charles Vess on a graphic novel prequel to *Bone*, called *Rose*, for which Vess wins an Eisner

2004   After Smith completes the last stand-alone issue of *Bone*, Cartoon Books issues the massive 1,300-page *Bone: One Volume Edition*, or, as it was nicknamed, "The Brick."

2005   *Time* magazine names *Bone* one of the ten greatest graphic novels of all time.

2007   DC Comics publishes Smith's *Shazam: The Monster Society of Evil* limited series.

2008   Ohio State University's Wexner Center sponsors an exhibit dedicated to Smith's work, "Bone and Beyond."

"Genre labels are a bit of a red herring," contends Jeff Smith, creator of the phenomenally successful *Bone* comics. He understands that the appeal of his comics lies in their effectiveness as a storytelling medium, and not necessarily the specific genre through which he chooses to tell them. And Smith should know, as his approach has won him a host of Eisner and Harvey Awards from within the industry, along with the accolades of critics, librarians, and booksellers from outside the industry. "Stories are information delivery devices. Each story contains the information it wants to convey, and also a metaphor to clothe it in," says Smith. In Smith's particular case, the funny animal metaphor wrapped around his epic series *Bone* involves three anthropomorphic cartoon cousins, Fone Bone, Smiley Bone, and Phoney Bone, who experience a heroic quest that took their creator twelve years and over 1,300 pages to tell. Despite using funny little Bone-folk, a motley band of human companions, and those "Stupid, Stupid Rat Creatures" as featured characters, Smith challenges the notion that funny animal comics cannot be sophisticated art. "People seem to think that some genres are more important or more legitimate than others. They are not. What matters is the story you are telling me." *Bone* uses humor and imagination to tell its story of heroism and loyalty. It has won fans of all ages and has been named one of *Time* magazine's ten best graphic novels ever.

Cont'd

In 1991 Smith and his wife, Vijaya Iyer, founded Cartoon Books as a vehicle for Jeff to begin self-publishing the black-and-white *Bone* comic. In 1993 Smith surprised the industry by reprinting the first several issues of his series in collected form. Until that time, publishers rarely reprinted older comics material in new formats, but Smith believed that comics deserved to have a longer shelf life than the monthly turnaround on comics racks. "When bookstores sell out of any other kind of book, they restock it with more copies," he explains. Why should comics be any different? Smith was already well on his way to making his *Bone* collections a perennial product in bookstores across the country when in 2005 Scholastic, the U.S. publisher of Harry Potter, began to release colored versions of the collections for the first time. This association with the world's largest children's publisher furthered the reach for Smith's comics, bringing them to new audiences through Scholastic's school-based book clubs and book fairs.

Although Smith resists being defined by genre, he cites as some of his greatest influences other cartoonists who specialized in anthropomorphic characters. Those influences include Carl Bark's Uncle Scrooge, Charles Shultz's Snoopy, and Walt Kelly's Pogo Possum. In fact, it was a 1967 paperback reprinting Kelly's Pogo comic strips that inspired Smith. "I collected Pogo books when I was a kid. When I started *Bone* in 1991, my goal wasn't the twenty-four-page comic books; I wanted to make my own Pogo books—with one twist: I wanted the entire comic, from the first page to the very last panel, to tell one giant, complete story—with a beginning, middle and end."

Horror

Tales of encounters with the supernatural have been fodder for the imagination since people first started storytelling, but the modern fascination with horror fiction can be traced most directly to Mary Shelley's 1818 novel *Frankenstein*. The novel speaks to the awful retribution that comes with disrupting the natural order of things. When the scientist Victor Frankenstein reanimates corpses in the form of his creature, he pays for transgressing the natural boundaries between life and death with his own ruination. Horror has been a popular genre in every mass medium, from novels, radio, and films to television, video games, and, of course, comics. Horror stories pick at our collective uneasiness with the unknown, with what lies beyond in the darkness, just out of reach of the revealing light of our primordial campfires. Reading horror stories allows an audience to play out what it fears and in the process allows some catharsis from those fears.

Given their familiarity in popular culture, it is not surprising that horrific figures like vampires appeared as villainous foils in early comics stories. But the first comic book devoted specifically to the genre was a one-shot from Avon titled *Eerie*, published in 1946. The first ongoing title came along within the next two years when the American Comics Group started *Adventures into the Unknown* in 1948, and continued to publish it until 1967. But the gold standard in horror comics came from the stable of Entertaining Comics, which published *The Crypt of Terror*—soon changed to the now more familiar title of *Tales from the Crypt*—alongside *Vault of Horror* and *Haunt of Fear* beginning in 1950. Under the guidance of publisher Bill Gaines and editor Al Feldstein, EC quickly gained a reputation for clever stories and superior artwork, and even popular fiction author Ray Bradbury allowed some of his works to be adapted by the EC staff. Although the entire run of EC horror comics lasted less than five years, those works have been reprinted again and again. They have even been adapted into film and television directly (e.g., HBO's *Tales from the Crypt*) and had an acknowledged influence on horror fiction in other media, including the works of Stephen King in his short stories and screenplays (*Creepshow*), R.L. Stine in children's books (the "Goosebumps" series), and George Romero and John Carpenter in their films (*Night of the Living Dead* and *The Fog*, respectively).

In the early 1950s EC's success inspired a stampede of imitators, many of whom thought the key to sales rested in increasingly gruesome scenes of violence and gore. The excesses of the horror genre helped fuel a national campaign against the entire comics industry, resulting in the Comics Code, an industry-sponsored censoring program that effectively neutered horror comics and sanitized most future comics exclusively for juvenile audiences (see Chapter 2). Among its prohibitions, the Code forbade the use of the words *horror* or *terror* in any comic book's title and prohibited the use of vampires, werewolves, and zombies in any comic's cast. Despite such restrictions, some of the former horror titles suffered on, but they were much tamer under the auspices of the Code, offering more fantasy and science fiction stories than outright horror. Fear-inducing giant monsters on the order of Godzilla became features in the late fifties and early sixties, offering comics readers some thrills but far fewer chills.

Horror comics eventually found an outlet outside traditional comics magazines, at least until the Comics Code could undergo revision. The reemergence of horror comics began in earnest in 1964 when Warren Publishing published the first issue of *Creepy*, an anthology attempting to replicate the EC formula for success. *Creepy* skirted the restrictions of the Comics Code by publishing its stories in a larger magazine size and in black and white instead of color. The success of *Creepy* led to companion magazines like *Eerie* and *Vampirella*, whose erotic vampire hostess went on to become an icon in her own right. By the mid-seventies, the success of the Warren publications had spawned a host of imitators crowding the magazine racks, including Skywald Publishing's *Nightmare*, *Psycho*, and *Scream*. Wanting to compete with the resurging horror market, comics publishers applied pressure to loosen the Code's restrictions.

When changes to the Code came, they also helped foment changes in the perception of the horrific creatures, as creators began to adopt a view of the monsters as somewhat sympathetic *protagonists* instead of the misery-inducing antagonists (Mishler, "Horror"). The turn began with the 1971 revised Code permitting some formerly restricted elements back into full-color comics, repealing the ban on supernatural creatures but still maintaining some taste-related restrictions. Marvel Comics quickly seized the opportunity to release a number of series featuring everything from werewolves to swamp monsters as their leads, the best of which was the *Tomb of Dracula* series written by Marv Wolfman and drawn by Gene Colan. During its run through most of the 1970s, *Tomb of*

Dracula was an intricately plotted serial, with the world's most famous vampire starring amidst a cast of dubious allies and righteous adversaries (including the later-to-be-famous Blade, the Vampire Hunter). Despite his titular role, Dracula was still evil in this series, but a more sympathetic monster would take shape over at DC Comics, where Len Wein and Bernie Wrightson introduced the Swamp Thing character (*House of Secrets* #92, 1971). In 1984 emerging super-star writer Alan Moore took the reigns of the Swamp Thing and used the char-acter to move horror comics more from the physical to psychological, emphasizing mood over gory spectacle. A similarly intellectual take on horror came from Neil Gaiman's acclaimed *Sandman* series (1989).

However, not all horror comics subsequent to the Code's revision were more cerebral than visceral. The rise of the direct market meant that comics' producers did not have to seek Code approval for newsstand distribution, allowing creators to push the envelope of graphic horror far further than it had been since the Code's introduction in the 1950s. The 1990s saw more blood-soaked series like *Evil Ernie* and *Lady Death* from Chaos! Comics on sale at comics specialty shops alongside the more moody titles of DC's Vertigo line. The emphasis on the horror as the hero, though, would continue to dom-inate the genre, with successful titles like DC's *Hellblazer*, Mike Mignola's *Hellboy*, and Marvel's *Man-Thing* thrusting the supernatural protagonists into the forefront.

As a genre, horror's most obvious characteristic is the insertion of the super-natural into the commonplace. Using fantastic creatures like ghosts or monsters accomplishes this quite readily, especially when their depictions are taken to the extremes of eeriness or distortion. Of course, what makes these representations really pop is their contrast with ordinary surroundings. So when a werewolf shows up at a movie theater, or a typical home becomes haunted by a screaming poltergeist, the shock scares an audience who fears that such monstrosities could be within their own commonplace reach. With its emphasis on the visual storytelling elements, comics is an ideal medium for horror stories, as the reader can be reminded of the presence of the supernatural frame after frame, and linger over them as they move through the story at their own pace (Gravett, *Graphic Novels*).

A second element common to stories within the horror genre is the element of suspense, the dramatic tension that comes from not knowing the survival of a character or the resolution of a stress-filled situation. Typically, this tension rises throughout the story with additional twists and turns compounding the pressure until the very end of the story. Al Feldstein was particularly revered for the twist endings he would give in EC's horror comics. He would generally provide a comeuppance for some deviant or evil character in the form of poetic justice. For instance, a butcher selling spoiled meat in order to increase his own profits would receive just punishment for his misdeeds, finding himself carved up and displayed in his own meat case by the story's end (*Tales from the Crypt* #32, 1952). Though usually gruesome, horror comics could also aim to be moralistic, intoning a message against greed, jealousy, and other vices. Whether such loftier messages get lost in the spectacle of the accompanying gore is open to debate.

Because the tension and gore can be so intense, some horror comics have often subscribed to a third common feature, softening the delivery of their gruesome tales by having them served up by a host with a sense of humor. Once again EC innovated this trend in horror comics, though Gaines and Feldstein had taken it from early radio programs. In popular radio series like the *Witch's Tale* and *Inner Sanctum*, a creepy narrator introduced and closed each episode. EC did the same with each story, framing their tales with three "GhouLunatics" named the Crypt-Keeper, the Vault-Keeper, and the Old Witch. Each of these characters provided punny segues into and out of the intense stories. For instance, at the end of one tale, the Crypt-Keeper reminds the reader of his own mortality and asks, "Why the *grave* look?" here using *grave* to play on both the deathly theme of the story and to strike an ironic chord about the anticipated seriousness of the reader's reaction. Later horror comics would embrace the GhouLunatics approach, with Warren Publishing giving both its Uncle Creepy and Cousin Eerie similar personalities for its black-and-white magazines. DC later cast sparring siblings Cain and Abel as the hosts of its leading horror books, and Charlton Comics featured a whole gang of offbeat hosts, from Dr. Graves to Baron Weirwulf. The hosts also gave those horror comics that featured anthology tales a recurring character to retain audience loyalty from issue to issue. After all, with a number of the featured characters left beheaded, dismembered, or disemboweled by the end of just one story, the host might be the only one in any shape to return with the next issue.

FIGURE 9.9. EC's Horrible Hosts, the GhouLunatics, © William M. Gaines Agent, Inc. Used with permission.

Memoir

Of the genres we've discussed so far, you may well have noted that most originated in comics' formative years, taking root sometime between the late 1930s and early 1950s. The variety of genres available to comics storytelling is not constrained to that one creative period in the medium's history, however, and to emphasize that point we turn to the example of memoir comics, which have a relatively more recent genesis. Such non-fiction comics in general have recently enjoyed a surge in both creative and commercial popularity.

The first American comic book to present its own cartoonist's life story was an underground comic titled *Binky Brown Meets the Holy Virgin Mary* (1972). In it, Justin Green (alias Binky Brown) provides a frank account of his psychological troubles growing up within the sexually repressive Catholic Church. Thereafter, a number of other underground cartoonists, including Robert Crumb and

S. Clay Wilson, began to explore their own life stories within the comics art form. As a genre, memoir comics have had little success with the mainstream publishers like Marvel or DC, and have instead found outlets through smaller presses or through self-publishing. One enduring example of the latter approach is Harvey Pekar's *American Splendor*, which since 1976 has chronicled the mundane life experiences of this Cleveland file clerk. An even more poignant memoir began to come together in the pages of Art Spiegelman's *Raw*, when Spiegelman began to publish chapters of his experiences coming to terms with the Holocaust experience of his father, Vladek. Ultimately *Maus* was reprinted as a graphic novel (1991), and it became one of the most honored works of graphic storytelling. More and more memoir comics have followed *Maus*'s turn to the graphic novel format. Examples include: *One! Hundred! Demons!* (2002), Lynda Barry's collection of vignettes of her growing up; *Blankets* (2003), Craig Thompson's recollections of growing up in an Evangelical family; *Epileptic* (2005), David B.'s documentation of the strain his brother's epilepsy placed on his family; and *Fun Home* (2006), Alison Bechdel's account of dealing with her own sexuality and that of her closeted father.

The graphic novel format has been especially conducive to memoir comics, particularly at a time when bookstores and libraries are making room on their shelves for the hardcover and trade paperback comics formats. Moreover, wider audiences seem to be more attracted to this genre than the traditional comics fare offered at comics specialty shops, given that the subject matter is often grounded in recognizable themes of family and day-to-day living, as opposed to the supernatural trappings of the superhero or horror comics.

Towards that end, scholar Craig Hight points out that one distinguishing characteristic of memoir comics is their quest for authenticity in the account of one's life, an honest realism of one's experience. Cartoonists who choose to work in this genre seek to lay bare the details of their experience, even if they are unflattering. Harvey Pekar is a prime example of this, readily chronicling in the pages of *American Splendor* admissions of his own unflattering behavior, including the petty crime of stealing albums for his record collection from a local radio station. Confessing such details may move the comic closer to this desired goal of authenticity, but in admitting one's imperfections, the creators of memoir comics come across as far less heroic than the superheroes who dominate the medium. That, however, is often the intention.

FIGURE 9.10. Chester Brown recalls a dishonest exchange with his onetime girlfriend in his memoir *The Playboy*. © 1992 Chester Brown and used with permission.

Interestingly, in their quest for authenticity, memoir comics actually present more of a self-caricature than an objectively realistic self. Rather than rely on a photo-realistic depiction, many cartoonists render themselves more abstractly, appearing as a cartoon rather than a more accurate effigy. Professor Charles Hatfield argues that such abstraction may serve to help creators of memoir comics acknowledge their own subjective role in re-presenting their life events. The caricatured self becomes self-referential, acknowledging that the story of one's life, as told by oneself, is always a subjective rather than an objective account. Through such an admission, the accounts may move closer to a truth about the story than a more varnished, attractive presentation would. For example, this effect is pronounced in *Maus*, where Spiegelman casts himself as a mouse, which is as abstract a self-representation as one is likely to find.

Memoir comics have been criticized for being too self-indulgent, focused as they are on the cartoonist's life. They have also been criticized for dwelling on life's tragic side. Still, these stories seem to ring true with sympathetic audiences, who respond to the intimate portrayals by buying and reading what the genre has to offer.

OTHER EXAMPLES OF COMIC BOOK GENRES		
Genre	**Characteristics**	**Example Titles**
Crime Comics	One of the most infamous comics genres because the depictions of crimes—some of them adaptations of real-life criminal activity—led to public outcry against their often all-too-graphic content.	*Crime Does Not Pay*, Lev Gleason (1942–1955) *Crime Suspenstories*, EC (1950–1955) *Mr. District Attorney*, DC (1950–1959)
Detective Comics	The first genre to have comics magazines expressly devoted to it. Hardboiled private eyes had their heyday in the 1930s but were largely supplanted by superheroes.	*Detective Comics*, DC (1937–present) *Dick Tracy*, Dell & Harvey (1948–1961) *Ms. Tree*, Eclipse & others (1981–1993)
Educational Comics	Comics have been used to train people on a variety of tasks, raise awareness of health and social issues, and adapt literature.	*Picture Stories from American History*, EC (1945–1947) *Classics Illustrated*, Gilberton (1947–1951) *Amazing Spider-Man Battles Ignorance*, Marvel (1992)
Jungle Comics	Inspired by Tarzan, white jungle kings and queens garbed in animal-print swimsuits protected the jungles and white prerogative.	*Jumbo Comics*, Fiction House (1938–1953) *Korak, Son of Tarzan*, Gold Key & DC (1964–1976) *Shanna the She-Devil*, Marvel (1972–1973)
Kid Comics	Innocent and funny, kid comics began in newspaper pages with Rudolph Dirks' *Katzenjammer Kids*. They and their imitators promoted imaginative interaction with the adult world around them.	*Little Lulu*, Dell & others (1948–1984) *Richie Rich*, Harvey (1960–1994) *Little Archie*, Archie (1957–present) *Cont'd*

Genre *(Cont'd)*	Characteristics *(Cont'd)*	Example Titles *(Cont'd)*
Kung Fu Comics	In the mid-seventies "everybody was kung fu fighting" in the mass media, including the lead characters of these martial arts–inspired periodicals.	*Master of Kung Fu*, Marvel (1974–1983) *Yang*, Charlton (1973–1976) *Karate Kid*, DC (1976–1978)
Movie Comics	Just as Hollywood has adapted comics material into films, comics have adapted popular features and stars into print. In addition to feature films, radio programs, television series, and even video games have supplied comics with inspiration.	*Adventures of Jerry Lewis*, DC (1952–1971) *Star Wars*, Marvel & others (1977–present) *Predator*, Dark Horse (1989–present)
Promotional Comics	Usually distributed as giveaways, promotional comics help to advertise a product or conviction or are a reward for having made a purchase.	*Funnies on Parade*, Proctor & Gamble (1933)—the first modern comic book *Captain America Goes to War Against Drugs*, Marvel (1990) *King James*, DC (2004 promo for Powerade)
Science Fiction Comics	Science fiction is a broad genre, popular in many media, but always involves some speculation about actual science or technology. Stories can feature everything from alien invaders to intelligent machines.	*Planet Comics*, Fiction House (1940–1953) *Weird Science*, EC (1950–1955) *Kamandi, the Last Boy on Earth*, DC (1972–1978)
Sword-and-Sorcery Comics	Sword-wielding heroes, scantily clad heroines, powerful wizards, and exotic locales characterize entries in this fantasy genre.	*Conan*, Marvel and Dark Horse (1970–present) *Warlord*, DC (1976–present) *Elfquest*, WaRP Graphics (1978–present)
Underground Comix	In every imaginable social taboo, from sexuality to scatology, underground comix have pushed the boundaries and worked in defiance of the puritanical Comics Code.	*Zap Comics*, Apex Novelties (1968–2005) *Fabulous Furry Freak Brothers*, Rip Off Press (1971–1992) *Wimmen's Comix*, Last Gasp & others (1972–1989)
War Comics	Stories in this genre make the most of the life-and-death struggle of combat. Some examples glamorize the heroics, while other stories suggest the futility of war.	*Two-Fisted Tales*, EC (1950–1955) *Sgt. Rock*, DC (1959–present) *The 'Nam*, Marvel (1986–1993)

ANALYZING: HYBRID FORMS

Although talking about genres requires us to define them in some static ways, the reality of media products is that they are always evolving. In part, this evolution may be attributed to the creative impulses of the cartoonists who are developing new stories to tell. Many of them want to experiment with pushing boundaries by introducing new storytelling elements into their work. The evolution may also be attributed to publishers wanting to find more distinct materials to appeal to their audience in a crowded marketplace. For instance, when the first horror comics appeared, they were nowhere near as gruesome as they would become by the midfifties and no one could have foreseen the turn to more moody, psychological horror later in the twentieth century. Put simply, genres evolve.

One of the ways to see the evolution of genre take shape is to note how some comics experiment with hybrid forms. A hybrid might take the familiar character types of one genre and drop them into the narrative pattern of another. For example, in the early 1950s, when both western and romance comics were at the heights of their popularity, a number of publishers experimented with cross-breeding the genres, producing titles like *Western Hearts*, *Western Love*, and *Cowgirl Romances*. Similarly,

FIGURE 9.11. Cowboys discover love on the range in the pages of the short-lived hybridization of western and romance comics (*Cowboy Love* #31, 1955). © 1955 Charlton Comics

publishers in the 1970s attempted to mix the chills of horror comics with the thrills of love comics, presenting gothic-romance hybrids in titles like *The Dark Mansion of Forbidden Love* and *Haunted Love*. Of course, by far the most experimentation has taken place with the dominant superhero genre, as nearly every conceivable match has been attempted at one time or another:

- Superhero + western = the original *Ghost Rider*
- Superhero + teen humor = *Archie as Pureheart the Powerful*
- Superhero + romance = *Young Heroes in Love*
- Superhero + funny animals = *Captain Carrot and His Amazing Zoo Crew*
- Superhero + horror = *Spectre*

And the list goes on and on.

Whether it is for aesthetic exploration or commercial exploitation, the attempts to create and market hybrids have produced some entertaining results.

Most of these combinations do not last long, though they can subtly influence a genre. Although a spate of western romances filled the newsstands in early 1950s, the hybrid was fleeting and the western soon returned to its conventional focus on the male hero, while romance anthologies only occasionally found themselves presenting a love story in a western setting. Other hybrids have been more successful. The combination of horror and superheroes in the pages of *Marvel Zombies* has sold a lot of comics and related merchandise over the past several years. Yet whatever their commercial success or longevity, hybrids serve to remind us that comics, as with other popular arts, allow creators to play with their most familiar storytelling techniques.

Discussion Questions

1. How do genres influence your consumption of media? For instance, are you more likely to tune in to a program because it's on the Sci-Fi Channel? Or would you pick up a paperback because it's a Harlequin Romance? Explain how your own preference(s) for genre(s) influence your selection of media products.
2. Are comics genres products of their times, or do they transcend the times? If you find that they are reflections of their eras, what does a given genre's popularity say about its time (e.g., the rise of sword-and-sorcery or kung fu comics in the 1970s)? If you perceive that genres transcend their era, what qualities make a given genre popular from generation to generation (e.g., why has Archie's teen humor been able to stay in publication for so long)?
3. Identify two comics genres and then propose a hybridization of them. What features of each would be most relevant to your hybrid narrative? Why do you suppose that the combination would be appealing to an audience?

Activities

1. Conduct a genre analysis of a recent graphic novel. First select one of the genres described in depth in this chapter's readings (e.g., teen humor, romance, funny animals, horror, memoir) and note well the qualities we have discussed that help to define that particular genre. Then select a graphic novel that you perceive as fitting into that genre. (Your instructor may be able to help with some suggestions.) Next, read the graphic novel, noting how it fulfills the characteristic of the genre, such as familiar character types, narrative patterns, genre conventions, and themes (recall that this is all a function of standardization). Also be aware of ways in which it deviates from the genre or other examples within the genre (differentiation). Consider how genre both enables and possibly constrains the storytelling going on in your graphic novel; in other words, what are the advantages and limitations of working within a genre? Your instructor may ask you to

submit this analysis as either a written report or an oral presentation explaining how the work fits the genre.

2. It is said that you can't judge a book by its cover, and yet countless impulse purchases at grocery store checkout lanes and bookstore window displays are predicated on the assumption that a good cover *can* sell a publication. Visit your local comic book specialty shop or the graphic novel section of your local library or bookstore in order to locate examples of one of the genres outlined in Figure 9.11. Scan the covers of a number of comics within your selected genre and then pick three covers to analyze in greater depth. Note what you are seeing in terms of genre conventions being displayed on the cover art. How do you know that a selected work actually fits into a given genre? Do the language choices of the title or on any backmatter (e.g., summaries, reviewers' comments, etc.) confirm your inclination that the book fits a specific genre? Do these choices inspire you to want to pick up that particular comic? Come to class prepared to share at least three talking points about how the shorthand of visual communication can be used to successfully (or perhaps even unsuccessfully) suggest a particular genre fit to a passing audience.

Recommended Readings

Comics:

Cochran, Russ, ed. *EC Archives*. 8+ vols. Timonium, MD: Gemstone Publishing, 2007.

EC aficionado Russ Cochran has partnered with Gemstone Publishing to reprint the entire EC library in sturdy hardbound editions. Thus far, three volumes of the genre-defining horror classics from *Tales from the Crypt* and one volume of *Vault of Horror* have been published. Also joining them in the series are volumes of EC's *Crime Suspenstories* and sci-fi favorite *Weird Science*.

Rosa, Don. *The Life and Times of Scrooge McDuck*. Timonium, MD: Gemstone Publishing, 2005.

Rosa won an Eisner Award in 1995 for Best Serialized Story with his comical biography of one of comicdom's most beloved funny animals. Rosa exercised great care with remaining true to the previously published stories by his predecessor and Scrooge creator Carl Barks when crafting this entertaining story.

Scholarly Sources:

Benton, Mike. *The Taylor History of Comics*. 5 vols. Dallas, TX: Taylor Publishing Company, 1991–1993.

Benton created some of the deepest explorations of comics genres in this series, which contains individual volumes dedicated to Golden Age superheroes, Silver Age superheroes, science fiction, horror, and crime comics. Each details the origins, characteristics, and representative series within each genre through the late 1980s.

Gravett, Paul. *Graphic Novels: Everything You Need to Know*. New York: Harper-Collins, 2005.

Gravett provides an introduction to both a variety of genres, ranging from memoir to romance, and individual examples of graphic novels published within each category. These examples include panel-by-panel analyses of notable works like *A Contract with God* and *Sin City*, among dozens of others. For those curious to sample some representative works within various genres, this introduction is a helpful primer.

Comic Book Genres:
The Superhero Genre

"A hero is someone who has given his or her life to something bigger than oneself."

—JOSEPH CAMPBELL, PROFESSOR OF MYTHOLOGY AND COMPARATIVE RELIGIONS, 1988

Software engineer Matthew Atherton's concept for a superhero called Feedback has taken on a life of its own since he first developed the character with the help of his wife Sarah Blevins. Atherton took the concept along with his homemade costume design to audition for a reality television program on the

Sci-Fi Channel. As Feedback, he went on to win *Who Wants to Be a Superhero?* and was immortalized in a comic book written by Stan Lee and published by Dark Horse Comics. His likeness has been cast in the form of an action figure, and he's starred in his own online radio serial. But what's more important to Atherton is the good that being Feedback has allowed him to do. As Feedback, he's raised thousands of dollars for the Make-A-Wish Foundation and Recording for the Blind & Dyslexic, and he has inspired many people to discover, as he did, the potential of the superhero everyone has within.

Feedback is far from the only real-life superhero. There are dozens of costumed crusaders, including promotional characters, people just having fun, and a few serious crime fighters, listed at the World Superhero Registry. In 2007 there were two

FIGURE 10.1. Feedback embodies the superhero role in real life. Courtesy of Matthew Atherton.

documentaries—*Super Amigos* and *Your Friendly Neighborhood Hero*—about people leading dual lives as superheroes. What possesses people to assume goofy names, don bizarre outfits, and devote themselves to helping others? Why is it that the concept of the superhero can capture the imagination and fortify the sense of right and wrong? In this chapter we will examine the nature of the superhero and consider why this concept, so firmly rooted in the American comic book industry, is so powerful.

OBJECTIVES

In this chapter you will learn:

1. the roots of the superhero concept;
2. the defining characteristics of the superhero;
3. the conventions of the superhero genre;
4. how the superhero genre has evolved; and
5. explanations for the enduring popularity of the major superhero characters.

ROOTS OF THE SUPERHERO CONCEPT

Although Superman was and still is the purest embodiment of the superhero, the concept was not born fully formed that spring day in 1938 when Superman made his debut in *Action Comics* #1. The familiar aspects of the superhero—the powers, the costume, and the dual identity—had all existed before Superman made the scene, albeit not quite in that combination. Even the superhero's penchant for individual initiative and "regeneration through violence" has always been engrained in the American mythos (Mark Nevins, 27; Early 71), and the extraordinary adventures of the buckskin-clad heroes of early American literature such as Natty Bumppo and larger-than-life pioneers like Daniel Boone prefigure the superhero. According to researcher Peter Coogan, the earliest comic book superheroes were derived from three primary streams of adventure-narrative figures: the science-fiction superman, the pulp magazine *übermensch*, and the dual-identity vigilante. Most of these figures first appeared in novels or pulp magazines. The Shadow, the Lone Ranger, and the Green Hornet were born on radio. Lesser-known characters like Dr. Occult and the Clock originated in comic books. Some characters, such as the comic strip strongman Popeye and the swashbuckling film heroes played by Douglas Fairbanks, which Joe Siegel and Jerry Shuster acknowledged as influencing their creation of Superman, do not fit easily into any of Coogan's categories. And, while the list in Figure 10.2 contains only the major characters in these three streams, it does provide an overview of the development of the superhero formula that became codified with Superman and soon after Batman.

Science Fiction Supermen	Pulp Übermensch	Dual Identity Vigilantes
		Robin Hood 1377
Frankenstein 1818		
		Nick of the Woods 1837
	Nick Carter 1886	
		Scarlet Pimpernel 1905
John Carter 1912	Tarzan 1912	
		The Gray Seal 1914
		Zorro 1919
Hugo Danner 1930		
		The Shadow 1931
		The Lone Ranger 1933
	Doc Savage 1933	The Spider 1933
		The Bat 1934
		Dr. Occult 1935
		Green Hornet 1936
		The Phantom 1936
		The Clock 1936
	Superman 1938	The Batman 1939

FIGURE 10.2. Peter Coogan has traced the development of the superhero as flowing from three streams of adventure-narrative figures.

Superman is the culmination of all three traditions, including similarities he shares with other science fiction supermen. Superman's abilities are directly influenced by a character named Hugo Danner, who appeared in Phillip Wylie's 1930 novel *Gladiator*, a book which Jerry Siegel had given a very favorable review in his fanzine. Early in the novel young Danner tells his father, "I can jump higher than a house. I can run faster'n a train. I can pull up big trees an' push 'em over" (Wylie 44). Later, when Danner goes to war, he finds that his skin is invulnerable to bullets, and only exploding mortar shells can wound him. In his early adventures, Superman's more limited powers were described in a similar way. In *Action Comics* #1 (1938), Clark Kent discovered he could "hurdle a twenty-story building . . . raise tremendous weights . . . run faster than an express train . . . and that nothing less than a bursting shell could penetrate his skin!" Hugo Danner's father cautions him that when people find out about his strength they will fear him, just as Pa Kent warns young Clark, "This great strength of yours—you've got to hide it from people or they'll be scared of you!" (*Superman* #1). Professor Danner goes on to assure Hugo that "some day you'll find a use for it—a big, noble use" (Wylie 46), just as Ma Kent charges Clark: "But when the proper time comes, you must use it to assist humanity" (*Superman* #1). In explaining the nature of his son's strength, Professor Danner asks, "Did you ever watch an ant carry many times its weight? Or see a grasshopper jump fifty times its length? The insects have better muscles and nerves than we have. And I improved your body till it was relatively that strong" (Wylie 46). In their explanation for Superman's phenomenal powers, Siegel and Shuster support the idea of the inhabitants of Superman's home planet having an advanced physical structure by pointing out that "The lowly ant can support weights hundreds of times its own!" and "The grasshopper leaps what to man would be the space of several city blocks" (*Action Comics* #1).

Superman's early displays of power are also similar to the prodigious feats of strength Earthman John Carter (from the 1911 Edgar Rice Burroughs novel *A Princess of Mars*) was capable of on Mars due to the lesser gravity. In fact, the explanation of Superman's powers was modified in *Superman* #1 (1939) with the addition of "The smaller size of our planet, with its slighter gravity pull, assists Superman's tremendous muscles in the performance of miraculous feats of strength!"

Over the years Superman writers and editors have borrowed a number of elements from the pulp magazine hero Doc Savage, including the name Clark, a fortress of solitude in the Arctic, and a code against taking life. Superman creators also seemed to have been inspired by the Scarlet Pimpernel, who is perhaps the most direct progenitor of the dual identity convention. Just as Percy Blakeney is despised by a wife who loves his dashing alter ego, the Scarlet Pimpernel, Lois Lane (in the first forty years of stories) feels disdain for Kent, but swoons over Superman.

The creation of Batman looks to have been inspired by a number of pulp magazine adventure heroes, most notably Nick Carter, Doc Savage, and the Shadow. Nick Carter made his debut in 1886 in the dime novels that preceded

FIGURE 10.3. Jim Lee's study in contrasts shows how the iconic figures of Superman and Batman complement one another, champions borne of the primordial forces of light and darkness. © DC Comics

the pulps, and it is likely that he served as a template for some aspects of Doc Savage. Nick Carter's first case is avenging his father's murder, as are the first adventures of Doc Savage and Batman. Young Bruce Wayne's parents are murdered in front of him, and he makes a vow to fight crime. That vow eventually leads him to assuming the identity of Batman. To prepare for his war, Bruce "becomes a master scientist" and "trains his body to physical perfection" (*Detective Comics* #33, 1939). Both Carter and Doc Savage were scientifically raised to attain the peak of human mental and physical perfection. Doc maintains his remarkable physical and mental prowess the hard way, through a daily regimen of exercises, just like the Caped Crusader. Batman has no superpowers with which to wage his war on crime, but he does have a utility belt full of weapons and tools and a fleet of technologically advanced vehicles at his disposal. Doc Savage also has vest pockets filled with scores of gadgets he invented and a fleet of impressive vehicles, including a souped-up roadster, an autogyro, and an amphibian jet. Carter adopts a fourteen-year-old boy who becomes his sidekick in solving crimes, much like Bruce Wayne makes the orphaned Dick Grayson his ward and crime fighting partner, Robin.

Pulp magazine heroes the Spider, the Shadow, and the Bat are all probable inspirations for Batman's modus operandi of striking fear into the hearts of criminals as a creature of the night. The Shadow and the Spider, with their intense eyes burning beneath slouch-brimmed hats, create identities meant to terrorize the criminal underworld, but they do not seem to be as direct an influence as the Bat. Five years before Batman's first appearance, Dawson Clade decides that in order to pursue the criminals who had framed him, he "must become a figure of sinister import," a "strange Nemesis" to criminals. Just then a bat flies into the room and he exclaims, "That's it! I'll call myself 'The Bat'!" (qtd. in Jess Nevins). Clade then dons a bat costume to become a vigilante crime fighter. After years of preparation, Bruce Wayne sits in his mansion contemplating how to undertake his war on crime. He reasons that to strike terror into the hearts of criminals he "must be a creature of the night, black, terrible." Just then a huge bat flies into the room and Bruce exclaims, "A Bat! That's it! It's an omen. I shall become a bat!" (*Detective Comics* #33)

Batman's daytime persona is similar to those of the Spider and the Shadow. The Spider is really wealthy Richard Wentworth, who appears to be a carefree playboy. It suits the purposes of the Shadow to take over the identity of millionaire playboy Lamont Cranston, who obligingly takes up residence overseas so the Shadow can use his identity. Although Bruce Wayne has been all work and no fun from the instant his childhood was shattered, no one suspects that Wayne is Batman because he adopts a demeanor that originated with the Scarlet Pimpernel and has been employed by a number of the dual-identity pulp heroes—a very wealthy man who seems self-absorbed and much more interested in seeking pleasure than adventure.

Shortly after the appearance of Batman, "the floodgates opened, and a host of long-underwear characters began cavorting across the four-color pages of comic book after comic book" (Harvey 21). If they hoped to emulate the financial success of Superman and Batman, "a publisher had to make sure of instant product identification. In the years just before the War a superhero needed a bright costume, a dual identity, and a wild talent" (Goulart, "Second Banana" 229). In the next section we will look more closely at defining characteristics of the superhero. We will also consider the conventions of character types, themes, and narrative patterns that have come to define the superhero genre in comic books since its inception with Superman and Batman.

CONVENTIONS OF THE SUPERHERO GENRE

Any genre which has had the time to develop over the course of seven decades is bound to have a wide variety of conventions that distinguish it. In the following section, we focus on the character types, themes, narrative patterns, and visual conventions that have come to define the superhero genre in comics.

Character Types

The most essential character type of the superhero genre is, of course, the hero. Coogan examined previous definitions of "superhero" and reduced them to three key elements he believes are emblematic of the superhero: mission, powers, and identity.

The pro-social **mission** of the comic book superhero was established in the early tales of the genre. Young Clark Kent's mother tells him he has a responsibility to use his powers to benefit humanity. Young Bruce Wayne vows he will wage a war on criminals to avenge his murdered parents. It is a well-established convention of the genre that when a character creates a superhero identity and dons a costume, he or she is making a commitment to help those in need and fight evil. By the time of the Fantastic Four's origin story in 1961, the convention was so well established that in the scene where they realize they have gained superpowers from being bombarded by cosmic rays, the gruff Ben Grimm interrupts the long-winded Reed Richards with, "You don't have to make a speech, big shot. We understand. We've gotta use that power to help mankind, right?" (*Fantastic Four* #1, 1961).

The cosmic rays transform Ben Grimm into the monstrous Thing, whose gruesome appearance gives him an understandably bad attitude. He is a radical departure from the typical superhero, who is a specimen of physical and moral perfection. However, the Thing is part of a longstanding tradition of tragic superheroes with deformed bodies and tortured psyches (a fraternity which includes characters such as the Heap, Hulk, and Swamp Thing). Another variation, the **anti-hero**, began with the easy-to-anger Namor the Sub-Mariner, who, from the time he first appeared in 1939, alternated between ally and enemy of the surface world. An anti-hero typically lacks one or more of the qualities associated with the heroic ideal. In the 1970s the Punisher and Wolverine led the way in popularizing a new breed of violent anti-heroes. Yet even the tragic heroes and the anti-heroes, while bitter, angry, or otherwise tainted, will, in the end, "do the right thing" and serve the cause of justice.

The second distinguishing characteristic of superheroes is their **powers**. This element sets superheroes apart from Tarzan, Zorro, Doc Savage, and all the other admittedly extraordinary adventure heroes who preceded them. Super-heroes possess fantastic abilities or skills far superior to those of ordinary humans. Part of the appeal of superheroes, and one of the reasons they have always worked better on printed paper than in any other medium, is that many of the powers, such as shooting energy beams from their eyes or light-ning bolts from their fingertips, make for an exciting visual display on the page. The generations of children who have tied towels around their necks, extended their arms, and pretended to fly are testimony to the fundamental appeal of superpowers.

There are a few recognized superheroes (e.g., the Phantom, the original Sandman, the Vigilante, and, most notably, Batman) with no superpowers. However, not only is Batman an incredible athlete, a master of all forms of com-bat, and able to endure massive amounts of punishment and keep going, he is also the world's greatest detective. In addition, his vast wealth allows him to employ the latest technology in his war on crime. Clearly he is superior to any human being in the real world; he can do things we only wish we could.

Interestingly, the more awesome the superhero's powers, the more necessary it is, for purposes of dramatic narrative, that the hero have a limitation. The most famous Achilles' heel in comic books is Superman's adverse reaction to kryptonite, shards of his shattered home world, Krypton. Most DC superheroes, following the Superman model, are limited by some external force. For example, Martian Manhunter passes out in the presence of an open flame, and for many years Green Lantern's power ring could not affect anything yellow. Few Marvel characters have such artificial, external weaknesses. Their limitations are rooted in their own personalities: pride (Thor), brashness (Human Torch), addictive personality (Iron Man), self-doubt (Spider-Man), and even some instances of self-loathing (Hulk).

The third distinguishing quality is the **identity**. As Coogan explains it, superhero identity consists of "the codename and the costume, with the secret identity being a customary counterpart to the code-name" (32). Generally, the superhero name relates to the hero's powers (Flash), attitude (Daredevil), or role (Captain America). The costume is often an externalization of these

FIGURE 10.4. Invincible conforms to the conventions of the super-hero. It is his *mission* to defend Earth from extraterrestrial and crimi-nal threats. He has the *powers* of invincibility, super-strength, and flight. His costumed *identity* conceals the fact that he is teenager Mark Grayson. Invincible was created by writer Robert Kirkman and artist Cory Walker and debuted in Image Comics' *Invincible* #1 (2003). Used with permission.

aspects of the character. For example, Daredevil's costume is solid red with horns on the cowl, and Captain America is virtually draped in the flag. The costume also marks out the superheroes (and supervillains) from ordinary people.

The secret or dual identity usually involves a stark contrast. In their civilian identities (which are not always their true identities) superheroes often feign some weakness of character, such as being a coward or a dissolute playboy. The dual identity is also a way for the ordinary person to identify with extraordinary characters. Perhaps one of the most alluring aspects of the Superman mythos is that Clark Kent is an average guy. Editor Danny Fingeroth believes "the appeal of the secret identity is as primal as ever" and rooted in that feeling most of us have experienced when we feel the world is not giving us enough respect: "Don't underestimate me. I may not be who you think I am" (*Superman* 60). Or, as Umberto Eco explains the appeal, "any accountant in any American city secretly feeds the hope that one day, from the slough of his actual personality, there can spring forth a superman who is capable of redeeming years of mediocre existence" (146).

Of course, not every superhero has a dual identity. Marvel Comics has always been less invested in the secret identity than has DC, but the element of a superhero identity is still present in their characters. Namor has no other identity, but he is given the superhero-sounding moniker the Sub-Mariner. The Fantastic Four are celebrities whose civilian identities are well known. Yet, while everyone knows Johnny Storm is the Human Torch of the Fantastic Four, Johnny does still have the codename and costume that constitute the superhero identity. The secret identity was more important in the early decades of the genre, when superheroes were presented as exceptional beings in a world of ordinary people. Modern stories feature superhero action on a grand scale, with few ordinary humans in evidence.

Supporting Characters: Sidekicks

The introduction of Robin in 1940 began the rather illogical tradition of adult superheroes taking on teenage sidekicks, often with no powers, in the dangerous fight against the very powerful forces of evil. By many accounts, Robin was introduced to "lighten up" the Batman feature, whose editors were worried that the book might be too intense for some kids. The sidekick was also a convenient device by which writers could have a hero's thoughts expressed in conversation rather than in thought balloons or stilted monologues. Editors and writers hoped the sidekick would provide powerful wish fulfillment for young readers who could project themselves onto the adolescent hero.

During the 1940s and 1950s there were a number of male and female superheroes who fought as a duo, but the female partners tended to be relegated to sidekick status. Not only did the heroine often serve as the damsel in distress for the hero to rescue, but despite the fact they were the same age, the male's superhero name usually ended in "-man" while the superheroine's named ended in "-girl" (e.g., Bullet*man* and Bullet*girl*, Hawk*man* and Hawk*girl*).

When writer Stan Lee and the artists at Marvel Comics began creating a new universe of superheroes in the early 1960s, they abandoned the sidekick convention. In fact, teenagers such as Spider-Man, the new Human Torch, and the X-Men were some of the most prominent and independent heroes in the Marvel Universe, although the X-Men did have an adult mentor in Professor Xavier. In 1964 DC let their sidekicks step out of the mentors' shadows and form the Teen Titans. As the sidekicks grew up, they took on new superhero identities. None of the original five Teen Titans kept their sidekick names: Robin became Nightwing; Wonder Girl went through a number of name changes, starting with Troia; Kid Flash took over the role of the Flash; Aqualad became Tempest; and Speedy opted for the more formidable moniker Arsenal for a while, but has since become Red Arrow.

Supporting Characters: Supervillains

Most of the early antagonists in comics were much less colorful than either the hero or his aide-de-camp. Superman began his career fighting gangsters and corrupt politicians, but it was soon apparent he was not even going to break a sweat that way, and before long he had to contend with villains like Lex Luthor, "the mad scientist who plots to dominate the Earth" (*Superman* #4, 1940). Other extraordinary menaces soon followed. Batman contended with bizarre villains such as Doctor Death, the Monk, and the Scarlet Horde quite early in his adventures. During the 1940s he encountered a colorful, and now familiar, array of Gotham City–based supervillains, among them Penguin, Catwoman, Riddler, Poison Ivy, and, of course, his arch-nemesis, the Joker. Each of the

major superheroes has a similar **rogues gallery** of villains who return to plague the hero time and time again. Soon, these menaces reached the distinction of being labeled supervillains, making them counterpoints to the superheroes.

FIGURE 10.5. Robin, the Boy Wonder, started the trend in sidekicks, but many more superheroes took on apprentices. Several of them eventually banded together as the Teen Titans. From *Secret Origins Annual* #2 (1989), words by George Perez and art by Irv Novick and Ty Templeton. © DC Comics

What makes a supervillain different from any other antagonist a hero might encounter? Superpowers and a garish costume certainly contribute to the supervillain persona, but according to scholars Gina Misiroglu and Michael Eury, it is the supervillain's propensity to scheme in operatic proportions that distinguishes him from ordinary criminals. The original Brainiac set out to shrink the city of Metropolis and steal it for his collection, Dr. Doom tries to supplant all other political leaders and establish himself as ruler over the world, and Galactus wants to eat entire planets. The supervillain is a powerfully evil opponent worthy of the incredible power and uncommon virtue of the superhero.

The villain is often more integral to the plot than the hero. As scholar Richard Reynolds points out, superheroes are largely conservative figures, usually content with the status quo. They typically do not seek to redistribute wealth, change sitting governments, or otherwise alter the existing social order. Supervillains, on the other hand, are out to change the world. They may well aim to take from the rich to give to the poor (albeit themselves) or unseat elected presidents in order to establish new forms of government (again benefiting themselves, presumably as dictators). Such provocative actions call the comparatively passive heroes into action, moving the story forward in exciting ways. Supervillains are active; superheroes are reactive. In the best of these stories, the hero discovers that defending the status quo challenges him to overcome obstacles he has never cleared before, further refining his qualities as a hero.

Themes

For decades superhero stories have been dismissed as power fantasies for adolescent males. Certainly, for children who might consider themselves powerless in the adult world, a part of the appeal is the freedom and power superheroes display once they cast off their ordinary identities. But there has always been more going on under the surface. What makes these protagonists heroic is not their power, but their persistence. The superhero is often the underdog, facing a more powerful foe or superior numbers, and experiencing temporary defeat. Superheroes are often beaten in the first encounter with a supervillain, or when the odds seem overwhelming they will briefly give in to their doubts, fears, or selfish desires. Yet they always return to the fray, exhibiting a strength of will that reaffirms the strength of the human spirit. "Whether a 'miraculous' return from

FIGURE 10.6. Dr. Doom and Mr. Fantastic find themselves locked in perpetual conflict. Doom will never give up until he has bested the Fantastic Four and conquered the world. From *Fantastic Four* #200 (1978), with words by Marv Wolfman and art by Keith Pollard and Joe Sinnott. © 2008 Marvel Entertainment, Inc. and its subsidiaries

seeming death, or a return to the right path, the values they embody are too strong to quell or kill" (Fingeroth, *Superman* 167).

Superheroes have always been driven by the ethic of "what one can do, one should do," or as it was stated in the final panel of the first Spider-Man story, "With great power there must also come . . . great responsibility" (*Amazing Fantasy* #15, 1962). Perhaps Batman is doing all he can to fight street crime in Gotham City, but more powerful superheroes do not seem to be living up to their responsibilities. Certainly dealing with gangsters or even reacting to the threats posed by supervillains does not tap Superman's full potential. As Eco points out, from a being of Superman's power, "one could expect the most bewildering political, economic, and technological upheavals in the world," from "the solution of hunger problems" to "the destruction of inhumane systems" (163). In the 1999 comic book *Superman: Peace on Earth*, Superman dedicates himself to ending hunger in the world, but ultimately fails, finding that more often than not, his efforts create distrust, hatred, or greed. Superman realizes he cannot impose solutions on mankind without compromising his own innate decency and forcing his values on others. Part of the responsibility that comes with great power is the responsibility to hold that power in check, to avoid fascist extremes. In the superhero genre it is only permissible for heroes to use power to impose their wills on the criminal element. And that is never done without great effort.

By their actions, superheroes teach the lesson that justice is more important than law. Superheroes are essentially outlaws, masked vigilantes violating rights and committing assault to bring evildoers to justice. Not surprisingly, the superhero concept has been decried as fascist for nearly seventy years. Some of the most interesting and ambitious superhero comic books have examined the implications of powerful beings taking the law into their own hands. In *Miracleman* (1985) and *Squadron Supreme* (1985), superheroes essentially conquer the world in order to make it better. One of the superheroes in *Watchmen* (1986) commits mass murder for the greater good of humanity. In *Black Summer* (2007) a superhero decides justice would best be served by violently removing the president of the United States from office. Marvel Comics' *Civil War* (2006) crossover event provides an allegorical exploration of superhero vigilante justice. The carnage caused by superhero battles prompts some members of the superhero community to advocate becoming officially sanctioned heroes under government supervision, while other superheroes, led by Captain America, fight to maintain their freedom from government control. The storyline is a thinly veiled commentary on the debate about sacrificing personal freedom for the sake of security in post-9/11 America. These themes are regularly, albeit not universally, presented in superhero stories.

Narrative Patterns

Because far more people are familiar with superheroes from movies than from comic books, and the first movie tends to explain how the hero came to be, the **origin story** is probably the most familiar superhero narrative. The origin story is necessary to explain the fantastic nature of the superhero. The tale usually involves a transformative experience that is often both physical and emotional in nature. Comic book historian Ron Goulart claims, "The most appealing idea to a kid was the short-cut origin, with magic powers thrust upon you. Doing pushups and studying chemistry were too much like school" ("Second Banana" 230). Accordingly, superpowers are often acquired in a flash of lightning. A lightning strike created the powers of Blue Bolt (with a radium chaser), the Human Top, the second Flash (who was simultaneously doused by chemicals), and when Billy Batson says his magic word there is a flash of lightning as he transforms into Captain Marvel. Yet cartoonist Paul Chadwick believes the origin tales that resonate most strongly with us are those that "mine the vein of trauma" because "Nobody travels to the extremes of human character without great suffering. In fact, nobody changes much at all without it" (34).

Many of the great hero tales of Western culture follow a mythic pattern similar to the one scholar Joseph Campbell has described as the classical **monomyth**. Coogan points out that most superhero origin stories follow the separation-initiation-return structure of the monomyth. The typical monomyth tale ends when the hero returns from his initiation with some wisdom or treasure that will benefit his community. The superhero does emerge from an ordeal, or a happy accident, with power and purpose that can be used to benefit the community, but, due to the serial aesthetic of most comic books, the transformation is only the beginning of the superhero's tale, a tale that will be told in monthly installments as long as there is a market for the adventures.

The month-to-month comic book adventures of the typical superhero are more likely to follow the pattern of what academics Robert Jewett and John Shelton Lawrence call the American monomyth:

1. a community is threatened
2. a selfless hero emerges
3. the hero renounces temptation
4. the hero wins a victory (through superheroism)
5. the hero restores harmony to the community
6. the hero recedes into obscurity (qtd. in Coogan 123; Lang and Trimble 159)

The majority of superhero stories in the first few decades of the genre's existence clearly followed this template, but by the mid-sixties new elements were being added to the simple pattern of defeating a menace and restoring order.

Comic book writer Nat Gertler has identified some broad trends in the evolution of superhero stories over the decades:

1. First Generation: Heroes strive to stop badness

   As Coogan points out, "in a narrative sense, villains are proactive and heroes are reactive. The villain's machinations drive the plot. The hero reacts to the villain's threat" (110).

2. Second Generation: Why the heroes strive to stop badness

   The soul-searching Marvel Comics heroes of the 1960s were some of the first to wrestle with the question of why someone would choose to put on a costume and battle evil.

FIGURE 10.7. Peter Parker reflects on the lesson he has learned from a poor decision that changed his life forever. Stan Lee scripted and Steve Ditko drew this in *Amazing Fantasy* #15 (1962). © 2008 Marvel Entertainment, Inc. and its subsidiaries

3. Third Generation: The results of the heroes striving to stop badness

   Works such as *Marvels*, Kurt Busiek's *Astro City*, and Gertler's own *The Factor* speculate about how our world would react to the presence of superheroes. Works such as *Batman: The Dark Knight Returns* and *Watchmen* examine the fascist implications of superhero vigilante justice taken to the extreme.

4. Fourth (Lost) Generation: Heroes are attacked by villains

   Supervillains and superheroes have become veritable Hatfields and McCoys, locked into their own feud with little connection to or concern for the world of ordinary humans. The battling superbeings, including the heroes, often seem cavalier to the collateral damage they are causing. The heroes will, of course, always save bystanders from falling debris, but they don't seem much concerned about the massive property damage resulting from their feuds. Gertler calls this a "lost generation" because he believes these tales have lost the true essence of the superhero concept and exist only for the display of bodies, costumes, and powers. Image Comics of the 1990s, such as *Youngblood*, fall into this category.

Some comics theorists believe there is no particular narrative pattern in superhero comic books, and that strong narrative structure is not even a necessary element of the genre. Brian Camp observes that "essentially, superhero stories as we know them are soap operas interrupted by slug-fests," and the "never-ending 'über-soap operas'" are collapsing under the weight of their own accumulated continuity. **Continuity** is the relatedness among characters and events said to inhabit the same fictional universe, and it can pose a problem for creators trying to deal with decades of backstory. Marc Singer believes it is not a story which persists in the minds of superhero comic book readers, but rather a state of being. Expanding on a term he borrowed from comics scribe Neil Gaiman, Singer refers to the alluring aspect of unchanging superheroes as a "state of grace" that consists of the hero's power, appearance, and behavior (Bissette, Gaiman, and Veitch 195). For example, over the years readers have not so much expected or responded to a particular tale of the Hulk, but rather to "Hulkness"—a huge green guy in purple pants who gets stronger as he becomes angry.

Perhaps no other distinct superhero tale besides the origin story developed because superheroes, whether they appeared in pulp magazines, comic strips, comic books, or radio, were born into a serial aesthetic. As Eco points out in his analysis of Superman, readers of superhero tales encounter "events happening in an ever-continuing present" (156) in which the hero overcomes obstacles, but does not affect real change in his environment because change would ground the superhero in the temporal and move him one step closer to death (150). As commodities that corporations want to continue to exploit for as long as possible, popular superheroes cannot grow old, die, or fundamentally change; "economics therefore denies any 'definitive' take on a hero" (Taylor 350).

At the end of their fourth encounter, Batman knocks the Joker over the rail of a ship and into the swirling waters below. Batman looks over the rail and ponders, "I wonder if this is really the end of the Joker at last! I wonder!" (*Detective Comics* #45, 1940). Fifteen issues later the Joker was back, and has, of course, returned to bedevil Batman hundreds of times since. The resolution of a typical superhero story provides at least a temporary triumph of good over evil. This usually means that once the hero has pummeled the villain into submission, the authorities haul him off to a prison from which he will soon escape, but every so often a villain, usually due to his own recklessness, seems to perish. As with the Joker example, the circumstance of the death, an explosion or fall into water, means no body is ever found and there is the possibility the villain might have survived. Some minor villains might remain "dead" for years, but when a popular villain suffers a visible and undeniable death in full view, the deceased is soon revealed to be a robot, a hapless henchman wearing the villain's costume, the occasional twin, or, in recent decades, a clone.

Superhero deaths are rarer in occurrence and more dramatic in execution, but no less temporary. The first superhero to die, MLJ Comics' the Comet, remained dead for twenty-five years. For forty-one years of Marvel Comics' publishing history, Captain America's sidekick, Bucky, appeared to have died in World War II attempting to defuse a missile. In 2005 a grown James Buchanan "Bucky" Barnes was reintroduced to Marvel continuity, and has since taken over the identity of Captain America in the wake of the apparent death of the original Cap. Most superheroes do not stay dead nearly as long. As stated, major superheroes are marketable commodities, and a storyline that keeps a character dead for too long can be bad for business. In the instance of the much-publicized death of Superman in 1992, it was only due to the carefully planned contrivances of an extended funeral and the possibility that one of the four replacement Supermen might be the real deal that DC was able to have their flagship character dead for a full year.

Figure 10.8. Jim Starlin imitates Michelangelo's *Pieta* for the cover of *The Death of Captain Marvel* (1982), a graphic novel in which the superhero dies in bed from cancer. © 2008 Marvel Entertainment, Inc. and its subsidiaries

Superman died very visibly in a heroic and bloody battle with Doomsday. Rather than disappearing into swirling waters, most superhero bodies are visible in death. In fact, one recurring visual motif associated with superhero deaths is showing the fallen hero in the arms of a comrade in an approximation of Michelangelo's Pieta sculpture of Mary holding the crucified Jesus.

Visual Conventions

The visual "vocabulary" and "grammar" of the superhero genre was established primarily by two artists. Burne Hogarth never drew true superheroes, but he took over the Tarzan comic strip from Hal Foster in 1936. The detailed musculature—sometimes referred to as the **flayed look**—and dynamic movement Hogarth used in rendering Tarzan influenced generations of comic book artists. The other artist was Jack Kirby (see profile below). While Kirby's figures might seem blockish and stiff compared to the lithe Tarzan of Hogarth, Kirby was even more of a force in creating the visual dynamic of the superhero comic book. Kirby's characters were seldom static; anyone in a costume was either moving or poised to spring into action. "I tore my characters out of the panels," Kirby once said. "I made them jump all over the page" (qtd. in Eisner, *Shop Talk* 211).

Another aspect of the look of superhero comics is the eroticism of skintight spandex stretched over impossibly muscled and improbably proportioned bodies. In the early decades of the genre, the emphasis was on the eroticism of tight, and often skimpy, costumes on curvaceous superheroines. While the male superheroes were obviously big, powerful guys, they were often drawn as blockish and without much muscular definition. In the 1960s artists like Neal Adams and Jim Steranko revived Hogarth's flayed look, in which every muscle stands in sharp relief, as if the covering skin had been removed. Adams and Steranko were highly influential artists in the genre, and most artists who followed devoted

FIGURE 10.9. Cartoonist Don Simpson pokes fun at the unrealistic anatomy of some superhero depictions in his Megaton Man caricature. Megaton Man © Don Simpson.

themselves to lovingly rendering bugling muscles, including many that cannot be found on the human body. The distortion of the superhero body accelerated during the eighties and nineties to the point that, if there is any eroticism left, it is based on an abstraction of breasts and biceps rather than emulation of the human form. While there has in recent years been some turning back to more reasonable portrayals of super-bodies, one can still find plenty of female superheroes with long stick legs and huge breasts, and plenty of male superheroes with such distorted "colossal anatomies" that they "are moving toward unconscious self-parody" (Taylor 351).

Because comic books are a visual medium, the ritualistic display of a hero's power has become another stylistic convention of the superhero genre. Numerous panels over the years have been devoted to Flash running on water and Thor calling down lightning bolts. Certain poses are often associated with the display of power. The image of Superman with one arm fully extended and one bent, flying up, up, and away, is familiar from both comic books and merchandise. And when Spider-Man swings around New York, he does so in a distinctive, if somewhat awkward-looking manner, with his knees up to his shoulders.

One additional visual convention to consider is the use of color. Comics have long been referred to as the "four-color" medium because of the use of color printing processes that employ black, red, blue, and yellow inks. Color was first introduced in newspaper comic strips to heighten their marketing appeal. The earliest comic books reprinted the strips in the same four-color process, sometimes adding color to strips that had previously been printed in black and white. In order to make the most out of the colors' visual appeal, most of the earliest superheroes came decked out in brightly colored uniforms. Since that time, the use of bold, primary colors has become synonymous with superheroes. For instance, both Superman and Spider-Man wear costumes that make use of vibrant blue and red. The connection between color and superheroes is so prominent that some creators working in other genres have consciously avoided the use of color, choosing to work in black and white in order to distance themselves from the juvenile connotation of bright color. Taken together, then, the body types, movement, and costuming contribute to the code that makes superheroes both recognizable and enduring.

Profile: Jack Kirby

born: Jacob Kurtzburg
        August 28, 1917
        New York City

"The secret of my success is the fact that I gave to it. I gave it all I had. There is blood and bone and sinew behind the whole thing."

Career Highlights

1941   The team of Joe Simon and Jack Kirby have their first big hit with *Captain America Comics*.

1942   Simon and Kirby move to DC and produce another hit, *Boy Commandos*.

1947   Simon and Kirby innovate the romance genre with the debut of *Young Romance*.

1950   The team creates *Boys' Ranch*.

1958   Kirby experiments with science fiction in the *Challengers of the Unknown*.

1961   Stan Lee and Kirby revolutionize the industry with *Fantastic Four*.

1962   Lee and Kirby introduce the Mighty Thor in *Journey into Mystery*.

1970   Kirby launches the Fourth World in *Superman's Pal Jimmy Olsen*.

1971   *The New Gods* expands the Fourth World Saga.

1976   Kirby returns to Marvel and creates *The Eternals*.

1980   Kirby designs characters for *Thundarr the Barbarian* for Saturday morning cartoons by Ruby-Spears Productions.

1981   Experiments with the direct market by *Captain Victory and the Galaxy Rangers* for Pacific Comics.

1993   Topps Comics issues "Kirbyverse" characters.

Many comics creators have been given nicknames over the years, but only one has earned a title: Jack "King" Kirby. He produced more than 20,000 pages of comics art, probably the most published of any professional cartoonist in the medium (Benton, *Masters* 28). But more than for his productivity, it is for his creativity that Kirby is best remembered. Indeed, "Jack Kirby didn't invent the comic book. It just seems that way" (Evanier, *Kirby* 15). Either in collaboration with men like Joe Simon and Stan Lee, or on his own, Kirby created some of the most iconic and successful superheroes in the medium's history: Captain America, the Fantastic Four, Hulk, Thor, the X-Men, Silver Surfer, Black Panther, the New Gods, and many other characters.

Kirby virtually created the visual language of superhero comics. His style conveyed motion, grandeur, and action that broke the panels, with heroes practically leaping off the page. He drew characters in their most extreme positions and then choreographed the action that followed.

Cont'd

Kirby began his career in animation working on *Popeye* shorts for Fleischer Studios in the 1930s. When Fleischer moved to Florida, Kirby stayed in New York and worked in the legendary Eisner & Iger Shop for a couple of years. By 1939 he was doing some of his earliest work with superheroes, drawing the *Blue Beetle* comic strip for Fox Features Syndicates and also picking up work for Fox's line of comic books. It was at Fox that Kirby met Joe Simon. The Simon and Kirby team created Captain America for Timely Comics (later Marvel Comics) in 1941. The two went on to collaborate on a number of projects, including creating the very first romance comic, *Young Romance*, in 1947. Kirby's versatile talent made possible all manner of genre storytelling, from westerns to horror comics, but he always seemed to come back to superheroes.

FIGURE 10.10. The dynamism of a Kirby panel as seen in *Jimmy Olsen* #133 (October 1970). © DC Comics

Perhaps Kirby's best work began in 1961 when he and writer-editor Stan Lee transformed the faltering Atlas Comics into the pop culture powerhouse Marvel Comics with the creation of quirky heroes such as the Fantastic Four and the X-Men. After nearly a decade of helping to build the Marvel Universe of characters and concepts, Kirby turned his considerable talents to creating his "Fourth World Saga" for Marvel's chief rival, DC Comics, in the 1970s, producing not only a cast of superheroes, but a whole new mythology. Concepts developed by Jack Kirby are still mined by both the major American comic book publishers to this day.

Cartoonist and filmmaker Frank Miller has said, "In the history of American comic books, there has been no single talent of greater importance and influence than that of Jack Kirby. It would be impossible to exaggerate his contribution to the evolution of the superhero, or to calculate exactly how much he personally advanced the art form. . . . Single-handedly, he developed the visual dialect, tone, and spirit of the modern superhero comic" (qtd. in George 96).

FIGURE 10.11 Jack Kirby displayed unparalleled creativity and productivity in his career. Photo courtesy of the Jack Kirby Museum.

ENDURING APPEAL OF SUPERHEROES

In 1989 comics historian Mike Benton identified what he called the "Significant Seven" superheroes. Benton claims that "out of the hundreds of superhero characters, seven stand out as the most historically important: Superman, Batman, Wonder Woman, Spider-Man, Captain America, Captain Marvel, and Plastic Man" (*Comic Book* 178). Benton's list does not allow for significant superhero teams, such as the Justice Society of America or the Fantastic Four, and one might be able to make an argument that the list should be expanded to include Wolverine, the Black Panther, Spawn, or even Rorschach from *Watchmen*. However, Benton's Significant Seven have stood the test of time—even the "new kid," Spider-Man, has been around for more than four decades. Let's take a brief look at the importance and appeal of each of these characters.

Superman (debuted in *Action Comics* #1, 1938)

Superman began as a champion of the oppressed and an avenger of the corruption in society. However, during World War II, and even more so postwar, he became less of a vigilante and more an upholder of law and order. Superman's mission was most memorably articulated when the opening of the 1940s Superman radio show declared that Superman has "sworn to devote his existence on Earth to helping those in need." Superman is a creature of light. He wears a brightly colored costume. His face is unencumbered by a mask. He seldom operates at night. In fact, he is powered by the rays of the sun. Superman is a shining beacon who calls to our better nature. As author Harlan Ellison put it, "He is courage and humanity, steadfastness and decency, responsibility and ethic. He is our universal longing for perfection, for wisdom and power used in the service of the human race" (qtd. in Dooley and Engle 12).

As Kal-El, born on the distant planet Krypton, Superman is an immigrant who exemplifies the melting pot metaphor of the early twentieth century; as Clark Kent he "makes good" by adopting traditional American values. While Superman was drawn to the city of Metropolis by his sense of duty (there is much to be done there and many people to be helped), his spiritual roots are in his hometown of Smallville, Kansas. Clark returns to Smallville in times of personal crisis, and in the alternate-reality *Kingdom Come* storyline, after Smallville has been destroyed, Clark takes refuge in a holographic simulation of farm life. It was while growing up in the heartland that he learned the value of hard work, humility, and concern for humanity.

Batman (debuted in *Detective Comics* # 27, 1939)

It is difficult to find a common essential aspect of the character in such disparate incarnations of Batman as the late fifties/early sixties science fiction adventurer, the mid-sixties tongue-in-cheek hero escaping traps and trading quips with his chum Robin, the seventies creature of the night, and the grimly obsessed dark knight of the eighties and beyond. Perhaps the core of the character is to be found in the reason Batman exists. Artist and former DC editor Dick Giordano believes Batman's origin is "intrinsic to his believability, popularity, and longevity" (7). As Giordano explains, "The Batman was born in a few brief, violent moments in which a young Bruce Wayne was forced to watch the brutal murder of his parents at the hands of a street thief," and "we all can understand his need to do something to avenge the deaths of his parents" (8). It is the origin, grounded in "an emotion that is primal and timeless and dark," that is the enduring and compelling essence of the character (Giordano 8). Some critics have argued that "every Batman story is to some extent an extension of the origin story" (Reynolds 67), and "every encounter with a criminal . . . raises the spectre of that original encounter" (Uricchio and Pearson 194).

Wonder Woman (debuted in *All-Star Comics* #8, 1941)

The first page of Wonder Woman's first appearance proclaimed her to be "As lovely as Aphrodite—As wise as Athena—With the speed of Mercury and the Strength of Hercules." Wonder Woman was created by psychologist William Moulton Marston, who wanted to provide a powerful positive role model for girls. He seems to have succeeded: When feminist and longtime Wonder Woman fan Gloria Steinem began *Ms.* magazine in 1972, she featured Wonder Woman on the cover of the first issue. Comics historian and occasional Wonder Woman cartoonist Trina Robbins believes "the most powerful humanistic message in Wonder Woman" is that "through personal development, any girl could become a wonder woman" (*Great Women* 10). Actress Lynda Carter, who portrayed Wonder Woman in a television series from 1975 to 1979, saw her as "a symbol of all the glorious gifts that reside in the spirit of Woman" (9).

Spider-Man (debuted in *Amazing Fantasy* #15, 1962)

When nerdy teenager Peter Parker gets fantastic powers from the bite of a radioactive spider, he attempts to use his abilities to make money. When he fails to stop the thief who later kills his beloved Uncle Ben, Peter realizes that with power comes responsibility. Spider-Man must "not only redeem himself, he must save the world in general and his aunt in particular, especially since she embodies his last connection to his parents and his uncle" (Fingeroth, *Superman* 76). Defined by loss and driven by responsibility, he still manages to take joy in swinging through the city and wisecracking his way through fights. Spider-Man embodies the complexities and contradictions we can all recognize in our own lives. The superhero Everyman, "it is his simple humanity, rather than his exotic talent, that has won him millions of enthusiastic fans" (Daniels, *Marvel* 96).

Captain America (debuted in *Captain America Comics* #1, 1941)

Writer Roy Thomas declares, "what made *Captain America* take off like a rocket were its two not-so-secret ingredients: A couple of guys named Joe Simon and Jack Kirby" ("Introduction" viii). Simon and Kirby presented Captain America's adventures "with all the subtlety of an exploding buzz bomb" (Steranko, *History* 51). The United States had not yet entered World War II, but right there on the cover of the first issue, the red, white, and blue clad hero was landing a solid right cross on Hitler's jaw. The Germans, and especially the Japanese, that Cap fought were not just villains, but sadistic, slobbering grotesqueries. Cap seemed to fight all of his battles at a full run, bursting out of the panels.

With the departure of Simon and Kirby, Captain America became a less exciting character, and with the end of the war he became less relevant. Save for a brief stint in the mid-fifties as a "commie smasher," Captain America disappeared from comic books for over a decade. Since his revival in 1964 he has become not only one of the best known superheroes in the world, but has realized his potential as an icon and a symbol. From the moment he socked Hitler in the jaw, Captain America was the embodiment of American idealism. As such, he has changed as the nation has changed: fighting the Axis powers in the forties, opposing the spread of communism in the fifties, questioning authority in the (late) sixties, and becoming disillusioned by the government corruption he uncovered in the seventies. In 2007 Captain America was assassinated, an event obviously fraught with symbolism but open to a wide range of interpretation. Of course, with comic book "deaths" being what they are, by the time this book sees print, Cap is likely to have made a miraculous return and thrown his mighty shield to oppose the evils that plague contemporary America.

Captain Marvel (debuted in *Whiz Comics* #1, 1940)

Teenage newsboy Billy Batson utters a magic word and turns into the powerful adult superhero Captain Marvel. It was a powerful and accessible fantasy (certainly easier than coming from another planet or lifting all those weights) for adolescent readers. Captain Marvel stories were a fanciful blend of magic, myth, and pseudo-science. The lighthearted adventures of the Big Red Cheese, as he was affectionately known, outsold Superman during the 1940s and gave the English language one of its great interjections: "Shazam!"

Plastic Man (debuted in *Police Comics* #1, 1941)

A botched robbery at the Crawford Chemical Works radically changes the life of hoodlum Eel O'Brian (later O'Brien). First, being drenched in acid while escaping the scene gives him a rubbery body he can mold into any shape, and then the kindly monks who nurse him back to health inspire him to use his abilities to fight crime as Plastic Man. Plas, as he is known to his friends and fans, soon acquires the lazy, bumbling, but mystically protected Woozy Winks as a sidekick. Plastic Man stories were a fast-paced blend of action and humor. Creator Jack Cole's talent and Plastic Man's power combined for a relentless stream of visually inventive sight gags. "Plas literally embodied the comic book form: its exuberant energy, its flexibility, its boyishness, and its only partially sublimated sexuality" (Spiegelman and Kidd 38).

Of course, Superman, Batman, Wonder Woman, Spider-Man, and Captain America continue to appear in multiple monthly comic books and are further merchandised through all conceivable media from television series to lunchboxes. Though both Captain Marvel and Plastic Man have faded as marquee stars and find themselves limited to guest-starring roles and periodic—though

FIGURE 10.12. Though they may not have claimed much of the limelight in recent years, both the original Captain Marvel and Plastic Man were foundational figures in the development of the superhero genre. Captain Marvel art by C.C. Beck and Plastic Man art by Jack Cole. © DC Comics

inevitably short-lived—revivals, the figures are no less iconic. All seven figures are the predecessors to whom all subsequent superhero creations owe a debt.

ANALYZING: SUPERHEROES AS MODERN MYTHS

The superhero genre is arguably the most important of the comic book genres. It has certainly been the most enduring. Superheroes established the comic book as a commercially viable medium in the United States, and it is superheroes who have defined the comic book in popular perception. Certainly the idea of the superhero is ubiquitous. A citizen of a modern industrial society cannot go a day without being exposed to superhero imagery. From Sesame Street's "Hero Guy" and "Super Grover," to Eminem's music videos "Superman" and the Batman and Robin homage "Without Me," to "Orkin Man" commercials, the concept of superheroes pervades our culture (Fingeroth, *Superman* 169). But beneath this superficial imagery, what is there that drives creators to continue telling tales of superheroes, and what keeps fans devoted to their adventures?

In the late 1930s, when the first comic book superheroes began to appear, many individuals were facing the economic devastation of the Great Depression and felt overwhelmed by the mighty machinery and vast structures of the modern world. In Superman and his ilk, they found mythical characters who could rise above the skyscrapers that dwarfed the ordinary human and transcend the forces of modernity that besieged humanity (Regalado 1). Writer Christopher Knowles contends, "All superheroes are essentially savior figures," and that is why they "traditionally enjoy greater popularity—with children and

FIGURE 10.13. Writer Kurt Busiek and artist Alex Ross explore the meaning of superheroes to the lives of ordinary people in *Marvels* #4 (1994). © 2008 Marvel Entertainment, Inc. and its Subsidiaries

adults—in times of national stress" (111). Superhero tales are not so much a fulfillment of a wish for power as they are an optimistic statement about the future and an act of defiance in the face of adversity (Regalado 12). Writer Jeph Loeb and scholar Tom Morris believe superheroes can serve as "moral examples. Superman can inspire us. Batman can keep us going even when the going is very tough. Spider-Man can help us understand that the voice of conscience is always more important than the cacophony of voices around us, who may be condemning us, belittling us, or just dismissing what we think of as so important" (19).

The superhero is recognized as a particularly American creation and is often seen as an embodiment of American **ideology**. However, many beyond America's shores mistakenly interpret the superhero as merely a symbol of power. The meaning of superheroes on their native soil can be found in Will Kane, of the movie *High Noon*, who stays to face the gunmen seeking revenge even though no one in town will stand with him or appreciates what he is doing. The meaning can be found in Raymond Chandler's private detective Phillip Marlowe, who risks his life in the service of justice, even though he seldom has a client paying him to do so. The superhero is the same Emersonian hero who strode down the main streets of western towns and the mean streets of Los Angeles, leading a life of duty, courage, and individual effort.

Discussion Questions

1. If you could have one superpower, what would it be? What do you find appealing about this power? How does what you find exciting about the power relate to the supposed "power fantasy" appeal of superheroes?

2. Apply one or more of the definitions of "superhero" presented in this chapter to a fictional hero who has not normally been labeled as a *super*-hero (e.g., Buffy the Vampire Slayer or Rambo). What does your comparison reveal about the qualities that make a superhero? What does it reveal about the hero you have chosen?

3. Would you revise Benton's "Significant Seven" to include other, more contemporary characters (e.g., Wolverine or the Punisher)? What contributions to the genre would justify the inclusion of your additions?

Activities

1. In *Superhero: The Secret Origin of a Genre*, Peter Coogan mentions a number of early twentieth century science fiction novels that dealt with the concept of the superman: *The Food of the Gods and How it Came to Earth* (1904) by H.G. Wells, *The Overman* (1907) by Upton Sinclair, *The Hampdenshire Wonder* (1911) by J.D. Beresford, *Alias* (1913) by Varick Vanardy, *Men Like Gods* (1923) by H.G. Wells, *Gladiator* (1930) by Philip Wylie, *The New Adam* (1939) by Stanley Weinbaum, and *Odd John* (1936) by Olaf Stapledon. Read one of these books and write a brief analysis of how the superbeing depicted in the book conforms to or differs from the definition and conventions of the superhero genre. Also consider the ways the character might have influenced aspects of the superhero genre or influenced the development of a particular character.

2. For a while now, superheroes have permeated American culture, in movies, in the toy aisle, and emblazoned on everything from cereal boxes to Underoos. Consider the more subtle ways superheroes have entered the popular culture in slang, songs, advertising, and just as part of the background of our popular culture (for instance, in the sitcom *Big Bang Theory*, one of the characters wears a different superhero T-shirt every episode). List at least half a dozen examples and bring one audiovisual example in to share with the class.

Recommended Readings

Comics:

Busiek, Kurt, and Brent E. Anderson. *Kurt Busiek's Astro City: Life in the Big City.* La Jolla, CA: Homage Comics, 1995.

Kurt Busiek lovingly crafted the fictional Astro City and its numerous superheroic inhabitants in homage to the superheroes he grew up admiring. Within these city limits, he explores both the heroism and the humanity of beings with powers and abilities far beyond those of mortal men.

Gold, Mike, and Robert Greenberger, eds. *The Greatest Superman Stories Ever Told.* New York: DC Comics, 1987.

This trade paperback collects a sampling of some of the most entertaining Superman stories published during the character's first fifty years, including selections from creators Jerry Siegel and Joe Shuster, definitive artist Curt Swan, and comic greats Jack Kirby, Alan Moore, and John Byrne.

Scholarly Sources:

Klock, Geoff. *How to Read Superhero Comics and Why.* New York: Continuum, 2002.

Klock examines the evolution of the superhero genre through recent works like those by Grant Morrison (*JLA, New X-Men*) and Alan Moore (*America's Best Comics*), using the tools of literary analysis.

Misiroglu, Gina, and David A. Roach, eds. *The Superhero Book: The Ultimate Encyclopedia of Comic-Book Icons and Hollywood Heroes.* Detroit: Visible Ink, 2004.

Misiroglu and Roach's phonebook-sized review of the genre offers both detailed entries on many of the genre's enduring figures and a broad perspective on how the superhero has appeared in other media. Coverage includes hundreds of individual superhero entries and features on such diverse topics as the antihero and Spider-Man in the media.

Comic Books and Ideology

"[T]he people who make comics have never existed in a vacuum. They instead live within a surrounding culture, a culture that is naturally reflected in their work."

—FREDRIK STRÖMBERG, HISTORIAN, 2003

The United States' involvement in Vietnam in the late 1960s and early 1970s was unquestionably one of the most controversial and painful chapters in American history. In the decades after American forces pulled out of that conflict, popular culture has revisited the troubled era in film, music, literature, and, of course, comics. In 1986 Marvel Comics began publishing *The 'Nam*, a monthly comic book series written by Vietnam veteran Doug Murray, focused on the lives of American servicemen at the time of conflict, and promoted as operating in "real time." That is, when a month passed between issues of the comic book, a month of time would have passed for the characters in the series as well, thus circumscribing the age-defying quality of most comic book series where titular characters rarely grow older, or do so at a protracted rate. Thus the creators promised to address the Vietnam experience in realistic terms, or at least as realistic as they could portray in a Comics Code–approved book in the eighties.

FIGURE 11.1. The cover of *The 'Nam* #67 (1992) presents the beefy Marvel anti-hero, the Punisher, attacking the much more meekly portrayed Vietnamese. Art by Jorge Zaffino. © 2008 Marvel Entertainment, Inc. and its subsidiaries

But in a close reading of the series, critic Annette Matton questions how much *The 'Nam* actually reconsidered the era. What Matton saw in her reading was a publication that seemed to do more to justify the American policy of the time than to present multiple, and thus inherently complex, perspectives on it. Such a conservative rendering by the publishers "follows the tradition of earlier war comics in supporting the established ideology"

(155). Adding support to her claim, Matton points out that the portrayal of the American soldiers in *The 'Nam* is nearly always flattering. The Americans are strong and handsome, but the Vietnamese are portrayed as weak and thin. The Americans are technologically savvy; the Vietnamese struggle on without advanced weaponry. Moreover, the rightness of America's cause is presented as sound, while most Vietnamese are portrayed as the enemy. Ultimately, *The 'Nam* violated its own avowed promises of realistic portrayals of the war when editorial pressure mandated guest stars from Marvel's stable of superheroes, including two story arcs starring the shoot-'em-up Punisher. But well before Marvel super-heroes began to guest star, the series had already been unrealistic in that it pre-sented a perspective on Vietnam that was already biased, offering an idealized view of the experience that favored American heroism and morality.

OBJECTIVES

In this chapter you will learn:

1. the concept of ideology and the reason for exploring its function in society;

2. how propaganda is a manifestation of ideology put into practice;

3. the ways in which the dominant ideology is served through certain representations of gender and race; and

4. some ways in which comics creators have taken up social causes in opposition to prevailing ideologies.

Matton's reading of *The 'Nam* illustrates how critical inquiry identifies con-cepts of ideology in comics. **Ideology** refers to a set of sense-making ideas about how the world works. Ideologies aren't hidden—unless they may be con-sidered to be hiding in plain sight—as they are composed of taken-for-granted assumptions about the way the social world is supposed to work. For instance, most of us hold some ideas about people's gender roles, sexual preference, class distinctions, racial characteristics, ethnic qualities, and national origin, among other markers, that inform how we perceive and interact with them. Ideologies emerge as groups of people develop ways of thinking about relationships between themselves and others in the world. A given set of ideas—an ideology—then helps them manage the world, and thus becomes equipment for living. The longer that these ideologies have a hold, the less likely anyone is to question their premises. Thus, an ideology takes on the appearance of common sense among those within a culture that embraces it. However, critical reflection or feedback from those outside an ideology's influence can expose an ideology's biases. Matton's reading is certainly an instance where critical interrogation points out the assumptions displayed in a comics narrative.

Why is identifying ideology an important intellectual undertaking? Because issues of ideology are entwined with issues of power. Those who benefit from a dominant idea often wield power in a society. Consider the idea, still dominant in numerous societies around the world, that men should enjoy more rights and privileges than women. In these societies, this idea is used to benefit the dominant group, in this case males, and subordinate another group, in this case females. Such an ideology is perpetuated through a number of institutions within a society: the customs of the family unit, the laws imposed by the state, the practices of the religion, and the messages coming from mass media outlets. All of these institutions may be critiqued for perpetuating a given ideology, but our focus is on how the mass medium of comic books shapes and shares such ideas.

Like other artifacts of mass media, comics are produced by individuals or groups of individuals who bring to their works their own preexisting ideas. Whether intentionally or unintentionally, creators' work in comics embodies elements of their ideologies. Some ideological messages find a welcoming audience who accept the creators' stated assumptions as true. This interpretation is called the **preferred reading** and occurs when the creators' intent matches the readers' understanding of the message. Readers whose ideologies favor American intervention in foreign affairs probably read *The 'Nam* through the preferred reading. However, not everyone who reads a comics narrative supports the same ideology. Those with a different, if not outright contradictory, set of ideas to those presented by the creators might interpret the messages quite unlike the way they were intended. These are **oppositional readings**, and they lay bare the assumptions presented in the narrative. For instance, a person of Vietnamese heritage might look at the depiction of Vietnam in *The 'Nam* and see an unflattering presentation of her people. Such a reader would likely have a very different take on the narrative. A word of caution here: Readings are not all or nothing, and a **negotiated reading**, where some assumptions are accepted and others rejected, is also possible. The essential point is that ideological assumptions are not always accepted at face value.

This chapter seeks to lay bare some of the ideological assumptions presented in comics. We begin by examining comics that have functioned as instruments of propaganda, particularly those that endorse government policies. Next we turn to issues of representation and focus on how ideologies of gender and race function as instruments of oppression to certain groups of people within society. Our third and final section will look at comics that have taken up social causes, promoting ideologies that call for social change.

PROPAGANDA

Propaganda is a series of related communication acts that *propagate*, or spread, a particular interpretation of an event. Propaganda tries to reach a large audience through the use of mass media and attempts to create a uniformity of interpretation among audience members by using what are arguably manipulative techniques. At any given time there exists an intricate web of diverse propaganda messages competing to become the prevailing interpretation or myth within a culture, and like all popular culture, the comic book "is a child of propaganda" engaged in a "cycle of quotation and cross-quotation" from "the myths that circulate in culture" (Murray 147). Propaganda works best when audiences are not aware they are being exposed to it. Cartoonist Peter Kuper believes "comics are a perfect medium to address portentous subjects; the title 'comics' already suggests something funny, light, kid-friendly, so the reader doesn't see the POW! coming" (28).

And, of course, the perception of propaganda is very subjective. If we perceive that a comic book is advocating an ideology we do not support, we are likely to view that comic as propaganda. A number of readers have described vigilante superheroes, who use power to impose their own idea of social order, as fascist. Fascism is a political philosophy that promotes devotion to authority and subverts individual rights to the interests of the state. To one reading, the typical superhero story "shows a democratic face in that the protagonist is an Everyman, yet has a pop-fascist dimension in that these unelected, law-transcending figures exercise superpowers to overcome foes" (Jewett and Lawrence 29). Scholar Walter J. Ong even went so far as to label Superman a Nazi (qtd. in "Are Comics" 67)! Other readers worry that comic books are espousing a secular progressive agenda and will serve as "a gateway medium into heavy metal music, soft-core pornography, and anti-religious propaganda" (Fulce 32).

Some of the most blatant propaganda is produced during times of war. In the following section we will consider how comic books have employed propaganda images and concepts both in support of American war efforts—chiefly during the Second World War and the Cold War that followed—and in powerful explorations and condemnations of the tragedy of war. The war comic book has existed since 1940, but it has generally been a marginal genre, and even during the years of World War II, the most vigorous propaganda was found not in war comics but in superhero comics.

Superheroes at War

Scholar Chris Murray believes that "even a brief look at superhero comics from the 1940s leaves little doubt that the genre as a whole fed off of the American government's programme of domestic propaganda" and reflected "the ideology of the dominant power structures and institutions" (142–143). Some of the propaganda was public-spirited and lighthearted, as with the smiling heroes who encouraged kids to get involved in paper drives and reminded parents to buy war bonds. Covers that would appeal to rowdy schoolboys, depicting raucous treatment of Nazis such as punching Adolf Hitler in the jaw or stuffing Herman Goering in a trash can, facilitated shifts in attitudes toward the enemy. Yet some of the older schoolboys would soon be on the front lines, inflicting far more serious violence on the enemy, and part of their psychological preparation had come from the pages of the growing number of comic books actively engaged in dehumanizing the Germans, and especially the Japanese. "Comic books became an integral part of the Allied propaganda machine, emphasizing the need for a maximum war effort by portraying the enemy as the inhuman offspring of a vast and pernicious evil" (Savage 10).

The most explicitly propagandistic comic books dehumanized and demonized the enemy. Arrogant Germans wearing monocles leered as they branded their captives with a red-hot swastika. Superheroes were constantly rescuing teenage sidekicks or beautiful women just as their partially naked bodies were about to suffer under a German lash. German officers were arrogant, the common soldiers were often barbaric, and they all delighted in cruelty. Yet the distortions of form and character they suffered were nothing compared to the deformities visited upon the Japanese. "The Japanese all wore glasses and had buck teeth (or, often, fangs) and claw-like fingernails. Their skins were usually yellow, often greenish-yellow" (Don Thompson 112). Drawn as fanged, clawed, and drooling, the Japanese villains hardly appeared human, and, in fact, were often depicted as some sort of animal: rats and snakes with slanted, squinty eyes were popular. They were reduced to a form of vermin that it seemed only natural to exterminate.

Depictions of a depraved and hideous enemy were soon contrasted with stalwart, handsome heroes with patriotic names and red, white, and blue costumes. The Shield (*Pep Comics* #1, 1940), the first of the patriotic heroes embodying the spirit of America, was the only such character for half a year. But as the war in Europe continued to dominate the headlines in America, the Shield was followed by star-spangled, freedom-defending heroes such as Uncle Sam, the Patriot, American Eagle, and Liberty Belle. Comics historian Michelle Nolan has identified sixty-one patriotic superheroes who debuted in comic books from 1940 to 1944, and forty-seven of those characters appeared before Pearl Harbor and the United States' entry into the war ("Patriotic"). Before America was at war with Germany, Captain America had punched Hitler in the jaw (*Captain America Comics* #1, 1941), the Flag had toppled Nazi tanks (*Our Flag Comics* #2, 1941), and U.S. Jones had "plummeted into the midst of the Nazis" (*U.S. Jones* #1, 1941). The patriotic hero comics were clearly advocating for America to step up and deal with a manifest evil. Once America did make a declaration of war, DC superheroes generally contented themselves with protecting the homeland from spies and saboteurs, but the Timely superheroes (Captain America, Sub-Mariner, Human Torch, etc.) were in the thick of the war, sinking a prodigious number of Japanese cruisers and German U-boats. Nor were the Timely superheroes merely fighting a sanitized war against machinery; the human enemy often felt their righteous wrath in gruesome ways. Because the enemy was so often presented as inhuman vermin deserving of extermination, "it was

FIGURE 11.2. Asians were often presented as subhuman in drawings such as this one from *Captain America Comics* #6 (1941). © 2008 Marvel Entertainment, Inc. and its subsidiaries

once a common sight to behold the Human Torch burning the arm off a grotesquely deformed Japanese while a pretty girl gleefully cheered him on" (Don Thompson 112). Through such images, the comics industry did its part to perpetuate the government's desired aim of inciting the population to stand against the enemy.

War Comics

Most early comic books in the war genre were not as blatantly racist as the superhero comics, but they generally supported the righteousness of the American cause and glorified the act of war. The vast majority of war comics presented the heroic adventures of soldiers amidst the thrilling action of war. It is not surprising that comic books during "the good war"—that is, World War II—were presented in simple terms of good and evil, and that the good guys, chiefly the Americans, always achieved victory. A few of the more ambitious stories might detail the struggles of an individual soldier overcoming inner conflict before engaging in an act of courage. The causes or impact of war were seldom considered.

Many comic book creators were no doubt motivated by patriotism or support of a just cause, but there was also some pressure to adhere to the dominant ideology of the time. Government agencies, aware of the power of images to support or subvert the American cause in World War II and the Cold War, devoted most of their effort to scrutinizing the output of the American film industry, but war comics did not totally escape their notice. Some comic books deemed contrary to the best interests of the United States war effort were banned from distribution on military bases. After one banning incident, the Navy received "the assurance of the publishers that all gory and pacifist features have been removed from their product" (U.S. House 29).

In the ideological struggle between democracy and communism that developed in the aftermath of World War II, "The cold war ideology of American comic books was nakedly displayed in the war and espionage comics of the early 1950s" (Rifas, "Cold War" 3). The Blackhawks, a squadron of pilots representing most of the Allied nations, made their first appearance in 1941 (*Military Comics* #1) and spent the rest of the war besting a multitude of outlandish Nazi opponents. With the end of World War II, the Blackhawks soon found a new purpose: opposing the threat of "invasion and tyranny" from an unnamed "aggressor nation," "dictator nation," or "peoples' dictatorship." Even when the opponents were called marauding pirates, they clearly served as surrogates for the Soviet Union, as illustrated by one series of panels in which the skull and crossbones of the pirate flag subtly morphed into the hammer and sickle of the Soviet flag.

Hostilities with the communists were more open when it came to the Korean Conflict. While most of the popular culture of the time ignored the war in Korea, war comic books reached the peak of their popularity in the early 1950s, and more than one hundred different titles featured the conflict in Korea. While artists often depicted the North Koreans and Chinese as "subhuman caricatures," much as they had done with the Japanese in World War II, the exuberant pro-war propaganda of the previous war was often muted in Korean War tales

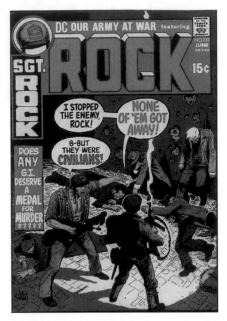

FIGURE 11.3. A 1971 Sgt. Rock story raises the specter of war crimes by American soldiers, a topic that would have been unimaginable in earlier comic books. © DC Comics

that "tended to be grim and ironic" (Bradford Wright 114–115).

Decades later, as the nation became ever more conflicted about the war in Vietnam, the change of tone in mainstream war comics became more pronounced. DC began to include the "Make War No More" slogan on the final page of each of its war comic books. In the story "Head Count" (*Our Army at War* #233, 1971), Sgt. Rock, the best-known recurring character in the war comics, encountered a massacre of civilians that was evocative of the actual My Lai massacre in Vietnam. DC also began to publish a sympathetic portrayal of a World War I German fighter pilot, Hans von Hammer, the Enemy Ace, who feels it is his duty to fight for his country, but also feels anguish about the lives he must take in battle. Many mainstream comic books of the Vietnam era took a more complex view of war and often undercut the concept of heroism, but they were not quite anti-war comics.

Anti-war Comics

Anti-war comics focus on the horrors of war and question not only the justifications for a particular war, but the morality of war in general. In this way, they may oppose the dominant ideology of their times. A number of scholars cite Harvey Kurtzman as the earliest anti-war creator for his work as writer and editor of EC Comics' *Frontline Combat* (1951–1954) and *Two-Fisted Tales* (1950–1955). The EC war books featured battle tales from a wide variety of eras and conflicts, but the vast majority of stories were set in the then-current Korean conflict, and Kurtzman thought the Korean War was justifiable. Kurtzman even worked with the Air Force's public relations civilian unit in making *Frontline Combat* #12 an Air Force tribute issue. While most of Kurtzman's stories focused on the men who fought the battles, he also became fascinated by the technical aspects of war and wrote some EC war stories that "celebrate the lifesaving capabilities of America's war technology" (Witek, *Comic Books* 42).

What made Kurtzman's war comics different from most on the market was that he resisted glorifying war and employing racist stereotypes of the enemy. Standard war comics portrayed death as a noble sacrifice, but "Kurtzman uses death to indicate the futility of war" (Versaci 167). Scholar Leonard Rifas believes "Harvey Kurtzman's reputation as an anti-war cartoonist is largely based on the unusual degree to which he insisted in his stories that the enemy is as human as ourselves" ("Cold War" 11). Kurtzman refused to romanticize or blunt the horror of war, and he never let readers forget the human cost of war on both sides.

Some of Kurtzman's most powerful tales explored how war impacts the noncombatant, the average people. In "Rubble" (*Two-Fisted Tales* #24, 1951), Chun, a young Korean farmer, builds a home on land he has inherited. Kurtzman devotes most of the story to detailing Chun's months of arduous labor, then, when the war impinges on the lives of the Chuns, the house is reduced to rubble in a matter of moments. Later, the foundation of what was once a home is used as the base for a piece of artillery. Buildings being destroyed are a familiar backdrop to the action of war comics, but in this story the destruction is experienced as a very personal tragedy. In the 1960s, Archie Goodwin, the writer of Warren publication's *Blazing Combat*, had an approach to war comics that was obviously inspired by Kurtzman's work. Goodwin's story "Landscape" (*Blazing Combat* #2, 1966), reminiscent of "Rubble," opens with Luong, an elderly Vietnamese farmer working in his rice fields as his small village is "freed," first by one side, then by the other. Luong does not care about the politics of either side, and even when the attacks and counter-attacks leave his family dead and his village in flames, he finds solace in working his rice crop (see Figure 11.4, panel 1). In the end, even that is taken when soldiers burn his rice paddy to flush out the enemy. The stark final panel (see Figure 11.4, panel 2), with its condemnation of war's brutality to civilians, is perhaps the chief reason the comic book was banned from Army bases. Neither Kurtzman nor Goodwin were creating stories that were blatantly anti-war, but they were both interested in conveying the horrors of war.

A more overtly anti-war comic book was written and published by Julian Bond, the man who went on to help found the Southern Poverty Law Center and become chairman of the NAACP. In 1967 young Julian Bond was elected to the Georgia House of Representatives, but the legislature voted not to seat him because he was an outspoken critic of America's involvement in Vietnam. While Bond was fighting in the courts for his right to take his seat in the legislature, he teamed up with artist T.G. Lewis to produce a comic book, *Vietnam*, that sought to show why the military action in Southeast Asia was immoral, and that young black men were doing a disproportionate amount of the fighting and dying.

FIGURE 11.4. Two separate panels from *Blazing Combat* #2 (1966) show the horrors of war inflicted on the innocent. Script by Archie Goodwin and art by Joe Orlando. © 2008 J. Michael Catron.

Of course, as products of the counterculture, many underground comics railed against the war in Vietnam, but one of the most bizarre publications was *The Legion of Charlies* (1971), written by Tom Veitch and drawn by Greg Irons. The book opens with a parallel between Charlie Manson and his "family" murdering people in their homes and Charlie Company's massacre of hundreds of Vietnamese civilians at My Lai and other villages. In this story Charlie Manson is executed for his crimes, and when traumatized Vietnam veterans return home, hundreds of them are possessed by the spirit of Manson. The transformed vets embark on an orgy of cannibalistic violence in which they devour world leaders, except for President Nixnerk, who is baptized in the word of Charlie.

A number of more temperate anti-war comic books appeared in the 1980s. In the spirit of the undergrounds, creators Peter Kuper and Seth Tobocman founded *World War 3 Illustrated* in 1980 as a home for political comics dedicated to exposing injustice and opposing violence and war. In 1982, Leonard Rifas' EduComics published *I SAW IT*, an English translation of Keiji Nakazawa's firsthand account of the atomic bombing of Hiroshima, in hopes of inspiring "urgent efforts to eliminate the threat of nuclear war" (Rifas "Introduction" 1). Also in 1982, Raymond Briggs, formerly known primarily as an illustrator of children's books, produced a harrowing tale of an innocent elderly couple caught up in the devastation and suffering of nuclear war in *When the Wind Blows*. Briggs followed that graphic novel a few years later with a condemnation of British militarism in the Falklands War in the bitingly satirical adult "nursery rhyme" *The Tin-Pot Foreign Dictator and the Old Iron Woman* (1984). The Joyce Brabner–edited anthology *Real War Stories* (1987) was sponsored by the Central Committee for Conscientious Objectors and published by Eclipse Comics to "present a viable alternative to militarism" for young men and women being targeted by Department of Defense advertising (Mullaney, inside cover). These examples represent a valiant effort to counteract the propaganda of the government, but their reach often paled in comparison to the extent to which the better-financed state could disseminate its pro-war messages.

Government-Produced Comic Books

Occasionally, the government has created comic books meant to deliver a persuasive message to allies or enemies during a conflict. For instance, in the late 1960s the CIA's Phoenix Program distributed the comic book *Mr. Ba's Family and the Phoenix Operation* throughout the Vietnamese countryside in hopes of encouraging villagers to inform the U.S. military about enemy Viet Cong secretly operating out of their communities.

The title of *Grenada: Rescued from Rape and Slavery*, a 1984 CIA-produced comic book that was distributed on the island of Grenada in conjunction with U.S. military operations, sets the tone for this heavy-handed propaganda of the late Cold War. The three panels on the front cover summarize the plot inside. In the first panel a village is burning, the ground is strewn with corpses, and communist soldiers are shooting defenseless Grenadians in the head. In the second panel U.S. troops are freeing lean Grenadian prisoners from jail cells. In the final panel U.S. soldiers stand among a throng of cheering Grenadians holding signs declaring "Down with Communism," "We are Free," and "Thanks to the USA" (Victims).

The United States government continues to show an interest in using the comic book medium as a vehicle for influencing the ideology of target populations, and some of its efforts are not even very covert. In 2005 the U.S. Army Special Operations Command advertised for a contractor to produce Arabic-language comic books with characters and plots developed by the Army. The advertisement calls for the books to present adventures of security forces, military, and police and provide the youth of the Middle East positive role models and moral lessons ("D.C. Comics"). The continuation of such efforts represents the perpetuation of propaganda. Of course, there are ideologically charged messages in addition to propaganda that help sustain the power base of the dominant group in society, as we shall see in our next section.

REPRESENTATION

In 1999 comics writer Gail Simone posted a list on the internet outlining a number of female leads and supporting characters who had been maimed or killed in mainstream superhero comics. She titled the list "Women in Refrigerators," naming it after a scene in a *Green Lantern* comic book where the protagonist returns home to find his girlfriend's dead body stuffed into a refrigerator. The list also included characters like the former Batgirl, Barbara Gordon, whose spine was shattered when she was shot by the Joker in Alan Moore and Brian Bolland's graphic novel *Batman: The Killing Joke* (1988), and a host of other female characters who had similarly had their identities and powers taken away or otherwise been left for dead. Simone wanted to start a conversation about the treatment of strong female leads in a genre dominated by male characters and presumably catering to a male audience. Were these just derivative plot devices used to stir the male heroes into action, with a Green Lantern

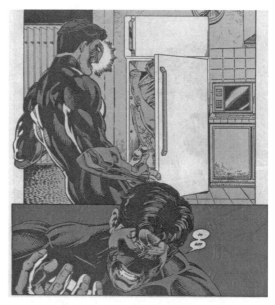

FIGURE 11.5. Green Lantern Kyle Rayner discovers the mutilated body of his feisty girlfriend, Alex DeWitt, murdered by the villainous Major Force to draw the hero into battle. Her grisly fate begs questions about the role of strong women characters in comics. From *Green Lantern* #54 (1994) written by Ron Marz with art by Daryll Banks and Romeo Thangal. © DC Comics

or a Batman meting out righteous justice to the perpetrators of these violent attacks? Or were male creators oblivious to their female audience and their needs for identification with strong characters too? Simone's posting of the Women in Refrigerators list became a flashpoint in issues of gender and comics, refocusing consideration of women in comics, both from the perspective of characters on the comics page and producers behind the scenes.

One of the ways that ideology works to serve the interests of the dominant group is to define them in contrast to other, less powerful groups in a society. For example, in American society the dominant group has been white males, leaving women and people of color in a subordinate position. Of course, there are additional social groupings that have defined the privileged group, including characteristics defined by social class, ethnicity, sexual preference, nationality, etc., but we will focus on biological sex and race, as they are among the most often studied discriminators. Such subordinate groups are often portrayed in popular culture as **"Other,"** a designation that makes them seem strange, unusual, and distant. This designation helps the dominant group define itself through negation (i.e., we know what we are by labeling what we are not), and as these definitions are repeated over time, they become increasingly difficult to dismiss. Those who seek to resist such definitions are therefore very concerned when portrayals that affirm the dominant group's definitions appear in the mass media, as these depictions seemingly verify the depiction's legitimacy. Left unchallenged, these images may be accepted as legitimate, and thus the issue of **representation** becomes central to the practice of ideological critique of the media.

Because depictions in comics are abstracted from reality to one degree or another, the selection of traits that a character embodies—both in terms of personality and physical appearance—runs the risk of relying on stereotypical qualities. Most of us are trained within our culture to recognize the shorthand symbols that seek to capture differences in biological sex. Consider, for instance, the restroom signs that use a simple stick figure with protrusions reminiscent of a skirt to indicate the ladies' room. As familiar a figure as this image has become, emerging back in a time when it was considered a norm for women to wear skirts, today's reality is that women do not wear skirts quite as often, and many favor slacks and jeans. Certainly it is not a particular garment that gives one social sanction to enter that particular restroom (else many a kilted Scotsman would be in for an unwelcome reception through those doors). Instead, the symbol is shorthand, a convenience for communicating quickly. While we might not object to such inaccurate abbreviations on the doors of public restrooms, when simplistic and unflattering stereotypes appear in more developed messages, like comics, the reliance on stereotypical representations sparks objections.

FIGURE 11.6. People accept this oversimplified depiction as representative of women in the context of a public restroom, but oversimplification is less welcome in more complex symbolic exchanges, like narratives.

Images of Women in Comics

The aforementioned trope of women being typecast as victims is, of course, only one of the stereotypes to note. Another objectionable stereotype in mainstream comics is to be found in the physical appearance of the women illustrated. The misrepresentation of women, especially in the last twenty years or so, as extremely thin with disproportionately large breasts has drawn the ire of many critics. Going all the way back to comics' Golden Age, artists have a tradition of drawing "good girls"—so-called for how well they were drawn, not how virtuous they were—featuring women with protruding breasts and provocative poses. Some comic book covers of the 1940s were scandalous because they depicted women in form-fitting outfits, accentuating their breasts (a.k.a., "headlights") in particular. However, the effect seems more pronounced in recent years, with even more unrealistic proportions being displayed. In the 1990s, Catwoman

FIGURE 11.7. Wonder Woman seems almost prudish in an early appearance rendered by 1940s artist Harry G. Peter when compared to the "cheesecake" rendition by Adam Hughes in 2000. © DC Comics

was put into an improbable costume that looked as if it was somehow shrink-wrapped to her top-heavy body. At the same time, buxom, scantily clad women became a house style for Image Comics, Marvel released a series of swimsuit specials that cast their heroines in bikinis, and the independent producers of comics like Lady Death took "**cheesecake**"—the depiction of females in suggestive clothing and poses—to the level of anatomical impossibility.

Even comics that do not cast women into the role of sex objects are still apt to define a woman's role as subservient. In a classic study of the ideological implications of the popular British comic *Jackie*, researcher Angela McRobbie found that the young women were consistently being subjected to an agenda that stressed traditional sex roles. Stories dealt with preparation for a domestic role in marriage, notions of idealized romance, and devotion to fashion and beauty. The problem with this, as McRobbie explains, is that "girls are being invited to join a closed sorority of shared feminine values which actively excludes other possible values" (70). In other words, the comics magazine's message foreclosed rather than opened possibilities, rather clearly suggesting that happiness followed becoming a homemaker, and not even mentioning the option of becoming a physician. Consequently, the closure focused young women on adopting values that served the interests of the dominant group: men. American comics fared little better in this regard, though they opened limited possibilities in terms of careers. Some of the most prominent and enduring female icons in comics represent such limited career choices as actress (Archie's *Katy Keene*) and model (Marvel's *Millie the Model*).

Part of the problem with the presentation of women in the comics may be attributed to the lack of participation among women in the industry. Throughout American comics history, the medium has been disproportionately populated by male creators working for male owners, although not always dominated by male readers. In the heyday of comic books in the 1940s, reader surveys suggested nearly an even split among male and female readers (Witty). Still, even comics' most enduring female icon, Wonder Woman, was created by a male—William Moulton Marston—and her stories were principally written by male storytellers for the first nearly fifty years of her publishing history. There have been professional women cartoonists, of course, but only a handful achieved notoriety at any give time, such as *Miss Fury* creator Tarpe Mills in the 1940s, EC colorist Marie Severin in the 1950s, and *Metamorpho* co-creator Ramona Fradon in the 1960s. Strides for an expanded role for women cartoonists came through the comix underground (edited by Trina Robbins, *It Ain't Me, Babe*, 1970) and the alternative press (Wendy Pini, *Elfquest*, 1978). The industry arguably achieved a milestone when Jeanette Kahn was appointed the high-profile role of publisher of DC Comics in 1976. Since that time, numerous women writers, artists, and editors have contributed their talents to the industry, though their surest ally has been the growth of the graphic novel market that has allowed women to work in genres other than superheroes, with particular success in terms of creating autobiographical comics (e.g., Marjane Satrapi's *Persepolis*, 2002, and Alison Bechdel's *Fun Home*, 2006). Complementing these efforts is an increasingly vocal fan community, such as the Friends of Lulu and GirlWonder.org, who strive to bring recognition to female creators, characters, and readership. Still, given the prevalence of male creators, male characters, and male themes in contemporary comics, it would be erroneous to assume that the dominant ideology has relinquished its hold on its audience's thinking entirely.

Profile: Karen Berger

Born: Karen Berger
       February 26, 1958
       Brooklyn, NY

"I don't have a comic book background. I have a literature background, a history background, a film background. I love story. As an editor, I've always wanted to work on material that appealed to a larger audience."

Career Highlights

1979   Graduates from Brooklyn College with a major in English literature and a minor in art history.

1979   Starts as Paul Levitz' editorial assistant at DC, working on books such as the horror-based *House of Mystery*.

Cont'd

1983   Edits *Amethyst, Princess of Gemworld*, a twelve-part fantasy maxi-series.

1984   Takes over editing *Saga of the Swamp Thing*, which was just beginning to flourish under British writer Alan Moore.

1987   Serves as editor on the re-launch of *Wonder Woman*.

1989   Neil Gaiman initiates *Sandman* under Berger's editorial guidance.

1993   Becomes founding editor of the Vertigo imprint, which would go on to publish acclaimed series like *Preacher, Y the Last Man*, and *Fables*.

1993   Wins the first of three Eisner Awards for Best Editor.

2006   DC promotes Berger to Senior Vice President–Executive Editor, Vertigo as she continues to develop the Vertigo line.

Karen Berger's tenure as one of comicdom's most influential editors suggests that comics don't have to be a medium dominated by males. For nearly three decades, Berger has provided the editorial direction to some of the industry's most acclaimed comic books, including *Swamp Thing, Y the Last Man*, and the much-honored *Sandman*, books that have reached well beyond the traditional comics readership of juvenile boys to appeal to a much wider audience. "I want to offer comics that I would want to read myself," says Berger. "I am lucky enough to work in an environment where I could."

FIGURE 11.8 Vertigo editor Karen Berger has been one of the defining forces in comics publishing in the past three decades. Photo courtesy of DC Comics.

Despite a long career working within the medium, Berger readily admits that she was not a comic book reader growing up. Aside from occasionally picking up a copy of her brothers' *Mad* or other comics, she had little interaction with the medium coming into the industry. Thus, when her friend and comic book writer J.M. DeMatteis recommended an opening as an editorial assistant in DC Comics' New York offices, Berger brought little baggage to the position. Berger joined DC's staff in the late 1970s, while the company was still publishing comics in genres other than superheroes, including mystery (i.e., horror) and fantasy series, and such titles gave her a sense of the wider storytelling potential of the medium. And though she has edited several superhero comics, she has built a reputation on developing series that are far more edgy. In 1993 she took a half dozen such titles, which included such atypical fare as *Shade, the Changing Man, Animal Man*, and *Hellblazer*, and founded the Vertigo imprint. Since that time, Vertigo has continued to widen its appeal: "We've broken out from dark fantasy to books that are more contemporary statements about the world in which we live. We use different genres to talk about the world at large." Among its successes, the imprint counts the noir-inspired *100 Bullets*, the cyberpunk *Transmetropolitan*, and the irreverent *Preacher*.

Vertigo's appeal has drawn wide acclaim, earning Berger herself and the titles she edits praise from within and beyond the industry, including multiple Eisner Award

Cont'd

wins for her and her collaborators. One of her strengths as an editor is identify rising talent, including recruiting Neil Gaiman to write American comics. "I'm looking for storytelling ability as well as novelty of ideas and the way they are portrayed. I'm looking for unconventional work, including deep character portrayals," notes Berger.

Perhaps it is the emphasis on characterization that attracts audiences to Vertigo comics, but it is clear to Berger that the balance between male and female creators is beginning to shift in the industry. "People like to write and draw what interests them," she points out, and more and more women are finding their voices through the medium. "The industry is still predominantly male because of the male readership," Berger explains, "but there are more opportunities for women to do comics that are not superhero related."

Images of Blacks in Comics

Another minority often represented as Other in the pages of American comics are blacks. In this instance, it is the interests of the white majority that are served by existing representations. The earliest depictions of people of color were almost always shaped by the openly racist sentiments of the early twentieth century. For blacks, this meant that they appeared in particularly harsh caricatures, often featured as either ignorant savages in need of enlightening by a white hero such as Tarzan, or as comic relief for an otherwise all-white cast. Even the venerable comics innovator Will Eisner included a character of the latter type in his 1940s *Spirit* series, casting the young boy Ebony White as the hero's sidekick. Like other minstrel-like figures of the time, Ebony had thick lips and spoke with an exaggerated accent. After World War II, depictions of African Americans all but disappeared, as the population of mostly white creators attempted to figure out how to portray the minority without relying on insulting stereotypes (Strömberg).

It wasn't until 1966 that the first black superhero, the Black Panther, debuted in the pages of Marvel Comics' *Fantastic Four*. Thereafter, a modest number of black characters began populating mainstream comics, some of them influenced by Hollywood's blaxploitation films like *Shaft*, with *Luke Cage, Hero for Hire* becoming the first black superhero with his own title in 1972. As time passed, additional African American heroes joined in, including the Falcon, Storm, Cyborg, and Vixen, characters who functioned as a part of an ensemble rather than featured characters in their own titles. African Americans did get their chance to star on occasion, though that function might be in the role of a "hand-me-down hero" taking over the previous identity of a white character, such as when John Stewart was promoted to Green Lantern or Jim Rhoades took over as Iron Man (Jennings and Duffy). A much bolder experiment in comics publishing came along in 1993, when four African American entrepreneurs, Denys Cowan, Michael Davis, Derek T. Dingle, and Dwayne McDuffie, launched Milestone Media. In titles like *Static* and *Icon*, the Milestone creators sought to present a multicultural view of heroism by casting people of color in lead roles. Though Milestone lasted only four years in comics publishing, it offered a meaningful step forward in terms of representation.

While some might think that no representation at all is better than a medium full of stereotypically unflattering portrayals, a state of under-representation is fraught with its own undesirable implications. Whether people are looking to media for entertainment or information, they are also looking to identify with the figures depicted therein. When a particular minority is under-represented, and thus essentially invisible in the medium, a message is sent about the normality of the presence of that minority in society (Haynes). For example, for decades an all-white Justice League of America sent a message about self-worth to young black readers looking for African American role models: There are none! Though the Justice League ultimately recruited various minorities, it wasn't until Vixen joined in 1984, more than twenty

FIGURE 11.9. Will Eisner's *The Spirit* was destined to break artistic ground in its run, but it began with reliance on some stereotypes, including that of a heavily caricatured African American sidekick, Ebony White. *The Spirit* is a registered trademark of Will Eisner Studios, Inc. Reprinted with permission. All rights reserved.

years after the league was founded, that a person of color took membership among "The World's Greatest Super-Heroes."

As it has been with women, part of the problem with African American representation may lie in African American participation in the industry—or lack thereof. Early pioneers, such as the legendary Matt Baker, contributed to a number of mainstream comics, breaking through the color barrier that kept African Americans segregated in other popular media of the era. However, the number of black creators, especially those working on high-profile assignments, has historically been very modest, and rarely has the work involved characters of color. Exceptions exist, like Trevor von Eden's tenure as artist of *Black Lightning* in the 1970s, but until recently most mainstream comics *about* black characters have not been done *by* black creators. Even the most successful comic book series to star a black protagonist, Image Comics' *Spawn*, is the production of a white creator, Todd McFarlane. Milestone Media certainly broke with that tradition when it employed a multicultural creative team to produce comics about multicultural characters in the late 1990s. Since then, African Americans have made strides in creating high-profile comics. Ho Che Anderson was hailed for *King* (1993–2003), his multi-volume biography of Dr. Martin Luther King, Jr.; Robert Morales and Kyle Baker garnered national media attention for adding a black predecessor to the mythos of Captain America in the 2003 limited series *Truth: Red, White & Black*; and another high-profile creative run began when Reginald Hudlin, President of Entertainment for the BET cable channel, took on writing Marvel's *Black Panther* series.

FIGURE 11.10. Behind the cover of *Truth: Red, White & Black* (2003), with art by Kyle Baker, lies the story of Isaiah Bradley, an African American hero created to be a patriotic "super-soldier" like Captain America. © 2008 Marvel Entertainment, Inc. and its subsidiaries

Such examples of progress should not suggest that comics are fully integrated, or that problems with representation for women, people of color, or any other minority have been fully addressed. While inroads in terms of positive representation for minority groups are being made, the reliance on stereotypes in comics—and this is true for most all mass media—still persists. So long as white males are the dominant group in terms of ownership and creative control, most media messages will most likely continue to be shaped for them and by them, in ways that perpetuate their privileged status. But however pervasive the influence of the dominant ideology may be in the media, messages of resistance still manage to work their way into those same media.

SOCIAL CAUSES

Judd Winick built a reputation among comic book fans for his high-profile work on DC Comics series like *Batman*. Before that, he was famous among the MTV generation for his role on the cable channel's reality program *The Real World*. While a member of the series' third season cast, he met AIDS educator Pedro Zamora, who also happened to be HIV positive. The charming Zamora won over his cast-mates and their television audience, and he became a national spokesperson for understanding the disease and tolerance for those it infected with it. Zamora died later that year, but the friendship that he had developed with Winick inspired the cartoonist to retell the story of their lives, their friendship, and their shared crusade, which Winick took up after his friend's passing. In 2000 Winick released the graphic novel *Pedro and Me: Friendship, Loss, and What I Learned*, which won a number of national awards, including one from the Gay and Lesbian Alliance Against Defamation (GLAAD). Winick went on to win further accolades for his portrayal of a homosexual supporting character in the pages of DC's *Green Lantern* and a teenage sidekick who happens to be HIV-positive in *Green Arrow*. These comics have challenged the dominant heterosexual/homophobic ideology and sought to educate even while they entertain. Similarly, other comics creators have sought to promote ideas that run contrary to the interests of the dominant ideology and thus advance social causes.

It is difficult for mainstream comics creators to challenge the dominant ideology, in part because these ideas enjoy the benefit of being familiar and, consequently, widely accepted over a period of time. An Italian social theorist named Antonio Gramsci called the perpetuation of dominant ideology, even by those whose interests it ran counter to, **hegemony**. Gramsci argued that the most powerful group in a society (in America this would be white male capitalists) wield their influence to convince the rest of society (that is, anyone who isn't a white male capitalist) that leaving power relations as they were was in everyone's best interest, disparities and all. Gramsci said that as folks accept and then pass along these notions, an acceptance of certain relationships and social hierarchies continues from one generation to the next. That is, of course, unless or until someone reconsiders the notions more critically.

While the comics art form has always been and will continue to be a useful tool for subversive messages, mainstream comics publishers have traditionally observed very conservative positions on society and social relations. Newspaper cartoonists have a longstanding tradition of critiquing those in power, but comic books have traditionally been less inclined to join in the conversation, preferring to peddle mostly juvenile, apolitical fare. Certainly material that favors the dominant ideology appeals to a common denominator in a society and is, consequently, often the safest bet in terms of marketing a product, regardless of genre. Consider how the superhero upholds the status quo of a social order within his genre. Romance comics almost always end with promise of a heterosexual union. Horror comics feature stories where punishment is meted out to social deviants. Thus it becomes not only uncomplicated but commercially beneficial to "play it safe" and support society's hegemonic concepts.

Perhaps the comics art form's most blatant challenge to hegemony came in the 1960s with the emergence of the underground comix movement. As detailed in Chapter 3, the underground movement unleashed cartoonists who explored all manner of social and political satire, resulting in material that offended existing standards regarding everything from the depiction of sexuality to scatology. The social taboos that underground cartoonists were willing to break even emboldened mainstream comics to venture into consideration of topics like drug abuse, race relations, and government policy towards Native Americans. The so-called "Era of Relevancy," which we also reviewed in Chapter 3, was embodied by Stan Lee and Gil Kane's drug abuse story in *Amazing Spider-Man* #96–98 (1971) and Dennis O'Neill and Neal Adams' run on *Green Lantern* (1970–1972). Arguably, though, there is only so far that mainstream comics will challenge the dominant ideology, given that they are owned and operated by conglomerates whose interests are served by hegemonic notions. Some apparent exceptions exist, of course, such as when Bob Layton and David Michelinie explored alcoholism in the pages of *Iron Man* in 1979 or when Grant Morrison addressed issues of animal rights and vegetarianism in the page of DC Comics' *Animal Man* in his run that began in 1988. The longevity of such pro-social messages is somewhat limited, usually enduring as long as the tenure of the creative team who advocate it, and sometimes subverted by the marketing needs of the publisher who wants to keep mass appeal for these potentially lucrative properties. Thus, in Iron Man's case, a second bout with alcoholism in 1983–1984 was the last prolonged exploration of the issue for the character in the last

FIGURE 11.11. Tony Stark succumbs to his alcoholism in this sequence from *Iron Man* #128 (1979) with words by David Michelinie and art by John Romita, Jr., and Bob Layton. © 2008 Marvel Entertainment, Inc. and its subsidiaries

two decades. Because social issues rarely remain the focus of most mainstream comics, special issues that take on the problems can come across as looking somewhat exploitative, rather than seeming to be sincere efforts at promoting sustained social change. DC's 2006 revelation that its latest Batwoman would be a lesbian suggests an effort at greater diversity among its characters, but some critics have faulted DC for both the way it announced the character's revelation and the subsequent handling of her earliest depictions.

However, the prospect of more outright resistance to hegemonic forces, carrying on the spirit of the sixties underground movement, is less likely to be found with the largest publishers and more likely with smaller publishers willing to take such risks. Here, comics are more frequently and freely used by creators to oppose dominant thinking and take up social causes that are not in step with the dominant thinking of their time. For example, EC Comics is well remembered for stories that confronted the rampant bigotry of 1950s America, and these stories have proven to hold a timeless charm thanks to recent, successive reprints. More recently, Dark Horse Comics has published a number of stories by Paul Chadwick featuring his Concrete character dealing with issues of the environment. In the 1996 miniseries *Concrete: Think Like a Mountain*, Concrete finds himself working with the controversial protest group Earth First! to challenge deforestation. In other stories he has spoken on behalf of Earth Day and for the need to recycle, among other ecologically minded themes.

Independent comics also challenge hegemonic forces when they question existing political institutions and practices. In attacking such powerful institutions, though, cartoonists have often relied on the veneer of science fiction and fantasy to help disguise the point of their jabs. In 1983, First Comics began to publish Howard Chaykin's satirical science fiction fantasy, *American Flagg!*, an indictment of the influences of corporations over government and media in American society. Set fifty years in the future, *Flagg!* critiqued contemporary corporate power even amidst the Martian colonies and talking cats that populated its universe. Another independent publisher, Eclipse Comics, offered up a more dystopian future by cartoonist Timothy Truman through his comic book series *Scout* (1987). The series was set in a post-apocalyptic America, where the United States was defeated in the Cold War not by Soviet military superiority, but by its own apathy. According to critic Brian Cremins, behind the series' unnerving setting lies a critique of eighties consumer culture. Eclipse also published a less allegorical but no less scathing indictment of America's political institutions and the Central Intelligence Agency's activities in the Joyce Brabner–edited graphic novel *Brought to Light* (1988), which featured a story written by comics icon Alan Moore. Such efforts evidence the role that comics can play in advocating greater social awareness by presenting interpretations of institutions that run contrary to the prevailing favorable opinion of those institutions.

While comics, like other forms of art, can function as catalysts for the raising of social consciousness among their readers, the industry that produces them has a less consistent record for taking more direct action to change existing disparities in power relations. For instance, the first mainstream initiative to use the medium as a fundraiser to benefit the less fortunate did not materialize until the mid-eighties when first Marvel (*Heroes for Hope*, 1985) and then DC (*Heroes against Hunger*, 1986) attempted to raise money for famine relief in Ethiopia by sponsoring "jam" issues of some of the industry's top talents (a jam issue is one in which a number of the industry's top talents collaborate on the creation of a story). While the effort—using the collaboration of high-profile talent to elicit funds to aid the less fortunate—was certainly well intentioned, it would be a while before similar widespread efforts were put forth again. It did happen, though, in the wake of the terrorist attacks of September 11, 2001. Within weeks of the attacks, Marvel Comics released *Heroes* #1 as a fundraiser, and it brought in over $1 million in support. Shortly thereafter, Alternative Comics, Dark Horse, and DC all released anthologies with stories by everyone from the venerable Will Eisner to contemporary top talents like Jeff Smith. All of these publications earned considerable money to benefit the 9/11 victims, relief agencies, and charities. Perhaps it was the prevalence of patriotic spirit in post-9/11 America or the boldness of a new generation of editors that spurred these projects onward, but their success shows how the comics industry, despite its historic skittishness with such engagement, can be a considerable participant in advancing social concerns if it chooses to be.

ANALYZING: COMICS JOURNALISM

For many who seek to change oppressive ideologies, the ability to raise people's awareness of inequalities is a welcome step towards dismantling the systems that perpetuate them. The emerging practice of comics journalism certainly has acknowledged many under-represented voices by drawing attention to oppressed

FIGURE 11.12. Comics journalist Joe Sacco caricatures himself in his accounts, but the events he documents are based on his own experiences and eyewitness testimony. Used by permission of Fantagraphics Books.

groups. **Comics journalism** features the accounts of actual events put into comics form. Unlike the traditionally dispassionate accounts of objective journalism, comics journalism offers a subjective interpretation of a story. In many ways it cannot help but do so, as the account is shaped by the perceptions and artistic style of the cartoonist/reporter. In fact, the comics often feature the cartoonist/reporter as a figure in the narrative, and we come to know the story through that individual's experiences. Comics journalism offers an account that brings both the words and the images of the cartoonist's experience into the reader's scrutiny. It also delivers both a verbal and visual representation of the people involved in the situation while recounting their story.

The most acclaimed comics journalist is Joe Sacco, whose two-volume work *Palestine* (serialized beginning in 1993) presented his experiences in exploring the Israeli-Palestinian Conflict from within the Palestinian territory. Respected intellectual Edward Said praised this work: "With the exception of one or two novelists and poets, no one has ever rendered this terrible state of affairs better than Joe Sacco" (vi). Sacco followed up this work with his accounts of the civil war in the former Yugoslavia in *Safe Area Goražde* (2000), which detailed the oppression of the Muslim minority in Bosnia. Besides Sacco, other comics journalists have published books, including Ted Rall's account of the early war in Afghanistan in his travelogue *To Afghanistan and Back* (2003), which shows the effects of the American invasion on the Afghan people. Even veteran cartoonists like Art Spiegelman, author of *Maus*, have explored the potential of comics journalism, and in his innovative *In the Shadow of No Towers* (2004), Spiegelman documents his experiences with the September 11, 2001, terrorist attacks on New York. Respected outlets of traditional journalism from the *New Yorker* to *Time* magazine have made a forum for comics journalism as it develops. Of course, accounts of recent events aren't the only means to illuminate social inequalities. The works of underground comix great Jack "Jaxon" Jackson also give voice to historic peoples who were treated inhumanely by the dominant ideologies of their times. He has done so in graphic novels like *Comanche Moon* (1979), where he provides an account of the Native American perspective on westward expansion, and *Los Tejanos* (1982), which details the lives of Mexicans who fought for Texas independence. Still, whether documenting past inequities or current disparities, comics are a viable means for shining the light of inspection upon the presumptions and practices of the dominant ideology. Their power to raise readers' awareness and thus contribute to a more understanding and equitable society is only beginning to be realized.

Discussion Questions

1. Select an audience that the United States government would be interested in spreading a propagandistic message to. What words and images directed towards this audience would be "fair game"? What tactics might be considered manipulative? Why so?

2. Issues of representation in comics often focus on the misrepresentation of groups of people. While women and African Americans have received unflattering portrayals, other minority groups have appeared rarely, if at all. Can you identify some groups that have been absent from comics? Which treatment would be more preferred: to be misrepresented or not be represented at all?

3. Does the comics format lend itself to advocating certain social causes better than others? For what causes would comics seem to be a good advocate? A poor one? What qualities of comics do you see contributing to the art form's ability to sway opinions (or not) in each case?

Activities

1. Browse through a set of wartime or war genre comic covers to examine how ideology was marketed to America's youth. A number of published cover collections exist, such as Ernst Gerber's two-volume *Photo-Journal Guide to Comics Books* or the Grand Comic Book Database (*www.comics.org*). Select an intriguing cover to analyze and plan to share both the cover art and the points of your analysis your classmates. Consider the following questions: How did the creators seek to demonize America's foes? What kind of oppositional reading might someone from that other culture render? How might a disinterested third party view the images and text?

2. Create a thumbnail version of your own comic designed to elicit support for a social cause. First, select a cause that either you have strong personal identification with or one that is of timely importance on your campus. Then, using both sides of an 8½ × 10 sheet of paper broken into quadrants, sketch out thumbnails for an eight-page comic book to the best of your artistic ability (even if that's only stick figures). Bring your thumbnails to class for a discussion about how you chose to pitch your cause: What story did you elect to tell about your cause? How did you plan to influence your intended audience? What images were you willing to show and what ones did you avoid?

Recommended Readings

Comics:

Anderson, Ho Che. *King.* 3 vols. Seattle, WA: Fantagraphics, 1993–2003.

Anderson gives an unvarnished account of Dr. Martin Luther King, Jr.'s life and labor and is unafraid to show even some of the shortfalls of "M.L." as he grows into his role as America's premier human rights advocate. *King* provides a fresh perspective on Dr. King's life story and serves as a testimony of the possibility of comics to bring representation to disenfranchised groups.

Chadwick, Paul. *Concrete Vol. 5: Think Like a Mountain.* Milwaukie, OR: Dark Horse Books, 2006.

Chadwick's Concrete stories started with a bit of a sci-fi riff when an everyman found his brain transplanted into an animated concrete shell, but the series has more often delved into the world of human politics than the world of the fantastic. This volume collects numerous ecologically minded stories, promoting a social agenda that was "green" before going green was trendy.

Scholarly Sources:

Dorfman, Ariel, and Armand Mattelart. *How to Read Donald Duck: Imperialist Ideology in the Disney Comic.* Translated by David Kunzle. New York: International General, 1975.

Amidst the political revolution of 1970s Chile, Dorfman and Mattelart produced one of the earliest and most influential ideological critiques of a comic book property. You are sure to have a new perspective on the Disney corporate machine after reading their interpretation of what Donald Duck and company are espousing regarding capitalism, sexuality, and childhood, among other ideologies.

Robbins, Trina. *From Girls to Grrrlz: A History of Comics from Teens to Zines.* San Francisco: Chronicle, 1999.

Robbins chronicles the representation of females in comic books from the 1940s to the 1990s, tracing both mainstream and underground depictions in an amply illustrated review of the changing face of women in comics.

Researching Comic Books

"Once intellectuals start appreciating something, like comics, it's usually dead."

—HARRY HARRISON, SCIENCE FICTION WRITER, 1973

Many pundits figured that the outcome of the 1948 presidential election was a foregone conclusion. Poll after poll indicated that Republican nominee Thomas E. Dewey would unseat incumbent president Harry S. Truman in the November contest. Despite these dour predictions, the Democratic National Committee (DNC) campaigned on, and among its promotional materials released the first ever comic book biography of a presidential candidate, the sixteen-page *The Story of Harry S. Truman*. The DNC commissioned more than 3 million copies of the comic book and released them in October, just before the election, hoping to bring around undecided voters. In releasing the comic books, the DNC targeted those groups of people most likely to turn to Truman: farmers, African Americans, labor unions, and veterans. Veterans, in particular, were fans of comic books, and the novelty of the unusual venue surely piqued the interest of many other potential voters. The four-color account of Truman's life highlighted many of his most heroic actions—including his own military service, his watchdog activities on behalf of taxpayers in the United States Senate, and his leading America to the conclusion of World War II—with none of his faults. While it is impossible to say if the comic book was ultimately responsible for winning over the hearts and minds of undecided voters, Truman won the election by a margin of 1,188,054 votes, which was well within the parameters of the three million copies of the comic book that the DNC had distributed. The pollster who had predicted Dewey's win did so too quickly. Many Americans did not make their choice for chief executive until the crucial last weeks of the campaign—weeks when *The Story of Harry S. Truman* had the chance to circulate among many of these voters (Szasz).

FIGURE 12.1. *The Story of Harry S. Truman* may have influenced some undecided voters to cast their ballot in favor of the incumbent president in a race that was so close that the *Chicago Tribune* famously printed an erroneous edition declaring "Dewey Defeats Truman." Reprinted with permission from the Democratic National Committee.

OBJECTIVES

In this chapter you will learn:

1. how early social scientific research explored the connection between comic books and juvenile delinquency;
2. what literacy experts have claimed in terms of comics' potential to help with reading skills;
3. about the use of content analysis as a tool for quantitative analysis of comics texts; and
4. how mythic criticism is employed to examine comic texts from a qualitative perspective.

Did *The Story of Harry S. Truman* win the election for the president? Can a comic book have that much influence on voter decision-making? For that matter, can comics—or any mass medium—produce such direct effects on its audience? Initially, critics attacked comics as inferior, even dangerous, products of culture, stirring fears that they affect their readers in negative ways. Alternatively, proponents of comics have hailed them as effective pedagogical tools for enhancing literacy and second language learning. More recently, critics and scholars have presented a less impassioned response to comics as artifacts of culture, commenting on their symbolic meanings. Though the approaches—and conclusions—have varied since the 1940s, researchers have tried to better understand the comics and their audiences through scholarly inquiry.

What do we mean when we say something is "scholarly"? Scholarship is publicly shared understanding that comes from systematic ways of knowing. Scholarship is subject to review from others, most especially those who have a background in the same area or on the same topic, and is commonly shared in public ways, such as through presentations and publications. Scholarship is more than merely reporting that a phenomenon exists or offering editorial opinion on it. Scholarship seeks to probe and know a phenomenon using methods that go beyond superficial acknowledgement of the subject or simple responses to its existence. Thus, scholarship is a more rigorous way of perceiving subjects and is typically, though not exclusively, the work of experts within a field.

This chapter explores several key elements in the scholarly tradition of comics over the past seven decades. Research into comics comes from a host of disciplinary perspectives, including particular interest from those in the fields of communication, psychology, education, and literature. We will begin with a consideration of effects research and how social scientists have examined the impact, for worse and better, comics have upon their readers. Then we shall turn our attention to studies into the contents of comics, sampling just two of many possible methods: content analysis and mythic criticism. By this chapter's end, you should have a broader picture of the investigations that have gone on and those that are proceeding in the interdisciplinary realm of comics art studies.

Discovering: Milestones in the Development of Comics Art Studies

The following chronology recognizes only a few of the many pioneering American comics scholars and the accomplishments that have contributed to our understanding of comic books. A larger survey would take into account many more scholars, expanding to include international scholars and those whose work in comic strips and political cartoons also enriched the larger study of comics as an art form.

1947	Cartoonist Frederick Coulton Waugh authors *The Comics*, one of the first histories of the comics to include an examination of comic books.
1954	Dr. Fredric Wertham publishes *The Seduction of the Innocent*, the most influential—and devastating—book about comic books ever published.
1965	Cartoonist Jules Feiffer produces one of the first critical essays about comics accessible to a wider public audience, published by Dial Press as *The Great Comic Book Heroes*.
1967	The inaugural issue of the *Journal of Popular Culture*, a peer-reviewed academic periodical, is launched under the guidance of founding editor and Bowling Green State University professor Ray B. Browne. *JPC* and the Popular Culture Association, founded thereafter, help to promote the scholarly study of all popular culture, comics included.

Cont'd

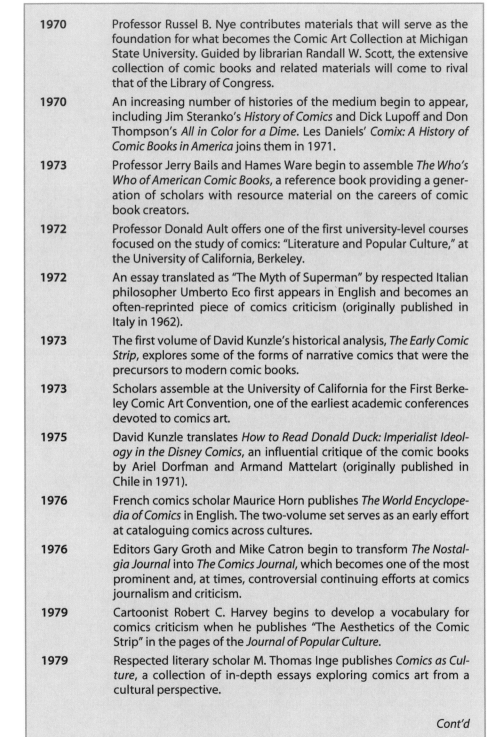

1970	Professor Russel B. Nye contributes materials that will serve as the foundation for what becomes the Comic Art Collection at Michigan State University. Guided by librarian Randall W. Scott, the extensive collection of comic books and related materials will come to rival that of the Library of Congress.
1970	An increasing number of histories of the medium begin to appear, including Jim Steranko's *History of Comics* and Dick Lupoff and Don Thompson's *All in Color for a Dime*. Les Daniels' *Comix: A History of Comic Books in America* joins them in 1971.
1973	Professor Jerry Bails and Hames Ware begin to assemble *The Who's Who of American Comic Books*, a reference book providing a generation of scholars with resource material on the careers of comic book creators.
1972	Professor Donald Ault offers one of the first university-level courses focused on the study of comics: "Literature and Popular Culture," at the University of California, Berkeley.
1972	An essay translated as "The Myth of Superman" by respected Italian philosopher Umberto Eco first appears in English and becomes an often-reprinted piece of comics criticism (originally published in Italy in 1962).
1973	The first volume of David Kunzle's historical analysis, *The Early Comic Strip*, explores some of the forms of narrative comics that were the precursors to modern comic books.
1973	Scholars assemble at the University of California for the First Berkeley Comic Art Convention, one of the earliest academic conferences devoted to comics art.
1975	David Kunzle translates *How to Read Donald Duck: Imperialist Ideology in the Disney Comics*, an influential critique of the comic books by Ariel Dorfman and Armand Mattelart (originally published in Chile in 1971).
1976	French comics scholar Maurice Horn publishes *The World Encyclopedia of Comics* in English. The two-volume set serves as an early effort at cataloguing comics across cultures.
1976	Editors Gary Groth and Mike Catron begin to transform *The Nostalgia Journal* into *The Comics Journal*, which becomes one of the most prominent and, at times, controversial continuing efforts at comics journalism and criticism.
1979	Cartoonist Robert C. Harvey begins to develop a vocabulary for comics criticism when he publishes "The Aesthetics of the Comic Strip" in the pages of the *Journal of Popular Culture*.
1979	Respected literary scholar M. Thomas Inge publishes *Comics as Culture*, a collection of in-depth essays exploring comics art from a cultural perspective.

Cont'd

1983	Frederik L. Schodt authors *Manga! Manga! The World of Japanese Comics*, bringing the study of manga to the attention of English-speaking audiences well before manga would surge in popularity in America.
1983	Under the editorial direction of Thomas Andrae and Geoffrey Blum, the first of the thirty-volume *Carl Barks Library* appears, launching one of the earliest collections of comics and criticism in English.
1985	Cartoonist Will Eisner publishes his first textbook on how to create comics, *Comics & Sequential Art*.
1985	Trina Robbins and Catherine Yronwode publishes *Women and the Comics*, a book-length examination of the contributions of women creators to the medium.
1989	Under the editorial direction of M. Thomas Inge, the University Press of Mississippi begins to publish a series of books devoted to comics art studies, beginning with Joseph Witek's *Comic Books as History*.
1992	Peter Coogan and Randy Duncan found the Comic Arts Conference, the first annual American academic conference devoted exclusively to the study of comics which, since 1998, has been held in conjunction with San Diego's Comic-Con International.
1993	Cartoonist Scott McCloud authors *Understanding Comics: The Invisible Art*, a book of comics theory told in comics form that garners critical acclaim and widespread interest.
1994	Under the editorial direction of Lucy Shelton Caswell, curator of the Cartoon Research Library at Ohio State University, *Inks: Cartoon and Comic Art Studies* becomes the first American academic journal focused exclusively on the comics medium.
1997	The International Comic Arts Festival convenes, bringing together comics scholars from around the world in its first annual meeting.
1997	Historians Robert L. Beerbohm and Richard D. Olson begin to open new perspectives on comics' historical development in the United States with articles on the "Platinum Age" (1883–1938) and then the "Victorian Age" (1828–1883) published in the *Overstreet Comic Book Price Guide*.
1999	Professor John A. Lent launches the *International Journal of Comic Art*, a scholarly journal devoted to the study of comics across cultures.
2004	The University of Florida posts the first online refereed academic journal about comics, *ImageTexT: Interdisciplinary Comics Studies*.

AUDIENCE EFFECTS RESEARCH

Each mass medium seems to come under attack shortly after it becomes popular, and comic books were no exception. The first widely published critique came in 1940, when Sterling North, the literary editor for the *Chicago Daily News*, publicly condemned them in an oft-quoted editorial:

Badly drawn, badly written and badly printed—a strain on young eyes and young nervous systems—the effect of these pulp-paper nightmares is that of a violent stimulant. Their crude blacks and reds spoil the child's natural sense of color; their hypodermic injection of sex and murder make the child impatient with better, though quieter stories. Unless we want a coming generation even more ferocious than the present one, parents and teachers throughout America must band together to break the 'comic' magazine. (56)

North outlined a litany of charges against the nascent comic book industry: comic books were aesthetically an inferior publication, they caused eye strain, and they corrupted America's youth by exposing them to violence and sex. Critics who followed his lead would argue that such exposure prompted children to commit wanton antisocial acts. While North was certainly entitled to his opinion about the artistic merits of the comic books, any claims about the effects of them on the physical and mental well-being of America's youth lacked objective study and confirmation at the time. Indeed, much of the initial condemnation of comics stemmed from superficial perceptions of comics' shortcomings rather than a more thorough investigation of their contents or their effects upon their audiences. The research conclusions that followed would challenge the claims that comic books caused impressionable minds to pursue violent, even criminal activities. A consensus of media scholars has since agreed that violent media do heighten violent reactions (Rifas "Fredric Wertham"), though the conditions under which audiences react to such stimulation is still subject to continued investigation and further understanding. As the comic book was coming of age in America, the first issue to be addressed among the medium's earliest researchers was whether a link existed between the consumption of comic books and increased juvenile delinquency among America's youth.

Delinquency

In the years after World War II, adult Americans were increasingly concerned with the criminal activities being committed by a portion of the country's youthful population: acts of vandalism, theft, and even murder. The term **juvenile delinquency** came to define this phenomenon, and concerned minds across the nation set about to figure out the causes of a reported upsurge in this antisocial behavior. The search led some community leaders and pundits to default to a rather simplistic "monkey see, monkey do" explanation, and comic books, whose popularity was exploding at the time, seemed a likely culprit as an influence in young people's lives. If impressionable minds consumed comics containing violence, sex, mayhem, and gore, then these fragile psyches would be inspired to indulge in their basest drives. Of course, a similar *direct effects* explanation had been offered a generation earlier, when Hollywood's gangster films were attacked as promoting similarly ruinous impulses, yet those claims had been largely debunked by an intensive research initiative. However, the public's memory is often short, and few voices spoke up to remind people that comics were being attacked just like motion pictures had been before them, and other mass media before that. As they had with those earlier media, experts proposed that comics had limited effects. Additional early research argued that "comics satisfy a real developmental need in normal children and are harmful only for children who are already maladjusted and susceptible to harm" (Wolfe and Fiske 50). Accordingly, a debate over the effects of comic books ensued.

In opposition to optimistic conclusions, the loudest voices were pointing to comics as a causal factor in juvenile delinquency. Popular sources from the National Education Association to *Reader's Digest* came out condemning comics. And the most influential of these voices came from Dr. Fredric Wertham, a New York psychiatrist who saw comic books as one manifestation of a culture that put commercial interests ahead of children's best interests. Beginning in the 1940s, Wertham became an outspoken opponent of comics magazines, advocating that legislation be enacted to curtail the sale of comic books to children in order to protect them from exposure to the comics' often sensational depictions of crime. In the course of his clinical work, Wertham had discovered that his juvenile patients commonly had been exposed to comic books. As Wertham investigated the content of the publications, he was alarmed by what he perceived to be inappropriate depictions of violence, sexism, racism, and other dubious messages. Wertham spoke and published in a number of public venues, including widely circulated outlets like *Ladies' Home Journal*, but he is best known for the case he made in *Seduction of the Innocent* (1954), a book that sealed his reputation as an opponent of the comic book industry. But even before the book's publication, Wertham's reputation brought him before the Senate Subcommittee on Juvenile Delinquency to testify as an expert witness against comic books.

In *Seduction of the Innocent* and his other writings, Wertham charged that comic books, especially those he labeled as "crime comics," promoted juvenile delinquency and a host of developmental problems ranging from insecurity to racial prejudice. In the course of seven years of research on the topic, Wertham had read comics, kept case studies of juvenile patients who had experience reading comics, and conducted psychological tests on several of those patients. While Wertham objected to the violence he saw depicted, he was alarmed that some comics went a step further and provided actual techniques for criminal activity, outlining everything from how to shoplift to how to commit murder. In Wertham's view, imitation followed instruction, and his fears were confirmed by accounts such as the following:

> Three boys, six to eight years old, took a boy of seven, hanged him nude from a tree, his hands tied behind him; then they burned him with matches. Probation officers who investigated found that they were reenacting a comic book plot. (150)

While this and other cases of juvenile violence were matters of record, Wertham indicated that the effects of comics were generalized to the reading public. In contesting Wertham's conclusions decades later, media scholars Shearon Lowery and Melvin DeFleur (1988) counter that these lurid cases were extremes and that Wertham's assertion that the effects were more widespread were simply not supported by his research. First, there was no systematic inventory of comics, and *Seduction* selectively reprinted only the most unsavory examples of comic books on sale at the time. Second, most of the patients used in Wertham's study were referrals—juveniles in the mental health or court systems. There was no control group of well-adjusted children outside of this system to compare the claims against. Other research found that delinquents did read more of the sensational crime comics material but hesitated to conclude "that there is any casual relationship between juvenile delinquency and the reading of crime . . . comic books" (Hoult, 283).

Still, Wertham was no simplistic censor and was not lashing out at a medium he neither understood nor appreciated. Rather, he saw comic books as just one mass medium, but certainly the worst in his estimation, which taught children that violence was a solution rather than a problem. In Wertham's estimation, the media were parts of a complex social matrix, but deleterious parts that were prone to being used to introduce antisocial behaviors. Accordingly, he objected to the glorification of violence he saw rampant in the crime, horror, and even superhero comics of his time. Since publishers

FIGURE 12.2. Fredric Wertham's name became the most infamous in comics history for his public condemnation of comics and advocacy of restrictions on their sale to children. This caricature appeared in the November 1953 issue of *Ladies' Home Journal.*

had shown no restraint in what they would sell to children up till that point, Wertham adopted a public position against the most popular and influential medium for children of his day. Unfortunately, while Wertham failed to bring about any actual legislation to regulate the comic book industry, his efforts did contribute to the formation of the Comics Code Authority, a self-censoring agency that effectively made comics suitable *only* for children for the next several decades—the opposite result of Wertham's goal to keep comics out of children's hands.

The initial focus and furor over comics' role in delinquency was shortly thereafter eclipsed by the rise of a medium that came to dominate the national consciousness even more: television. Consequently, social scientific research into comics' possible deleterious effects subsided for some time. However, interest in comics as an influence on our negative emotions does return periodically. For example, one study found that consumption of the violent content in mass media, including comic books, desensitized children to the effects of crime and violence (Lovibond). More recently, Stephen Kirsh and Paul Olczak (2003) investigated how consumption of violent media content influences people with a disposition towards hostility. They conducted an experiment with two groups of college students, who were first measured for their attitudes towards seeking vengeance. One group read comics with graphic violence, like *Curse of Spawn* and *Evil Ernie*, while the other group read less violent material like the innocuous *Archie* and *Dexter's Laboratory.* The researchers then presented the participants with different scenarios (e.g., being cheated on by one's significant other) and asked them to rate the likelihood of seeking vengeance in each of these situations. When the results were tallied and compared to the initial measures, Kirsh and Olczak found that after having read the violent comics, people who were high in trait hostility were more likely to consider vengeful responses.

Such conclusions are in sync with other research findings indicating that mass media that offer antisocial messages can—but not necessarily will—encourage those dispositions, and comics seem as likely to promote such responses as any other mass medium. Thus, while the scholarly community might not have affirmed a causal link between comic books and delinquency, eventually it did forward evidence of a connection between comics and other negative responses. Around the same time that researchers were making inquiries into the effects of comics on their audience's social behavior, interest in comics' effect on audience's reading abilities was also underway.

Literacy

While a climate of fear seemingly motivated the initial research into comics' possible negative impact, it appears that an attitude of hope sustains social scientific research into the medium's educational implications. In particular, a number of scholars have investigated the hope that comics can be used as tools to aid in educating, especially in terms of improving literacy. Research over the past seven decades has demonstrated that comics have the capability to motivate readers, to enhance reading skills, and to aid those engaged in learning a second language.

One of the chief virtues of comics seems to be their ability to motivate readers by turning them on to reading in the first place (Haugaard). Bonny Norton argues that it is ownership of one's reading material that encourages people, especially young people, to read more. If one is allowed to read what gives one pleasure, then one tends to read more. In the case of children, a problem arises when parents and teachers fail to acknowledge what children enjoy reading. Consequently, other researchers have found that "Those who reported more comic book reading also reported more pleasure reading in general, greater reading enjoyment, and tended to do more book reading." (Ujiie and Krashen, 51). Noted literacy expert Stephen Krashen claims comics have the benefit of functioning as a bridge to other kinds of reading, as they help young readers develop linguistic competence and an interest in books.

Second, contrary to the criticisms of those who feared that reading comics handicaps a child's ability to read text-only materials, research has confirmed that comics actually do more to promote than retard reading ability. In fact, one of the earliest studies into comics readership found that children who read a lot of comics and those who read few comics actually read about the same amount and types of materials, leading researcher Paul Witty to conclude that comics were not harmful so long as they remained a part of a well-balanced reading program. Likewise, teacher Florence Heisler found that reading comics is not indicative of a lack of intelligence; one study by reading specialist Emma Halstead Swain even found that in comparing groups of students with poor grades to those with good grades, comics were more often read by students earning good grades! Reading experts like Gary Wright and Robert Thorndike have found that mainstream superhero comics tend to be written somewhere around the sixth grade level—about the same level as the average American newspaper—making reading comics something of a challenge for any child less developed than that. Comics may not be a panacea, though, for struggling readers. Marshall Arlin and Garry Roth caution that poor students may spend more time consuming the pictures than attending to the words, requiring educators to do more than merely distribute comics if they are to promote literacy.

Still, recent research has further suggested that comics may enhance readers' understanding of material and abilities to work with language. Ġorġ Mallia reported on students involved in an experiment where different groups were asked to read a historical text. One group got a text-only version, a second group got the text with illustrations, and a third group got a comics version of material. After each group read the material, they were tested for their recollection, comprehension, and knowledge of the history lesson. Statistical analysis of the results showed that students recalled the content of the comic as well as the text with illustrations; those who read the text-only treatment fared the poorest in the comparison. Mallia concludes that comics are at least as effective as the other two options as teaching tools. Similarly encouraging results were found in an experiment run by Michael Bitz with more than seven hundred students involved in an after-school program that encouraged them to write and draw their own eight-page comic book as a means for improving their expressiveness. A survey of the students found that 86 percent of them believed that the experience helped their writing ability. Even more impressively, 90 percent of the instructors reported that they thought the students' writing had improved after participating in the project.

Third, comics seem to help facilitate the acquisition of a second language. Researcher Neil Williams found that the depiction of nonverbal activities provided by comics helps second language learners to understand the text within context. Comics are also attractive as they are culturally current, using the common vernacular rather than artificially perfected grammar and vocabulary, giving the students a less formal entrée into the other culture. Bonny Norton and Karen Vanderheyden found that Archie comics were particularly helpful to their second language learners, perhaps because their readers could easily relate to the high school social situations depicted in those comics. They found that the pleasure and enjoyment the readers got from the comics engaged their interest more than some other texts. Moreover, when they could discuss these comics with others in their class, the connection further encouraged their engagement with the language.

Given that comics seem to help with reading motivation, reading development, and second language acquisition, why are they not a more familiar feature in language arts curricula? One argument is that the campaign against comics in the 1950s did such a thorough job of discrediting comics in the public eye that for decades thereafter most respectable researchers steered clear of advocating for the comics. Presumably, most instructors are reluctant to face the scorn of introducing materials that are perceived to be morally and developmentally questionable. However, James Bucky Carter cautions that we do not know exactly why the vast majority of instructors are hesitant to introduce comics in the classroom and that is an attitude education researchers should investigate.

Another possible explanation lies in the different sets of interpretive skills that today's teachers and today's students possess. Many current teachers were trained to privilege text-based narratives as the only legitimate cultural material worth studying. Thus, educators have not only advocated for traditional, text-based literacy, they have taught it to the exclusion of other forms of literacy. Today's students, however, are immersed in a **multimodal** culture, learning about their world from more than just prose sources. They also communicate through multiple interpretive systems: Just consider how a given website uses textual, visual, and aural stimuli simultaneously to communicate its message. Educators like Adam Schwartz and Elaine Rubinstein-Avila have taken note of this difference and begun to advocate for the teaching of forms of literacy that go beyond just text-based literacy, such as visual literacy and the more far-reaching critical literacy. In order to help educators begin to address these different literacies, a number of academics have begun to publish books that provide guidance to composition instructors (see James Bucky Carter), language instructors (see Stephen Cary), and librarians (see Michele Gorman) to help them facilitate the integration of comics into their instruction.

There is certainly increasing interest in many areas of education about the power of comics to engage readers. For example, the state of Maryland is engaged in the Maryland Comic Book Initiative, employing graphic storytelling in curricula ranging from elementary schools to correctional education. Developed in partnership with Diamond Comic Distributors, the largest distributor of comics in America, the initiative adds credence to the growing body of research indicating that that comics motivate readership and encourage creativity. Likewise, a diverse body of instructional materials are coming forth for the educational market.

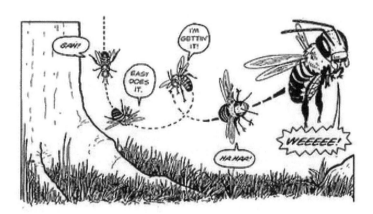

FIGURE 12.3. Dr. Jay Hosler teaches his readers about the life cycle of the bee while weaving a narrative around one bee in the hive, Nyuki. From *Clan Apis* © Jay Hosler

Dr. Jay Hosler is a college biology professor and cartoonist who has illustrated books on topics as diverse as the life cycle of the bee and the theories of Charles Darwin. Such examples are only the tip of the iceberg in terms of the range and possible applications of comics in educational settings.

Discovering: Educational Comics

The colorful adventures of Superman, Captain Marvel, and the Sub-Mariner may have propelled the early comics market towards popular success, but their flights of fancy did not meet the approval of discerning parents and educators, many of whom accused them of being a waste of perfectly good reading time. However, the attraction of the comics form left many of its critics no choice but the classic reaction: If you can't beat 'em, join 'em! Accordingly, comics with intentionally educational aims began to compete with other genres of comics. One of the first of these publications came from the publishers of *Parents Magazine*, who issued *True Comics* beginning in March 1941. The idea of *True Comics* was to provide an alternative to the superhero, substituting in his stead such real-life heroes as Winston Churchill or Dwight D. Eisenhower (the cover blurb read: "Truth is stronger and a thousand times more thrilling than fiction"). Clearly the market responded to educational comics, as competitors began producing similar ones. Comics innovator Max Gaines even launched a whole company under the banner of Educational Comics, ushering in titles like *Picture Stories from the Bible* and *Picture Stories from American History*.

But the most enduring of the educational comics came in the form of *Classic Comics*, launched in Fall 1941 and continuing on as *Classics Illustrated* from 1947 until 1971. The brainchild of publisher Albert Kanter, *Classics* adapted works of prose into comics form, "Featuring stories by the world's greatest authors" such as Jules Verne (*A Journey to the Center of the Earth*), Alexandre Dumas (*The Three Musketeers*), and James Fenimore Cooper (*The Last of the Mohicans*). Although its initial few issues were crudely drawn, even by the standards of the time, *Classics Illustrated* rose to distinguish itself by markedly improving the quality of its presentation in time, eschewing outside advertising, and making available a catalogue of its run. Unlike most comics, which were issued as one-shot periodicals, initial printings of *Classics Illustrated* would be followed up with reprint runs that educators and interested readers could request using a mail-order form in each issue. And when its original publisher canceled the magazine after several decades of success, subsequent attempts to capitalize on the reputation of the title were mounted by First Comics in 1990 and Acclaim Books in 1997. In 2007 Marvel Comics began experimenting with adaptations of prose works, capitalizing on the "illustrated" brand name by launching its own line of *Marvel Illustrated* comics.

While *Classics Illustrated* may have endured as an icon, it was not without its critics. Educators like Elinor Saltus complained that while educational comics might have the right intent, the format diminished the quality of the content of the original works. In most cases the comics had to abbreviate the original works, removing the

Cont'd

FIGURE 12.4. Publishers tried to win the favor of teachers, parents, and young readers in the pages of educational comics like *Classics Illustrated*, *True Comics*, and *Picture Stories from the Bible*. *Classics Illustrated* ©Jack Lake Productions Inc.; *True Comics* © Parent's Magazine Press; *Picture Stories from the Bible* © William M. Gaines, Agent, Inc. Used with permission.

richness of the content. In all cases, providing the reader with illustrations robbed that reader of the opportunity to visualize the story more fully on his own. Moreover, the lure of substituting comics for the original prose seemed to be motivated more by crass commercialism, as the great works of Western literature simply became fodder for the mass consumption. Indeed, according to historian Jed Rasula, the selections seemed to pander heavily towards one audience and be geared towards boys and adventure stories, despite the fact that girls made up nearly half of all comics readers at the time.

But as *Classics Illustrated* fan turned historian William B. Jones, Jr., explains, "the series was never intended to replace the original works. . . . It is unlikely that anyone who read the sequential-art abridgements of *The House of the Seven Gables* or *Silas Mariner* as a means of avoiding Nathaniel Hawthorne or George Eliot would have read those authors in the first place." Instead what the series did was "to make the realms of the literary and historical imagination accessible and immediate" to generations of readers (6).

Using comics to educate even while they engage their readership persists to this day, with creators like Leonard Rifas, Jim Ottaviani, Fred Van Lente, and Ryan Dunlavey independently producing educational comics. Rifas has created a number of topical comics such as *All-Atomic Comics* and *Food Comics* through his EduComics label. Ottaviani's G.T. Labs is responsible for comics such as *Two-Fisted Science* and a number of biographies of famous scientists. Van Lente and Dunlavey are publishers of Evil Twin Comics and won acclaim by documenting the lives and ideas of great thinkers in their *Action Philosophers!* series. While these comics certainly will never sell as prodigiously as superhero comics, they prove a loftier utility for the medium that goes beyond merely making publishers money.

TEXTUAL METHODS OF ANALYSIS

While some questions posed by researchers about comics and their role in society are best answered by measuring their effects on audiences, other questions have more to do with the content of the comics and are best explored by methods of investigation that facilitate closer examination of the substance of the publications themselves. There are numerous methods for conducting such explorations, far more than we could ever hope to catalog in one chapter, but we offer a sample of them here to demonstrate the diversity of possible approaches for analyzing comics. We begin with the method of content analysis and then turn to mythic analysis. For each method, we also present an example of published research using that approach.

Content Analysis

Researchers who use content analysis are interested in the patterns of meaning as they appear across mediated messages. To them, there are insights to be found in counting the number of times a particular portrayal is offered or a certain act is performed in the media. Thus, content analysis involves examining the frequency of selected variables presented in media messages. For example, a researcher might review how often acts of physical violence are portrayed in a genre of graphic novels or consider what roles minorities fill in a comic book series. Content analysis is a quantitative methodology, meaning that concepts are counted, tabulated, and discussed in terms of statistics. By quantifying their discoveries, researchers can compare and contrast phenomena in pronounced ways.

Like other studies, a content analysis begins with the researcher posing a question. A research question should always guide the selection of a method to study a phenomenon, and content analysis works particularly well for answering questions dealing with patterns and trends across the media. If indeed the question lends itself to content analysis, the researcher proceeds with determining what kind of sample to work within (e.g., what kind of comics should be examined and how many should be reviewed?). The researcher must also define the units for analysis. The key to producing effective content analysis is to work with carefully defined categories (e.g., what qualifies as an act of violence?). From here the researcher uses a coding sheet to begin collecting data by reading the actual media messages and recording the findings. Once all of the examples in the sample have been reviewed, the results are tabulated, interpreted, and reported.

An example of a content analysis of comic books comes from Russell W. Belk, who reported the findings of his research in the *Journal of Consumer Research*. A professor of business administration, Belk began his project with an interest in how comics might influence young people's expectation of and reflect America's preoccupation with material possessions. He asked questions like, "Are the wealthy portrayed positively, or are they treated ambiguously or even negatively?" and "Do [the portrayals] change over time or remain constant?" (26). In order to answer these questions, he conducted a content analysis of five comic book characters associated with wealth: the miserly Uncle Scrooge McDuck from *Donald Duck*, heiress Veronica Lodge from *Archie*, funny animal adversaries *Fox and Crow*, and the world's richest boy, *Richie Rich*. In order to come up with a manageable sample of the hundreds of stories published about these popular characters, many of whom had been in publication since the 1940s, Belk selected a sample of at least twenty published stories from each decade of the characters' publishing history. After an initial review of many of the stories, he then crafted a coding sheet with categories covering seventy themes, values, and character traits that he wanted to count. Assistants, called coders, helped him to review more than 230 samples for quantitative analysis, looking to determine the frequency of activities such as "trying to earn money at a job" and qualities such as "who is portrayed as selfish?" (39).

FIGURE 12.5. The laughs in *The Fox and the Crow* came from the Crow trying to con the Fox, but the lesson of each story underscored the virtue of honest dealings. © DC Comics

Belk found a number of interesting portrayals among the individual characters from this analysis and was able to conclude that the comic books taught lessons consistent with accepted values about wealth, namely that wealth should be earned honestly and used responsibly, and that those who did not follow this model suffered misfortune accordingly. For example, while Uncle Scrooge might not be frequently generous, he is shown to have earned all his money through hard work. In contrast, his adversaries, the burglaring Beagle Boys, have their schemes to swindle their way to fortune foiled each time. Because of the extent of his sample, which covered several decades and characters from many different publishers, Belk's thoroughness sustains the strength of the claims he makes about comic book portrayals of wealth. A systematic content analysis allows researchers to lay some claim to a better understanding of the trends presented within the content of the medium's messages.

Mythic Criticism

The previous sections considered methods of examining comics audiences and the comics themselves using quantitative methods of investigation. As an alternative, **qualitative** methods emphasize understanding without necessarily counting. Instead, the researcher's focus is placed on interpreting meaning. Some qualitative methods are designed to look at meanings as interpreted by the audiences, and others explore the meanings constructed by symbols within the text itself. We saw examples of scholarship in the qualitative tradition aimed at discovering meanings as read by audiences in Chapter 8. We now turn to just one example of the many qualitative methods aimed at identifying meanings represented within the text itself.

Mythic criticism is a type of rhetorical criticism that examines a given text for its culturally symbolic meanings. The symbols used in the course of a narrative often stand in for other figures or values in a given cultural tradition. All rhetorical criticism is concerned with meaning, and in mythic criticism the researchers carefully review the text to identify how key symbols presented in the text are addressing additional culture concerns. *Myths* are the stories that a culture tells itself to remind its participants of key values and traditions. The ancient Greeks, for instance, clearly valued humility, as they had numerous myths that told of misfortune that followed pride, like the story of Ariadne, whose pride in her weaving led her to brag that she was better than Athena, the goddess who turned Ariadne into the first spider as punishment for her boast. Cultures all over the world still have myths that they espouse today, and the researcher's goal in mythic criticism is to help others see just how such contemporary myths underscore deeper messages. Critics seek to uncover what such stories say that people value. Their work helps the rest of us reflect on the significance of these portrayals of values.

In mythic criticism, the researcher begins by selecting a text, usually one that has already made an impression upon the researcher or one that has garnered a lot of critical or popular attention. The investigator reads this text carefully, often multiple times, noting familiar themes that come through upon each review. This scholar also brings to bear her own familiarity with the larger culture in which the narrative is told, drawing connections between the symbols in the story and the meanings that they connect to in the larger culture itself. The researcher then writes an argument, or a case, for the presence and significance of the meanings that she believes are present in the text. This argument is then shared with others through an oral presentation or by publication.

One publication that illustrates mythic analysis comes from Tim Blackmore and was published in *The International Journal of Comic Art*. Therein, Blackmore argues that Frank Miller's limited series turned graphic novel, *300*, is mythic in nature, speaking to America's value of selfless heroism. As many readers know, *300* retells the story of the three hundred soldiers led by King Leonidas of Sparta who defended the narrow mountain pass at Thermopylae from invasion by a significantly larger Persian army in 480 BC. According to Blackmore, the information that served as Miller's source material, the writings of the Greek historian Herodotus, was itself already highly mythologized, with recent historians casting doubt on several of Herodotus' details, such as his inflation of the Persian army from about 100,000 actual troops to 5 million in the account. Miller himself added to the symbolic, rather than realistic, portrayal in his retelling of the tale by adding details such as making the traitorous Ephialtes monstrously deformed. Whether it is the overwhelming opposition or a horrific appearance, such symbols are included to provide contrast to the bravery and attractiveness of the Spartan

FIGURE 12.6. A mythic analysis of Frank Miller's *300* argues for the connection between the heroism portrayed in the graphic novel and the value of heroism in American culture. *300* © 1998 Frank Miller, Inc. *300* and the *300* logo are trademarks of Frank Miller, Inc. Published by Dark Horse Comics, Inc.

heroes. In myths, the story isn't concerned with historical accuracy but with making its point as clearly as possible.

The point Blackmore sees in Miller's tale is that Americans should do the heroic thing regardless of personal cost. Interestingly, Miller wrote *300* while America was at peace, not at war. "America's hero, argues Miller, should be heroism," writes Blackmore; *300* "is a story of manners, a didactic text about the unimaginable courage it takes to act in a truly civil way" (347). The graphic novel depicting the heroic sacrifice of the Spartans is thus a myth for modern audiences, meant to stir within the members of a free society the desire to stand and defend their way of life. Mythic critiques like Blackmore's help us to appreciate and understand the complexity and sophistication of comic narratives within their cultural context.

Profile: Charles Hatfield

born: Charles William Hatfield
April 16, 1965
Elmendorf Air Force Base, Alaska

"Both socially and aesthetically, comics are likely to remain an unresolved, unstable, and challenging form."

Cont'd

Career Highlights

1994 First professional publication in *The Comics Journal*.

1995 Presents first comic-related project at the Popular Culture Association conference in Philadelphia.

1997 Joins the newly formed Executive Committee of the annual International Comics and Animation Festival, now the International Comic Arts Forum (ICAF).

1997 Publishes first refereed academic article in *Inks: Cartoon and Comic Art Studies*.

2000 Completes his doctoral dissertation "Graphic Interventions: Form and Argument in Contemporary Comics" at the University of Connecticut.

2000 Writes the introduction for *Streetwise: Autobiographical Stories by Comic Book Professionals* with TwoMorrows Publishing.

2001 Joins the faculty at California State University Northridge and begins teaching courses on comics as literature.

2005 Publishes *Alternative Comics: An Emerging Literature* through the University Press of Mississippi.

2007 Guest co-edits a special issue on "Comics and Childhood" for *Image-TexT: Interdisciplinary Comics Studies*

FIGURE 12.7 College professor Charles Hatfield helps promote comics scholarship by teaching about comics in his classroom, authoring scholarship for both academic and popular publications, and participating in research conferences. Courtesy of California State University, Northridge, and Lee Choo.

Professor Charles Hatfield represents a new generation of teacher/scholars working in the interdisciplinary field of comics art studies. Although Hatfield finds himself situated in a traditionally defined department of English, his interests go beyond the normally defined canons of literature, as he examines storytelling outside the narrow dictates of high-culture staples such as Shakespeare and Hemingway. "I enjoy bringing the everyday and popular into focus and not just the elevated material," he says, explaining the use of works by cartoonists Harvey Pekar or the Hernandez Brothers. "I want students to recognize that popular forms may be wrestling with the same issues as other, so-called higher forms of culture." Indeed, Hatfield has labored to do just that, challenging himself to apply the tools and techniques of literary criticism to comics and inviting his students to do the same. The results of his efforts go beyond his classroom and can be seen in scholarly outlets, such as presentations he makes at academic conferences, and in publications like his well-received 2005 book *Alternative Comics: An Emerging Literature*.

Cont'd

Like many other comics scholars, Hatfield had a lifelong passion for reading comics for pleasure, but was motivated to make them his life's work while a graduate student. He explains that his studies in literary theory gave him a new perspective on comics' innate complexity. "So many of the things we study in literature are applicable to comics," he notes. But the study of comics offers more than just a new venue for the application of text-borne theories, as the study of images adds another interpretive level. "Students gain a greater sensitivity to the word and image relationship through the study of comics that they can apply to other media like billboards, blogs, etc. Comics are a laboratory for what's going on in the larger visual culture."

While Hatfield is actively helping the next generation of students to appreciate comics more fully, he credits the previous generation of comics scholars for helping him get his start. "The people who thrive in academia are those who were mentored. No career path is obvious and that's what makes mentoring so important." He credits forerunners in comics studies like Joseph Witek, M. Thomas Inge, John Lent, and a host of colleagues from across disciplines for lending him the benefit of their experience. "One of the things about comics studies is that it is necessarily multi-disciplinary. It's good for me to associate with those outside of my own discipline." As comics studies continues to widen its appeal, such positive interactions would ideally benefit other teacher/scholars and their students as well.

ANALYZING: COMICS CRITICISM COMES OF AGE

Perhaps the most exciting development in comics scholarship involves work in building a language for critiquing the art form on its own terms. Other media already benefit from the long-standing tradition of developing and using concepts to talk about the storytelling devices in their art forms. For example, the field of film studies has over the past century developed a vocabulary for talking about framing, editing, lighting, and setting within a motion picture. Terms like *mise-en-scène* and *noir* are familiar examples of this vocabulary for those who may have already taken a film appreciation course. In similar fashion, scholars in comics studies are now developing a vocabulary to talk about their medium.

According to comics scholar Joseph Witek ("Comics Criticism"), this is a relatively recent development in the field and the third in series of phases in the development of a distinct comics criticism. The first phase was characterized by comics appreciation and exemplified in such early works of sustained study as Martin Sheridan's 1942 book, *Comics and Their Creators*, which basically cataloged the comic strip's creations. The second step towards a distinct comics criticism came when comics began to be used as evidence for arguments about larger social trends. The method of content analysis, discussed above, would fall within the parameters of this phase, and works such as Arthur Asa Berger's 1973 *The Comic-Stripped American* would exemplify it. The third and most mature phase in this process came when thinkers began to approach comics as a narrative medium on its own terms. Witek credits legendary cartoonist Will

Eisner with producing the first full-length treatment of this approach in his 1985 *Comics and Sequential Art.*

The groundbreaking work of cartoonists like Eisner, along with others like Robert C. Harvey and Scott McCloud, have certainly laid much of the foundation for this current work. We have considered concepts like Eisner's encapsulation, Harvey's blending, and McCloud's closure in Chapters 6 and 7, where we discussed the encoding and decoding of the comics narrative content. Additional language for interpreting comics is also coming from academics. Among those scholars and works offering language for consideration on the domestic side are Neil Cohn's *Early Writings on Visual Language* and David Carrier's *Aesthetics of Comics,* while more and more international theorists are making their influence felt through translations, like the recent addition of Thierry Groenstein's *System of Comics.* Through these and other works, we are witnessing the beginning of a more formal approach to comics criticism, one that promises to enrich our understanding and appreciation for the comics art form on its own terms.

Discussion Questions

1. Occasionally news reports of youth imitating some extreme behavior they have witnessed in a mass medium gain the national spotlight (e.g., re-creating a bloody pro wrestling match). Such occurrences seem to counter research conclusions that say media generally have limited rather than direct effects on most of their audiences. How would you explain these instances to those who would point to them as proof of the media's corrupting influence?

2. What qualities of the comics form do you find appealing as a reader? How could these qualities help motivate others to want to read comics and other forms of literature more?

3. What questions are still unanswered about comics' content or their effects on audiences? How could researchers go about finding answers to the questions you have posed?

Activities

1. Using your university's databases (e.g., EBSCOhost) and online search engines (e.g., Google), develop an annotated bibliography for one of the figures introduced in this chapter's sidebar, "Discovering: Milestones in the Development of Comics Studies." An annotated bibliography provides both a citation for a scholarly publication and a brief summary/commentary on the contents of each entry. Be prepared to discuss the major contributions of your figure to the field of comics studies.

2. Conduct a content analysis that closely examines a set of comics for the patterns of messages they send about an ethnic group, profession, institution,

etc. The following is an example of the elements that must be defined and the steps that one follows in conducting a content analysis.

Step One: Formulate Your Research Question
Example: "How are journalists portrayed in Marvel superhero comic books?"

Step Two: Identify Your Genre
Example: "Marvel superhero comic books"

Step Three: Outline Your Sample
Example: "Six months worth of Marvel's ten best-selling superhero titles"

Step Four: Designate Your Unit of Analysis
Example: "Depictions of journalists"

Step Five: Create a Coding Sheet of the Categories to be Analyzed
Example:

Type of journalist:	___ editor	___ reporter	___ photojournalist
Look:	___ well-dressed	___ scruffy	___ casual
Personality:	___ ethical	___ unethical	___ brave
	___ cowardly	___ angry	___ dispassionate
Bad Habits:	___ cigarettes	___ coffee	___ alcohol

Step Six: Review Each Comic in Your Sample and Record a Count of Each Appearance of Your Categories

Step Seven: Write a Paragraph or Two Explaining the Answer to Your Research Question Based on the Patterns Seen in Your Results

Note: **This is just an example!** You need to formulate your own question, select your own universe and sample, construct your own coding sheet, and draw your own conclusions.

Recommended Readings

Comics:

Hosler, Jay. *Clan Apis*. Columbus, OH: Active Synapse, 2000.

Clan Apis tells the story of Nyuki the bee in a clever mix of comic adventure and biological fact. Hosler's efforts go to show that comics can be both entertaining and educating.

Thomas, Roy, and Mario Gully. *Marvel Illustrated: Treasure Island*. New York: Marvel Comics, 2008.

With the original *Classics Illustrated* out of print, any of Marvel Comics' recent efforts to revitalize the adaptation of prose literature to comics form will give you a sense of the *Classics'* legacy. Of course, it doesn't hurt that this particular adaptation is by Roy Thomas, one of the most seasoned writers in comics.

Scholarly Sources:

Carter, James Bucky, ed. *Building Literacy Connections with Graphic Novels: Page by Page, Panel by Panel*. Urbana, IL: National Council of Teachers of English, 2007.

Carter and his collaborators provide guidance for the teaching of language arts lessons that pair traditional prose narratives like Dickens' *Oliver Twist* with graphic novels like Eisner's *Fagin the Jew*. Given its support from the NCTE, this book demonstrates the progress comics are making in being accepted by the educational mainstream as tools from promoting literacy.

Heer, Jeet, and Kent Worcester, eds. *Arguing Comics: Literary Masters on a Popular Medium*. Jackson, MS: University Press of Mississippi, 2004.

Heer and Worcester collect more than two dozen historic essays about comics written by such notable critics as E.E. Cummings, Dorothy Parker, and Marshall McLuhan. Contributions from Gilbert Seldes and Robert Warshow are reprints of some of the most influential of the early critiques of the art form.

Comics Culture
Around the World

"Now we are living in the age of comics as air."

—OSAMU TEZUKA, JAPAN'S PREEMINENT COMICS CREATOR, N.D.

Most people familiar with popular culture are aware of the annual film festival that takes place each year in the French town of Cannes. Hundreds of thousands of film fans descend upon the town to catch a glimpse of their favorite filmmakers as the industry screens its newest and most artistic productions for eager audiences. The festival is an electrifying event, and that excitement is certainly communicated to a distant American audience thanks to coverage in television programs like *Entertainment Tonight* and photographs in the pages of *People* magazine. Now imagine the same excitement, but this time the focus is not on documentaries and directors but instead on comics and cartoonists. That is the scene in the French town of Angoulême each year. Up to 300,000 people from across Europe and around the world descend upon this municipality each winter for the International Comics Festival, or, as they say in French, *Festival International de la Bande Dessinée*. The festival features exhibits of comics artwork, lectures, seminars, and workshops, and creators receive celebrity treatment throughout the celebration. Though similar festivals are held across Europe, the event in Angoulême has grown to be the preeminent showcase for the comics arts and comics artists since it began in 1974. So central has the town become to the art form that it is also home to permanent museum and research center, the Cité Internationale de la Bande Dessinée et de l'Image (CIIBDI). Along with the festival, this center, which is partially funded by the cultural ministry of the French government, has become emblematic of the French's interest in and respect for the medium, and it demonstrates a markedly different attitude towards comics than we are accustomed to in America.

FIGURE 13.1. Crowds of comics lovers take to the streets of Angoulême, France, each winter for the Festival International de la Bande Dessinée. Admirers at the 2008 festival gather around the Smurfs to celebrate the fiftieth anniversary of the characters' debut in the Belgian comic book *Le Journal de Spirou*. © 2008 Paul Gravett: *www.paulgravett.com*

OBJECTIVES

In this chapter you will learn:

1. about several different comics traditions in cultures beyond the United States;

2. the ways in which those other traditions have reacted to and interacted with the American comic book tradition;

3. the importance of cultural identity and the struggle to establish or preserve that identity through indigenous cultural products; and

4. how the process of cultural imperialism threatens to erode native cultures.

B *ande dessinée. Fumetti. Historietas. Komiks. Lianhuantos. Manga. Manhua. Tebeos.* Whatever they are called locally, comic books have taken hold in cultures across the globe. The example of Angoulême, France, serves as just one possible starting point for us to talk about comic books in cultures other than that of the United States, as the medium is truly worldwide in its appeal. In the preface to this book, the authors admitted to an inherent perception of comics borne of our American background. In most of the previous chapters, we have focused on the American comics industry and used examples largely pulled from American publishers. Yet we would do a disservice to students of the medium if we failed to acknowledge that comics exist and thrive in cultures other than this one. Thus, this chapter introduces a number of comic book traditions operating outside of the United States, so that we may situate the study of American comics in its broader international context.

As one begins to look at different indigenous comics industries around the world, one notices that three comics producing cultures wield extraordinary influence. One of these cultures is, as you might have guessed, the United States. There is no denying that American comic books have been among the most influential in the world, having either served as the de facto comics traditions in some places or impressing their stylistic or genre influences in others. A combination of high production values, such as four-color printing and massive print runs, coupled with highly effective distribution systems, has exposed comics featuring American characters like Donald Duck and Superman to nearly every corner of the world. As you will see in this chapter, many cultures have defined their comics industry by the influence of or in outright opposition to the American comic book industry. The other two of the three most influential comics cultures are the Franco-Belgian region of Europe and the Asian nation of Japan. The French and Belgians were among the first cultures to treat comics with respect, valorizing modern cartoonists and their works, and thus have produced some very mature, highly regarded comics. On the other hand, the Japanese have one of the largest comics-consuming cultures in the world, giving them one of the most diverse and widely appealing array of comics material in any market. In truth, some combination of production values, maturity, and diversity have been factors in the rise of all three traditions.

While these three traditions are undeniably influential, they are themselves susceptible to outside influences as well. Simply pause and take a second look at some of the most prominent figures in American comic book publishing, and you would find that many of them were not born in America. Imagine how much poorer American comics would be without the contributions of notables such as *Watchmen* author Alan Moore (United Kingdom), WildStorm founder Jim Lee (South Korea), or *Cerebus* creator Dave Sim (Canada). Indeed, there may not have even been an American comics industry as we know it if Superman co-creator Joe Shuster hadn't emigrated from Canada. Given the interrelationships that exist and have, of late, accelerated on the world's comics scene, this chapter will examine how five different comics cultures emerged and have both been influenced by and provided influence upon the industry we know best, the American. We begin our tour with the other two of the Big Three international players, the Japanese and the Franco-Belgian traditions. Then we examine how America's two nearest neighbors, Canada and Mexico, have created and extended their own unique comics traditions, given their close proximity to the U.S. and its considerable influence. Finally, we examine the United Kingdom's comics industry. While the U.K. is far from the U.S. shores, common political and linguistic connections link these two nations. In the last three decades these strong bonds have facilitated the ascent of British talent within the American comic book mainstream. By the time our tour is complete, you should be able to better understand the American comic book industry's close relationship with the rest of the world's comics.

Considerable Influence, Part I: Japanese Manga

The word *manga* translates as "irresponsible pictures," but despite that name, the Japanese are anything but dismissive of their comics. Nowhere else in the world do comics appeal to a wider audience or achieve greater financial success than in the land of the rising sun. While certain comics are targeted to young boys there, as in the rest of the world, so-called *shōnen manga* are not the only comics products available to eager audiences. Manga addresses diverse audiences, including young girls (*shōjo*) and more mature women (*redikomi*), and they offer subjects as varied as historical drama and cooking. There are even many popular sports manga featuring the intricacies of a mahjong game or the thrill of a high school basketball team's season (e.g., the popular series *Slam Dunk*). Such diversity has given manga an appeal that penetrates nearly all aspects of Japanese society and has made manga a considerable economic force among the country's media industries. According to comics aficionados Tim Pilcher and Brad Brooks, manga makes up an estimated 40 percent of the Japanese publishing industry. In comparison, the comics industry in the United States is merely 3 percent of the publishing trade. Given its diversity and economic clout, manga has largely avoided the biases that plague Western comics, and readers unashamedly consume manga like they can in no other society on Earth.

Manga, or *gekiga* ("dramatic pictures"), tend to be published in formats quite different from those familiar to most American comics readers. The majority of manga have relatively low production values, and their contents are published in black and white, rather than full color as in America. Most manga are published as anthologies of several hundred pages in length, with some as thick as telephone directories. Each publication may contain a number of serialized features, and these features may run for many years and literally thousands of pages. Given the freedom to tell a story in that kind of space, creators tend to relate stories at a slower pace than that with which Western audiences are familiar. This also means that manga are intended to be read relatively quickly compared to Western comics. And, unlike American publishers who rely on their ownership of characters to perpetuate their business (e.g., Superman, Archie), manga features are rarely continued beyond the tenure of the original creator once that cartoonist is finished with the story.

Like other comics traditions, the origins of manga have been influenced by a number of historical precedents, though it is fairly clear that the title of *manga* stems from the works of an artist named Katsushika Hokusai. Famed for his woodblock prints, Hokusai published a set of self-caricatures in 1814 that he dubbed "irresponsible pictures": manga. Over the next century and a half, other forms of cartooning would appear in print, but the industry as it is known today really took hold after World War II. At that time, a nation struggling to recover from the devastation of war sought temporary escape in the pages of materials rented out by Japan's pay libraries. So-called "red books," cheaply produced manga with red ink on their covers, became a staple of these vendors. The pay libraries' popularity helped make manga accessible to a much wider audience. Timed with this newfound audience was an emerging talent who helped define the medium.

Unquestionably the most influential figure in manga is Osamu Tezuka, who lived from 1928 to 1989, and was dubbed by his fans "The God of Manga." Tezuka had trained to be a medical doctor but instead pursued his dream to become a cartoonist and, eventually, an animator. He took inspiration from the animated films of Fleischer Studies and Walt Disney and succeeded in conveying the same energy in storytelling on paper that these pioneers had on film. Tezuka drew on these sources for both stylistic and thematic ideas. For example, his early manga featured characters with large eyes, a convention Tezuka adopted from Disney animated characters (and a convention often imitated by Tezuka's successors). His first full-length manga, *New Treasure Island* (1947), demonstrated his innate storytelling sensibilities and established

FIGURE 13.2. The popular manga series *Bleach* exhibits many of the popular conventions of Japanese comics, including an emphasis on warrior heroes and depiction of doe-eyed heroines.

his popularity among consumers. Further well-liked series included *Kimba the White Lion* (1950), the story of the ruler of the animal kingdom learning to live in harmony with humankind, and *Astro Boy* (1952), a re-imagining of the Pinocchio story with a robot boy in place of the traditional wooden one. Tezuka's later works explored additional genres and included the philosophical epic *Phoenix* (1967) and the medical drama *Black Jack* (1973) among many, many others. Not content to have mastered one medium, Tezuka translated many of his works into animated series, or **anime**, for television, also to great acclaim. In fact, it was because of the success and accolades won by Tezuka in his lifetime that it became acceptable for serious artists to work as professional makers of manga—or *mangaka*.

In Tezuka's wake, a host of *mangaka* began to experiment with the medium and explore a host of issues confronting post-war Japan, including the introduction of technology into society. Tezuka himself had introduced this issue with his *Astro Boy* series, when the atomic-powered little robot who is rejected by his inventor finds love and purpose in an adopted family. Astro Boy became indicative of the Japanese attitude towards technology: Robots were at best helpful, like Fujiko F. Fujio's robot cat from the future, *Doraemon* (1969), and at the very least useful tools, like Go Nagai's "super robot" *Mazinger Z* (1972). While popular culture in the west often interpreted robots and their associated technologies as threats (think of Dave in *2001: A Space Odyssey*), Japanese manga and anime cast them as heroic tools. Super-robots like the heroes that later arrived in America as Voltron and the Power Rangers are inheritors of this ongoing legacy. Of course, not all technologies were warmly accepted by the Japanese, and the scourge of atomic bombings of Hiroshima and Nagasaki loomed large over the post-war consciousness. Keiji Nakazawa's *Barefoot Gen* (1973) provides one moving portrait of a survivor's tale of the Hiroshima bombing, the results of a technology whose consequences were experienced and not just imagined.

Although manga had enjoyed widespread indigenous popularity since World War II, it remained largely undiscovered by American audiences until the 1980s. In order to achieve acceptance, American translations first had to overcome some design differences. One difference is that the Japanese read from right to left instead of left to right. This meant that early translations had to print the page in reverse or cut and re-order individual frames into left-to-right sequences. Today, numerous purists have learned to read many imported manga in their original right-to-left fashion—"unflopped"—saving publishers such hassle. Early translations also had to alter the artwork to change Japanese sound effects, written in Japanese characters, into recognizable English characters. Also, numerous cultural idioms posed certain barriers to easy interpretations; for instance, Roger Sabin points out that *mangaka* conventionally represent a sleeping character with bubbles emitting from his nose, unlike American cartoonists who use a series of "zzzzzz" flowing within a speech balloon (*Comics, Comix*). One of the first efforts to market manga to the American audience came from American publisher First Comics, who in 1987 began to reprint Kazuo Koike and Goseki Kojima's *Lone Wolf and Cub* (which had begun its seven-thousand-page run in *Manga Action* in 1970). The series is about a *ronin*, a masterless samurai, who brings his baby son, the only other surviving member of his murdered family, on his quest for vengeance upon those who have framed him. The initial success of *Lone Wolf and Cub* was aided by the contribution of covers for the reprints from an American fan, cartoonist Frank Miller, who had already shown manga influences in his earlier work on the 1983 limited series *Ronin* for DC Comics.

Other publishers began to follow First Comics into testing the market with more manga offerings, but the real watershed event for manga in America came about thanks to anime and the proliferation of *Akira* (1988) through the early 1990s. Katsuhiro Otomo had begun this saga in the pages of *Young Magazine* in 1982, and some two thousand pages and eight years later, he wrapped up his tale of young psychics and bikers living in a post-apocalyptic Tokyo. In 1988 Otomo directed an anime version of *Akira*, whose higher production values gained the attention of international audiences. Eventually, Marvel Comics reprinted the original saga under its Epic imprint, helping to draw a whole new audience to manga. These markets opened wider in the 1990s as publishers specializing in reprinting manga imported from Japan, like Viz Media and Tokyopop, began to make headway in the placement and sale of manga. Along the way they have been aided and abetted by their anime counterparts. Indeed, not only are manga adapted to anime and original anime adapted to manga (so-called *cinemanga*), but the canny publishers have sized the manga books to the same dimensions as a DVD case so that the two can be shelved next to one another. This technique has helped facilitate the international popularity of series like *Dragonball* (1984), *Yu-Gi-Oh* (1996), and *Naruto* (1999), all now familiar staples for youthful American audiences who consume products from these franchises in their manga, anime, games, and numerous additional licensed products. Already having conquered the reading public at home, then, manga is poised to conquer the rest of the world as well.

CONSIDERABLE INFLUENCE, PART II: FRANCO-BELGIAN *BANDE DESSINÉE*

With perhaps even more regard than the Japanese for comics' value for self-expression, the French and Belgians have always embraced the comics medium as art. In fact, it was a French film scholar, Claude Beylie, who in 1964 proposed that comics deserved to be held as the "ninth art," putting it on an even footing with television and seven other arts canonized earlier in the century by Italian film critic Ricciotto Canudo: architecture, music, painting, sculpture, poetry, dance, and cinema. In the Franco-Belgian tradition, comics are called *bande dessinée* ("drawn strips") or simply *BD* (pronounced "bay-day"), and the vitality and diversity of their industry is second only to that of the Japanese.

While a considerable number of series have won distinction in this tradition, easily the most internationally recognizable and influential of the *bande dessinée* is *The Adventures of Tintin*. Its renown is based in part upon its style and in part because of the publishing tradition it helped establish. Developed by cartoonist Georges Rémi (1907–1983), under the nom de plume Hergé, Tintin debuted on January 10, 1929, as a supplement to a Belgian newspaper *Le Vingtième Siècle*. Tintin was a reporter, who, along with his dog Snowy and a cast of colorful supporting characters, traveled the world in thrilling adventure stories. Hergé drew Tintin in a style known as ***ligne claire*** ("clear line"), where each pen line is drawn with equal thickness and shadows are minimized. This creates a clean, simple-looking figure, but it actually takes a very methodical approach to achieve this clarity. As a result of the *linge claire* style, Tintin and his cast seem abstractly cartoonish, although their backgrounds are renowned for their detail. In fact, Hergé or members of his staff traveled to locales to be featured in Tintin's adventures before drawing them, to make the settings appear as authentic as possible. A *ligne claire* style was embraced by numerous other strips in the wake of Tintin's success, including a French imitation of *Tintin* named *Spirou*, whose title character was a bellboy who later becomes an adventurer, and *Asterix the Gaul*, a comedic strip featuring a cast of indigenous Gaul villagers, led by the diminutive Asterix, who resist Roman occupation of northern France at the time of Julius Caesar. Created by writer René Goscinny, who had worked in America on *Mad* with Harvey Kurtzman, and artist Albert Uderzo, *Asterix* is second only to *Tintin* as the most widely recognized *bande dessinée* character.

The successful reception of *Tintin*, *Spirou*, and *Asterix*, among others in serialized form, subsequently led to an important development in the solicitation

To the docks, Snowy... as quick as we can!

FIGURE 13.3. Hergé won acclaim for his *ligne clair* (clear line) style of drawing in *The Adventures of Tintin*. © Hergé/Moulinsart 2008

of *bande dessinée*, as collections of these serials were bound and sold in bookstores as **albums**. The hardbound albums gave the *bande dessinée* a permanence that newsprint periodicals lacked and helped foster a perception among people that they were keepsakes worth rereading rather than merely disposable ephemera. The album system helped nurture the professional standing of continental cartoonists and fostered favorable repute for the burgeoning *bande dessinée* industry. Sabin points out that this system prospered because of three synergistic reasons (*Comic, Comix*). First, because the cartoonist were both paid for their serialized work appearing in periodicals and then later enjoyed royalties from their album reprints, it became possible to make a respectable living as a cartoonist. In contrast, repackaging of comic books in the U.S. didn't really pick up steam until late in the twentieth century. Second, copyright laws enshrined a cartoonist's ownership of a character or strip, so the agreement to have a publisher print a strip was not tantamount to surrendering one's ownership of the material, as was most often the case in the United States. Third, because a cartoonist could make a living at his profession and was inalienably linked to a creation, notoriety and prestige began to emerge around the most talented producers in the field. These factors helped contribute to the emergence of a culture where comics could be taken seriously.

The progression towards maturity for *bande dessinée* was both hindered and helped by a 1949 law establishing a review board for the censoring of French comics. The law reacted to the flood of imported comics flowing into France after World War II and sought to stem the flow of outside influence, particularly from America. Interestingly, the law resulted from a pair of politically uneasy allies: the Catholic educators on one hand, who abhorred the violence in American comics, and the Communist Party on the other, who feared the imperialist influence of outside cultures replacing native French values. The prohibitions set forth by the review board set limits on the amount of material that could be imported for publication, forcing French publishers to employ native talent. Such a mandate further encouraged the domestic talent pool for the industry. The board's influence was eventually undermined, as members of the French countercultural movement of late 1960s turned their attentions outside of France, and especially to American underground cartoonists like Robert Crumb, for material. Consequently, French artists began to take cues from the American underground and developed more mature themes in their works.

Such a mature approach is embodied in the works of one of France's most famous artists, Jean Giraud, who signs his work "Gir" or "Moebius." Giraud rose to prominence as the artist of the series *Lieutenant Blueberry*, which was published in an influential *bande dessinée* titled *Pilote* beginning in 1963. This western series featured Blueberry, a cavalry officer, in adventures set in the post–Civil War American west. The artwork was gritty but realistic and unlike what Giraud would produce for his science fiction and fantasy work under the alias of Moebius. Under that pseudonym he published numerous strips, including those appearing in *Métal Hurlant*, that he helped co-found—and one that was eventually franchised in the U.S. as the magazine *Heavy Metal*. This work, such as the pterodactyl-flying journey in Arzach, was a departure from his *Lieutenant Blueberry* material and featured a rejection of traditional realistic depictions, instead favoring a *nouveau réalisme* born of a deft use of airbrushed colors, exotic landscapes, and dominating panels that could stand as individual works of art apart from their narrative (Screech 95). Revered in France and abroad, Moebius is among the few French artists known by American audiences, thanks in part to a 1988 collaboration with Stan Lee on a Epic Comics project.

The maturing of the Franco-Belgian comics took place both within the medium and thanks to a critical response outside of it. It was the French intellectuals who had earlier led the western appreciation of film as a significant medium for human expression, and today that medium is widely accepted

FIGURE 13.4. French cartoonist Jean "Moebius" Giraud came to the attention of American audiences when he teamed up with Stan Lee to do a Silver Surfer story for Epic Comics. © 2008 Marvel Entertainment, Inc. and its subsidiaries

insofar as academic departments teach film studies and prestigious awards are given valorizing the works of filmmakers. It has also been the French who have championed the appreciation of comics. In part, this appreciation was fostered by the founding of societies for the study of the medium, and the eventual establishment of academic journals devoted to the serious discussion of the material, beginning with *Les Cahiers de la Bande Dessinée*. High-profile exhibitions like the one held at the Louvre in 1967 also helped raise the profile of comics, as did the establishment of festivals, like the one in Angoulême discussed in the chapter's opening. Today Europeans continue to lead the world in the critical appreciation of the medium, even as their works are being discovered by new audiences in America. These discoveries include the works of French publishers like l'Association, who brought forth both David B's *l'Ascension du Haut Mal* (published stateside as *Epileptic*) and Marjane Satrapi's *Persepolis*, who though born Iranian, published in France—further demonstrating the international confluence of artists France is now host to.

OUR NEIGHBOR TO THE NORTH: CANADIAN COMIC BOOKS

While oceans distance America from Japan and continental Europe, the border between America and her nearest neighbors is far more immediate. Canada, for one, is a nation seeking to get out from under the shadow cast by the popular culture industries of its more influential southern neighbor. Yet among nations, Canada's proximity to the United States has made America's influence particularly powerful. Canada's quest to claim a distinct cultural identity has thus been a difficult one, most especially in the English-speaking parts of the country, as American influence and imports have long dominated (if not at times obliterated) indigenous efforts to foster creativity and independent voices communicating through the comics medium. The story of Canadian comic books is a history of give and take that has, with time, led to the acceptance of Canadian talent and publishing as an integral, although barely distinct, part of the North American comics publishing industry.

English-speaking Canadians first encountered comic books in the form of American imports in the late 1930s and became hooked. American comics were in high demand until circumstances blocked their further importation. In late 1940 the Canadian government closed off the import of fictional material like comic books. Canada was already engaged in the expensive process of fighting World War II at that time and was facing a trade deficit that forced the government to take some protective measures against foreign imports. Thus, the War Exchange Conservation Act stopped the import of non-essential materials like comic books, which unintentionally opened the door for Canadian publishers to fill the void in the market. By March 1941, Maple Leaf Publishing had rushed Canada's first indigenous comic book, *Better Comics* #1, to market. Other publishers quickly followed and began to offer comics with everything that the American books had offered: sports, secret agents, humor, westerns, war, jungle, adventure, detective, and of course, superheroes. Some publishers simply printed comic titles borrowed from America. For instance, Anglo-American purchased scripts for *Captain Marvel* from Fawcett Comics and had Canadian artists redraw them before publishing and distributing them north of the border. Other publishers, like Bell Features, developed their own corral of characters, like Thunderfist, the Brain, and the Penguin. But the real standouts were those heroes who were distinctly Canadian, among them Nelvana of the Northern Lights, Johnny Canuck, and Dixon of the Mounted. Nelvana was the first Canadian national hero, and her debut predated America's Wonder Woman by several months. Nelvana was created by Adrian Dingle and first appeared in *Triumph-Adventure Comics* #1 (1941) and ran until 1947. Historian Alan Walker claims that these heroes

FIGURE 13.5. Adrian Dingle's national heroine, Nelvana of the Northern Lights, was a goddess who fought crime using her superpowers, which included the ability to ride the lights of the Aurora Borealis. © Nelvana Limited. Used with permission. All rights reserved.

became potent and powerful wartime symbols and matters of national pride for a generation of youthful Canadians.

Although Canada's "Golden Age" certainly captured the imagination of the American comic book industry, it couldn't necessarily capture the same production values. In fact, after a few initial experiments with color printing, Canada's publishers simply printed the interior pages of their comics in black and white, which was both less technical and less expensive. For this reason, the comics became known as **Canadian whites**. Despite their lack of full color, the Canadian whites prospered, at least until the end of the war brought with it the end of the protectionism that had kept American comics at bay. Within a year of the war's end in 1945 most of the Canadian publishers had stopped producing original material, and by 1947 the American comic book industry had reasserted itself as the dominant source of material for mass market comic books, a position that would go unchallenged throughout most of Canada until 1969. During this period, Canadian publishers might reprint American material for their domestic audience, but virtually no original Canadian-made material was commissioned. The outlets for Canadian creators during this period lay in either heading south of the 49th Parallel to work in the American comics industry or helping to produce the occasional promotional comics for the government or marketers eager to target children (e.g., Kentucky Fried Chicken's *Colonel Sanders Comics*).

According to historian John Bell, Canadian comics would experience a resurgence in the late 1960s and early 1970s, thanks to the contributions of adult comics made by those involved in the counterculture, the rise of the literary small press, and the emergence of comics fandom. Experiments with additional nationalistic superheroes led the way, and soon one flag-draped hero after another tried to capture the wonder of the original Canadian whites: Captain Canada in 1969, the Northern Light in 1974, Captain Canuck in 1975, and Northguard in 1984. None of these attempts were long-lasting. But Canadian comics really gained its footing in 1977, when Dave Sim launched his sword-and-sorcery parody *Cerebus the Aardvark*. Self-publishing through his Aardvark-Vanaheim Press, Sim gradually shifted the focus of the series from sword-and-sorcery to a number of social and political commentaries, and in the center of it was, absurdly enough, a talking aardvark. *Cerebus the Aardvark* became the longest-running Canadian comic book series, lasting a planned three hundred issues when it wrapped up its run in 2004. Interestingly, Sim's series found its audience through the emerging comics specialty shops that had begun to spring up across North America (see Chapter 4). Alternative presses like Aardvark-Vanaheim could viably compete for shelf space in these shops and establish a presence for Canadian material at home and even abroad in America. In these footsteps followed Chris Oliveros' Montreal-based Drawn and Quarterly, a publisher that entered the alternative press arena in 1990 and has grown to be one of the most influential alternative presses in contemporary comics publishing. Drawn and Quarterly not only publishes its own anthology, but regularly prints the works of noted cartoonists like Chester Brown. With comics like his experimental *Yummy Fur* to his credit, Brown has achieved an even wider audience through album reprints of his work, including such acclaimed graphic novels as his autobiographical *The Playboy* (1992) and the historical *Louis Reil* (2003). The successes of Sim, Oliveros, and Brown point to the best compromise that the Canadian industry has achieved: It cannot establish a completely separate comics scene given the influx of American products, but it can be a contributing part of a larger North American milieu.

While English language comics are more widespread in Canada and beyond, a separate comics tradition has existed in the French-speaking province of Quebec. Historian Michael Viau explains that like their English-speaking neighbors, Quebecois were subjected to American comics imports (albeit in translated forms), but were additionally targeted by Franco-Belgium albums. Consequently, a body of uniquely Quebecois comics, or *bande dessinée Québécoise* (BDQ), emerged during the twentieth century and continues to be published today. This tradition has been shaped both by the strong sense of a distinct Quebecois identity and the influence of the Catholic Church, though the most popular and enduring material has been lighthearted (e.g., the humor anthology *Croc*). Given the limits of an even smaller readership base than the rest of Canada, though, BDQ face an even more difficult struggle to sustain a distinct cultural tradition. One recent attempt at reinforcing a distinct Canadian national identity is the establishment of the Joe Shuster Canadian Comic Book Creator Awards in 2005, which recognizes the accomplishment of both English and French Canadian efforts. With nominees limited to Canadian natives or residents, the awards seek to recognize and publicize the nation's contributions to the broader North American comics industry.

And certainly, Canadians have helped shape that broader comics industry, thanks to the longstanding and continual flow of Canadian talent to American publishers. Such a current stretches all the way back to the very foundation of the American comic book industry, with Superman co-creator and original artist Joe Shuster, who was born in Canada before immigrating to the United States to help shape the most influential of all comic book characters. Likewise, cartoonist John Byrne turned Canadian expatriate in order to make his mark on Marvel and DC Comics. Interestingly, Byrne created perhaps the best-known Canadian superheroes, the members of Alpha Flight, while working for an American audience on Marvel's *X-Men* series in the early 1980s. And quite possibly the most financially successful cartoonist to work in comics in North America is of Canadian origin: Todd McFarlane, who not only created the bestselling *Spawn*, but was instrumental in the founding of upstart Image Comics in the 1990s (see Chapter 3). Indeed, today cartoonists like Darwyn Cooke (*The New Frontier*), Chris Bachalo (*Generation X*) and Dale Keown (*Pitt*) are part of a steady stream of Canadian talent that helps supply the American comics mainstream.

OUR NEIGHBOR TO THE SOUTH: MEXICAN HISTORIETAS

Unlike the Canadians, whose efforts at producing an indigenous comics industry have ebbed and flowed through the years, Mexico has sustained a vibrant comics industry of its own despite the threat of American competition. While Mexican comics, or *historietas* ("little stories"), have suffered from less impressive production values than their American counterparts, they have long been extremely popular among the Mexican people, including adults. Like the Japanese, generations of Mexicans have found little shame in enjoying tales told through graphic storytelling and have demonstrated their enthusiasm through their support of a number of distinct genres, including adventure, romance, humor, horror, and detective comics. The success of the Mexican *historietas* may be partially attributed to the language barrier between the Spanish-speaking Mexico and the English-speaking United States, but there are also economic and cultural differences that have helped Mexico's own comics to thrive.

One of the earliest factors contributing to the rise of a distinct Mexican comics industry was the simple need for material. Getting comics to Mexican publishers for translation and reprinting seemed to be a low priority for American syndicates in the early days of comics, ascent to popularity. And so in 1921, the editor of one Mexican newspaper, *El Heraldo*, simply commissioned Salvador Pruñeda, a local artist, to create a strip that happened to be about a cowboy, *Don Catariño*. Within a few years a number of other homegrown strips were running in newspapers across the country. Such strips tended to resonate more with Mexican readers, relying on themes and characters more familiar and identifiable to Mexicans. By 1934 the newspaper publishers began to reprint comic strips and sell these comic books on newsstands. The first of these publications was called *Paquín* ("Frankie"), but the most popular of these anthologies, *Pepín* ("Joey"), debuted shortly thereafter in 1936. *Pepín* eventually became so popular that it was published daily, Monday through Friday, and twice on Sundays! To this day, some Mexicans refer to comics as *pepines* in testimony to *Pepín's* impact on the industry. Early Mexican comics such as these were printed in black and white and surrounded by a full-color cover. In time, Mexican comics would continue to be printed in a single color ink, though the publishers began to color-code the comics by genre (e.g., romance comics were printed in a reddish-brown ink). The *historietas* were much shorter than their American counterparts—thirty-two pages or fewer compared to sixty-four— which is understandable given their daily schedule as opposed to American comics' monthly schedule.

Mexican *historietas* were also distinct in terms of their contents and their orientation towards their readers. Unlike most American comics of the time, where the approach was to produce self-contained "done-in-one" stories, the Mexican publishers preferred episodic serials, continuing a storyline over a number of issues, with some storylines running for years. These continuing story arcs encouraged audiences to return day after day or week after week to see what the next chapter in the saga would tell. It would be several more decades before American publishers began to experiment with episodic series, though today most mainstream comic book titles in America embrace the approach. Certainly, attracting the audience's attention with serials was one way Mexican comics retained their audiences, according to researcher Anne Rubenstein. Another was the community orientation that the publications adopted. Again, long before American publishers would adopt such conventions, Mexican comics were publishing their readers' letters, introducing profiles of their creators (engendering a "star" system of cartoonists), and sponsoring contests to engage their audience. The *historietas* thus became an interactive, communal experience. Decades later, Stan Lee would employ a similar set of appeals in promoting Marvel Comics among America's youth, long after Mexican publishers had won their audiences over with their common appeals.

Of course, the popularity of Mexican comics was also helped by their use of some scandalous materials, such as the appearance of *chicas modernas*, modern women living independent of the traditional male-dominated hierarchies favored in Latin American cultures. Such breaks with traditional values, as well as depictions of scantily clad women and graphic depictions of violence, raised the concerns of more conservative segments of Mexican society, leading the Catholic Legion of Decency to wage a campaign against the comics industry in the early 1940s. The Mexican government sought to mediate the conflict between the conservative movement and the publishers, attempting to appease the former by introducing the *Comisión Calificadora de Publicaciones y Revistas Ilustradas* (the Qualifying Committee for Publications and Illustrated Magazines) in 1944. The charge of the *Comisión Calificadora* was to review all comics titles and related publications once they were issued. It was within this commission's power to levy fines, revoke publishing licenses, and recommend prosecution for violations of decency laws. In many cases, publishers summoned before the commission would be forgiven for their transgressions with the promise that they would mend their ways—which they did not always do. Other publishers might simply cancel a persecuted title and restart under a new title, temporarily evading the commission's reach. An unintended effect of this censoring body was the protection it afforded local production efforts. The *Comisión Calificadora* simply refused to grant licenses to publish to a number of foreign publishers on grounds ranging from being too pornographic to depicting notions contrary to the national interests. The determination of these standards was at the commissioners' discretion, but many potentially competitive products from other countries found themselves blocked by the *Comisión Calificadora*'s decisions, decisions that ultimately helped Mexican publishers prosper.

Within this environment, a number of prominent series have emerged. For more than half a century, cartoonist Gabriel Vargas has entertained Mexican audiences with his humorous take on family life in the pages of *La Familia Burrón*. Much of the humor in the Burrón family comes from class distinctions, as Burola, the wife in the family, attempts scheme after scheme to raise her lower middle class family up from the modest living provided by her husband Don Regino's barber's salary. In addition to family fun, Mexico has also had its share of native superheroes, the best known of which is Kalimán. Originally introduced on radio, *Kalimán: El Hombre Increíble* debuted in comics in 1965, the creation of Modesto Vásquez González and Rafael Cutberto Navarro. Kalimán possess great physical prowess and an array of superhuman mental powers (e.g., telekinesis), all of which were perfected by training he received from Tibetan lamas. Dressed in a white outfit and a white turban, he travels the world pursuing justice in the name of the Hindu goddess Kali and in the company of a sidekick named Solín. Additionally, romance comics have been a staple of the Mexican industry. Titles like *Lágrimas, Risas y Amor* ("Tears, Laughter and Love") have delivered formulaic stories about courtship in serialized story arcs. A variation on the *historieta*, the *fotonovela*, is also a popular vehicle for romance stories. *Fotonovelas* feature photographs or movie stills of actors superimposed over backgrounds drawn into the frame. All of these are examples of periodicals that typically met with approval of the conservative forces in Mexican society.

An example of a cartoonist who has not met with conservative approval is Eduardo del Río, who works under the pen name Rius. He came to prominence in 1966 when he created *Los Supermachos* ("The Super-Virile Men"), which was ostensibly a humorous look at rural life but also became a vehicle for Rius to criticize government policies and corruption. After a falling out with his publisher, Rius started a similar series, *Los Agachados* ("The Stooped Ones") beginning in 1968. His popularity and his politics led him to be abducted by military forces and, after being hauled before a firing squad and made to witness his own mock execution, he was warned to soften his rhetoric. Rius did just the opposite and has become an outspoken critic of government abuse and a proponent of leftist politics. In addition to his political cartoons, Rius has written a number of educational books on leftist ideology using the comics medium. One such book,

Figure 13.6. Rius inaugurated the "for beginners" series with his treatises on leftist ideology like *Marx for Beginners*. From *Marx for Beginners* by Rius, translated by Richard Appignanesi. Translation © 1976 by Richard Appignanesi. Used by permission of Pantheon Books, a division of Random House, Inc.

Marx Para Principiantes ("Marx for Beginners"), was an international success and helped launch a series of "for beginners" books introducing complex philosophical figures in comics form.

Mexicans may have read more comics per capita than any other culture, but recently the huge audience for comics has begun to slip away. Increased foreign competition and the introduction of new media have decreased its once-large audience. In a desperate attempt to win back some of its readership, one of the largest publisher has turned to creating **ghetto librettos**, "a particular mixture of Mexican soap opera melodrama with softcore porn and pulp fiction" (Blackaller). These *historietas* are nearly pornographic in their depictions of curvaceous women, who are often situated in suggestive positions and/or menaced by sex-starved men. These ghetto librettos offer a stark contrast to the traditionally conservative content of Mexican *historietas* and ultimately make for an unflattering coda to an industry that largely held very high standards for decades.

THE TALENT EXCHANGE: BRITISH COMIC BOOKS

A closer look at one final comics tradition illuminates another aspect of America's relationship to the rest of the comic book industries in the world. The comics tradition in the United Kingdom predates that in the United States, with the first regular comics magazines having already become fixtures of British newsstands by the time famed American cartoonist Robert F. Outcault was debuting his "Hogan's Alley" in the 1890s. In fact, the British had pioneered the modern cartoon format in the pages of the humor magazine *Punch* beginning in 1841, more than half a century before Outcault's experiments with the form captured America's interest. Indeed, British humor magazines regularly featured cartoon characters like the bulbous-nosed con man Ally Sloper, who appeared in the pages of one of *Punch*'s rival humor magazines, *Judy*, beginning in 1867. Sloper eventually became the first character to have a comic magazine devoted to his antics, *Ally Sloper's Half Holiday*, which premiered in 1884 as an inexpensive black-and-white weekly. Other comics magazines followed suit, such as *Comics Cuts* in 1890 and *Illustrated Chips* in 1896, establishing a tradition of the medium as a humorous diversion. This expectation continues today in comics magazines like *Viz* (started in 1979), which features humor catering to adult sensibilities, not unlike American's *Mad* magazine.

The British comics magazines were quite different from their American counterparts. For one thing, British comics tended to be published as weeklies rather than monthlies as they were in the states. As a result, British comics tended to be considerably shorter than American comics, running perhaps as few as eight pages an issue. They also tended to have black-and-white instead of four-color pages, with the typical exception of a color cover. Their shorter page count and lack of expensive color processes resulted in a comparatively lower cover price per issue. Also of

A. SLOPER, ESQ., M.F.K.O.M.I.E.
(Most Frequently Kicked Out Man in Europe.)

FIGURE 13.7. Ally Sloper's name is a period idiom for a rent dodger. Such dishonest renters would be said to "slope on down the ally" to avoid paying their landlords.

interest is the different ways in which comics magazines and newspapers related. In the states, comics held early sway in newspapers, and only ventured out into their own magazines decades later; in Britain, comics were successful first in their own periodical publications and only later became features of respectable newspapers.

While the earliest British comics magazines were concerned with entertaining adults, the medium eventually became considered the province of childhood. In contrast to their earliest years when they were intended for adult consumption, Sabin notes that most comics made between 1914 and 1960 targeted the children's audience (*Adult Comics*). Long running magazines like *The Dandy* and *Beano*, both in print since the late 1930s, have continued what grew to become a rather innocuous tradition in British comics. The publishers eventually offered fare that was more than just simple humor strips. Accordingly, the publishers often tailored content to more mature girls and boys. One example of the latter tailoring was a magazine aimed at boys called the *Eagle*, which featured the popular "Dan Dare, Pilot of the Future," a strip in the tradition of Alex Raymond's "Flash Gordon." Eventually, more adult fare rose to challenge this dominant paradigm, questioning a commonly-held assumption among the Brits that comics were a medium of interest only to children.

According to Sabin, by the 1960s several circumstances had contributed to the rise of more mature offerings in British comics (*Adult Comics*). First, comics fans began to organize themselves, holding swap meets and networking to nurture their mutual interest in the medium. Second, this fandom helped support the emergence of comics specialty shops that sold both back issues and highly demanded American imports. Third, some of these imports included underground comics with their mature themes and graphic portrayals. One of the first magazines to respond to these circumstances was a Pat Mills production called *Action*, which proved to be too controversial to survive for long. *Action* featured strips like "Hookjaw," about a carnage-spewing shark in the *Jaws* lineage, and "Kids Rule O.K.," depicting a juvenile attack on police officers. A national flurry urged the publishers of *Action* to clean up their act, which they did, only to find their audience abandon the magazine when the content was toned down. *Action* may have been more graphic than British sensibilities for the time would have allowed, breaking with expectations that comics should be juvenile material, but it paved the way for additional attempts at more mature applications of the medium. Mills' next attempt would succeed where *Action* had failed.

In 1977, Mills began to publish *2000 A.D.*, one of the most significant British comics. *2000 A.D.* managed to avoid much of the controversy *Action* had drawn by telling its tales through science fiction, thus concealing any of the more objectionable political comments under the veneer of fantasy. Heavily influenced by American superhero comics, *2000 A.D.* became closely associated with its lead feature, *Judge Dredd*. Dredd told the violent story of a police officer living in the dystopian future of Megacity One and used black humor to satirize the concept of authority, says British comics observer David Roach. The success of *2000 A.D.* spawned a number of imitators, including Dez Skinn's *Warrior*, a series notable for having published the initial chapters of Alan Moore and David Lloyd's *V for Vendetta* series. Magazines like *2000 A.D.* and *Warrior* not only came to represent a new, more mature face for comics in the United Kingdom, they also became a talent showcase for potential export to the United States.

There has been a long cross-pollination of ideas and talents between the U.S. and the U.K. comics industries. In 1936 *Mickey Mouse Weekly* arrived in the United Kingdom as a popular import, buoyed in advance by Mickey's fame in animated films. After World War II, America's Captain Marvel proved to be as popular in Britain as he was in the United States. In fact, when Fawcett Publications gave up producing new material for Captain Marvel in 1953, the British publisher commissioned a thinly veiled imitation, Marvelman, to continue the series. In the 1970s Marvel Comics opened a United Kingdom office, a move that helped turn an American-created *Captain Britain* series around, once homegrown talent refashioned him. While American influence has been substantial in the U.K., it has not been a one-sided affair, especially in the last several decades when an influx of British talent has come to dominate mainstream American comics. Barry Windsor-Smith cracked the international divide when he was hired to produce the art for Marvel's *Conan the Barbarian* in 1970. A decade later a whole crop of British talent found themselves recruited, beginning when DC Comics began to hire talents like artists Brian Bolland (*Camelot 3000*) and Dave Gibbons (*Green Lantern*), and writer Alan Moore (*Saga of the Swamp Thing*). Moore and Gibbons would go on to create one of the seminal graphic novels in American comics publishing, *Watchmen*, in 1986. Since the critical and commercial success of *Watchmen*, imported talents

FIGURE 13.8. Brian Bolland won acclaim at home carrying out the art chores for *2000 A.D.* before taking on assignments for American publishers. Judge Dredd & 2000 A.D. © & ® Rebellion

from the British Isles have had considerable impact on the American comics mainstream. These talents include writers like Neil Gaiman (*Sandman*), Warren Ellis (*The Authority*), Mark Millar (*Civil War*), and Grant Morrison (*JLA*). Some of the artists have included Mark Buckingham (*Fables*), Alan Davis (*Excalibur*), Bryan Hitch (*Ultimates*), Dave McKean (*Sandman*), and Kevin O'Neill (*League of Extraordinary Gentlemen*). As it stands, even while American-made comics are still in demand among British audiences, many of those makers are Brits themselves.

Discovering: Lost in Translation

Everyone is familiar with the story of Spider-Man: Awkward Pavitr Prabhakar was raised by his kindly Aunt Maya and Uncle Bhim to know that with great power comes great responsibility. Everyone also knows how a mysterious man bequeathed upon him the costume and powers of Spider-Man to fight foes like Doctor Octopus in the streets of Mumbai. Okay, so maybe the details aren't exactly what everyone remembers, but that's the reinterpretation of the Spider-Man story that the creative team of Jeevan Kang, Suresh Seetharaman, and Sharad Devarajan of Gotham Entertainment offered audiences in their 2004 limited series, which aimed to make your friendly neighborhood Spider-Man fit into a new neighborhood: India.

For the most part, foreign publishers of American material have stuck to the relatively simple (and inexpensive) process of translating the word balloons and captions in American comics from English into their own tongue before releasing them in their home markets. While these translations might adapt the characters' dialogue to local language and idiom, they typically don't adapt to their audience's customs and values, or consider their taboos, and thus these comics still reflect American iconography and ideals in their presentation of characters and

Cont'd

FIGURE 13.9. The experimental *Spider-Man: India* re-envisions Spider-Man in order to make him more resonant for audiences in another culture. © 2008 Marvel Entertainment, Inc. and its subsidiaries

stories. Experiments like *Spider-Man: India* present an interesting hybrid of a highly recognizable concept (Spider-Man) within a different cultural milieu (India), trying to market to an indigenous audience by making the figure even more identifiable than before.

Of course, *Spider-Man: India* isn't the first attempt at such market adaptation. Marvel Comics franchised its most recognizable icon to Japan's *Monthly Shonen Magazine* back in 1970, where *mangaka* Ryoichi Ikegami took the lead in producing a serial for a very different Spider-Man named Yu Komori, who spun his webs in Tokyo. Interestingly, these stories resurfaced in the late 1990s, when, in a fascinating twist, Marvel reprinted them in English translations for an American audience who was becoming obsessed with manga. A similar process is presently underway with the manga adaptation of Top Cow's *Witchblade* series. *Witchblade Tekura* began to run in Japan's *Champion Red* in 2006, with the titular character, Tekura, set in Japan, in contrast to the American original Sarah Pezzini in New York. The change was meant to help the property better relate to its target audience in Japan, and now the manga is set to cross back over to American audiences.

Such efforts may suggest some moderate progress in terms of cultural sensitivity, as local characters, customs, and themes receive greater attention in the pages of these comic books. However, the branding of popular American concepts in foreign markets may also be seen as yet another attempt to exploit lucrative international markets, as American publishers pursue new paths to sell and re-sell their properties time and again.

ANALYZING: CONSIDERING CULTURAL IMPERIALISM

In 1936 cartoonist Lee Falk debuted his long-running syndicated comic strip, *The Phantom*, in the pages of America's newspapers. According to his origin, the Phantom is the latest in a family of crime fighters who have opposed piracy and villainy since the sixteenth century, operating from a base somewhere in the heart of the African jungle. At the start of this heroic legacy, the man who would become the very first Phantom was rescued by a group of African pygmies called the Bander tribe. He, in turn, would help free them from slavery after adopting a costume that invoked the image of their slaver's demon god. The current Phantom continues to provide protection to the Bander tribe. If you read this series from a Western point of view, it may seem like a story that is in keeping with accepted cultural values and norms. Americans in particular are fond of heroic individuals who make a comeback against the odds and manage to not only save themselves but to single-handedly rescue the larger society. However, taken from another perspective, that of the African native, the story is less flattering. Africans are portrayed as either superstitious villains or helpless victims in this story. Either way, it takes a white man to figure out how to free and protect them for centuries; no champion of equal stature to the seemingly immortal Phantom emerges from among their own people.

The idea of a beneficent white hero was a common theme in fiction at the time of the Phantom's debut. White heroes like Tarzan, Sheena, and dozens of other jungle kings and queens were often the stars of novels, newspaper strips, and comic books. Yet the portrayal of these Western-born champions almost always places them in a superior position to the native peoples around them. To readers from these parts of the world, and often those descended from them, such portrayals are insulting. The portrayals devalue both the peoples and the cultures depicted in them. In addition, the portrayals also work to reinforce existing notions of dominance. Thus, to Western readers, such portrayals perpetuate beliefs about the superiority of the white race and Western know-how. In the case of the Phantom, Falk tells us that one white man can do what an entire village of Africans could not: secure the Banders' freedom. Moreover, the continued protection of the Phantom legacy over the tribe for centuries echoes a Western notion that developing nations are childlike and need the supervision of white people.

This, of course, was part of the rationale for European colonialism in the past. While the desire for resources and territory drove colonizers forward, European intellectuals argued that they were doing native peoples of the Americas, India, African, Australia, and the Asian Pacific Islands a favor by delivering them from savagery and bringing them the superior European language, religion, and culture. Of course, the delivery of such "gifts" was most often made at the end of a gun barrel, as Western militaries first conquered and then "tamed" native people by forcing Western culture upon them.

While nearly all nations once under colonial rule have won their political independence, some academics argue that the process of colonialization has only changed tactics, having moved from the use of militaries and missionaries to the tools of mass media. The concern with this new form of colonialism, called **cultural imperialism**, is that dominant cultures can supplant native cultures through the widespread use of broadcast, electronic, and print technology. The dominant invading cultures often produce very attractive media products, which is no surprise given that these are often created using superior technology (e.g., computer-assisted coloring programs) and under the direction of long-term professionals. They also tend to have a head start in learning the business of media when compared to emerging homegrown producers, particularly in terms of establishing and maintaining distribution systems to get the media products into the hands of consumers. Dominant cultures also have typically covered their production costs in their domestic market long before the same product is released abroad. Western publishers can make substantial profits by distributing their products thusly, even if the charges to consumers in a developing country

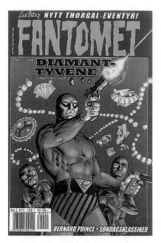

FIGURE 13.10. The Phantom is published widely abroad, including his series in Norway, where he is know as *Fantomet*. © King Features Syndicate

are considerably lower than that for their domestic audience. With much of its overhead covered by sales in its country of origin, a media product can be priced so low in a foreign market that it will even undersell a native product. In the competitive world of media production, the reality is that those who have already made money at it are better positioned to make more money. The unforeseen cost, though, is the erosion of indigenous cultures, as the slicker, cheaper, and more widespread media products provide messages about values, norms, and roles that are different from (if not outright contradictory to) those of native culture. Certainly America has been charged with cultural imperialism thanks to its highly influential film, television, and, yes, comic book industries. Likewise, we are now seeing Japan exhibiting a similar influence through the widespread distribution of manga.

This brings us back to the *Phantom*, a strip still running today, many years after its creator's passing. The enduring popularity of "The Ghost Who Walks" in newspaper strips eventually led to his appearance in comic books and other media, at home and abroad. In fact, while *Phantom* comic books have been published off and on in America over the years, the Phantom has achieved his greatest popularity abroad. The Phantom is something of a phenomenon in the countries of Scandinavia (Norway, Sweden, Finland), in Australia, and, curiously enough, in India. In these countries, the comic books have been in continuous publication for more than fifty years, ever since their first introduction, and have been among the bestselling comics in their respective markets. The Phantom can be seen then as an example of imperialism in terms of both the content of its stories and the effect of its distribution. Although the Phantom is not self-consciously propaganda trying to convert readers to adopt its notions of white, Western superiority, it nonetheless propagates that very message through its use of characters and setting. The financial benefits that King Features Syndicate, the owner of the copyright, has garnered through the licensing of Phantom comics around the world is considerable. And while the Phantom may have entertained, if not inspired, audiences in many lands, the lingering question is: at what costs to native identity? Then there is the additional question left in the wake of all characters—including the Phantom, Donald Duck, and Superman—who displace native series: But for the intervention of these commercial endeavors, what alternative heroes might have been imagined around the world?

This chapter hasn't answered that question definitively, but it has attempted to show you how certain cultures have responded to the incursion of other nation's comic books into their own cultures. At times these arrivals have been eagerly welcomed, and at other times they have been fiercely opposed, but for much of the world a seemingly inevitable exchange of concepts and cartoonists has occurred. This chapter shows that such exchanges haven't always been balanced, but history has taught us that it ultimately proves very difficult to stem outside influence indefinitely. The richness of the comics scene in the world today owes much to both the fostering of native comics and the interchange of ideas among different traditions. Their ability to help build a given culture's identity and the propensity they have to build bridges between cultures are but two more manifestations of the power of comics.

Discussion Questions

1. What values do you think are most often represented in American comic books? Why would these values be attractive to people in some other parts of the world? Why would such values be perceived as a threat to certain cultures?

2. If you could distribute an American graphic novel or comic book series to people in other cultures, which one(s) would you send? What about the example(s) you chose do you think makes them suitable for a wider world audience? On the other hand, if you could withhold the distribution of any graphic novel or comic book series on the world market, which would you stop? What about this example makes you reluctant to distribute it?

3. Is there room for both indigenous and imported comics in developing countries? If so, what steps can be taken to ensure that indigenous comics have a chance to nurture native talent and develop a domestic audience in the face of imported comics that often come with higher production values, more widespread distribution systems, and almost universally recognizable characters?

Activities

1. This chapter presented a limited number of comic book traditions in countries other than the United States, and in doing so it only scratched the surface when it comes to the worldwide comics scene. Select a country not explored in detail in this chapter and research the comics tradition within it. Some examples include China, Argentina, South Africa, and Australia, but there are many, many others you can explore as well. As you investigate these traditions, consider the following questions: Do these countries have revered figures like Japan's Osamu Tezuka? Do they have influential characters like Belgium's Tintin? Do they have pivotal titles like Britain's *2000 A.D.*? Prepare the results of your research in the form of an oral report to be shared with your classmates. Feel free to use visual aids to help your peers conceptualize the distinct tradition you have researched.

2. Pick up an album or trade paperback from another culture (many possible titles for you to consider are listed in this chapter) and read it. Note how the storytelling and not just the culture it represents differs from the American

models that you have been exposed to in previous chapters and activities in this book. What elements stand out in particular to your reading? List the differences as you read and compare them to the norms of storytelling in American comics. Then prepare a short essay response to the following inquiry: Are comics a truly universal form of communication, or do differences make each culture's comics a unique language of its own?

Recommended Readings

Comics:

Hergé. *The Calculus Affair*. Translated by Leslie Lonsdale-Cooper and Michael Turner. Boston: Little, Brown and Company, 1976.

Hergé's often-imitated style can be seen in this album collecting one of the most acclaimed storylines from his long-running series *The Adventures of Tintin*. In addition to demonstrating the *ligne claire* technique, the album features Tintin and crew in international intrigue, racing to save their friend, Professor Calculus, from spies who want him to perfect a devastating ultrasonic weapon.

Tezuka, Osamu. *Phoenix*. 12 vols. San Francisco: Viz, 2002.

Any volume in the series will reveal the imaginative storytelling that made Tezuka into the most revered storyteller in modern Japan. If Tezuka is Japan's answer to Walt Disney, then this epic series of life, death, time, and space is his *Fantasia*.

Scholarly Sources:

Gravett, Paul. *Manga: Sixty Years of Japanese Comics*. New York: HarperCollins, 2004.

Gravett provides a thorough review of manga, including its history, genres, and audiences, with a great many full-color illustrations. Whether you've never picked up a manga before or you've been reading them for years, Gravett's treatment reveals interesting details about the medium, its messages, and its makers.

Rubenstein, Anne. *Bad Language, Naked Ladies, and Other Threats to the Nation: A Political History of Comic Books in Mexico*. Durham, NC: Duke University Press, 1998.

Rubenstein presents an insightful analysis of the development of comics south of the border. The examination capably details how the Mexican comics industry was shaped through a confluence of economic, government, and religious forces.

Glossary

affective response—emotional reactions (e.g., excitement, pity, fear) that arise without conscious effort

album—a collection of previously serialized comics in a bound edition

alternative—non-mainstream comic books usually created by a single cartoonist and presenting a very personal vision

amplification—the heightening of meaning that comes when people communicate about an act of communication

anime—Japanese animated films

anthropomorphism—literary device where non-human creatures are given human qualities, and usually human failings

anti-hero—a protagonist who lacks some of the qualities of an idealized hero

apa—an amateur press alliance, whose members publish collections of their works and distribute them to each other

art form—a type of creative expression governed by its own materials, techniques, and limitations

artisan process—production method that involves principally individual execution of the writing and drawing (and perhaps other roles) in the creation of comics

asynchronous—the depiction of sound (dialogue, sound effects, or music) in a panel that is not occurring at the same moment as the events pictured in the panel

auteur—the primary "author" of a work who provides a unifying artistic vision, even within a collaborative production process

back issues—stocks of comic book magazines older than the most current issue offered for sale by comics specialty shops

bande dessinée—"drawn strips" or comics from the Franco-Belgian tradition

broadsheet—an early form of mass communication consisting of a single page of printed material usually with both words and images

Canadian whites—comic with black and white interior pages published during World War II

canon—a definitive list of the most worthwhile works or most talented creators

cartoonist—creator who both writes and draws comics

chiaroscuro—a stark contrast of light and dark

closure—applying background knowledge and an understanding of the relationships between encapsulated images to synthesize (or blend) sequences of panels into events

cognitive response—the process of perceiving, organizing, and interpreting the symbols on the page in order to construct meaning

comic book—a volume in which all aspects of the narrative are represented by pictorial and linguistic images encapsulated in a sequence of juxtaposed panels and pages

comics—juxtaposed images in a sequence

Comics Code Authority—an industry-sponsored board tasked with reviewing the contents of comic books before approving them for distribution

Comics Guaranty, LLC (CGC)—limited liability corporation that offers the services of a third-party evaluation of a comic book's grading

comics journalism—accounts of actual events presented in comics form

composition—the selection and placement of visual elements on a comics page and within a panel

content analysis—research method in which the frequency and patterns of selected variables are investigated across media messages

continuity—the consistent relationship among different comics stories

copyright—the legal control that the owner has over intellectual property

cultural imperialism—the erosion of native cultures, including their value systems, language, and traditions, due to the influence of more dominant cultures through the distribution of mass media

diegetic images—pictures and words that depict characters, objects, and sensory environment of the world of the story

differentiation—the process of distinguishing a narrative from others within its genre

direct effects—theory of mass media consumption that says audiences imitate what they see portrayed in media messages; also known as the "magic bullet theory" of media effects

Direct Market—the system of comic book distribution to specialty shops

disjointed panel—the words and images that constitute the panel are not contiguous

distribution—stage in the mass media industry where entities deliver media products from the producer to the exhibitor

encapsulation—selecting images that capture the flow of experience and putting them in a panel

exhibition—stage in the mass media industry where entities sell media products to the consumers

fan—an audience member engaged in the dialogue about comic books

fanboy—a term for fans that may be either insulting or used for self-deprecation

fandom—the community of fans produced by organized activity

fanzine—a fan-produced magazine

flayed look—artistic style that emphasizes detailed musculature

fotonovela—a comic whose panels consist of a mixture of still photography and text; also known as *fumetti* in Europe

freelancer—an independent contractor who accepts work on particular assignments

gatekeeper—anyone who has the authority to select or modify messages communicated through the media

genre—a class or type of an art form as determined by the appearance of similarities with other works

ghetto librettos—Mexican comics emphasizing sexuality, crime, and melodrama

Golden Age—reference to the comic book era of earliest mass popularity, roughly dated 1938–1945

Good Girl Art—style of comic art in which shapely, stereotypically attractive women are provocatively posed for the pleasure of the male viewer

graphic novel—a label applied by creators and publishers to distinguish a comic book, which in practice is longer and perhaps self-contained, in contrast to most periodical comic books

ground level—non-mainstream comic books that allowed creators to tap into the underground sensibility and work in genres other than superheroes

gutter—the space between panels

hardcover—a book published with a comparatively durable cover

hegemony—the perpetuation of power disparities in a culture through the capitulation of those disadvantaged by the system

historietas—"little stories" or comics from the Mexican tradition

hybrid—a narrative that combines qualities from two or more genres

icon signs—visual cues that represent things similar in appearance (e.g., a simple drawing of a car meant to conjure the idea of an actual car)

ideology—a set of ideas that function as sense-making tools for groups of people

independent—smaller publisher that attempts to compete with the established publishers by offering genre fiction comic books intended for a mainstream audience

index signs—visual cues that have relationship to ideas or things not explicitly depicted (e.g., a gasp indicates surprise)

industrial process—production method that involves collaborators performing specialized tasks in the creation of comics

intellectual property—an original work of words, images, or ideas that is legally recognized as being owned by its creator

interanimation of meaning—images (picture or text) appearing in proximity (in a panel or on a page) can each affect the meaning of the other, and together create a meaning beyond what is communicated by each separate image

intertextual image—a picture that reminds the reader of something he or she has encountered in other media (movies, books, paintings, TV shows, etc.)

juvenile delinquency—a social condition in which youth engage in illegal activities such as vandalism, theft, and murder

juxtapose—to place items side-by-side

layout—the relationship of a single panel to the succession of panels, to the totality of the page, and to the totality of the story; involves choices of size, sequence, and juxtaposition

licensing—the assigning of rights by a trademark holder to a licensee to use a character for a marketing application

ligne claire—style of drawing that assigns equal value to all the lines within the frame and de-emphasizes shading

literacy—the ability to understand and interpret a symbol system, traditionally associated with reading text but now regarded as including visual and other cultural symbols as well

limited series—a comic book series launched with definite conclusion planned

mainstream—comic books produced by the most established and profitable publishers

manga—Japanese comics; translated as "irresponsible pictures"

mangaka—professional cartoonists working in Japanese manga

Marvel method—a collaborative production which vests most control over the story-telling dynamics upon the artist rather than the writer

medium—a channel for communication

metonymy—the use of an associated detail to represent the whole

mini-comics (or mini-comix)—originally designated a 3½ x 4" eight page comic, but the term has come to refer to small, homemade comic book.

mint condition—a state lacking any detectable flaws

monomyth—the archetypical story of the hero's journey repeated across multiple versions

monopoly—a marketplace characterized by only one provider and no competition

multimodal—a text which communicates through more than one symbol system such as comics (visual and textual) or television (visual and aural)

mythic criticism—a research method wherein texts are reviewed for their culturally significant meanings

narrative problematic—the challenge that must be overcome or resolved before a happy ending can be reached in a story (e.g., a rival's diversion)

negotiated reading—an interpretation of a message that accepts some of the intent of the creators while rejecting other elements

newwave (also new wave)—half or quarter page mini-comics produced by cartoonists independent of any publisher

ninth art—title assigned to the comics art form by scholar Claude Beylie, who argued comics and television deserved standing with seven other arts: architecture, music, painting, sculpture, poetry, dance, and cinema

noise—any interference that distorts the message

oligopoly—a marketplace characterized by relatively few competitors

onomatopoeia—invented words that mimic sounds

oppositional reading—an interpretation of a message that is counter to the creators' intent

origin story—narrative that explains the fantastic nature of the superhero and involves a transformation; also referred to commonly as the "secret origin"

Other—social group that is defined in contrast to the qualities of a preferred group in a society

panel—a discernible area that contains a moment of the story

paradigmatic choice—the chosen images and all the images that could have made sense or communicated nearly the same meaning at the same point in the panel

paralanguage—qualities of our spoken communication (volume, emphasis, rate, quality, etc.)

parasocial relationship—the perception of a relationship with figures in the media that develops over time and may have an emotional intensity similar to that of actual shared relationships

preferred reading—an interpretation of a message that matches the intent of the creators

primary movement—the implied movement of people or objects in the frame

production—stage in mass media industry where entities create media products

proliferating narrativity—the focus of interest does not reside in the building and resolution of dramatic suspense spanning the entire text (story), but in the narrative verve displayed in relating adventures from the life of the hero (mythos)

propaganda—a series of related communication acts that spread a particular interpretation of an event

prozine—a fanzine with higher production values and produced by a staff with more of a professional than amateur standing

psychological image—an image that represents some aspect of a character's personality or state of mind

pulps—magazine made of cheap paper and featuring sensational fictional stories (e.g., detective, science fiction, adventure)

quantitative—analysis of phenomena using numerical data

reboot—starting a series over with revisions to the mythos established in the previous incarnation(s) of the series

representation—the depiction (or lack thereof) and definition of a social group in mass media messages

rogues gallery—a superhero's collection of foes

scarcity—the relatively limited availability of an object, which helps drive up its value

scene—a unit of the story that usually, but not necessarily, has unity of time and space to portray a continuous action.

secondary movement—the implied movement of the frame itself

sequence—the compilation of related and usually consecutive scenes

sequential art—any artwork with elements arranged in a sequence to tell a story

shop system—an arrangement where independent contractors produced content for the major publishers, often in an assembly line where different production steps were divided among artists

sign—something, such as an image, meant to represent something else, such as a quality

Silver Age—reference to the comic book era coinciding with the second surge in popularity in superhero comics, roughly dated 1956–1969

slabbed—referring to the state of a comic book that has been evaluated and then sheathed between two sheets of plastic by the Comics Guaranty, LLC

slash fiction—stories authored by fans that place same-sex fictional characters into sexual situations

specialty shops—stores offering comics and comics-related paraphernalia

speculators—collectors who purchase comic books as investments

splash page—full-page panel, usually at or near the beginning of a comics narrative, used to establish context or mood

standardization—the process of including enough recognizable elements so that a narrative clearly fits within a genre

state of grace—a set of powers, appearance, supporting characters, and behaviors that are preserved in a recognizable form for the economic interests of the corporation that owns the character

stereotype—a recognizable generalization of a type

symbol signs—arbitrary patterns, such as words, that reference an idea or thing

synchronous—the depiction of sound (dialogue, sound effects, or music) in a panel that emanates from and is occurring at the same moment as the events pictured in the panel

synecdoche—a part of something that stands for the whole or vice versa

synergy—the coordinated release of products tied into a media property to maximize exposure and increase profitability

syntagmatic choice—the process of selecting which panels to present from the possible progression of story images that could occur

Tijuana Bible—crude sex comic books

trade paperback (TPB)—a comic book usually with more pages than most monthly issues and bound by a cover that is of higher durability than a paper cover but not quite as durable as hardcover

underground comix—independently produced comic books, often socially rebellious

virtual community—a group of people in relationship to one another who rely on mediated communication because of a lack of geographic proximity to one another

visual metaphor—a picture of one thing to evoke the idea of something else

work-for-hire—an arrangement with a cartoonist in which the publisher retains copyright over characters and story

Yellow Kid Thesis—a disputed assertion that the comics medium began with the work of Richard Felton Outcault's *Hogan's Alley*, featuring the character of the Yellow Kid

Bibliography

Allen, Todd. "Online Comics vs. Printed Comics: A Study in E-Commerce and the Comparative Economics of Content." *www.businessofcontent.com/dojo/215/v.jsp?p=/comics-ecommerce/index* (accessed July 10, 2007).

Alls, Rob. "Marvel Press Conference Transcript." *Comics Continuum*, May 17, 2001, *www.comicscontinuum.com/stories/0105/17/marvelindex.htm* (accessed May 12, 2008).

Ames, Winslow, and David M. Kunzle. "Caricature, Cartoon and Comic Strip." In *The New Encyclopedia Britannica*, vol. 15, Macropedia 15th ed., 539–552. Chicago: Encyclopedia Britannica, Inc., 2007.

Anderson, Brent. Personal Interview. August 13, 1999.

"Are Comics Fascist?" *Time*, October 22, 1945: 67–68.

Arlin, Marshall, and Garry Roth. "Pupils' Use of Time while Reading Comics and Books." *American Educational Research Journal* 15 (1978): 201–216.

Arlington, Gary. "A Recollection." In *The Official Underground and Newave Comix Price Guide*, edited by Jay Kennedy, 35. Cambridge: Boatner Norton Press, 1982.

Bails, Jerry, and Hames Ware, eds. *The Who's Who of American Comic Books*. 4 vols. Detroit, MI:, 1973–1976.

Bakwin, Ruth Morris. "Psychological Aspects of Pediatrics: The Comics." *The Journal of Pediatrics* 42 (1953): 633–635.

Barrier, Michael. "Comic Master: The Art of Will Eisner." *Print* Nov–Dec 1988: 197–198.

Beard, David. "Deceptive Data: How Diamond Best-seller Lists Distort the Comics Industry." *The Comics Journal* 283 (May 2007): 19–24.

Beerbohm, Robert Lee. E-mail to Comics Scholars' Discussion List, December 4, 1997.

———. "The Originator of Comics." In *The Adventures of Obadiah Oldbuck*, edited by Alfredo Castelli, 50. Napoli: Comicon, 2003.

———. "Secret Origins of the Direct Market: Part One: 'Affidavit Returns'—The Scourge of Distribution." *Comic Book Artist* 6 (Fall 1999): 80–91.

Beerbohm, Robert Lee, and Richard D. Olson. "The Platinum Age: The American Comic Book: 1883–1938: Further Concise History & Price Index of the Field as of 2008." In *The Official Overstreet Comic Book Price Guide*, 38th ed., edited by Robert M. Overstreet, 367–375. New York: House of Collectible, 2008.

Belk, Russell W. "Material Values in the Comics: A Content Analysis of Comic Books Featuring Themes of Wealth." *The Journal of Consumer Research* 14 (1987): 26–42.

Bell, Blake. "Ditko and Stanton." *Ditko Looked Up.* N.d. *www.ditko.comics.org/ditko/crea/crerstan.html* (accessed June 11, 2008).

Bell, John. *Invaders from the North: How Canada Conquered the Comic Book Universe.* Toronto: Dundurn Press, 2006.

Bell, John, ed. *Canuck Comics.* Montreal: Matrix Books, 1986.

Bender, Lauretta, and Reginald S. Lourie. "The Effect of Comic Books on the Ideology of Children." *American Journal of Orthopsychiatry* 11 (1941): 540–550.

Benson, John. "Is War Hell? The Evolution of an Artist's Viewpoint." *Panels* 2 (1981): 18–20.

Benton, Mike. *The Comic Book in America: An Illustrated History.* Dallas, TX: Taylor Publishing Company, 1993.

———. *Horror Comics: The Illustrated History.* Dallas, TX: Taylor Publishing Company, 1991.

———. *Masters of Imagination: The Comic Book Artists Hall of Fame.* Dallas, TX: Taylor Publishing Company, 1994.

Berger, Arthur Asa. *The Comic-Stripped American: What Dick Tracy, Blondie, Daddy Warbucks and Charlie Brown Tell Us about Ourselves.* New York: Walker & Co., 1973.

Berona, David. "Picture Stories: Eric Drooker and the Tradition of Woodcut Novels." *Inks* 2, no. 1 (1995): 2–11.

Bignell, Jonathan. *Media Semiotics: An Introduction.* Manchester: Manchester University Press, 1997.

Bissette, Stephen, Neil Gaiman, and Tom Veitch. "Change or Die! The Revisionist Roundtable Discussion." In Rick Veitch, *The One,* 188–209. Windham Hill, VT: King Hell Press, 1989.

Bitz, Michael. "The Comic Book Project: Forging Alternative Pathways to Literacy." *Journal of Adolescent & Adult Literacy* 47 (2004): 574–586.

Blackaller, Luis E. "Sexy Comics of Mexico." Henry Jenkins. *www.henryjenkins.org/2007/05/ghetto_libretto.html* (accessed October 10, 2007).

Blackmore, Tim. "*300* and Two: Frank Miller and Daniel Ford Interpret Herodotus's Thermopylae Myth." *International Journal of Comic Art* 6, no. 2 (2004): 325–349.

Bloomberg News. "Spider Cents Boost Marvel Profits." *Ottawa Citizen,* May 9, 2007, D8.

Blumberg, Arnold T. "'The Night Gwen Stacy Died': The End of Innocence and the 'Last Gasp of the Silver Age.'" *International Journal of Comic Art* 8, no. 1 (2006): 197–211.

———. "Promotional Comics: The Marketing of a Medium." In *The Official Overstreet Comic Book Price Guide,* 35th ed., edited by Robert M. Overstreet, 285–288. New York: Gemstone Publishing, 2005.

Boichel, Bill. "Batman: Commodity as Myth." In *The Many Lives of the Batman: Critical Approaches to a Superhero and His Media,* edited by Roberta E. Pearson and William Uricchio, 4–17. New York: Routledge, 1991.

Bolhafner, Stephen. "Art for Art's Sake: Spiegelman Speaks on *Raw*'s Past, Present and Future." *The Comics Journal*, 145 (1991): 96–99.

Boxer, Sarah. "Comics Escape a Paper Box, and Electronic Questions Pop Out." *New York Times*, April 17, 2005, E1.

Branch, Jeffrey C. "Everything's . . . Archie: The Inside Story of Archie Comics." *Comic Book Marketplace*, October 1997, 32–36, 45–51.

Brooks, Tim, and Earle Marsh. *The Complete Directory to Prime Time Network TV Shows, 1946–Present.* 5th ed. New York: Ballantine, 1992.

Brown, Jeffrey A. *Black Superheroes, Milestone Comics, and Their Fans.* Jackson, MS: University Press of Mississippi, 2001.

———. "Comic Book Masculinity and the New Black Superhero." *African-American Review* 33 (1999): 25–42.

Bynre, John. "Superman: A Personal View." *The Man of Steel* 1 (1986): inside back cover.

Camp, Brian. "What is the Superhero Genre Tale?" Paper presented at the Comic Arts Conference, San Diego, CA: July 21, 2000.

Campbell, Richard, Christopher R. Martin, and Betina Fabos. *Media and Culture: An Introduction to Mass Communication.* 5th ed. Boston: Bedford/St. Martin's, 2006.

Carlson, Johanna Draper. "Online Comic Fandom in 1995." *Comics Worth Reading*, December 15, 2005. *http://comicsworthreading.com/2005/12/15/online-comic-fandom-in-1995* (accessed May 6, 2008).

Carrier, David. *Aesthetics of Comics.* University Park, PA: Penn State University Press, 2001.

Carter, James Bucky. "Introduction—Carving a Niche: Graphic Novels in the English Language Arts Classroom." In *Building Literacy Connections with Graphic Novels: Page by Page, Panel by Panel*, edited by James Bucky Carter, 1–25. Urbana, IL: National Council of Teachers of English, 2007.

Carter, Lynda. "Introduction." In *Wonder Woman: The Complete History*, by Les Daniels, 9. San Francisco: Chronicle Books, 2000.

Cary, Stephen. *Going Graphic: Comics at Work in the Multilingual Classroom.* Portsmouth, NH: Heinemann, 2004.

Chadwick, Paul. "Not That Old Chestnut!" *Comics Buyer's Guide*, December 12, 1997, 34–35.

Chiarello, Mark, and Todd Klein. *The DC Comics Guide to Coloring and Lettering Comics.* New York: Watson-Guptill Publications, 2004.

Clancy, Shaun. "Hex . . . and Other Blessings: Tony DeZuñiga, the CBA Interview." *Comic Book Artist* 4 (2004): 40–45.

Coale, Mark. *Breaking the Panels: Over 75 Short Interviews from around the Comics Industry.* Colora, MD: O-Goshi Studios, 1998.

Cohn, Neil. *Early Writings on Visual Language.* Carlsbad, CA: Emaki Productions, 2003.

Contino, Jennifer M. "A Touch of Vertigo: Karen Berger." *Sequential Tart* 4, no. 1 (2001). *www.sequentialtart.com/archive/feb01/berger.shtml* (accessed January 24, 2008).

Coogan, Peter. *The Superhero: The Secret Origin of a Genre*. Austin, TX: MonkeyBrain Books, 2006.

Cooke, Jon B. "Vengeance, Incorporated: A History of the Short-lived Comics Publisher, Atlas/Seaboard." *Comic Book Artist* 16 (December 2001): 14–19.

Cremins, Brian. "'I Asked for Water (She Gave Me Gasoline)': Tim Truman's Scout and Social Satire in the Independent Comics of the 1980s." *International Journal of Comic Art* 5.2 (2003): 339–350.

Crist, Judith. "Horror in the Nursery." *Collier's*, March 29, 1948, 22–23.

Crumb, Robert. "Twenty Years Later." *R. Crumb's Head Comix*. New York: Simon & Schuster, 1988: 1–5.

Crumb, Robert, and Peter Poplaski. *The R. Crumb Handbook*. London: MQ Publications, 2005.

Cruse, Howard. "Digging the Underground." Lecture to the Cartoonists Guild, Inc. New York, 1980.

Daniels, Les. *Comix: A History of Comic Books in America*. New York: Bonanza Books, 1971.

———. *Marvel: Five Fabulous Decades of the World's Greatest Comics*. New York: Harry N. Abrams, Inc., 1991.

"D.C. Comics." *Harper's Magazine Online*. June 2005. *http://harpers.org/archive/2005/06/0080579* (accessed February 13, 2008).

Dean, Michael. "Fine Young Cannibals: How Phil Seuling and a Generation of Teenage Entrepreneurs Created the Direct Market and Changed the Face of Comics." *The Comics Journal*, July 2006, 49–59.

Deppy, Dirk. "Suicide Club: How Greed and Stupidity Disemboweled the American Comic-Book Industry in the 1990s." *The Comics Journal*, July 2006, 68–75.

Dooley, Dennis, and Gary Engle, eds. *Superman at Fifty: The Persistence of a Legend*. Cleveland, OH: Octavia, 1987.

Duin, Steve, and Mike Richardson. *Comics between the Panels*. Milwaukie, OR: Dark Horse Comics, Inc., 1998.

Duncan, Randy. "Toward a Theory of Comic Book Communication." *Academic Forum* 17 (1999–2000). *www.hsu.edu/default.aspx?id=3508* (accessed May 19, 2008).

Durwood, Thomas A. "Jack Kirby, Fritz Lang and Balance." *The Harvard Journal of Pictorial Fiction* 1.1 (1974): 1–3.

Dziedric, Nancy, and Scot Peacock, eds. *Twentieth Century Literary Criticism*, vol. 66. Detroit, MI: Gale, 1997.

Early, Gerald. "The 1960s, African Americans, and the American Comic Book." In *Strips, Toons, and Bluesies: Essays in Comics and Culture*, edited by D. B. Dowd and Todd Hignite, 60–75. New York: Princeton Architectural Press, 2004.

Eco, Umberto. "The Myth of Superman." In *Arguing Comics: Literary Masters on a Popular Medium*, edited by Jeet Heer and Kent Worcester, 146–164. Jackson, MS: University Press of Mississippi, 2004.

Eisner, Will. *Comics & Sequential Art*. Tamarac, FL: Poorhouse Press, 1985.

———. *Graphic Storytelling*. Tamarac, FL: Poorhouse Press, 1996.

———. Personal conversation. May 4, 1993.

———. "Shop Talk with Jack Kirby." In *Will Eisner's Shop Talk*, edited by Diana Schutz and Denis Kitchen, 193–223. Milwaukie, OR: Dark Horse Comics, 2001.

Endres, Clifford. "Jaxon Returns: The Long Road Back to Austin." *Austin Sun,* 7 November 1974, 13, 20, 23.

Estren, Mark James. *A History of Underground Comix.* 4th ed. Berkeley: Ronin Publishing, 1993.

Evanier, Mark. *Kirby: King of Comics.* New York: Abrams, 2008.

Fingeroth, Danny. *Disguised as Clark Kent: Jews, Comics, and the Creation of the Superhero.* New York: Continuum, 2007.

———. *Superman on the Couch.* New York: Continuum, 2004.

Fiske, John. "The Discourses of TV Quiz Shows, or School + Luck = Success + Sex." In *Television Criticism: Approaches and Applications*, edited by Leah Vande Berg and Lawrence Wenner, 445–462. White Plains, NY: Longman, 1991.

Fulce, John. *Seduction of the Innocent Revisited.* Lafayette, LA: Huntington House, 1990.

Garriock, P.R. *Masters of Comic Book Art.* New York: Images Graphiques, 1978.

Garrity, Shaenon. "The Gail Simone Interview." *Comics Journal* 286 (2007): 68–91.

Geerdes, Clay. "Comix Wavola." *Comix F/X,* May 1990: n.p.

———. "The Evolution of the Minicomix in the Bay Area, Part 4." *Comix F/X,* May 1990: 6–7.

Geipel, John. *The Cartoon: A Short History of Graphic Comedy and Satire.* South Brunswick: A. S. Barnes and Company, 1972.

George, Milo, ed. *The Comics Journal Library, Volume One: Jack Kirby.* Seattle: Fantagraphics Books, 2002.

Gerber, Ernst. *The Photo-Journal Guide to Comic Books.* 2 vols. Minden, NV: Gerber Publishing Co., 1989–1990.

Gertler, Nat. "What Is the Superhero Genre Tale?" Paper presented at the Comic Arts Conference, San Diego, CA, July 21, 2000.

Giordano, Dick. "Introduction: Growing up with the Greatest." In *The Greatest Batman Stories Ever Told*, edited by Mike Gold, 6–11. New York: DC Comics, 1988.

Goethe, Johann Wolfgang von. *Conversations of Goethe with Eckermann and Soret.* Translated by John Oxenford. London: George Bell, 1875.

Gordon, Ian. *Comic Strips and Consumer Culture 1890–1945.* Washington, D.C.: Smithsonian Institution Press, 1998.

Gorman, Michele. *Getting Graphic! Using Graphic Novels to Promote Literacy with Preteens and Teens.* Worthington, OH: Linworth Publishing, Inc., 2003.

Goulart, Ron. *Comic Book Culture: An Illustrated History.* Portland, OR: Collectors Press, 2000.

———. *Great American Comic Books.* Lincolnwood, IL: Publications International, Ltd., 2001.

———. *Over Fifty Years of American Comic Books.* Lincolnwood, IL: Publications International, Ltd., 1991.

————. *Ron Goulart's Great History of Comic Books*. Chicago: Contemporary Books, 1986.

————. "The Second Banana Superheroes." In *All in Color for a Dime*, edited by Dick Lupoff and Don Thompson, 229–239. New Rochelle, NY: Arlington House, 1970; Iola, WI: Krause Publications, 1997.

Gramsci, Antonio. *Selections from the Prison Notebooks of Antonio Gramsci*, edited by Quintin Hoare and Geoffrey Nowell Smith. New York: International Publishers, 1971.

Grand Comic Book Database. 1994–2008. *www.comics.org* (accessed August 3, 2008).

"Graphic Novels Hit $375 Million." *ICv2*, April 18, 2008. *www.icv2.com/articles/news/ 12416.html* (accessed May 18, 2008).

Gravett, Paul. *Graphic Novels: Everything You Need to Know*. New York: HarperCollins, 2005.

————. *Great British Comics: Celebrating a Century of Ripping Yarns and Wizard Wheezes*. London: Aurum Press Limited, 2006.

————. *Manga: Sixty Years of Japanese Comics*. New York: HarperCollins, 2004.

Groensteen, Theirry. *System of Comics*. Translated by Bart Beaty and Nick Nguyen. Jackson, MS: University Press of Mississippi, 2007.

————. "Töpffer, the Originator of the Modern Comic Strip." In *Forging a New Medium: The Comic Strip in the Nineteenth Century*, edited by Pascal Lefevre and Charles Dierick, 105–114. Brussells: VUB University Press, 1998.

Grossman, Lev, and Richard Lacayo. "*Time*'s Critics Pick the 100 Best Novels 1923 to Present." *Time* 2005. *www.time.com/time/2005/100books* (accessed May 29, 2008).

Groth, Gary. "Black and White and Dead All Over." *The Comics Journal*, July 2006, 60–67.

————. "Independent Spirits: A Comics Perspective." In *Below Critical Radar: Fanzines and Alternative Comics from 1976 to the Present Day*, edited by Roger Sabin and Teal Triggs, 17–27. Hove, U.K.: Slab-O-Concrete, 2000.

Gustines, George Gene. "Where Superheroes Go for Industry News." *New York Times*, August 2, 2005. *www.nytimes.com/2005/08/02/books/02sham.html?_r=2&oref= slogin&oref=slogin* (accessed April 21, 2008).

Harrison, Randall. *The Cartoon: Communication to the Quick*. Beverly Hills, CA: Sage Publications, 1981.

Harvey, Robert C. *The Art of the Comic Book: An Aesthetic History*. Jackson, MS: University Press of Mississippi, 1996.

Hatfield, Charles. *Alternative Comics: An Emerging Literature*. Jackson, MS: University Press of Mississippi, 2005.

Haugaard, Kay. "Comic Books: Conduits to Culture?" *The Reading Teacher* 27 (1973): 54–55.

Haynes, Amanda. "Mass Media Re-Presentations of the Social World: Ethnicity and 'Race.'" In *Media Studies: Key Issues and Debates*, edited by Eoin Devereux, 162–190. Los Angeles: Sage, 2007.

Heisler, Florence. "Comparison of Comic Book and Non-Comic Book Readers of the Elementary School." *Journal of Educational Research* 41 (1948): 541–546.

Hight, Craig. "*American Splendor*: Translating Comic Autobiography into Drama-Documentary." In *Film and Comic Books*. Jackson, MS: University Press of Mississippi, 2007.

Hinds, Harold E., and Charles M. Tatum. *Not Just for Children: The Mexican Comic Book in the Late 1960s and 1970s*. Westport, CT: Greenwood Press, 1992.

Horn, Maurice. *Comics of the American West*. New York: Winchester Press, 1977.

———. "Hogarth, William." In *The World Encyclopedia of Comics*, edited by Maurice Horn, 320–321. New York: Avon, 1977.

———. *Sex in the Comics*. New York: Chelsea House Publishers, 1985.

Hoult, Thomas F. "Comic Books and Juvenile Delinquency." *Sociology and Social Research* 33 (1949): 279–284.

Houston, Frank. "Stan Lee." Salon.com, August 17, 1999. *www.salon.com/people/bc/1999/08/17/lee* (accessed June 11, 2008).

Infantino, Carmine, and J. David Spurlock. *The Amazing World of Carmine Infantino: An Autobiography*. Lebanon, NJ: Vanguard Productions, 2001.

Inge, M. Thomas. *Comics as Culture*. Jackson, MS: University Press of Mississippi, 1990.

———. Preface to *The American Comic Book: An Exhibition at the Ohio State University*. Columbus, OH: Ohio State University Libraries, 1985.

Jackson, Jack. "A Phenomenon." *Infinity Four* 1972: n.p.

Jacobson, Nels. "The Maverick Tradition: Postering in Austin, Texas." *OFFtheWALL* 1, no. 2 (1991): n.p.

Jenkins, Henry. "Quentin Tarantino's *Star Wars*? Digital Cinema, Media Convergence, and Participatory Culture." In *Rethinking Media Change: The Aesthetics of Transition*, edited by David Thorburn & Henry Jenkins, 281–312. Cambridge, MA: The MIT Press, 2003.

Jennings, John, with Damian Duffy. "Finding Other Heroes." In *Other Heroes: African American Comic Book Creators, Characters and Archetypes*, edited by John Jennings and Damian Duffy, 162–166. [S. I.]: lulu.com, 2007.

Jensen, Joli. "Fandom as Pathology: The Consequences of Characterization." In *The Adoring Audience: Fan Culture and Popular Media*, edited by Lisa A. Lewis, 9–29. New York: Routledge, 1992.

Jewett, Robert, and John Shelton Lawrence. *Captain America and the Crusade against Evil: The Dilemma of Zealous Nationalism*. Grand Rapids, MI: William B. Eerdmans Publishing, 2003.

Jones, Gerard, and Will Jacobs. *The Comic Book Heroes*. 2nd ed. Rocklin, CA: Prima Publishing, 1997.

Jones, William B., Jr. *Classics Illustrated: A Cultural History, with Illustrations*. Jefferson, NC: McFarland & Company, Inc., 2002.

Juno, Andrea. *Dangerous Drawings: Interviews with Graphix and Comix Artists*. New York: Juno Books, 1997.

Kane, Bob, and Gardner F. Fox. "The Batman Meets Dr. Death." *Detective Comics* #29 (July 1939): 1–10.

Kannenberg, Gene, Jr. "The Ad that Made an Icon out of Mac." *Hogan's Alley: The Online Magazine of the Cartoon Arts. www.cagle.com/hogan/features/atlas.asp* (accessed July 7, 2007).

———. "Graphic Text, Graphic Context: Interpreting Custom Fonts and Hands in Contemporary Comics." In *Illuminating Letter: Typography and Literary Interpretation*, edited by Paul C. Gutjahr and Megan L. Benton, 165–192. Amherst: University of Massachusetts Press, 2001.

Kefauver, Estes. Comic Books and Juvenile Delinquency: Interim Report of the Committee on the Judiciary; A Part of the Investigation of Juvenile Delinquency in the United States. Eighty-third Congress, first session pursuant to S. Res. 89, and Eighty-third Congress, second session pursuant to S. Res. 190, March 14 (Legislative Day, March 10), 1955.

Kelso, Megan. "New Voices in Comics 1998: A Roundtable." *International Journal of Comic Art* 1.2 (1999): 216–237.

Kendall, David, ed. *The Mammoth Book of Best War Comics*. New York: Running Press, 2007.

Kennedy, Jay. *The Official Underground and Newave Price Guide*. Cambridge: Boatner Norton Press, 1982.

Kidson, Mike. "William Hogarth: Printing Techniques and Comics." *International Journal of Comic Art* 1.1 (1999): 76–89.

Kirsh, Steven J., and Paul V. Olczak. "Comic Book Violence and Vengeance." In *Perspectives on Violence*, edited by Frederick K. Blucher, 81–92. Hauppage, NY: Nova Science Publishers, 2003.

Kirste, Kenneth K. *Drawn to Excellence: Masters of Cartoon Art*. San Francisco: Cartoon Art Museum, 1988.

Knowles, Christopher. *Our Gods Wear Spandex: The Secret History of Comic Book Heroes*. San Francisco: Weiser Books, 2007.

Krashen, Stephen. *The Power of Reading: Insights from the Research*. Englewood, CO: Libraries Unlimited, 1993.

Kunzle, David M. "Caricature, Cartoon, and Comic Strip," *The New Encyclopedia Britannica*, vol. 15. Macropaedia, 15th ed. Chicago: Encyclopedia Britannica, Inc., 1998: 52.

Kunzle, David. "The Comic Strip." In *Art News Annual XXXVI: Narrative Art*, edited by Thomas B. Hess and John Ashbery, 133–45 New York: The Macmillan Company, 1970.

Kuper, Peter. "Launching World War 3." In *The Education of a Comics Artist: Visual Narrative in Cartoons, Graphic Novels, and Beyond*, edited by Michael Dooley and Steven Heller, 28–31. New York: Allworth Press, 2005.

Kurtzman, Harvey. *From Aargh! to Zap! Harvey Kurtzman's Visual History of the Comics*. New York: Prentice Hall Press, 1991.

Lang, Jeffrey, and Patrick Trimble. "Whatever Happened to the Man of Tomorrow? An Examination of the American Monomyth and the Comic Book Superhero." *Journal of Popular Culture* 22, no. 3 (1988): 157–173.

Langer, Lawrence L. "A Fable of the Holocaust." *The New York Times Book Review*, November 3, 1991, 17.

Lee, Stan. *Origins of Marvel Comics*. New York: Simon and Shuster, 1974.

Leonard, Devin. "Marvel Goes Hollywood: Calling All Superheroes." *Fortune*, May 28, 2007. *http://money.cnn.com/magazines/fortune/fortune_archive/2007/05/28/10003446/index.html* (accessed June 3, 2007).

Levitz, Paul. Interview with author, San Diego, CA, July 18, 1997.

Lewin, Herbert S. "Fact and Figures about the Comics." *Nation's Schools* 52 (1953): 46–48.

Ling, Paul K. "A Thematic Analysis of Underground Comics." *Crimmer's: The Journal of the Narrative Arts* (1976): 39–43.

Loeb, Jeph, and Tom Morris. "Heroes and Superheroes." In *Superheroes and Philosophy*, edited by Tom Morris and Matt Morris, 11–20. Chicago: Open Court, 2005.

Lofficier, Jean-Marc, and Randy Lofficier. *Shadowmen 2: Heroes and Villains of French Comics*. Encino, CA: Black Coat Press, 2004.

Lovibond, S. H. "The Effect of Media Stressing Crime and Violence upon Children's Attitudes." *Social Problems* 15 (1967): 91–100.

Lowery, Shearon L., and Melvin L. DeFleur. *Milestones in Mass Communication Research*. 2nd ed. New York: Longman, 1983.

Luckiesh, Matthew, and Frak K. Moss. "Legibility in Comic Books." *Sight-Saving Review* 12 (1942): 19–24.

Lupoff, Dick, and Don Thompson. Introduction to *All in Color for a Dime*, by Dick Lupoff and Don Thompson. 1970. Iola, WI: Krause Publications, 1997.

Lustig, John. "The Terrible, Tragic (*Sob!*) Death of Romance (Comics!!)." *Back Issue* December 2005, 16–23.

MacDonald, Heidi, and Phillip Dana Yeh. *Secret Teachings of a Comic Book Master: The Art of Alfredo Alcala*. Lompoc, CA: International Humor Advisory Council, 1994.

Malan, Dan. "Introduction." In *The Labours of Hercules*, translated by Eric Bosch, 2. Paris: Aubert & Cie, 1847. St. Louis, MO: Malan Classical Enterprises, 1992.

Mallia, Ġorġ. "Learning from the Sequence: The Use of Comics in Instruction." *ImageText* 3 (2007). *www.english.ufl.edu/imagetext/archives/v3_3/mallia/* (accessed November 9, 2007).

Malloy, Alex. *Comics Values Annual*. Radnor, PA: Wallace Homestead, 1992.

Masters of Comic Book Art. Directed by Ken Viola. 1 hr, 1 min. Ken Viola Productions, 1987. Videocassette.

Matton, Annette. "From Realism to Superheroes in Marvel's *The 'Nam*." In *Comics & Ideology*, edited by Matthew P. McAllister, Edward H. Sewell, Jr., and Ian Gordon, 151–176. New York: Peter Lang, 2001.

McAllister, Matthew P. "Cultural Argument and Organizational Constraint in the Comic Book Industry." *Journal of Communication* 40 (1990): 55–71.

———. "Ownership Concentration in the U.S. Comic Book Industry." In *Comics & Ideology*, edited by Matthew P. McAllister, Edward H. Sewell, Jr., and Ian Gordon, 15–38. New York: Peter Lang, 2001.

McAllister, Matthew P., Edward H. Sewell, Jr., and Ian Gordon. "Introducing Comics and Ideology." In *Comics & Ideology*, edited by Matthew P. McAllister, Edward H. Sewell, Jr., and Ian Gordon, 1–13. New York: Peter Lang, 2001.

McCloud, Scott. *Making Comics: Storytelling Secrets of Comics, Manga and Graphic Novels*. New York: Harper, 2006.

———. *Reinventing Comics: How Imagination and Technology are Revolutionizing an Art Form*. New York: HarperCollins, 2000.

———. *Understanding Comics: The Invisible Art*. Northhampton, MA: Tundra Publishing, 1993.

McLuhan, Marshall. "Essay 11 [unnamed]." In *McLuhan: Hot and Cool*, edited by Gerald Emanuel Stern, 119–123. New York: Signet, 1967.

McRobbie, Angela. *Feminism and Youth Culture*. 2nd ed. New York: Routledge, 2000.

Meehan, Eileen R. "'Holy Commodity Fetish, Batman!': The Political Economy of a Commercial Intertext." In *The Many Lives of the Batman: Critical Approaches to a Superhero and His Media*, edited by Roberta E. Pearson and William Uricchio, 47–65. New York: Routledge, 1991.

Miller, Ann. *Reading Bande Dessinée: Critical Approaches to French-language Comic Strip*. Bristol, UK: Intellect, 2007.

Miller, Jeffery. Posting to Comics Scholars Discussion List, March 17, 2000.

Miller, John Jackson. *Comics Chronicles*. April 24, 2008. *www.comichron.com* (accessed May 18, 2008).

Miller, John Jackson, Maggie Thompson, Peter Bickford, and Brent Frankenhoff. *Comics Buyer's Guide Standard Catalog of Comic Books* 4th ed. Iola, WI: kp books, 2005.

Mishler, James. "Horror Comics: Tricks & Treats through the Ages." *Comic Buyer's Guide* January 2006, 24–26, 28–30, 32, 34.

Mishler, James, ed. "Overall Market Shares (in Percent) since 1997." *Comics & Games Retailer* June 2007, 27.

Misiroglu, Gina, and Michael Eury, eds. *The Supervillain Book: The Evil Side of Comics and Hollywood*. Canton, MI.: Visible Ink Press, 2006.

Monaco, James. *How to Read a Film*. New York: Oxford University Press, 1977.

Mullaney, Dean. "Publisher's Introduction." In *Real War Stories* no. 1. Forestville, CA: Eclipse Comics, 1987.

Murphy, T.E. "For the Kiddies to Read." *Reader's Digest*, June 1954, 5–8.

Murray, Chris. "Popaganda: Superhero Comics and Propaganda in World War Two." In *Comics & Culture: Analytical and Theoretical Approaches to Comics*, edited by Anne Magnussen and Hans-Christian Christiansen, 141–156. Copenhagen: Museum Tusculanum Press, 2000.

Nelson, Gayle, and Ron Truner. "The Last Gasp Story." *Last Gasp*, January 1999. *www.lastgasp.com/alg* (accessed June 11, 2008).

Nevins, Jess. "The Bat." *Pulp and Adventure Heroes of the Pre-War Years*. *http://geocities.com/jjnevins/pulpsb.html* (accessed November 29, 2007).

Nevins, Mark David. "Mythology and Superheroes." *Inks* 3, no. 3 (1996): 24–30.

Nolan, Michelle. "Collecting the Western Genre!" *Comic Book Marketplace*, July 1998, 23–26.

———. "Patriotic Heroes . . . the Red, White & Blue of WWII." *Comic Book Marketplace*, June 1997, 13–18.

Norrington, Stephen. *Blade*. New York: New Line Cinema, 1998.

North, Sterling. "A National Disgrace." *Chicago Daily News*, May 8, 1940, reprinted in *Childhood Education* 17 (1940): 56.

Norton, Bonny. "The Motivating Power of Comic Books: Insights from Archie Comic Readers." *Reaching Teacher* 57 (2003): 140–147.

Norton, Bonny, and Karen Vanderheyden. "Comic Book Culture and Second Language Learners." In *Critical Pedagogies and Language Learning*, edited by Bonny Norton and Kelleen Toohey, 201–221. New York: Cambridge University Press, 2004.

Nyberg, Amy Kiste. *Seal of Approval: The History of the Comics Code*. Jackson, MS: University of Mississippi Press, 1998.

Oliver, Glynis. Personal correspondence. March 15, 1988.

O'Nale, Robert. "The Gestalt Function of Comics." Paper presented at the 16th annual Comics Arts Conference, San Diego, California, July 24–27, 2008.

O'Neil, Dennis. "Green Thoughts." Introduction to *Green Lantern, Green Arrow: The Collection*, by Dennis O'Neil. New York: DC Comics, 1992.

O'Sullivan, Judith. *The Great American Comic Strip*. Boston: Bulfinch Press, 1990.

"Over 3,300 Graphic Novels Released in '07." *ICv2*, March 6, 2008. *www.icv2.com/articles/news/12186.html* (accessed May 18, 2008).

Overstreet, Robert M. "Introduction." *Comic Book Price Guide*. Cleveland, TN: Robert M. Overstreet, 1970.

———. *Official Overstreet Comic Book Price Guide*. 35th ed. New York: Gemstone Publishing, 2005.

Peeters, Benoit. "Les Adventures de la Page." *Consequences* 1 (1983): 32–44.

Pekar, Harvey. Interview by Gary Groth. "Stories about Honesty, Money, and Misogyny." *Comics Journal* 97 (1985): 44–64.

Phillips, Charles. *Archie: His First 50 Years*. New York: Abbeville Press, 1991.

Pilcher, Tim, and Brad Brooks. *The Essential Guide to World Comics*. London: Collins & Brown, 2005.

Pollman, Joost. "Shaping Sounds in Comics." *International Journal of Comic Art* 3.1 (2001): 9–21.

Pudovkin, Vsevolod I. "Film Technique." *Film: An Anthology*, edited by Daniel Talbot. Berkeley: University of California Press, 1975.

Pustz, Matthew. *Comic Book Culture: Fanboys and True Believers*. Jackson, MS: University Press of Mississippi, 1999.

Raeburn, Daniel. "Two Centuries of Underground Comic Books." In *Strips, Toons, and Bluesies: Essays in Comics and Culture*, edited by D.B. Dowd and Todd Hignite, 34–45. New York: Princeton Architectural Press, 2004.

Rasula, Jed. "Nietzsche in the Nursery: Naïve Classics and Surrogate Parents in Post-War American Cultural Debates." *Representations* 29 (1990): 50–77.

Raviv, Dan. *Comic Wars: How Two Tycoons Battled over the Marvel Comics Empire—and Both Lost.* New York: Broadway Books, 2002.

Reed, Robbie. "Secret Origins of the DC Implosion." *Dial B for Blog.* N.d. *www.dialbforblog.com/archives/252* (accessed June 11, 2008).

Regalado, Aldo. "The Superhero Genre: Revisited and Reinterpreted." *Partial Proceedings of the 8th Annual Comic Arts Conference*, San Diego, CA, July 20–22, 2000.

Reid, Calvin. "Graphic Novel Market Hits $330 Million." *PW Daily.* February 23, 2007. *www.publishersweekly.com/article/CA6419034.html?q=Graphic+novel+market+hits+%24330* (accessed March 25, 2008).

Reitberger, Reinhold, and Wolfgang Fuchs. *Comics: Anatomy of a Mass Medium.* 1971. Translated by Nadia Fowler. Boston: Little, Brown and Company, 1972.

Reynolds, Richard. *Super Heroes: A Modern Mythology.* London: B.T. Batsford Ltd., 1992.

Ridley, John. "Three Writers are Drawn by the Allure of Comics." NPR, October 17, 2007. *www.npr.org/templates/story/story.php?storyId=87867518*, accessed June 8, 2008.

Rifas, Leonard. "Cold War Comics." *International Journal of Comic Art* 2.1 (2000): 3–32.

———. "Fredric Wertham, Scientist." Paper presented at the Comic Arts Conference, San Diego, CA, 1992.

———. "Introduction." In *I SAW IT*, by Keiji Nakazawa, 1. San Francisco: EduComics, 1982.

Roach, David. "The History of British Comic Art." In *True Brit: A Celebration of the Great Comic Book Artists of the UK.* Raleigh, NC: TwoMorrows Publishing, 2004.

Robbins, Trina. *From Girls to Grrrlz: A History of Comics from Teens to Zines.* San Francisco: Chronicle Books, 1999.

———. *The Great Women Super Heroes.* Northampton, MA: Kitchen Sink Press, 1996.

Rogers, Mark C. "Beyond Bang! Pow! Genre and the Evolution of the American Comic Book Industry." Ph.D. diss., University of Michigan, 1997.

———. "Understanding Production: The Stylistic Impact of Artisan and Industrial Methods." *International Journal of Comic Art* 8, no. 1 (2006): 509–517.

Rosenkranz, Patrick. *Rebel Visions: The Underground Comix Revolution, 1963–1975.* Seattle: Fantagraphics Books, 2002.

Rovin, Jeff. *The Encyclopedia of Superheroes.* New York: Facts on File, 1985.

Rozanski, Chuck. "Death of Superman" promotion of 1992. *Tales from the Database.* *www.milehighcomics.com/tales/cbg127.html.*

Rubenstein, Anne. *Bad Language, Naked Ladies, and Other Threats to the Nation: A Political History of Comic Books in Mexico.* Durham, NC: Duke University Press, 1998.

Ryan, Marie-Laure. "The Modes of Narrativity and Their Visual Metaphors." *Style* 26.3 (1992): 368–387.

Sabin, Roger. *Adult Comics: An Introduction.* London: Routledge, 1993.

———. *Comics, Comix, & Graphic Novels: A History of Comic Art*. New York: Phaidon Press Inc., 1996.

Sabin, Roger, and Teal Triggs. *Below Critical Radar: Fanzines and Alternative Comics from 1976 to the Present Day*. Hove, U.K.: Slab-O-Concrete, 2000.

Said, Edward. "Homage to Joe Sacco." In *Palestine: The Special Edition*, edited by Kim Thompson, v–vii. Seattle: Fantagraphics Books, 2007. (Originally published in 2001.)

Saltus, Elinor C. "The Comics Aren't Good Enough." *Wilson Library Bulletin* 26 (1952): 382–383.

Saraceni, Mario. *The Language of Comics*. London: Routledge, 2003.

Sassienie, Paul. *The Comic Book*. Edison, NJ: Chartwell Books, 1994.

Savage, William W., Jr. *Commies, Cowboys, and Jungle Queens: Comic Books and America, 1945–1954*. Hanover, NH: Wesleyan University Press, 1990.

Schelly, Bill. *The Golden Age of Comic Fandom*. Seattle: Hamster Press, 1999.

———. *Sense of Wonder: A Life in Comic Fandom*. Raleigh, NC: TwoMorrows Publishing, 2001.

Schmitt, Ronald. "Deconstructive Comics." *Journal of Popular Culture* 25 (1992): 153–161.

Schreiner, Dave. *Kitchen Sink Press: The First 25 Years*. Northampton, MA: Kitchen Sink Press, 1994.

Schwartz, Adam, and Eliane Rubinstein-Avila. "Understanding the Manga Hype: Uncovering the Multimodality of Comic-Book Literacies." *Journal of Adolescent and Adult Literacy* 50 (2006): 40–49.

Scott, Naomi, ed. *Heart Throbs: The Best of DC Romance Comics*. New York: Simon & Shuster, 1979.

Screech, Matthew. *Masters of the Ninth Art: Bandes Dessinées and the Franco-Belgian Identity*. Liverpool, U.K.: Liverpool University Press, 2005.

Shannon, Claude, and Warren Weaver. *The Mathematical Theory of Communication*. Urbana, IL: University of Illinois Press, 1949.

Sharen, Bob. Personal correspondence. March 21, 1988.

Shaw, Scott. "The Secret Origin of (the San Diego Golden State) Comic-Con International (more or less)." In *Comic-Con International: San Diego Souvenir Book*, 94–95. San Diego: Comic-Con International, 1999.

Shelton, Gilbert, publisher. *The Austin Iconoclastic Newsletter* 1, no. 5, 1964.

Sheridan, Martin. *Comics and Their Creators*. Boston: Hale, Cushman & Flint, 1942.

Shooter, Jim. Foreword to *The Comic Book*, by Paul Sassiene. Edison, NJ: Chartwell Books, 1994.

Simon, Joe, and Jim Simon. *The Comic Book Makers*. Lebanon, NJ: Vanguard Productions, 2003.

Singer, Marc. "Invisible Order: Comics, Time and Narrative." Paper presented at the 29th Annual Popular Culture Association Conference, San Diego, California, March 31–April 3, 1999.

Slade, Michael. "Michael Slade: An Unconventional Biography." Darkworlds Productions. 1999–2000. *www.specialx.net/unconbio.html* (accessed July 1, 2000).

Smith, Craig R. *Rhetoric and Human Consciousness*. Prospect Heights, IL: Waveland, 1998.

Smith, Zack. "Jonathan Lethem on *Omega the Unknown*." *Newsarama*, July 20, 2007. *http://forum.newsarama.com/showthread.php?t=121762&highlight=omega+unknown* (accessed May 23, 2008).

Spiegelman, Art. "Those Dirty Little Comics." In *Tijuana Bibles: Art and Wit in America's Forbidden Funnies, 1930s–1950s*, edited by Bob Andelman, 5–10. New York: Simon & Schuster, 1997.

Spiegelman, Art, and Chip Kidd. *Jack Cole and Plastic Man: Forms Stretched to Their Limits!* New York: DC Comics/Chronicle Books, 2001.

Spurgeon, Tom. "Mini-Comics: Comics' Secret Lifeblood." In *The Education of a Comics Artist: Visual Narrative in Cartoons, Graphic Novels, and Beyond*, edited by Michael Dooley and Steven Heller, 133–137. New York: Allworth Press, 2005.

Stack, Frank. "Gilbert Shelton Interviewed by Frank Stack." *The Comics Journal*, 2002. *www.tcj.com/2_archives/i_shelton.html* (accessed June 11, 2008).

Stan Lee: ComiX-Man. Produced by A&E Biography. 42 minutes. A&E, 1995. Videocassette.

Steranko, James. "Foreword." In *The Superman Archives, Vol. 1*, edited by Mark Waid and Richard Bruning, 3–6. New York: DC Comics, 1989.

———. *The Steranko History of Comics, Vols. 1 and 2*. Reading, PA: Supergraphics, 1970–1972.

Stevenson, Daniel. "Year by Year Title Listing." Unpublished index. July 24, 2008.

Strömberg, Fredrik. *Black Images in the Comics: A Visual History*. Korea: Fantagraphic Books, 2003.

Sullivan, Vincent. On a Golden Age panel at San Diego Con 1999, Rm 4, 6:30 p.m.

Super Amigos. Produced and directed by Arturo Perez Torres. 1 hr. 22 min. Open City Works, 2007.

Swain, Emma Halstead. "Using Comic Books to Teach Reading and Language Arts." *Journal of Reading* 22 (1978): 253–258.

Sweeney, Bruce. "Jaxon." *Comics Interview*, March 1984, [pages?].

Szasz, Ferenc Morton. "The Comic Book that Changed the Nation!" *Comic Book Marketplace* June 2000, 48–52.

Tales from the Crypt: From Comic Books to Television! 2004. Written, produced, and directed by Chip Selby. 56 min. MONSTERS. DVD video.

Taylor, Aaron. "'He's Gotta Be Strong, and He's Gotta Be Fast, and He's Gotta Be Larger than Life': Investigating the Engendered Superhero Body." *The Journal of Popular Culture* 40, no. 2 (2007): 345–360.

Thomas, Roy. "Introduction." In *Marvel Masterworks: Golden Age Captain America, Vol. 1*, edited by Mark D. Beazley, vi–vii. New York: Marvel Comics, 2005.

———. "Stan the Man & Roy the Boy." *Comic Book Artist* 2 (1998): 6–18.

Thomas, Roy, and Bill Schelly. *Alter Ego: The Best of the Legendary Comics Fanzine*. Seattle: Hamster Press, 1997.

Thompson, Don. "OK. Axis, Here We Come!" In *All in Color for a Dime*, edited by Dick Lupoff and Don Thompson, 110–129. New York: Ace Books, 1970.

Thompson, Maggie. Interview with author, San Diego, CA, July 19, 1997.

Thorn, Matt. "Shôjo Manga—Something for Girls." *Japan Quarterly* 48 (2001): 43–50.

Thorndike, Robert L. "Words and the Comics." *Journal of Experimental Education* 10 (1941): 110–113.

Thrasher, Frederic M. "The Comics and Delinquency: Cause or Scapegoat." *Journal of Educational Sociology* 23 (1949): 195–205.

Töpffer, Rodolphe. "Essay on Physiognomy." In *Enter: Comics*, translated and edited by Ellen Wiese, 2–35. Lincoln, NE: University of Nebraska Press, 1965.

Ujiie, Joanne, and Stephen Krashen, "Comic Book Reading, Reading Enjoyment, and Pleasure Reading among Middle Class and Chapter I Middle School Students." *Reading Improvement* 33 (1996): 51–54.

Uricchio, William, and Roberta E. Pearson. "'I'm Not Fooled by that Cheap Disguise.'" In *The Many Lives of the Batman: Critical Approaches to a Superhero and His Media*, edited by Roberta E. Pearson and William Uricchio, 182–213. New York: Routledge, 1991.

U.S. Congress. Senate. *Juvenile Delinquency (Comic Books): Hearings before the Senate Subcommittee on Juvenile Delinquency*, 83rd Cong., 2nd sess., April 21–22, 1954.

U.S. House of Representatives. *Report of the Select Committee on Current Pornographic Materials, House of Representatives, Eighty-second Congress, pursuant to H. Res. 596: A Resolution Creating a Select Committee to Conduct a Study and Investigation of Current Pornographic Materials*, 1952. Washington, D.C.: USGPO, 1952.

Van Hise, James. *How to Draw Art for Comic Books: Lessons from the Masters*. Las Vegas, NV: Pioneer Books, 1989.

Versaci, Rocco. *This Book Contains Graphic Language: Comics as Literature*. New York: Continuum, 2007.

Viau, Michael. "Quebecois Comics." Library and Archives Canada. *www.collectionscanada.gc.ca/comics/027002-7000-e.html* (accessed September 30, 2007).

Victims of International Communist Emissaries. *Grenada: Rescued from Rape and Slavery*. 1984. *www.ep.tc/grenada/index.html* (accessed February 13, 2008).

Viola, Ken. "Will Eisner Interview." *The Masters of Comic Book Art*. VHS. Bogota, NJ: Ken Viola Productions, 1987.

Walker, Alan. "Introduction: Historical Perspective." *Alter Ego* 71 (2007): 4–13. Original material printed in *The Great Canadian Comic Books*, 1971.

Waugh, Coulton. *The Comics*. New York: Macmillan, 1947.

Weiner, Stephen. *Faster than a Speeding Bullet: The Rise of the Graphic Novel*. New York: Nantier, Beall, Minoustchine Publishing Inc., 2003.

Wertham, Fredric. "The Comics . . . Very Funny!" *Reader's Digest*, August 1948: 15–18.

———. "It's Still Murder: What Parents Don't Know about Comic Books." *Saturday Review of Literature*, April 9, 1955, 11–121.

———. *Seduction of the Innocent*. New York: Rinehart, 1954.

———. "What Parents Don't Know about Comic Books." *Ladies' Home Journal,* November 1953: 50–53.

Wheat, John. "Jack Jackson: A Tribute." *Southwestern Historical Quarterly* 110, no. 2 (2006): 272–275.

Wiese, Ellen. "Introduction: Rodolphe Töpffer and the Language of Physiognomy." In *Enter: Comics,* translated and edited by Ellen Wiese, ix–xxxii. Lincoln, NE: University of Nebraska Press, 1965.

Williams, Kristian. "The Case for Comics Journalism." *Columbia Journalism Review* (2005). *http://cjrarchives.org/issues/2005/2/ideas-essay-williams.asp.*

Williams, Neil. "The Comic Book as Course Book: Why and How." Paper presented at the Annual Meeting of the Teachers of English to Speakers of Other Languages (29th, Long Beach, CA, 1995).

Winick, Judd. *Pedro and Me: Friendship, Loss and What I Learned.* New York: Henry Holt and Company, 2000.

Witek, Joseph. *Comic Books as History: The Narrative Art of Jack Jackson, Art Spiegelman, and Harvey Pekar.* Jackson, MS: University Press of Mississippi, 1989.

———. "Comics Criticism in the United States: A Brief Historical Survey." *International Journal of Comic Art* 1 (1999): 4–16.

Witty, Paul. "Reading the Comics: A Comparative Study." *Journal of Experimental Education* 10 (1941): 105–106.

Wolf, Thomas. "Reading Reconsidered." *Harvard Educational Review* 47 (1977): 427.

Wolfe, Katherine M., and Marjorie Fiske. "The Children Talk about Comics." In *Communications Research 1948–1949,* edited by Paul F. Lazaerfeld and Frank N. Stanton, 3–50. New York: Harper, 1949.

Wolfe, Tom. *The Electric Kool-Aid Acid Test.* New York: Farrar, Straus, and Giroux, 1968.

Wright, Bradford W. *Comic Book Nation: The Transformation of Youth Culture in America.* Baltimore: John Hopkins University Press, 2001.

Wright, Gary. "The Comic Book: A Forgotten Medium in the Classroom." *Reading Teacher* 33 (1979): 158–161.

Wright, Nicky. *The Classic Era of American Comics.* Lincolnwood, IL: Contemporary Books, 2000.

Wylie, Philip. *The Gladiator.* New York: Manor Books, 1976. (Original work published in 1930).

Young, Michael C., and Richard Foltin. "Comics' New Wave." *Harvard Journal of Pictorial Fiction* (1974): 4–11.

Your Friendly Neighborhood Hero. Produced and directed by Sybil Drew. 1 hr., 8 min. Kojanpan Films, 2008.

Index